The Israelites in History and Tradition

LIBRARY OF ANCIENT ISRAEL

Douglas A. Knight, *General Editor*

The Israelites in History and Tradition

NIELS PETER LEMCHE

SPCK
LONDON
WESTMINSTER JOHN KNOX PRESS
LOUISVILLE, KENTUCKY

First published in the United States in 1998 by
Westminster John Knox Press
Louisville, KY 40202-1396

First published in Great Britain by
Society for Promoting Christian Knowledge
Holy Trinity Church
Marylebone Road
London NW1 4DU

Book design by Publishers' WorkGroup
Cover design by Kim Wohlenhaus

This book is printed on acid-free paper.

PRINTED IN THE UNITED STATES OF AMERICA
98 99 00 01 02 03 04 05 06 07 — 10 9 8 7 6 5 4 3 2 1

Library of Congress Cataloging-in-Publication Data

Lemche, Niels Peter.
     The Israelites in history and tradition / Niels Peter Lemche. — 1st ed.
          p.   cm. — (The Library of ancient Israel)
     Includes bibliographical references and indexes.
     ISBN 0-664-22075-4
     1. Jews—History—To 586 B.C.—Sources.   2. Jews—History—To 586
B.C.—Historiography.   3. Bible. O.T.—Historiography.   I. Title.   II. Series.
DS121.L446   1998
930′.04924—dc21   98-22300

British Cataloguing-in-Publication Data

A catalogue record of this book is available from the British Library.

ISBN 0-281-05227-1

Contents

Foreword

The historical and literary questions preoccupying biblical scholars since the Enlightenment have focused primarily on events and leaders in ancient Israel, the practices and beliefs of Yahwistic religion, and the oral and written stages in the development of the people's literature. Considering how little was known about Israel, and indeed the whole ancient Near East, just three centuries ago, the gains achieved to date have been extraordinary, due in no small part to the unanticipated discovery by archaeologists of innumerable texts and artifacts.

Recent years have witnessed a new turn in biblical studies, occasioned largely by a growing lack of confidence in the "assured results" of past generations of scholars. At the same time, an increased openness to the methods and issues of other disciplines such as anthropology, sociology, linguistics, and literary criticism has allowed new questions to be posed regarding the old materials. Social history, a well-established area within the field of historical studies, has proved especially fruitful as a means of analyzing specific segments of the society. Instead of concentrating predominantly on national events, leading individuals, political institutions, and "high culture," social historians attend to broader and more basic issues such as social organization, conditions in cities and villages, life stages, environmental contexts, power distribution according to class and status, and social stability and instability. To ask such questions of ancient Israel shifts the focus away from those with power and the events they instigated and onto the everyday realities and social subtleties experienced by the vast majority of the population. Such inquiry has now gained new force with the application of various forms of ideological criticism and other methods designed to ferret out the political, economic, and social interests concealed in the sources.

This series represents a collaborative effort to investigate several specific topics—societal structure, politics, economics, religion, literature, material culture, law, intellectual leadership, ethnic identity, social marginalization, the international context, and canon formation—each in terms of its social dimensions and processes within ancient Israel. Some of these subjects have not been explored in depth until now; others are familiar areas currently in need of reexamination. While the sociohistorical approach provides the general perspective for all volumes of the series, each author has the latitude to determine the most appropriate means for dealing with the topic at hand. Individually and collectively, the volumes aim to expand our vision of the culture and society of ancient Israel and thereby generate new appreciation for its impact on subsequent history.

Niels Peter Lemche addresses an issue that is too often merely presupposed among scholars and lay readers of the Bible—that we know who the ancient "Israelites" were. Lemche begins by discussing all explicit references to the people or their leaders in other ancient Near Eastern texts, and he then searches for the various indications, both biblical and archaeological, of the Israelites' own self-understanding or behavior as a distinct people throughout the various stages of their long history. The traditional touchstones of ethnicity—common blood, language, and religion—prove on closer examination to be inadequate for capturing the diversity and subtleties of Israelite reality. In line with current social-anthropological theory, Lemche attends to the fluidity of ethnic boundaries, affirming the extensive variations across time and region and concluding that our usual characterizations of this ancient people would certainly have struck them as strange in comparison with their own self-identities. He demonstrates how two key factors have influenced our pictures of the people: on the one hand the artful theological descriptions of Israel in the Hebrew Bible, and on the other the notions of nationality and group identity held by people of the modern Western world, including scholars. This book thus serves as a prerequisite to the writing of history, inasmuch as Lemche presses the question of how we are, at a fundamental level, to portray the "Israelites." His discussion contributes directly not only to today's historiographical debates but also to our appreciation of the very complex population and culture behind the biblical literature.

Douglas A. Knight
General Editor

Preface

After having published a study on the Canaanites back in 1991, and having claimed the biblical Canaanites to be the invention of ancient biblical historians, I soon found another volume missing, devoted to the image of Israel as found on the pages of the Old Testament. When Douglas Knight kindly offered me the opportunity to write a volume for his Library of Ancient Israel series directed at exactly the problem of ethnicity and ancient Israel, I was quite easily persuaded. It is my hope that this book will provoke a healthy discussion about the subject of ancient Israel. What was Israel really? A people? Or a state in ancient Palestine? Or something which only exists in the biblical narrative? Are all of these questions as a matter of fact simplifications or does every single question carry some part of the truth? While I have certainly not provided any definite answer to these questions, I at least hope to have stirred the interest of scholars and general readers alike. If the book is going to promote a more conscious approach to the identity of the ancient Israelites, it has done its job.

Several people have had their part in the realization of this volume: first of all, Douglas Knight, whose advice has always been welcome; the original editor, John Berquist, who was a great help during the initial stage of the production of the volume; and finally the present staff of Westminster John Knox Press—especially Amy Brack, for a very painstaking revision of my English manuscript. My colleague in Copenhagen, Thomas L. Thompson, read the book in its first form and provided many helpful suggestions. If anything went wrong, the blame is to be placed on my shoulders alone.

Inventing the Past

Ancient Israel—Ethnicity, Nation, and History as the Mode of Interpreting Ancient Cultures

THE HISTORICAL MODE OF READING BIBLICAL TEXTS

Recent developments in the study of ancient Israel have caused of a lot of concern. We hear rumors that biblical scholars have questioned the value of the Old Testament[1] as a source for the history of Israel, thereby dismissing the entire Old Testament as a book of guidance for Christian as well as Jewish believers.

To a certain degree this is true, at least as long as the Old Testament is used primarily as a historical textbook. It will be demonstrated in this book that it is hardly possible any more to uphold this idea of the Old Testament literature as a historical source in the classical sense of the word. According to the prevalent view, almost any written source should be given priority in the analysis of humankind's historical past. It is also the aim of the author, however, to demonstrate that this may not be as severe a loss as is generally maintained. In contrast to the generally skeptical evaluation of biblical studies among Christian as well as Jewish Bible readers, some scholars and theologians may prefer to look on the present tendency of Old Testament studies as representing a kind of liberation movement. This new trend seems to be liberating the Bible from the tyranny of having to be historically accurate in the most minute detail in order to remain a Bible for Christians and Jews. The shift of emphasis away from the predominant historical analyses of biblical texts has on the other hand led to a number of readings that sometimes seem far removed from the realities of the ancient world. It is as if the authors of such studies are convinced that the biblical books are to be read as modern literature, open to all kinds of modern reading techniques. In this way it also becomes true that the last traces of interest in the historical content of the books of the Old Testament have been lost at the same time as

1

the book itself has been liberated from the dominance of historical interpretation.

In order to appreciate the importance of the change of emphasis in Old
Testament studies over the last couple of decades, it is necessary to understand that historical readings of biblical literature which have dominated the
modern world for almost two centuries are certainly not exclusive. This way
of reading the Bible does not exclude other ways of interpretation. To the
contrary, the historical reading of the Bible is a comparative newcomer in
comparison to such venerable procedures as allegorical understanding or typological interpretation, both of which having been around for, in some
cases, more than two thousand years. The two traditional methods of extracting information from biblical literature differ somewhat. According to allegorical interpretation the meaning of a certain biblical text is never literal
but always something else hidden away in the text, which is in this way understood to be almost a secret code. On the other hand, the typological reading of the Bible takes the events of the biblical text to be paradigmatic for
present developments. The borderline between these two kinds of readings
is certainly vague. It is probably better to say that the genres are often mixed,
as in the antique Jewish commentaries on Old Testament prophetic literature found in the Dead Sea Library and especially in Jewish writings of the
Hellenistic age, such as the works of Philo from Alexandria. Well known,
however, are also the typological interpretation of Old Testament passages
in the New Testament, seeing the events narrated by the Gospels to be at
the same time a fulfilment of the prophecies of the Old Testament and rep-
etitions of events in the history of Israel. Examples of this abound in the
pages of the New Testament, as for example when Matthew understands the
sojourn of Jesus in Egypt in the light of Hosea's prophecy, "Out of Egypt I
have called my son."[2] In Matthew this is immediately followed by the story
of the slaughter of the innocents, which for its part is considered a fulfill-
ment of a prophecy of Jeremiah.[3]

This mode of reading biblical texts survived and developed until the Reformation in Europe, when the more elaborate and artful examples of allegorical interpretation were ostracized by the reformers. Since the
Reformation we find a marked trend toward a more literate interpretation,
which should not yet, however, be confused with a genuine historical interest. After the Reformation the main interest of the theologians did not center on the historical background of the narratives of the Old Testament. The
main subject of interest was still mostly the question of the importance of
the Old Testament for the daily life of the Christians.[4] The Old Testament
was, among other things, simply understood to provide guidance to Chris-

tian communities because it was understood to formulate the ethical laws to be followed by the true Christians, although this guidance was always seen as different from the demand on Jews to obey the Torah.

Critical scholarship, however, began as early as in the seventeenth century, and soon centered on the authorship by Moses of the five books carrying his name.[5] From this period and onward, an increasing amount of analytical work has fractured the church's traditional view of the Bible as the inspired word of God. In fact the liberalism of some of these early writers sometimes astonishes, only seldom, however, consistently. Advanced ideas often stand next to very traditional and conservative viewpoints.

The great divide in biblical scholarship came with the Romantic period, when the study of the Bible became modern in the sense that the romantic understanding of the Bible concentrated on two major issues, nationality and history. This was part of the general romantic construct, which could be called the national state. The nation-state, which was to take over after the former kingdoms of Europe, was dependent on the acceptance by its populace of belonging together. In order to achieve the necessary sense of ethnic identity, history was introduced as obviously the best medium, as it created the sense of something very old, that is to say, that the nation-state could trace its origin back to the early days of the people who happened to inhabit the state. It therefore became a truism in romanticism that the inhabitants of a certain area belonged to the same ethnos with an age-old history, and each ethnos displayed characteristic traits, which were particular to it in comparison with the neighboring nations. Other concepts developed in combination with this idea of history. We might mention the notion of a mystic connection between a nation and its territory. The territory is something holy and unchangeable. This means that the national territory could not be traded because the spirit of the nation was attached to its soil. In contrast to this it must be realized that in the eighteenth century the dominant political structure of Europe had been the patronage state, that is, a state not only ruled by a single person, the king, but considered to be the private possession of its king. The system was patriarchal and achieved its high point in the age of absolute monarchy between c. 1600 and 1800. It would thus be correct to say that the inhabitants of a certain territory in Europe, as for example Denmark, would first and foremost consider themselves to be the subjects of their king rather than Danish citizens. The borders between the states were accordingly extremely fluid, as possessions of land could be freely interchanged between the patron kings according to the vagaries of war or for some other reason,[6] a process that had but one minor consequence for ordinary persons: that they became the subjects of a new master.

With the ascent to power of the so-called third estate, the bourgeois class imprinted its definition of nationality and of nations on other parts of the society. This definition was, as we shall see, to a large extent inspired by classical political theory. In this connection, the idea of history was developed as a specific European political phenomenon in order to persuade the masses—most of all the peasants—that they belonged to a certain nation and therefore were obliged to fight for the preservation of their state. We accordingly find over the next century in Europe a development of the historical sciences that went hand in hand with the growing of European nationalism. That happened to such an extent that historical thinking in this century became the dominant mode of self-definition in the modern world.

In biblical studies, this development of historical and nationalistic thinking has had some remarkable consequences, the importance of which has only recently been acknowledged by biblical scholars. We should first and foremost point to the development during the nineteenth and at the beginning of the twentieth centuries toward the hegemony of the white man over the rest of the world. The process included the forcible colonization of large stretches of the inhabited world and brought about the feeling of superiority among Europeans and North Americans. We are normally brought up by tradition to consider ourselves to be the masters of the world, while we are at the same time denying the value of other traditions[7]—if we accept at all that other traditions may exist or should be worth preserving or even remembering.

The cradle of this European tradition was considered to be the classical world of Greece and Rome, a conviction that had struck root already during the Renaissance. We were used to deriving our civilization from Greece and Rome and to look on Europe (and later North America) as the true heir of Greco-Roman culture. To theologians whose position in society had never before been questioned, this could hardly be considered a satisfying situation. They were therefore in desperate need of another cradle of the Western world, to be sought in the ancient Near East, or rather in ancient Israel, where we should look for the origin of our religion. The intensified study of the Old Testament,[8] with its pronounced patriarchal idea of religion and civilization, did nothing except strengthen this impression of European excellence. As such, it damaged a proper European appraisal of modern Islamic culture of the Middle East, which has generally been and still is despised as being inferior to Christian and European civilization. In the course of the nineteenth century the civilizations of the ancient Near East changed character from being almost unknown prehistoric societies to becoming the homeland of the two great civilizations of ancient Egypt and

Mesopotamia. Now, this ancient world was not so much appreciated as the forerunner of Arab civilizations as it was understood to be the cradle of Israelite culture and through Israel of European civilization. By promoting ancient Israel as an important forerunner of our civilization, the theologians of the Western world created a competitor to the classical world of the humanists and thereby managed to remain—at least for the time being—important in modern society.[9]

Daniel Patte, a North American biblical scholar of French origin, has adeptly described biblical studies during the last two hundred years as being male, white, and North European North American.[10] This characterization is certainly correct. He suggests that modern biblical exegesis of the Western world with its remarkable historical predominance has become so dominating that any other method of reading the biblical text is considered secondary. This "Western" reading of the Bible has never allowed for the fact that the texts of both the Old and the New Testament were written by people who lived in a premodern world not necessarily sharing our belief and sentiments.

In the course of these developments in biblical studies, ancient Israel, however, changed character from being part of the ancient Near East to becoming almost a pre-European civilization. Keith W. Whitelam has recently described in more detail this metamorphosis of the Israel of the Bible populated by biblical Israelites into a forerunner of the modern European national state. In his study, Whitelam has explored the political consequences of the European creation of ancient Israel as a special civilization, whereby the pre-Islamic past of the Arab nations has almost been stolen away from them.[11] The assumed conflict between Arab and Israelite history is, however, not the subject of this study. The creation of ancient Israel as a society that belonged to the historical past of the landscape otherwise known in Christian tradition as Palestine or the Holy Land is, however, symptomatic of a conflict that has been around since the beginning of historical studies about two hundred years ago. This conflict has to do with the possibility of recreating the past as it really was, as it was programmatically formulated by the leading German historian of the nineteenth century, Leopold von Ranke.[12] Von Ranke, who is often praised as the father of modern history, insisted on the necessity of an objective history writing, which should base itself on contemporary documents and not rely on paraphrases of later sources. His object was certainly a positivistic one, that the past should be studied in an unbiased way in order to reconstruct what really happened in history. His shortcomings, on the other hand, had to do with a rather limited idea of the laws of history. Here he was classical in the sense that his history was a kind of metahistory, working only on the highest level of society; ordinary people had no role to play in his writings. Von Ranke's history had to be a history of the great men, and as such it was a very personalized form of history writing, often praised because of the psychological insight of its author into the characters to whom he allotted the major roles in the course of history.[13]

Von Ranke's spirit permeates the early histories of Israel, which were almost without exception—when talking about contributions by serious scholars—of German origin, from Heinrich Ewald's history of Israel, which first appeared in 1843–55,[14] to Ernst Sellin's, from 1924 to 1932.[15] They are with few exceptions oriented toward a description of the history of ancient Israel as based on the lives and destinies of its great characters, from Joseph (or Moses) until the time of Ezra and Nehemiah. Nowhere do we find any endeavor to understand history as a process, which was decided by forces other than the individual. For anything like a real history of the Israelite society, these authors showed little interest, simply because they were ill equipped for writing anything other than history in von Ranke's sense of the word. Sometimes this has had rather amusing consequences. One such example is when historians like Rudolf Kittel and Sellin try to characterize the inner self of their heroes, and it turns out that these have been described in a way more suitable for Prussian civil servants than for people living in the Near East in ancient times. It goes without saying that hand in hand with their psychological "familiarization" with the main characters of Israel's ancient history, these historians produced an extensive amount of paraphrases of the history of Israel as narrated by the authors of the historical literature in the Old Testament.

There are from this early period when the history of ancient Israel was formed few exceptions to the rule, and none of these really succeeded in changing the course of historical reconstruction laid down in the tradition of von Ranke. This is also true of Julius Wellhausen, although he in his famous *Prolegomena to the History of Ancient Israel* from 1878[16] chose not to produce another history of ancient Israel. As the title indicates, he concentrated on creating the prerequisites for the historian who would take on himself the reconstruction of this history. Wellhausen focused on the cult and the development of tradition and presented a picture of the Old Testament as a historical source that sees ancient Israel through the filter of later Judaism. He also tried to get behind this screen of Judaism by returning to the prophets of the Old Testament as representatives of genuine Israelite tradition from the time before the Torah, which was his programmatic characterization of the relationship between the preexilic Israelites and postexilic Jews. When it came to his own historical reconstruction, however, he hardly possessed the intellectual prerequisites to carry through this program of his, but at the end wrote another fairly conventional history of Israel.[17]

The period following the appearance of Wellhausen's *Prolegomena* witnessed the reestablishment of the more traditional line of biblical history as mainly a revision of the history as told by the Old Testament itself, whereby Wellhausen's radicalism was pacified.[18] In the spirit of von Ranke, histories of Israel were in abundance also after Wellhausen. Few scholars paid any attention to Eduard Meyer, a German historian of the ancient world of immense learning, who as early as 1906 had denounced the enterprise as problematic. Meyer had in a pointed way described the usual proceedings of Old Testament historians, which involved an unrestricted paraphrasing of the biblical text, as both naive and faulty.[19]

Only after the end of World War I a new development started, which is synonymous with the names of Albrecht Alt and Martin Noth. In their historical writings we find a much more conscious and methodical way of describing the history of Israel. It will at the same time be true to say that they definitely belonged in the previous romantic German tradition, both trying to remain faithful to the idea of the nation current in romantic Europe. Alt, however, presented a reconstruction of the historical development that is much closer to the demands of the professional historians of the twentieth century, for example by introducing a kind of long-distance perspective. This he described as territorial history, but it would not be incorrect to maintain that it closely resembles the notion of the long duration otherwise believed to be invented by a French school of historians, *les annales,* which has been dominating the field for the last generation. According to this school, historical investigations should not concentrate on individual figures, because they provide an unpredictable and unstable factor—we could also say unusual or unique—not necessarily representative for the historical development in a certain period in general. Instead of this, historians should concentrate on the constant features of a certain area—first and foremost the landscape in question and its population—and analyze changes that may have happened over a prolonged period in order to reconstruct the historical development that took place in this territory.[20] Alt combined the history of the territory of ancient Palestine from the Late Bronze Age to the Early Iron Age—a period spanning a couple of centuries—with a sociological approach to history. In this way he produced the necessary prerequisites for a proper modern history of Israel, although he never wrote one. Instead of this, he concentrated on the early history of the Israelite nation, especially the conquest of Palestine, which he saw as a gradual process during which pastoral nomadic tribesmen infiltrated Palestine. The proper Israelite conquest of Palestine belonged to a second phase of the Israelite settlement, when the tribes of Israel felt themselves so consolidated in their possession of the land that they decided also to assume political power over the whole territory of Palestine.[21]

A history of Israel written in the tradition of Alt was first to be authored by his student and spiritual heir Martin Noth.[22] Noth followed Alt most of the way, but was able to promote ideas only indicated in Alt's writing. Thus he proposed a new model for Israelite society in the period of the Judges, which was understood to be organized as a tribal league that could be analyzed in the light of the Greek institution of the amphictyony, which centerd in the sanctuary of Apollo at Delphi.[23] This was a brilliant choice, since it explained how early Israel could be a nation, in spite of the fact of its dispersed origin in the desert. It is obvious that Alt's view on the Israelite migration would prevent any talk about a coherent Israelite nation before or after the settlement, and then only as a result of a long history in Palestine. In the German tradition it could not be otherwise, as this tradition in its more radical shape had already bidden farewell to the age of the patriarchs as a historical period. It was also mostly extremely skeptical as to the historical content of the sojourn of Israel in Egypt and its liberation from the yoke of the pharaoh. The revelation on Sinai, where God for the first time revealed himself to the Israelite nation, could not be considered history and was thus impossible to accept as the true origin of Israelite nationality. However, the construction of the tribal society of the period of the Judges as a sacral tribal league centered on the common worship of Yahweh at a central shrine, served to rectify this situation. This organization provided the first and most important requisite for explaining how the idea of nationhood was achieved. From that point it was fairly easy to reconstruct the history of ancient Israel as a national history. It was certainly also in accordance with the German understanding of nationality that at the end of the existence of this tribal league the Israelite nation was cemented together by a more permanent and more centralized type of government, the monarchy. The empire of David and Solomon in this way became the greatest monument of Israelite nationality, and from this point it was possible to follow the history of Israel as narrated by the Old Testament almost from one end to the other. Ancient Israel had been proved to constitute a nation, an ethnos, with its own land and own particular religion.

WHAT IS A NATION OR AN ETHNOS?

The last sentence, however, shows how the classical idea of ethnicity[24] still dominates the thinking of biblical scholars of the modern age. In Herodotus's

History a nation is defined as a group of people who share a common blood, a common religion, and a common language.

> Again, there is the Greek nation—the common blood, the common language; the temples and religious ritual; the whole way of life we understand and share together.[25]

It is important that a common ancestor can be named who—should it only be in the shape of a metaphor—is considered the progenitor of the whole nation, as Jacob was the progenitor of twelve sons, the apical ancestors of the Israelite tribes. This is only one prerequisite, as it was also deemed necessary in order to maintain ethnic unity that the descendants of the common ancestor spoke the same language. Language therefore became a definitive mark of nationality. Finally, religion was the third prerequisite, as a nation could survive only if it shared common beliefs and common values. Otherwise the nation would fall apart.

Anyone acquainted with modern European history would realize that this definition was at the bottom of the romantic soul accepted as the foundation of the new nation-states that appeared after the French Revolution in 1789 and the Napoleonic wars. To German academics like Ernst Moritz Arndt (1769–1860), it was especially true not only as a definition of the nation but as a political program for the unification of the German nation. This goal was only, if ever, achieved in 1870. Arndt entertained a vision of a "Third Reich," following the Roman Empire as the first, and the Holy Roman (German) one as the second. This vision sadly became true only in a perverted form, when Hitler took up this ideology when molding his "empire." However, before 1870 the incredible number of small German states were united in different kinds of leagues, later dissolved by Bismarck into the German empire. The parallel between this history of Germany and the reconstructed history of ancient Israel is remarkable. It is certainly not to be excluded, or it is rather quite obvious that the molding of the Israelites into one nation was seen as a kind of corollary to the German unification in the nineteenth century, even where this was not expressly mentioned.

The impact of the Greek definition of a nation can still be shown to be operative as late as in the 1960s. At this time the North American anthropologist Raoul Naroll published what he considered to be the criteria to be used when trying to define a cultural, or ethnic, unit, which according to him

1. is largely biologically self-perpetuating,
2. shares fundamental cultural values, realized in overt unity in cultural forms,

3. makes up a field of communication and interaction, and
4. has a membership that identifies itself, and is identified by others, as constituting a category distinguishable from other categories of the same order.[26]

It is certainly not difficult to see that this definition of an ethnic group not only has much in common with Herodotus's classic one, but that its three first criteria are almost identical with Herodotus's definition. Naroll's first criterion, biological self-perpetuation, sounds like a modern paraphrase of the idea of a common blood. Naroll as a modern person will not speak about an apical ancestor—such as Abraham or Jacob in the biblical tradition—who was to become the progenitor of the Israelite people; instead he speaks about an ethnic group perpetuating itself biologically. However, the idea of a common blood is part of the ancient as well as the modern definition of ethnicity. Nevertheless, we are also induced into believing that the modern definition would have made sense in antiquity. Thus we think of Pliny's famous remark about the community at the Dead Sea as a special community that is able to perpetuate itself exclusively by attracting proselytes and *without* breeding children of its own.[27]

Naroll's second criterion speaks about shared fundamental cultural values. This is hardly anything but a secularized version of Herodotus's talk about a common religion, as it is well known that religion is used in a very broad sense in ancient times to denote culture, a concept not well understood by ancient man. An ethnic group should therefore consist of people who share common cultural values, that is, religion and whatever follows from having a common religion. Translated into Old Testament terms, this criterion can be seen to be operative, as the membership of the community of believers is characterized by a special bodily mark on the male members of the community, that is, circumcision. It also depends on the obedience to a communal set of laws, which are said to go back to Moses, the founder of the society.

Naroll's third criterion, which deals with communication, is related to Herodotus's concept of language; in fact, it is nothing except a paraphrase of it. Understood in this way, it has little to do with the way the biblical writers understood Israelite ethnicity. Here language is not normally understood to be an ethnic marker.

His fourth and final criterion is, however, more important because it claims that an ethnic group should be able to know who belongs to the group and who are to be reckoned nonmembers of the group. Here he touches on more modern definitions of ethnicity, as he has here included a dynamic element to his otherwise rather stable, not to say stiff, definition.

Before we continue with this discussion it is worthwhile for a moment to pause on the question of definition, first of all because the concepts nation/nationality and ethnos/ethnicity are sometimes considered to cover two different things. That this is hardly true as far as the two words nation and ethnos are concerned becomes clear when we look at the etymology and the development of the semantic fields of both words from their origin in Greek and Latin down to modern times. It does not say, however, that the distinction as such is of no use as a heuristic tool for further research into the concepts of nationalism and ethnicity. It might very well be that we have to mark out the differences between the two concepts in order to understand each of them in its own right.

Ethnicity is a derivation of the Greek word ἔθνος, which according to the standard Greek dictionary of Liddell and Scott[28] means "number of people living together, company, body of men." It need not mean anything else than, for example, "a company of comrades," or as ἔθνος λαῶν a "host of men" (λαός being the normal Greek word for "people"). The meaning of ἔθνος is not confined to human beings; animals can also be described as constituting an ἔθνος. The meaning "nation" is also known, for example in Homer, but only at a late date the meaning "foreign, or barbarous, nations" becomes part of the content of ἔθνος. Finally, the word can also be used to describe a class of men, for example ἔθνος κηρυκικόν, "the class of heralds," members of a tribe (in the Greek sense of that mysterious word[29]). In the New Testament the plural form τὰ ἔθνη achieves the derogatory meaning of heathens. In modern Greek, however, ἔθνος is usually translated as "nation" only.

In contrast the Latin *natio,* a derivative of *nascor,* takes the meaning of "a breed, stock, kind, species, race," which does also include animals. It sometimes also has the sense of a "race of people," something that in Latin is more often expressed by the word *gens.* Only in later Latin dependent on the usage of the church (which is for its part dependent on the New Testament use of τὰ ἔθνη) is it employed in the meaning of "heathen."[30] From this point a secondary, more neutral, meaning developed during the Middle Ages and the Renaissance as the term could be used of people living in different quarters of the earth, including all the connotations of its Latin origin, such as "race" and "breed." As such the use of "nation" did not contain anything "nationalistic" in the later nineteenth-century sense.

This means that as philosophers and political thinkers of the Enlightenment and the Romantic period initiated the path to true nationalism, they did so without already in advance carrying with them the particular nationalistic meaning of "nation." The reason why they chose the term is obvious, as this term had been known to them in the broad meaning of, on one side, the biblical language and, on the other, the classical literature. What was new was the connection made between nations and their territories. Political thinkers and social anthropologists have sometimes believed the idea of the nation to be part of the industrialized society.[31] It is hard to understand why this should be so, except as part of the propaganda of the new ruling class. This group was implanting in the minds of their anonymous workers, drawn to the cities from the countryside with the prospect of a better life, the idea of a communal ownership to the land. Formerly the peasants had entertained the idea of a personal ownership of the land—as far as they owned any land at all and were not anymore enslaved by the medieval feudal system. Even in this case, these destitute people had at least the feeling of belonging to a certain piece of land. The new idea of common ownership was, however, not tied to a specific strip of agricultural soil. It was about something much bigger, but also much more vague, such as the territory of the state.

The next stage in the development of the meaning of nation was to mold this idea of common ownership of a territory that was identical with that of a political structure, the state, into a concept that also said that the people inhabiting this territory was something special. According to this propaganda the people displayed special traits peculiar only to this people and different from comparable phenomena among other "nations." In von Ranke's work, already referred to above, this concept was developed as the *Völkergeist,* a mysterious peculiarity to, in his case, the German nation, which not only presented it in its own eyes as special but also rendered the Germans superior in comparison to other nations. The same happened in all other sovereign states of Europe. The idea of a nation was soon exported also to the parts of Europe under foreign (in practice, Turkish) domination, which led to a series of liberation wars and later internecine tribal-like wars, especially in the Balkans.

The classical origin of the concept should not be forgotten. It, however, also included the idea of a nation as a certain "people" with its own characteristics, which molded it into a nation, with a common language and common culture and with its own land belonging to it and to nobody else. In order to fulfill the requirements of the Greek forefathers, the concept must also contain the idea of common descent, which was a task given to the historians of the time, who set out to create national histories, even in places where such ones had never existed before.

France was, for example, originally inhabited by a hodgepodge of ethnic groups speaking several different languages, including two major forms of French, the langue d'oc and the langue d'oil, the Provençal and the Basque language. It had not in the Middle Ages formed a single state, but was the result of a deliberate policy of the French kings who had bit by bit reduced the different duchies of the country into one strongly centralized state. A common French history did not exist that could be said to be a *national* history, only a tale of the (more or less) heroic exploits of the kings of France. By decapitating this symbol during the revolution, every possibility of discord was let loose among the inhabitants of the country, which could have led to the dissolution of the state and endangered the survival of the nation. France, however, had the peculiar luck to be able to change its contemporary history into an origin history, including the tradition of the people's revolution (as a matter of fact, a typical example of a revolution "from the top") and the heroic (almost) present of the era of Napoleon.

Another example very different in character is made up by the formation of the Czech nation. The area of the Czech Republic belonged in the nineteenth century to the Hapsburg Empire, a truly multiethnic state embracing an enormous variety of different language groups and ethnic minorities. The territory of the Czechs—since the Middle Ages known on one hand as the Czech lands or territories and on the other as Bohemia (Böhmen)—had since the twelfth or thirteenth century been inhabited by a population partly of Slavonic, partly of German origin. Although the relations between the different populations had not always been harmonious, the idea of a separate Czech national identity did not arise before the nineteenth century. At this time the Austrian authorities introduced a nationalistic program. This should have led to the "Germanization" of the territory, but provoked intellectuals in Prague to formulate the idea about a Czech nation, something that only became true after the First World War when the Czechs—in an alliance with the Slavonic Slovaks—gained their independence. The question of being a Czech or a German was seen mainly as a matter of the language spoken. This problem was not solved, however, before the end of the Second World War, when the so-called Sudeten Germans were forced to leave the country. Total national independence and integrity was achieved only in the 1990s, when the second part of Czechoslovakia, Slovakia, decided to separate.[32]

So far the concept of the nation-state has dominated the political thinking into the present. Nation and state have, so to speak, become synonymous, as evidenced by the name of "The United Nations," the membership of which is made up of sovereign states only. In spite of its deficiencies, the concept is very much a political one. In this case the propaganda has experienced an overwhelming success. Most common men of the Western world who think of themselves in national terms have accepted the concept.

It doesn't really matter whether their nation is the same as the state (i.e., with its own independent territory) or one "without a land" (the gospel of many so-called liberation movements of the present).

The idea of a *Völkergeist* has also been perpetuated since the last century. This happened not least in social-anthropological writing dating from the period between the wars and was especially accentuated in periods of war. In such times the war propaganda was boosted by the notion of national superiority, often followed by generalizations that included a ridiculing of the enemy not only as inferior but as laughable.[33] In its more innocent form this occurred in the form of "ethnic jokes," with a special focus on special traits among neighbors considered to be peculiar to them, often connected with the kind of food consumed. In its crude form, however, it turned into a devastating piece of propaganda, making such atrocities as death camps and genocide legitimate.

How artificial this concept of a national coherence is can be seen in many parts of the world today, not least in the new states of Africa, supposed to be ethnic units but drawn up by the colonial powers without any idea about the ethnic composition of their colonies. Meantime in Europe, the cradle of the concept of the nation, this idea is crumbling, while at the same time still leading to horrible atrocities such as those experienced during the last decade in the former Yugoslavia. In France, the mother of nationalism, the phenomenon that is in Europe called "regionalism" is becoming a major factor creating local identities with very old "memories." Examples of this can be found in the Basque territories (in its more violent form), or (more peaceful) in Provence, where the local language having been almost extinguished is experiencing a revitalization. The same has happened on the Iberian Peninsula, where it could be said that it is only a political coincidence that Portugal remained an independent state, whereas the Catalan part of the country came under the sway of the Castilians. Regionalism is violently present in the Basque provinces in northern Spain, whereas it has so far manifested itself only in a much more benevolent way in Catalonia (which has its own language, Catalan) or in Andalusia. The present development in Italy is well known, with a political party simply propagating the dissolution of the Italian state, as is also the much more violent dissolution of Yugoslavia.

In Germany this development has followed a different route, as the sense of unity before the reunification in the 1990s was much stronger than it has developed to be after this event. Germany's history as a single political organization covers the short span of time from 1870 to 1945 only. The idea of German unity, however, survived and was continuously held in esteem. It did not matter very much that it became obvious how devastating this "unity" could be and it was not considered important that German-speaking Austrians (after 1945) and the German-speaking population of Switzerland and France were not longing for any kind of reunification with major Germany. The constitution of the Federal Republic even contains a paragraph guaranteeing German citizenship to any person who can prove to be of German descent. After the fall of the Communist states of Eastern Europe, this last paragraph has become a problem to many Germans living in Germany, as many immigrants have arrived with a German pedigree, but able to speak barely one word of German. Thus new regulations have been ordered to block this infusion of too many persons who might be part of the German heritage, but who are not any more accepted as true Germans by the people living in Germany proper.

Nationalism has obviously showed itself not to be an original part of the self-understanding of man. It has developed over the last two centuries in a peculiar environment, Europe of the late eighteenth, and the nineteenth and twentieth centuries. In Europe it may, however, disappear. It could be replaced on the one hand by a comprehensive political structure, "the European Union." This has no common history (except a very warlike one, every part fighting its neighbors for thousands of years). A substitute could also be regionalism, a centrifugal movement that concentrates on smaller units supposed to have an ethnic basis. This is a retrograde movement, so to speak, taking us back to where we started before the formation of the national states and even before the formation of the kingdoms of the past.

This development also says, however, that there is something to return to. This involves a kind of identity that is bound not to the existence of a national state with fixed and protected borders, but to something much more vague which could probably best be described as an indefinite sentiment of belonging to somewhere. In that case there are basically two possibilities: the first argues that this sense has a historical background—people do really belong to somewhere; or it could be imaginative, "mythic"—people think that they are belonging to somewhere. This is probably the core of the concept of ethnicity, which makes it at the same time a forerunner of the more comprehensive and political device understood here to be nationalism. Before we go farther, however, it is necessary to present a short survey of the discussion about this concept, as elusive as it may turn out to be.

It is basically possible to speak about ethnicity in two different ways. On one hand it can be considered an integral part of human nature. In this case it is assumed always to be present in any group of human beings. It is a kind of territoriality not absolutely different from the sense of territorial possession common among predatory animals, and especially birds. On the other hand, ethnicity could be something that cannot be taken to be there in advance, but something that might develop should the circumstances further such a development. The first point of view is sometimes called "perennialism," the second "modernism."

The British sociologist Anthony Smith and the North American political scientist John Armstrong represent perennialism, among others.[34] Thus Anthony Smith in his discussion of the subject relates the idea of ethnicity to the Greek and Roman way of understanding other cultures or to the Egyptian particularism, in contrast to western Asia or to Nubia.[35] He is certainly right. That kind of ethnicity truly existed. We find the same kind of ethnicity in many parts of the world where members of a certain group describe themselves as "*the* human beings." This is seen in contrast to other groups, whose members cannot—since members of one's own group have already usurped the position—logically be human beings.

There are plenty of examples of this, dating from ancient times, a very outspoken one being probably the legend about Naram-Sin of Akkad (twenty-third century B.C.E.) and the Umannanda, "the horde from the north." The royal administration are in doubt about the identity of these invaders, whether they are human beings or not, and has therefore sent an officer with a spear whose task is to pierce one of the invaders to see whether he bleeds. The invader actually does so, to the great relief of the Akkadians because this means that it is possible to fight the invaders.[36] Surely ethnic differences existed and were understood and discussed also in ancient times; this is not a thing to be debated. The existence of ethnicity is not the issue, but the origin of it. Was it something that existed in advance? Did it have definable borders, imagined or real? Was it founded in myths and symbols pertinent to a specific ethnos and its origins? Was it therefore as stable a phenomenon as could be expected in those days of the past or was it something invented, something that was always in a state of flux, something that depended on a decision taken by the members of an ethnic group?

Without doubt one of the most influential studies on ethnicity published since the Second World War is the introduction to a series of studies on ethnicity published by the Norwegian functionalist anthropologist Fredrik Barth in 1969.[37] According to Barth, ethnicity is a social way of organizing cultural difference. He says that ethnicity basically consists of two main elements, on the one hand a social group, and on the other a cultural unit. However, since both may develop independently, there is no necessary connection between a certain culture and a certain group of people. The relations are dynamic and always changing.[38]

This is not as easy as some may think. The following example from the history of social anthropology will suffice. In 1940 the British social anthropologist E. E. Evans-Pritchard published his famous and widely acclaimed study of the Nuer society in Sudan.[39] After the Second World War some of his students returned to Africa to take up their master's research among the Nuer people in southern Sudan and could not find them. It turned out that this ethnic group was recognized only by its neighbors, while it itself did not know of any identity to be connected with the name of the Nuer. "Nuer" was an ethnical tag attached on them by their neighbors, the Dinka.[40] We here have a classic example of the so-called emic/etic distinction, which implies a difference between what people think of themselves and what they are thought to be by other persons. This distinction, which has been borrowed by anthropologists from general linguistics (and may not be used in an absolutely precise sense), teaches the anthropologist to make a distinction between what he is told by his native informers and what he can "see with his own eyes." The anthropologist is in this way forced to treat both as two separate, however interrelated, sets of data, which have to be handled in two different ways.

In order to decide who might belong to a certain ethnic group and who are excluded from it, it is necessary to establish borders between the groups. This every student of the concept would admit. The interesting thing about Barth's concept of borders is that it is not limited to geographical lines more or less visible in the landscape of a certain region; it also includes linguistic and occupational as well as mental borders. This means that it is too easy to say that a certain region will provide the home for a certain ethnic group. Any region may in fact contain several ethnic groups, all of them with a home in the same region, which is the case when gypsy tribes are around, always constituting an ethnos of their own, irrespective of where they may travel. To a certain degree this could also be the case of nomads traveling through different regions during their yearly migrations. If such a region is under pressure from forces with a base outside the region itself, it is characteristic that the different ethnic groups may not unite in order to defend the region. Such a defense will normally be an obligation put on the *dominating* group.

Language can make up a difference, as already appreciated in antiquity, but it need not do so. Switzerland has been one federal state since the Middle Ages without changing its constituency since then, although four officially acknowledged languages are recognized. No one who has ever visited Switzerland will be in doubt that in spite of this difference the country is remarkably homogeneous and displays most of the features normally related to an ethnic group. While a common language is certainly an advantage to any ethnos, it is not mandatory. Regionalism can in fact mold groups with different linguistic backgrounds into one ethnic organization.

Occupation is another possibility of differentiation, and history and anthropology possess many examples of dividing lines being created by occupational diversity, often provoking animosity and even fierce struggle when two different occupational strategies compete in one and the same habitat. Thus it was formerly believed that tribalism was limited to one form of occupation (this was normally assumed to be nomadism). Now it has beyond doubt been demonstrated that one and the same occupation is not a prerequisite in order to keep a tribal organization together—nor for that matter is the physical limitation to one and the same region. The Baḫtiyari of Iran are not a tribe in any occupational sense; it is simply the name of the people who live in the Baḫtiyar region.[41]

Mental borders are at one and the same time difficult to pinpoint and very effective. Any person will be acquainted with some sort of mental borderlines drawn to create difference and distance between individuals and groups. In every case, a mental line of division has to go with any other criteria mentioned or forgotten in this place, because without mental borders the other criteria will not work. Differences of language will mean nothing if the persons speaking them will not accept or acknowledge this as creating an ethnic difference should other concerns be considered more important; neither will occupational differentiation. Mental borders have to do among other things with myths of origin, historical remembrance, real or imagined, religious differences believed to be important, and especially acceptance, which has turned out to be a key word in modern concepts of ethnicity.

As to geographical borders, these can certainly turn out to be decisive in the formation of an ethnos, although this will usually demand that a group be stable and able to survive for longer periods. This may happen in a remote valley where the inhabitants are cut off from regular communication with their neighbors living in similar valleys, and even help to create religious minorities such as the Waldensian community in Europe in the Middle Ages.[42] The presence and importance of this type of "Shangri-las" may, however, be exaggerated, and the assumption that they are out there somewhere more a modern myth that reflecting reality. As far as the ancient Near East goes, it has still to be shown that a total isolated community existed somewhere here, and this applies also to the remote nooks and corners of Palestine, Lebanon, or Syria.

Other places where geography is supposed to provide the borderline between ethnic units are areas dominated by agriculture and a fixed peasantry. Here it is not the lack of communication that may create the differences. It is, rather, the competition for the scant resources of the area and simply a lack of horizon, as the immobility of the peasants makes them unfit to survey a greater region than the landscape in which they are placed and where they are born, work, and die. In this case there could well be a difference in the understanding of local ethnicity if such an area also includes a hierarchical structure, where a squire may be considered the master of the population of peasants, as a patron of his clients. In such a case the geographical horizon of the squire would certainly be different from that of his peasants. He will in fact belong to a "different world"—another way of saying "a different ethnos"—as a member of a group that reaches farther out in society.[43] This is not limited to agrarian societies, where such differences may be explained as a difference of locality or residence; it can also happen in other sectors, for example among tribal societies whose leaders are sometimes elevated to high positions in the states where their kinsmen live.[44] It would also be possible to say that such persons are members of two different ethnic units, their tribal unit and the social group where most of their political activity will take place. They are, so to speak, changing their ethnic affiliation according to the circumstances of the day, and are thus pointing toward a more flexible definition of ethnicity than normally assumed, but one that is in accordance with Barth's and his students' definition. This is not only the case with members of the societal elite, however, as examples can be found where this also applies to the common man.

The concept of ethnicity will, in contrast to the artificial one of the state, have to be fluid with the acceptance of borders, which are multidimensional in character and always flexible. Ethnicity does not in itself imply a closed and self-contained social unit, although it can do so, for example in isolated villages in mountain regions, but is more often than not something that is always changeable according to circumstances. As long as the concept of a nation is kept away from the discourse of an ethnic group, it will be open for changes. These may be major ones, understood as important by every member of the community, or they may be minute, almost impossible to perceive, something that is only realized after some time has elapsed. Many elements come together in order to create an ethnos, including those of languages, symbols, religion, practices, food, and so on,[45] but in a living society none of these elements are stable, but are always being transformed into something else. Stability is an artificial element in the concept of ethnicity—probably the result of a sociological armchair theory, no more than a scholarly assumption in the past or of today as well.

The decisive factor is whether or not changes are accepted by the members of the community, no matter how such changes involve the exchange of habits or of persons. In reality the long-lasting discussion among social anthropologist in the 1970s and 1980s may have produced only one result. An ethnic group consists of the persons who think of themselves as members of this group, in contrast to other individuals who are not reckoned to be members and who do not reckon themselves to belong to this group. No ethnic group has ever been able to create a situation of stability that will last for centuries. Rather, ethnic groups are by definition unstable, with borders that can be transgressed in every possible way. As a matter of fact, any ethnic group is a part of a continuum of ethnic groups with overlapping borders, with probably many identities, held together by a founding myth or set of myths and narratives about how this particular group came into being. An ethnic group may probably also result simply from the existence of such myths with the ability to create identity among people.

... AND ANCIENT ISRAEL

Fifteen years ago I concluded a preliminary discussion about tribes and ethnicity in this way:

> However, the debate concerning such concepts as "tribe" or "ethnicity" underlines the fact that we must be prepared to describe tribes as flexible as possible. . . . To use Barth's definition, "*ethnicity*" in the case of Israel would signify the process which enabled people who understood themselves to be Israelites to distinguish between themselves and others. We must seek the reasons behind such an ability to differentiate in the available source materials. To focus in advance of such an investigation on a single element, especially the notion of a specifically Israelite religion, could well prove to have fatal consequences.[46]

It was the general idea that in studying human societies we should allow for all kind of dynamics to be involved in the development of society. A society is unstable, always changing, and always interwoven in a network of relations to other societies. But once written down, theories about societies are stable.

When approaching the description of the Israel of the Old Testament, it is obvious that this society is here considered to be of one blood, of common descent, with an apical ancestor, Israel, alias Jacob, the grandson of Abraham who traveled from Mesopotamia to the land of Canaan. It also is said to have one and the same religion deciding who is and who is not a member of this society, and with a divinely sanctioned constitution, which was given to this Israel at Sinai. It was supposed to be in the possession of a special land of its own, although this was not always so (here a dynamic element intrudes into the otherwise stable model). It also carried a special bodily symbol—circumcision—as a distinctive mark of its nationality. In short, the model of Israel to be found in the Old Testament has much in common with ideas of ethnicity and nationality expressed by scholars belonging to the political sciences and ethnography. It deviates, however, in a very serious way from modern definitions of ethnicity and shows absolutely no understanding for the processual character of this phenomenon.

This book will analyze the concept of Israel in order to see whether the Israel of the Old Testament is a reflection of a real society of this world or the negative contrast to the new Israel. This "new Israel" is understood to be an ideal society to be established sometime in the near future. In the eyes of many "scholars" of the past who have never looked out the window to perceive the world outside it, this biblical Israel was believed to have existed once. Therefore a theme also to be scrutinized is how this theme of Israelite ethnicity and nationality has been treated in modern historical studies. The aim will be to demonstrate whether such studies ever showed any independent concern about what historical Israel might have been like or whether they have just followed the ideas of nationality as developed in their own time.

CHAPTER 1

Playing the
von Ranke Game

Sifting the Sources

According to Leopold von Ranke, the historian who intends to re-create the past should always concentrate on the *acknowledged* contemporary sources and delegate all other kind of information to a second place.

When von Ranke and historians since his time are referring to an acknowledged contemporary source, they indicate first of all that kind of information which can be dated without problems. They also say that the source must physically belong to the period about which it is taken to be firsthand information. A slab of stone with an inscription found in situ, that is, where it was originally placed by the person who erected the stone to commemorate some event of his own day, is without doubt a primary and contemporary source. A description of the same item found in some ancient literary source is, however, not a contemporary source except in the case where it goes back to the same time as the stone inscription. Thus Livy's description of the Second Punic War is not a contemporary source, as it is removed by about two hundred years from the days of Hannibal and Scipio. Suetonius's life of August is not a primary source because it is about a hundred years later than the time of August. The *Monumentum Ancyranum*[1] can, however, be considered a firsthand piece of evidence from this period, since it relies on an official document from the days of August, and was placed on his temple in Ankara shortly after his death.

The situation in the ancient Near East is not different from this. Thus Manetho's description of the expulsion of the Hyksos is not a contemporary source, removed by at least twelve hundred years from the events referred to and only preserved as quotations in much later sources.[2] Documents from the time of the Eighteenth Dynasty in Egypt are much closer to the event, but they are not contemporary sources to this event.

Only an inscription from the days of Kamose, the last pharaoh of the Seventeenth Dynasty (middle of the sixteenth century B.C.E.) will be reckoned a firsthand source.

Seen from the perspective of its time of origin, it is of secondary importance whether an inscription represents royal propaganda or should be considered a general's report from the field. Every written document is a singular piece of evidence and has been written with a special purpose in mind. Still, contemporary documents may probably refer to events that in some form or the other "really happened." How and why they happened are, in comparison to this—although certainly important questions—secondary problems. Only the demonstration that an event recorded in a contemporary document never did happen may in a fundamental way shake our confidence in this basic distinction. Such cases are known, although only occasionally possible to pinpoint. One recent example of this is the disturbance caused among scholars of the history of the hometown of this author, Copenhagen, which according to a contemporary source was founded in 1167 C.E. New excavations in Copenhagen have demonstrated that the city may be a hundred years older than this official date.[3] Consequently, contemporary sources are per se infinitely better than documents from subsequent periods, but they must still be used with analytical care; the scholar must especially be aware of the pitfalls created by the difference between his cultural outlook and the one of the ancient authors.

An example of the reverse, the premature ascription of an ancient source to so-called historical events of the past, may be Manetho's aforementioned anecdotal description of the expulsion of the Hyksos. Scholars have tried to refer this "event" to the biblical story of the escape of the Israelite tribes from Egypt under Moses' leadership. They are unquestionably wrong. First of all, the tale of the exodus is in itself beset with so many historical problems that its historicity is more than questionable— rather, it is from a historian's point of view highly unlikely. Second, Manetho's description of the expulsion of the Hyksos is from a historian's vantage point only slightly better. Finally, the link between the biblical version of the exodus and Manetho's narrative was not a simple one as sometimes assumed. It is included in his description of the fate of the Hyksos people, but it is mixed up with notes and commentaries by the Jewish historian Flavius Josephus, in his *Contra Apionem,* a work that was composed in the second half of the first century C.E. If Manetho knew anything about the Israelite exodus—and this is not something added by Josephus—it is certainly not the version preserved in the present book of Exodus.[4]

THE OLD TESTAMENT
AS A HISTORICAL SOURCE

The Old Testament is not a primary source of the history of ancient Israel, since it is not preserved in a condition that physically goes back to the time described in its historical literature. We may decide to follow the dates of Archbishop James Ussher, placing the creation of the world in 4004 B.C.E.[5] Also in this case there will be a vast span between, say, the days of David and the earliest extant fragment of the books of Solomon found at Qumran and hardly older than the first century B.C.E.[6] Assuming a case can be made for dating King David to the tenth century B.C.E., an inscription from this century mentioning him would, however, have to be acknowledged as a source of the first rank, whereas an inscription from, say, as early as the ninth century is not.[7]

It is very important to accept this status of the Old Testament as a secondary source to the history of Israel. It is by all means, without forgetting the extensive *Jewish History* of Josephus, the most comprehensive written source to this history, but it is also always later—probably much later—than the events referred to by the biblical authors. Josephus's *Jewish History* is, as far as the pre-Hasmonaean time goes, mostly dependent on the biblical narrative and only occasionally presents independent material such as Moses' Ethiopian war[8]—an event never referred to in the biblical material.[9]

This does not automatically mean that the historical narrative in the Old Testament is devoid of historical information. This is a common misunderstanding when a late date of this narrative is argued, that the scholar in favor of such a position will at the same time deny that any historical recollection can be preserved in such a late text. Historicity and the status of a text as a primary or secondary source are two different subjects. It can easily happen that a later source is more reliable than a contemporary one, which is often the case when we talk about modern reconstructions of ancient history that are certainly modern renditions of the past as *we see it*. One such example of a contemporary source that has little to do with the real circumstances surrounding a historical event is the tale of King Idrimi's ascension to the throne of Alalakh (c. 1500 B.C.E.), a tale that was commissioned by the king himself and inscribed on his statue.[10] This narrative has a long time ago been shown not to tell us the realities connected with the career of this Syrian king. It is a kind of fairy tale structured according to the well-known tale of the male hero, the youngest among his brothers, who nonetheless decides to leave the house of his parents in order to win a kingdom and a princess for himself. A historical reconstruction of how Idrimi came to power in the kingdom Mukish shows that, instead of being a hero, he was obviously a foreign usurper, in fact an illegitimate king (although he may—as maintained by himself—have been of noble blood from the royal line of Aleppo).[11]

It is, on the other hand, almost always the modern historian—and only this person—who is endowed with the methodological remedies to analyze a story like Idrimi's and to extract historical information and distinguish between this and "noise." "Noise" means a kind of "screen" put up by the ancient author to conceal the brutal and unwelcome fact of the assumption of power by a tyrant of dubious origins. As a matter of fact, very few examples exist of an ancient author who calls into question what he has found in a written source, and the few examples that may be quoted hardly display a methodologically critical mind; rather, they are examples of so-called "common sense."[12]

The status of the Idrimi inscription should be borne in mind when approaching an ancient source that should by all means be considered contemporary evidence. Even in this case it is necessary to study the text not as representing the plain truth and nothing but it, but also as containing a potentially highly complicated message edited before publishing, with particular reasons in mind. People of ancient times were certainly not naive, brutish persons without sophistication. Conversely, the manipulation of texts—which also includes propagandistic distortions—was a well-known and widely used means of communication also in contemporary royal documents. This propaganda was often presented in a concealed way, so effectively done that it is easy to point at more naive modern scholars who have not been able to penetrate the propagandistic message to reach the so-called realities that may have provoked the message.[13] Much too seldom among our contemporaries are we met with the same ironic distance as displayed by King Hattushilish III of Hatti. In a letter to Ramses II of Egypt, Hattushilish asks him about his participation in the famous battle of Kadesh: "Was there really nobody with you!" referring of course to the well-known propagandistic descriptions by Ramses in both words and pictures of his glorious exploits in Syria against the Hittite army.[14]

Historical information may be present in a late text irrespective of how strongly edited this text may have been. It would be ridiculous to say the opposite. However, the criteria necessary for judging whether or not such a late textual witness may provide information must be severe, as it is unlikely that the producer of a late written source from antiquity would be in the position to present a kind of systemically correct picture of the past. At least such an example has still to be found. In general, it will be necessary to

provide contemporary evidence to say that a later source is delivering anything in the way of historical information.

In 2 Kings 18–19, Sennacherib's attack on Jerusalem in 701 B.C.E. is described in a way not very far removed from the version present in Sennacherib's narrative in his annals. There is no reason to deny that we in this
case have a biblical confirmation of the Assyrian attack. It is also true that
the biblical version of the campaign is placed within a network of legendary
motives. Consequently, the biblical interpretation of the outcome of the
siege is at one and the same time historically imprecise and mythic, and covers up the fact that Jerusalem may have been the only part of Hezekiah's
kingdom that was not destroyed by the Assyrians. It is therefore correct to
say that the great divinely inspired victory over the Assyrians recounted by
the biblical narrative has little to do with the events of the fateful year of 701
B.C.E. Second Kings 18–19 is not a historical narrative but a tale about the
past that includes, however, an isolated historical residue contained in the
narrative. This historical element does not, on the other hand, turn this tale
into history writing.[15]

Other examples could be mentioned, such as the conquest of Jerusalem
in 587 B.C.E. There is no reason to doubt the historicity of the conquest of
Jerusalem in 597 B.C.E., since the Babylonian Chronicle confirms this.[16] The
historicity of the one supposed to have happened in 587 B.C.E. relies only
on the description of the conquest of Jerusalem and the deportation of its
inhabitants in 2 Kings 25 and Jeremiah 39 and 52. As it has been shown, the
various Old Testament textual witnesses to this event are not in agreement
as to the exact date of this conquest.[17]

It is correct that more than a century of biblical research has tried to sort
out methods to carve out historical remembrances of the text of the Old Testament, which has been considered to be the result of a rather complicated
process of redacting and editing. The division of the Pentateuch into at least
three or four (or more) literary strata—the Yahwist, the Elohist, the Priestly
writer, and a Deuteronomistic appendix in the form of the book of
Deuteronomy—is well known and was for generations accepted almost
without questioning in one form or the other. Several different ways were,
however, employed to separate the various parts from each other: literary
criticism, tradition history, and redaction history. More recently the same has
happened to the so-called Deuteronomistic History, which is often split up
into two or three redaction phases, if not sources.

All of this may be employed according to the preferences of the individual scholar. The result will, however, always be the same, even when the
analyst may think that he or she has reached the oldest part of the text. It is

still not a contemporary document; it is still a secondhand source and not an eyewitness to the events described by the text in question.

The oldest part of the Pentateuch was thus considered to be the Yahwist source going back—according to the traditional opinion of Old Testament scholars from Julius Wellhausen to Gerhard von Rad—to the glorious days of King Solomon in the tenth century. However, the narrative in the Yahwist source covered the period from creation (remember Archbishop Ussher: 4004 B.C.E.) down to the point of entry of the Israelite tribes into Canaan. This event was supposed to have occurred no less than 250 years before the ascension of Solomon to the throne. There was accordingly no way of getting back to the original event and to consider any part of the Pentateuch a primary historical source of the patriarchs, the sojourn of Israel in Egypt, the exodus, and the drowning of the pharaoh in the Sea of Reeds. This could not be achieved even by invoking the specter of oral tradition, as was sometimes done, not least in the Scandinavian school of Old Testament research.[18] If anything, oral tradition is even more uncontrollable than ancient *written* information.[19] Neither could it be done by referring the prose narrative of the biblical text to an original epic version of Israel prehistory, something that is not uncommon among North American biblical scholars.[20]

When it comes to the Deuteronomistic History, which covers the books from Joshua to 2 Kings, from the immigration to the second fall of Jerusalem in 587 B.C.E. (probably with the book of Deuteronomy as its preamble), the same will have to be said. In this case the time factor is—according to the traditional view which places the composition of this work in the late part of the exilic period[21]—narrowed down for the last part of the period covered by this history. Therefore the Deuteronomistic History cannot claim to be considered a primary source to, say, the reign of David, usually dated to the tenth century B.C.E. Neither is it for that matter to any other event until exilic times. It has only one short note about this exile, the piece about the fate of Jehoiachin after 562 B.C.E. (2 Kings 25:27–30)—as a matter of fact the only and very reason for dating the History to the exilic period. Logically, this date can serve only as an upper line of its composition.

Sometimes the prophetic literature has been brought into the discussion as representative of firsthand knowledge of events narrated by 2 Kings. Thus Amos is supposed, by the heading to his book, to have prophesied in the days of Uzziah of Judah and Jeroboam II of Israel; Hosea in the time of Uzziah, Jotham, Ahaz, and Hezekiah of Judah and Jeroboam of Israel; Micah in the days of Jotham, Ahaz, and Hezekiah; Isaiah in the days of Uzziah, Jotham, Ahaz, and Hezekiah; Zephaniah in the days of Josiah; and Jeremiah in the days of Josiah, Jehoiachim, and Zedekiah. It is obvious, however, that these prophetic books contain many passages that it is impossible to place in the historical context of the prophets. For that matter, it is easy to point to texts that cannot belong to preexilic times, although placed by the composers of the prophetic literature in that context. Furthermore, it was also considered beyond doubt that many parts of these books had been reworked, some of them several times and over a long period. Therefore a number of methods were invented to distinguish between original material in the prophetic literature—the so-called *ipsissima verba* of the prophets[22]—and later additions.

It is certain that could it be demonstrated beyond doubt that a certain prophecy was once upon a time formulated by, say Isaiah, such a prophecy would be a primary source of the period to which it belonged. If the prophecy about the birth of Immanuel in Isaiah 7:14 really went back to the prophet, then we would be in the possession of firsthand evidence about the period in question supposed to have been the time of the Syro-Ephraimite War (according to a popular estimate to have happened between 734 and 732 B.C.E.). Again the problem is that this piece of prophecy is contained in a narrative that is heavily dependent—sometimes literally—on the narrative in 2 Kings 16. It cannot be left out of consideration that even if this prophecy went back to Isaiah himself (a thing that can, because of lack of evidence, never be proved), its place in its present literary context will invariably be secondary. The formulation of Isaiah 7, which opens with a quote from 2 Kings,[23] evidently belongs to a Deuteronomistic-inspired editing of the tradition of preexilic Israel and Judah. It is therefore at least two hundred years later than the war between Aram, Israel, and Judah.

The same verdict applies to the dating of the prophets to the reigns of named Israelite and Judean kings, as these dates clearly presuppose the history of Israel and Judah as presented by the books of Kings. In a stereotypical way these dates display Deuteronomistic phraseology. It may be that Hosea was really active as a prophet in the eighth century B.C.E. This cannot be proved or disproved on the basis of contemporary sources. It is, however, a fact that a redactor—if not simply the author—of the book of Hosea motivated by Deuteronomistic ideology placed him in this historical context. As a matter of fact, it is fundamentally the person who redacted the book of Hosea who claims that his prophet was the author of the prophecies in the book of Hosea. It is also the same person, however, who says that this book belongs in a historical context otherwise known only from the books of Kings. It is immaterial whether or not the modern scholars accept these claims to be correct, and does not concern the general question about the status of the prophetic text as a firsthand source of the period in question.

It cannot be considered such evidence, as it in its present form clearly belongs to another and later period.

Playing the game of von Ranke does not include the splitting of late sources into, on one side, material considered to be contemporary evidence, and on the other, secondary material. Evidence is either secondary, that is, removed in time from the period under discussion, or it is primary, belonging to this period. That cannot be decided on the basis of a majority vote among scholars. Evidence may be included in a textual context of, say, the fifth century (or later). It may refer to events of, say, the eighth century. It can only be elevated from the status of a secondary source to the one of a primary source of the eighth century, however, if it can otherwise, from contemporary sources, be proved beyond doubt that it really belongs to the eighth and not to the fifth century. This is a fact often overlooked by biblical scholars who sometimes think that late books like Ezra and Nehemiah include primary documentary material going back to, say, the time of Cyrus or other Achaemenid kings of Persia.

Although it certainly creates problems for the assumption that the Old Testament is a source for ancient Israelite history, this verdict has nothing to do with denying the historicity of the events narrated by the authors of the historical literature in the Old Testament. Everything narrated by them may in principle be historical, but the biblical text cannot in advance be accepted as a historical source or documentation; it has in every single case to prove its status as a historical source. Although it is sometimes maintained that a certain part of Old Testament scholarship is at the present characterized by a negative attitude toward the biblical texts as a historical source, this opinion is false. The text of the Old Testament is, for the simple reason that it is an old document, a historical source. The question is only about what. It might be that the description of the reign of David contained in the books of Samuel is historically correct, as seen from the perspective of its late author. It cannot be excluded. However, it has to be proved that the narrative in Samuel is historically reliable as far as the tenth century is concerned. It is not something that can be assumed in advance.

It is traditionally believed to be a respectable enterprise to try to show that a certain event narrated by the Old Testament really happened and that the narrative is for that reason a valuable source. It is at least as respectable, however, to try to show that the text does not carry any information about the period worth speaking about. In both cases the scholar should employ an identical set of methods and proceed from the same basic assumption, that the text of the Old Testament is not a primary source of the history of Israel. It is later than the events mentioned in it and therefore a secondary source to the past, the historical value of which has to be demonstrated and not accepted in advance of the historical analysis. To assume the historicity of a biblical narrative in advance is unscholarly and cannot escape influencing the analysis in a negative direction.

OTHER SOURCES

In traditional historical research, written sources always take precedence over all other types of evidence. These may include remnants of cities and villages, farmsteads, houses, artifacts, pictures engraved on monuments (when not accompanied by an inscription), and so on. Most of this has been unearthed by archaeological excavations in Palestine and its neighboring countries over a period of more than a hundred years. Modern archaeology is a highly complicated scientific discipline. It has assumed many shapes, including social archaeology and cognitive archaeology,[24] both of which aimed (among other things) at extracting historical information from an otherwise mute material. It has not been able, however, to bypass the problem that most of its results are based on material remains not accompanied by any written indication of the people who produced them. When a certain village of the Early Iron Age in the central Palestinian highlands dating from the twelfth century B.C.E. is called Israelite—or "proto-Israelite"[25]—this assumption is not based on the physical remnants themselves. It is a label attached to them on the basis of written sources, primary evidence from contemporary documents or secondary evidence as found in the Old Testament. It is not so that this village cannot be Israelite because we lack evidence to say so. It is only so that we don't know the ethnic composition of its inhabitants, except in the case that in the material remains of the village we can find references to a material culture that shows up at other sites and in contexts that are undeniably Israelite.

This village might reveal a material culture with a definite relationship to the culture of the cities of Palestine in the Late Bronze Age in the thirteenth century. In this case it is legitimate to think that the inhabitants of the village in question must somehow and to a certain extent trace their descent from these cities. Such cities might be called "Canaanite"—still the common name of the pre-Israelite inhabitants of Palestine used by most Orientalists, although no more than a conventional term borrowed from the Old Testament.[26] If so, it would be a correct deduction to say that a dominant demographic element in our village was in this respect "Canaanite." Of course, this ethnic tag is problematic and distorting because it owes its existence to the late biblical agenda of creating opponents to the biblical Israelites. The biblical term "Canaanite" has little, if anything, to do with ethnic realities of Palestine in, say, the Late Bronze Age. It simply has to be accepted that we have no idea about what the villagers thought of their own ethnic affiliation. "Canaanite" in this connection says only that the culture of the village in question derived from the one found in the area in the preceding period.

On the other hand, the culture of the village might also relate to the culture of a city of the ninth century that was undoubtedly situated inside the borders of the Iron Age state of Israel (Samaria). In that case it is possible to call the inhabitants of the village proto-Israelites, insofar as the culture of the village could be styled a "protoculture" of the later city. This does not say that the inhabitants of the said village were "Israelites." It indicates only that they shared a material culture otherwise found within the territory of the state of Israel in the Iron Age. The designation "proto-Israelite" is thus not a suitable ethnic tag. It should probably be avoided as infested with the same kinds of problems as concerned the Canaanites. It is a term borrowed from the Old Testament as part of the agenda of the biblical historians who also created the "Canaanites" as the adversaries of these biblical Israelites. The term "Israelite" understood as an ethnical tag placed on the material culture of our village only means that it belonged to "citizens of the historical state of Israel" between, say, 900 and 722 B.C.E. It is no more than a political term, and its biblical implications should be avoided.

The situation becomes immensely more complicated if the material culture described as "proto-Israelite" should turn up outside the territory of the Iron Age state of Israel, for example in Transjordan in regions otherwise known to be part of the Ammonite, the Moabite, or the Edomite states. In this case, there are no more excuses for naming it proto-Israelite. If in spite of this scholars continue to use the term "proto-Israelite," they use it contrary to the evidence. The so-called Israelite culture showed up to be nothing except in the first case a development of earlier local Bronze Age culture, and in the second a shared material culture, not exclusive to the kingdom of Israel and its inhabitants. The reason for assuming an ethnic exclusivity for the citizens of this kingdom has therefore totally vanished as far as the material remains are concerned.

This is not theory. As a matter of fact, the discussion concerning the two most famous examples of early "Israelite" material culture, the house type[27] and the collared-rim storage jars,[28] show how archaeologists on the basis of mute contemporary cultural remains and secondary written evidence try to establish historical links. At the same time their assumptions also make room for the establishment of ethnic groups and borderlines.

A dominant form of houses found in the villages of the Early Iron Age consists of a three-room compound. This house first showed up in excavations in the central highlands and was by the archaeologists related ethnically to the Israelites and historically to the nomads of ancient Syria and Palestine. They saw it as a reflection of the form of the tent popular among the Bedouins of the modern age. This tent consists of three apartments: one used as a public domain, where guests are received and entertained, the second the male's apartment, and the last one a territory exclusively used by the women of the household. This type of nomadic dwelling was extensively studied earlier this century by the Danish social anthropologist C. G. Feilberg,[29] who dated its appearance to the eleventh century B.C.E. based on biblical secondary sources of a much later date. Feilberg's conclusions and dating were, however, accepted by biblical scholars as a proof that the tent was an older prototype of the houses of the twelfth and eleventh century B.C.E. The argument is, of course, false and there is no reason to pay attention to it anymore. We have no idea of the date of appearance of the tent form. To trace the origin of the house form of the Early Iron Age back to a form of a tent that is attested only in much later contexts is simply, from a methodological point of view, ridiculous.

It has with more reason been argued that the house form represents a development of local house style that goes back to the Late Bronze Age. If this is the case, the burden has been removed from the shoulders of nomads that they should have invented new house forms almost as soon as they settled.[30] The house form cannot be an ethnic designator, and this is confirmed by the fact that the same style of housing has been found outside the territory ruled by the kings of Samaria in the Iron Age, that is, the kingdom of Israel.

The situation as far as the collared-rim jar is concerned is very much the same, although this jar may not represent a development of a pottery type in use in the Late Bronze Age.[31] Instead it has been found outside the territory of the later kingdom of Israel, in Transjordan and other places.[32]

The situation is more complicated because of the character of the Palestinian landscape with its many small units and short distances. When two material cultures are related, the reason might be that they represent ethnic relations: the people living in the first place are related to the people living in the second place. Therefore the material culture is more or less the same. As far as it is not due to a mutual lifestyle—basic agriculture—cultural similarity may also be caused by other influences like traveling, trade, or mutual interconnections between two population groups melting two originally independent groups together in one and the same cultural if not yet ethnic unit.

If, however, we can identify two isolated examples of systemic cultural similarity, separated by, say, a thousand miles, the reason for this similarity could, among other things, be common origin, or ethnic relationship. In this case trade and traveling of individuals are hardly the reason for cultural identity. Casual and infrequent visits may account for the borrowing of isolated common traits, but in the case of a general and systemic relationship between two material cultures separated in this way, the reason is likely to be common ancestry. In the Levant, southwestern Syria and Palestine, however, the distances are short and interconnection between separate groups easy and common. Cultural similarity may therefore not reflect common ancestry. It might only tell us about frequent interconnections between different groups living within a short distance of each other. It is therefore to be expected that a general cultural similarity will be present in a small-scale territory like this one, which also militates against the assumption that cultural similarity may by necessity be reflecting ethnic composition. Two very different and, from a genetic point of view, unrelated groups could be in the possession of a common material culture, a fact also supported by the general low standard of material culture of what was basically an agrarian society possessing little occupational differentiation.

This is not said in order to deny cultural diversity and change. It may of course be possible to point at regional differences. Such differences might involve, say, the material culture of Lebanese Iron Age villages and central Palestinian ones. They might also concern the city lifestyle of major Syrian cities and the one found in the insignificant urban settlements of Bronze and Iron Age Palestine.[33] They might also involve the cities in the Judean mountains and their neighbors in the coastal plain belonging to the so-called Philistine Pentapolis.[34] For the Philistines it seems rather certain that a series of components supports a theory about ethnic diversity. The support includes not only written documents from the ancient Near East, but ceramics, and also certain examples of house style such as the palace from Ekron displaying the "megaron-style" from the Greek mainland.[35]

It is an interesting fact that the presence of a basically cultural identity and continuity in the Levant as far as the material remains are concerned is paralleled by other phenomena attested in contemporary written documents. The population in this area spoke fundamentally the same West Semitic language, worshiped the same gods, and to a large extent carried identical names. Furthermore, this common language—although increasingly being pressed by Aramaic, the presence of which is first traced in inscriptions from the late tenth century—continued to be in use in the Iron Age, as did also the religion and the forms of names. As was the case of the material remains, this fact does not exclude the presence of numerous local variations—dialectal differences, different attitudes as to the gods to be worshiped, or the like. In the Late Bronze Age significant differences existed between the language spoken in Syrian cities like Ugarit, or Phoenician cities like Byblos, and the language in use in southern Palestine or inner Syria. In the Iron Age, the language in inscriptions from the kingdoms of Israel and Judah was not a hundred percent identical. Neither were their language and the one of Phoenician, Moabite, Ammonite, or Edomite inscriptions. They were all closely related, probably more closely than the dialects of modern national states like France or Germany, certainly more than the many local dialects that were artificially combined into "New Norwegian" only a few generations ago.

CHAPTER 2

Israel in Contemporary Historical Documents from the Ancient Near East

THE SO-CALLED "ISRAEL-STELE" OF MERNEPTAH

In 1896 the German Egyptologist Wilhelm Spiegelberg published an inscription commemorating Pharaoh Merneptah's (1213–1204 B.C.E.) victory over the Libyans.[1] In a few lines at the end—almost like an appendix—the inscription, however, also refers to a campaign of this pharaoh in western Asia, in the translation of John A. Wilson:

> The princes are prostrate, saying: "Mercy!"
>> Not one raises his head among the Nine Bows.
> Desolation is for Tehenu; Hatti is pacified;
>> Plundered is Canaan with every evil;
> Carried off is Ashkelon; seized upon is Gezer;
>> Yanoam is made as that which does not exist;
> Israel is laid waste, his seed is not;
>> Hurru has become a widow for Egypt!
> All lands together, they are pacified;
>> Everyone, who was restless, he has been bound.[2]

It goes without saying that many are the theories and hypotheses put forward on behalf of this Israel, which is by far the most likely transcription of the Egyptian text.[3] In the days of old—only a generation ago—this text was considered important evidence of the immigration of the biblical Israelites into Palestine, which was supposed to have taken place within a few years of the Egyptian campaign in Asia referred to in Merneptah's Libyan inscription. The date of the Libyan campaign was, according to this text, Merneptah's fifth year, 1208 B.C.E., which meant that the immigration of the Israelites would have happened, say, around 1225 B.C.E. The Israelites were therefore supposed to have arrived in Palestine in the interval between the Amarna period (middle of fourteenth century B.C.E.) and the end of the thirteenth century. Israel is not mentioned in the Amarna letters from Palestine, although several letters come from or concern the territory of the later kingdom of Israel.[4]

The victory stele of Merneptah, however, does not confirm the date of the Hebrew conquest of Palestine; in fact, it has no bearing on that topic. It testifies only to the presence in western Asia at the end of the thirteenth century B.C.E. of something that constituted some sort of ethnic unity, which was identifiable as far as it had its own name, Israel. What this entity precisely was is, on the other hand, not as easy to ascertain as people may be inclined to believe.

A few things, however, have to be settled in advance. First of all, the part of the text mentioning Israel is only an appendix to a major description of the victory over the Libyans. It is only a sideshow to this major military success of Merneptah. It could therefore be questioned whether there actually was a *military* campaign of Merneptah in western Asia during the first part of his reign. Although some of the names in this appendix are original to the inscription in question, not all of them are. Any rate, it seems to have been a local affair, no more than a "campaign" of some sort into the heartland of Palestine. It might not have included the territory to the north of the Carmel range or the Jordan valley up to Beth-shean, otherwise known to be an Egyptian stronghold in the days of the Nineteenth and Twentieth Dynasties.

Now it has been argued that there really was a campaign, as pictorial descriptions that can be related to the inscription prove this to have taken place.[5] These pictorial references are thought by Frank Yurco also to represent the battle against the Israelites who in Yurco's interpretation, however, are represented as Canaanites, that is, wearing the same garments and equipment as other conquered people shown in the reliefs attached to this battle scene.[6] Again we will have to say that, in spite of the fact that we here have a contemporary source, its testimonial is not unequivocal. There might have been a campaign, although hardly a major one—one to show the flag and to loot (if not just extracting "taxes" from) a few urban settlements.[7] Otherwise the inscription may refer to an act of submission to the Egyptian rule following the ascension of Merneptah just a few years before.

All this is, on the other hand. not important when it comes to the central point, the presence of Israel, written *ysri3r*[8] in this inscription. Israel is one of the original elements here, never mentioned by any Egyptian inscription before the days of Merneptah. Furthermore the way Israel is introduced is different from the preceding place names, Canaan, Askalon, Gezer, and Yano'am. Israel alone is determined by the hieroglyphic sign for "foreign people" 𓏤𓀭𓏥 something that may be taken as an indication of a different status of Israel in comparison to the other names on the inscription. These are normally provided with the determinative for a foreign place, ⟨ᴍᴍ⟩. It must, however, at the same time be taken into consideration that the inscription's use of determinatives is inconsistent, as emphasized among others by Gösta W. Ahlström in his discussion of this text.[9]

Ahlström argued in favor of a territorial understanding of the term as used by Merneptah, interpreting this part of his inscription as a "ring"-composition where Israel in the seventh line parallels "Canaan" in the fourth line.[10] Thus the text opens with and ends with a general statement without any names being mentioned. The next part has to do with the major geographical entities, real or fictive—the Nine Bows and Hatti at the beginning, Kharu (Hurru) at the end. These three names form the outer ring. The inner ring is composed of at the beginning Canaan and at the end Israel, and the center is occupied by the three Palestinian localities, Ashkelon, Gezer, and Yano'am. As Canaan is here a territorial designation, so Israel must also be one, and Ahlström points with good reasons at the northern part of the central highlands.

It is remarkable that other scholars have not taken up Ahlström's interpretation. It provides a safe haven for scholars who would like not only to see this early Israel as a special ethnic or territorial (or both) entity in Palestine at the end of the thirteenth century, but also to retain the biblical understanding of the distinction between Israelites and Canaanites. His interpretation is, however, based on a shaky foundation, as the Canaan mentioned here most likely means nothing except Gaza, the center of the Nineteenth Dynasty Egyptian province of Canaan,[11] which says that in this place Canaan is the name of a town, followed by other Palestinian townships. If this is correct, then there is a geographical line of the Egyptian approach into Palestine. The text opens with a general indication of the territory: "the Nine Bows." This has since the beginning of Egyptian written history been a well-known term for the foreign enemies of Egypt, and Hatti, now at the very end of its history.[12] Thereupon the inscription progresses from Canaan (Gaza), the natural point of departure in those days for an Egyptian expedition (whatever its purpose) into Palestine, to Ashkelon, a traditional stronghold and a wealthy urban settlement at the coast a day's traveling to the north of Gaza. From Ashkelon there was only another day's walk to Gezer at the plain of Ajalon, and from here probably another day in order to get to Yano'am, the identification of which is so far not absolutely secure but probably only a few miles to the north or northeast of Gezer. That is the end of the city line. The following is described as Israel, whether this reference is a reference to a specific population, a tribe or a tribal coalition, or just a territory carrying this name.

When mapping the route of approach of the Egyptian expedition, there can be no doubt that we have arrived at the western border of the central highlands, at the southeastern extension of what would in the Iron Age be situated at the southwestern border of the kingdom of Israel. The Egyptian army is said to have wasted the territory of this population group. We know nothing about this event from other sources, and it is a fair guess to maintain that it was probably an exaggeration in kinds. It is difficult to point to definite destruction layers in Palestinian cities to be put into connection with this Egyptian campaign, although William G. Dever has indicated that Merneptah's hand could be seen behind a destruction of Gezer at this time.[13] It would be a natural consequence of this campaign if, for example, the only major urban settlement in the northern part of the central highland, Shechem, had been destroyed by Merneptah's troops. However, in that case he would probably not have forgotten to mention the name of this city if he had penetrated the highlands as far as that.

Now the character of Merneptah's defeat of Israel cannot be outlined in any precise way. It is not, however, very important. The important evidence of the inscription is its reference to an Israel placed in the northern part of the central highlands, as this certainly indicates some sort of political or geographical or ethnic relationship between this Israel and the later kingdom of this name in the Iron Age. The biblical evidence is firm: it speaks of a relationship that is outspokenly ethnic, although in all likelihood it covers a vastly bigger area than the one referred to in the inscription of Merneptah. At best this evidence is representative of a much later interpretation of a tradition of Israel.

THE BETH DAVID INSCRIPTION

Probably every scholar who has been working with primary material such as inscriptions has felt the stir that is occasioned by the recognition of something that the scholar in question is supposed to know in advance. Every scholar is—in spite of repeated assurances to the contrary—a kind of treasure hunter, looking for booty in the form of new knowledge, improved knowledge, a reconfirmation of something we thought we knew in advance or had already guessed or argued in favor of. Often when a major inscription or collection of written material turns up in an excavation in the Near East and its content is revealed to the public, the first question will be how this new textual evidence relates to the Bible. Scholars have traditionally been all too ready to find such links, often on a very shaky background. The most famous example of this is, of course, the Dead Sea Scrolls, a major assembly of ancient manuscripts that became available after 1947 when the first texts are said to have been found.[14] Their value for the study of the Bible and of Judaism in the Hellenistic-Roman period and through that also of the background of Christianity is enormous. Nevertheless, it will also be correct to say that these texts have been a major disappointment to many believing Christians: so many texts so close to the time of Jesus (if not simply from his era), and not a single reference to Christ! No wonder that books were published with a sensational message about cover-ups by the Vatican or arguing a secret code that enables the texts to provide the vaunted evidence, in spite of their plain message having been widely read and having even made headlines of modern mass communication.[15] The Dead Sea Scrolls are, however, only one among many similar examples unearthed over a period of more than a hundred years. Whenever an important collection of texts appears, the interpretation of this discovery first has to pass through a process handled by biblical scholars who try, so to speak on the basis of this inscription, to prove "that the Bible is, after all, true."

A reception in some quarters almost comparable to that of the Dead Sea Scrolls was accorded the so-called "House of David" inscription found at Tel Dan in the northern part of the Huleh Valley in 1993. Other fragments supposed to belong to the same inscription were unearthed in 1995. Now this inscription has found its place of honor in the Israel Museum in Jerusalem.[16] It would, however, be wiser to speak about two inscriptions or fragments of inscriptions. It is still a matter of dispute among scholars whether or not these fragments belong to one and the same inscription. This has not prevented the curators of the Israel Museum from presenting the fragments as if a joint was found.[17] That the fragments belong to two different inscriptions is obvious when the two inscriptions are compared. First of all, it is clear that the lines in the two fragments do not match each other. Second, the style of writing is different from one fragment to the next, although the fragments were probably written at the same time.[18]

Tel Dan Fragment A

1: [ ] . . . . [	][	]	[ ]°עֹּ[רֹ]מֹא[ ]
2: [ ] . . my father . . [	][		[ ]°°סֹי.אבי[ ]
3: and my father died. He went to [	*Is*-][		[לֹא.ךֹהֹי.אבי.בכשׁיו]
4: rael was before in the country of my father [ ][			[יֹביאֹ.קֹראב.םֹדק.לֹאר]
5: I, and Hadad went before me [	][		[יֹמֹדק.דֹדהֹ.ךֹהיו.הנא]
6: . . my king and I killed . . [	*cha*-][		[לֹלמֹ.לֹתקֹאו.ידֹלמֹ.י]
7: riots and thousands of horse[men	][		[שֹרפֹ.יֹפלאו.בב]
8: king of Israel, and killed [	][		[לֹתקֹ.הֹ.לאראשׁי.ךֹלמ]

9: . . Betdawd, and I put [   ][ד.ביתדוד.ואשם]

10: their country was [   ][ית.ארק.הם.ל]

11: other and . . [   ][אחרן.ולה]

12: . . over . . [   ][לך.על.ישֹ]

13: siege upon [   ][ומֹצר.עלֹ]

Tel Dan Fragments B1 and B2

1: [ ] and cut . [   ][ ]°רֹזגו[   ]

2: [w]ar in [   ][   ]]לחמה.בא]°[ ]

3: [ ] . . and my king entered [   ][   ]והֹי.יעל.מלכֹיֹ[ ]

4: [ ] Hadad made king [   ][   ]המלך.הדד[ ]

5: and I went fro[m] . . [   ][ ]בֹ [ ]מ.קֹפא[   ]

6: [ ]. prisoners . . [   ][   ]א.ירסאֹ.ןֹ.ןֹ[ ]

7: [ ]rm son [   ][   ].רב.םרֹ[ ]

8: [ ]yhw son [   ][ ]רב.והֹיֹ[   ]

The fragments were found with an interval of approximately 8 meters in secondary use in the city wall of Tel Dan, close to the southern gate. It might probably be best to understand them as either two different sections of the same inscription (the material of the fragments being almost identical), with two engravers each responsible for his part, or as two separate, though related, inscriptions. The excavator Avraham Biran and his epigrapher Joseph Naveh dated the inscriptions to the middle of the ninth century B.C.E. They believed them to commemorate the victory of an otherwise unknown Aramaean king over a coalition of Israel and Beth David, understood to be the dynastic name of the state of Judah. In their second article, and based on their false joint of all the fragments, the two editors identified the Israelite and Judean kings who—according to their reconstruction—were killed by the author of the inscription as Jehoram of Israel and Ahaziah of Judah.[19]

Now this interpretation is highly doubtful, if for no other reason, then at least because we have no other sources telling us that Ahaziah of Judah was killed by an Aramaean king. In fact, according to the Old Testament the two kings of Israel and Judah mentioned by Biran and Naveh were victims of Jehu's purge in Jezreel (2 Kings 11:21–29). Now Jehu, according to the narrative in 2 Kings 11, was designated to become a king by the prophet Elisha while commanding the Israelite army in a war against the Aramaeans before he turned against his royal master and assumed the power for himself. If Biran and Naveh had really joined the two texts together and read them correctly, we would be in possession of a curious but important example of a contemporary text going directly against the evidence of the Old Testament.

Otherwise Jehu should be considered the author of this text; evidently a theory that would create more historical problems than it solves, as it would probably turn Jehu Ben Jehoshaphat Ben Nimshi into an Aramaean prince. This is certainly an interesting option, but hardly one many scholars are ready to choose.

Now the two texts are clearly not interrelated in the way proposed by its original editors, so we don't have to waste more space on historical speculations based on their reading of it. Instead, other problems attached to the inscription have to be settled before we try to see what kind of information about Israel in the Iron Age it may contain.

Biran and Naveh dated—ostensibly on paleographic reasons only—the inscription to the middle of the ninth century B.C.E. This would in their eyes make it almost contemporary with the Moabite inscription of King Mesha (see below) and a bit older than most of the Aramaic monumental inscriptions known so far, dating from the end of the ninth century B.C.E. and from the eighth century B.C.E.[20] The lack of contemporary Aramaic evidence makes the dating precarious, as the closest parallel would in that case be the Mesha inscription, which is, however, not in Aramaic but in Moabite and also paleographically rather different from the Tel Dan inscription.[21] As a matter of fact, a letter-by-letter comparison will in the opinion of some scholars show that a date of the Tel Dan inscription at the end of the ninth century B.C.E. would undoubtedly fit the style of the inscription better.[22] Other scholars would prefer to reduce this date by at least another fifty years.[23]

The inscription is kept in a kind of "pidgin" Aramaic, sometimes looking more like a kind of mixed language in which Aramaic and Phoenician linguistic elements are jumbled together, in its phraseology nevertheless closely resembling especially the Mesha inscription and the Aramaic Zakkur inscription from Aphis near Aleppo. The narrow links between the Tel Dan inscription and these two inscriptions are of a kind that has persuaded at least one major specialist into believing that the inscription is a forgery.[24] This cannot be left out of consideration in advance, because some of the circumstances surrounding its discovery may speak against its being genuine.[25] Other examples of forgeries of this kind are well known, and clever forgers have cheated even respectable scholars into accepting something that is obviously false.[26]

If we assume, however, that the text is genuine and belongs probably to a period no earlier than, say, 900 B.C.E., it still includes a very important although confusing testimony to the presence of a state of the name of Israel in northern Palestine in the ninth or eighth century, ruled by kings. We will never get to know the identity of the king of Israel mentioned in fragment

A line 8 unless other comprehensive fragments of the same text should subsequently appear. Otherwise we will have to be content with the statement
that Israel was the name of a kingdom in northern Palestine in the Iron Age.
How it relates to the earlier Israel of the Merneptah inscription, that is, what
kind of tradition led to the continuation of the name of Israel, is unknown.
As already maintained, it may be the result of a political continuity, that Israel (whatever it was and in spite of Merneptah's claim to the opposite) continued in some form physically to exist and was incorporated into the later
kingdom of this name as a sustaining element of the realm. It could, however, also be a traditional name that was remembered in northern Palestine
even though the institutions of the earlier Israel did not survive from the thirteenth to the ninth or eighth century. Any endeavor to choose between these
options or, for that matter to combine both of them into one and only one
hypothesis, is nothing except free speculation.

Most people would at this stage prefer to introduce the biblical narrative
to the discussion and by paraphrasing the biblical text create the missing
link between the two Israels. According to this, the tribal society of early Israel of the late second millennium B.C.E. developed into the monarchy of Israel in the first millennium. The procedure is, however, false and represents
a premature blending of primary and secondary sources which may, as already explained above, prevent any type of evidence—on one hand the external written sources, on the other the biblical narrative—from being
properly utilized.

Whereas the testimony of the Tel Dan inscription as to the existence of
the state of Israel in this period is unequivocal, its mentioning of the
"House of David" has created many problems so far unsolved. The im-
mediate reaction of the excavator and epigrapher was here to see a reference to the House of David as understood to be the dynastic name of
the kingdom of Judah. Most of the early contributors to the interpretation
of the inscription sided with them. They understood the inscription in line
8 to include a reference to a king of Israel and in line 9 as a parallel to
the king of the House of David. These two kings appeared as members
of a coalition destroyed by the author of the inscription, an Aramaean
king. Such a reconstruction, however, depends on the completion of a la-
cuna in the text. This text has no reference to a king of the House of David,
but only to something that can eventually be made to say so. This has, on
the other hand, never been thought of as a major disadvantage. Neither
was it understood to present any obstacle to the interpretation of the text
that we do not know how wide it originally was, and therefore cannot say
whether it is correct that Israel and the House of David stand as paral-

lels.[27] Names of states of the type "the house of NN" were widely known in Syria at the beginning of the first millennium B.C.E.[28] These names reveal the identity either of the tribe that formed the backbone of the state, of the founder of the state, or of the apical ancestor of the ruling dynasty of the state in question. Not a single example among them can be mentioned, however, that contains the combination "the king of Beth NN," as demonstrated by Ernst Axel Knauf,[29] something that has never disturbed the scholars who see behind the expression "[kin]g of Bytdwd" a reference to a king of Judah.

Finally it must be mentioned that some scholars have questioned the interpretation of the phrase *bytdwd,* supposed to mean the "House of David," expressing confusion because of the way this Beth David is written in this inscription, which uses word dividers, or small dots inserted between words. In biblical references to the House of David, *Bêt Davîd,* the name is always written in two words, as are also contemporary dynastic names of states in Syria and Mesopotamia like Bit Adini, Bit Gusi, or Bit Humriya (*Bêt Omrî;* cf. below) to mention just a few of them. We were accordingly to expect a word divider between the two words in Beth David. Otherwise, other name combinations including the word *Beth* are known from the Old Testament, including the city names of Bethel and Beth-shean. Such names are, however, normally written in one word, like the *bytdwd* of the Tel Dan inscription A. It could therefore well be that we here have a reference to a place name in the vicinity of Dan rather than a mentioning of the kingdom of Judah. As a matter of fact, there can be found other evidence that may be used in support of such a thesis, as will be seen when we come to the next inscription mentioning Israel.

In spite of these and other objections to the original interpretation of the Tel Dan inscription, it has to be said that most scholars have brushed aside such criticism with contempt. They have often paid no attention to the many objections that can be raised against their own interpretation and in spite of the fact that the reconstruction of the text(s) by Biran and Naveh creates a series of historical problems which none of the scholars seem able to solve. In this way the short history of the reception of the Tel Dan inscriptions constitutes a classic example of how biblical scholars are moved not so much by evidence from the inscription itself as by the wish to create links between the inscription and the biblical narrative. Such endeavors have often been pursued in a headless manner but have found support in many quarters for the simple reason that priority is given to the evidence of the secondary source, the biblical narrative, and not to the primary evidence, the inscription in question.

THE MESHA INSCRIPTION

The third time Israel is mentioned in an inscription from the ancient Near East is in the so-called "Mesha inscription" found at Diban in Transjordan in 1868.[30] The inscription has been dated to the middle of the ninth century B.C.E. on the basis of its reference to King Omri of Israel and his son, who is, however, not mentioned by name. It refers to a forty-year-long Israelite oppression of Moab, now brought to an end by King Mesha of Moab, who claims to have liberated Moab from Israel, "which has been destroyed forever" (the destruction of Israel seems almost to be a recurrent theme of the contemporary inscriptions!). A number of places, persons, and gods are mentioned by Mesha that are already known from the Old Testament, beginning with King Mesha himself, evidently the same king against whom a coalition of Israel and Judah under King Jehoram and King Jehoshaphat fought, without much luck (2 Kings 3), and King Omri, according to the Old Testament the founder of a dynasty including also Ahab. The supreme gods of both Moab and Israel are mentioned, Kemosh in Moab and Jahwe in Israel. There are references to the people of Gad, which King Mesha claims to have destroyed, and to several named localities in Transjordan, such as Ataroth, Dibon, and Nebo among others.

The similarities between the persons, deities, and places mentioned in the Mesha inscription and persons, deities, and places known from the Old Testament are numerous. Noting these, in combination with the many ambiguities concerning the circumstances of the discovery of the inscription, a number of scholars began to question the genuineness of the inscription. Scholars also pointed to its similarity to the Phoenician Eshmunazer inscription from Sidon, found in 1855.[31] This similarity between the Mesha inscription and the Eshmunazer inscription is, however, quite superficial. It may have been stressed because of the otherwise clear fraud of the Paraiba inscription "found" after the Mesha inscription had been published, however obviously a concoction of the Eshmunazer inscription and the biblical description of Solomon's sea trade from Ezion-geber (1 Kings 10:26–28).[32]

Now, the genuineness of the Mesha inscription having never in any serious way been disputed since the turn of the present century, its value as a source to Israel in the Iron Age is both important and limited at one and the same time. Its content of historical and topographical information as well as its placing Kemosh and Jahwe side by side, so to speak, is extremely interesting. Its mentioning of the dynasty of Omri, whether a precise reference or a more generic one to Israel understood to be the House of Omri (see below) is certainly also unparalleled, as is its reference to the kingdom of

Israel having political aspirations in Transjordan. The particulars are, however, placed in a legendary time frame of forty years, consisting of, according to Mesha, the reign of Omri and half the reign of his son. According to the Old Testament, though, the combined rule of Omri and his son Ahab did not span a full period of forty years.[33] Moreover, this reference to "forty years" is hardly a historical, but a mythical one. "Forty" is a round number that expresses a long span of time only.[34] Furthermore, the fact that Mesha does not mention Ahab, who was otherwise a well-known figure from this period (see on the Assyrian evidence below), probably reveals that he was fairly ignorant of conditions in the kingdom of Israel in his days. The mentioning of King Omri may therefore in this inscription not be solid evidence of the existence of a king of this name but simply a reference to the apical founder of the kingdom of Israel.[35] "King Omri" of Israel may be the only Israelite "king" known by name by Mesha, simply because Israel was in those days often or normally called "the House of Omri."[36] This may be of some importance for the exact date of the Mesha inscription. "Omri" in the Mesha inscription may be only a reference to the dynastic name of the state of Israel. It need not refer to a king of this name. If so, the mentioning of "his son" might involve any king of Israel right down to the destruction of Samaria, as this term "House of Omri" seems to have been a current name of the kingdom also after the fall of the Omrite dynasty itself. In this connection it should not be forgotten that the Assyrians reckoned Jehu to be a son of Omri.[37] In this way we may have much less reason to date the Mesha inscription to the middle of the ninth century B.C.E. than normally believed.[38]

Apart from this evidence, which says that Israel was in the ninth century a kingdom ruled by the House of Omri, the inscription mentions something that may refer to some item of the cult of Ataroth, in Moabite *'r'l dwdh*[39] (line 12). This enigmatic expression has been the subject of a long discussion, but scholars generally tend to see here a reference to the altar or a part of it.[40] More important is the second part of the expression, *dwdh,* which contains the same consonants as the *dwd* of what is considered by many interpreters to be the contemporary Tel Dan inscription that was believed to be a reference to the King David of the Bible. Now, David in the Old Testament is mostly used as a personal name, and the mentioning of the *dwdh* in the Mesha inscription cannot be a reference to David endowed with a personal suffix ("his David") as Semitic personal names do not carry personal suffixes. The *dwdh* of the Mesha inscription must be either a title of some sort, or the name of a thing probably belonging to the temple at Atarot, or an epithet meaning perhaps "his beloved." It may also be the name of a Moabite god called Daudo, as recently proposed by Nadav Na'aman.[41] A translation of the word as "leader," "governor," or the like would make sense if the name of King David of the Old Testament could be understood as a title or a second name, an epithet, his real name being perhaps Elhanan.[42] This suggestion seems out of the question, though, contrary to some scholars' opinions.[43] In this light the *dwdh* of the Mesha inscription could be understood as a surname or even the name of a local god (whoever this god might be).[44] If not the first choice, then this is at least a possibility that we also in the Tel Dan inscription have a reference to what might be a local temple of the same god, or a god carrying the same surname.[45]

OTHER TEXTUAL EVIDENCE
FROM PALESTINE IN THE IRON AGE

No other inscription from Palestine, or from Transjordan in the Iron Age, has so far provided any specific reference to Israel. A relatively large collection of small-scale inscriptions: seals and stamps, letters, inventories, burial inscriptions, or commemorative inscriptions exists dating from the tenth century and down to the end of the political independence of the states of Israel and Judah in the eighth and sixth centuries respectively. Their presence, among other things, tells us that writing was known and used at least in official quarters, although there is hardly any basis for the assumption that the majority of the population of the two states was literate.[46] Literacy would in a preindustrial society of the type found in Palestine in antiquity normally not have involved more than a few percent at most of the populace. This must be seen in the light of the main occupation, probably involving more than 90 percent of the population, basic agricultural production, where the ability to reduce experience into writing would not count for much. Much of this evidence has been brought into light in a more or less disorganized way by sheer luck or as isolated examples without a stratigraphic context. Never has a comprehensive archive been found in southern Syria and Palestine of the type normally associated with excavations in Mesopotamia or any other place where the basic material used for writing was a clay tablet. Many excavations have hardly provided any written material at all.[47]

Some of this evidence may point to private enterprises, but most of it belongs to official circles, the royal administration or officers with an official standing. Thus the Samaria Ostraca—mainly very small inscriptions of a few short lines each—from the eighth century B.C.E. throw some light on the royal administration of Israel in this period.[48] So do also the so-called *lemelek* stamps from Judah, not very far removed from the Samaria Ostraca in time and most likely to be connected with productions from royal farms in the kingdom of Judah.[49]

Very little of this material is extraordinary compared to what we were to expect from a civilization of the kind found in this area in the Iron Age. None of them tell us anything special about the society at large except that monarchs ruled Israel as well as Judah. Their organization may not have been very different from the political system found in Palestine in the Late Bronze Age, in fact better documented in contemporary documents of the second half of the second millennium B.C.E.[50]

As an exceptional example of an official inscription, we can only mention the Siloam inscription, placed at the point where two groups of workers met when cutting their way under Jerusalem and preparing the tunnel leading water from the Gihon spring to the Siloam pool.[51] The inscription says nothing about why and when and who constructed it. Most scholars have traditionally related this inscription to the reference in the Old Testament (2 Kings 20:20) to King Hezekiah's rearrangement of the water system of Jerusalem, probably on the eve of Sennacherib's attack on Judah in 701 B.C.E. This assumption of an Hezekian origin of the Siloam inscription may, in spite of a recent endeavor to disqualify this dating of the inscription,[52] not be totally off the mark. A good case can be made on the basis of the paleography to date the inscription in the Iron Age. The inscription itself, on the other hand, does not tell us this. It is only a secondary source, which in this case may be right but which can also be wrong, because nobody can really say on the basis of this anonymous inscription whether it was Hezekiah or some other Judean king from the eighth or seventh century who constructed the tunnel. As it stands, it is the only clear example of an inscription from either Israel or Judah commemorating a public construction work. As such it is a poor companion to similar inscriptions, not least from Egypt and Mesopotamia.

Documents concerning the daily life of the inhabitants of the kingdoms of Israel and Judah are, as is also the case of most of the southern Levant in the Iron Age, few and far between. Nothing like the piles of juridical documents pertaining to the life in court, or economic texts about sale and purchase of land, goods, and the like, found in several Mesopotamian places has been unearthed in Palestine. At most we are in possession of a few scattered glimpses of the life of ordinary man. One example is the Yavne Yam letter. In this a harvester complains to a magnate—probably a district commander or governor—about an officer who has appropriated his garment, evidently as a punishment for some crime which the writer claims he never committed.[53] Another text—this time from Gezer—contains a kind of a short calendar covering the agricultural year.[54]

Other assemblies come from, among other places, Arad in the northern part of the Negev, and from Lachish. The Arad ostraca deal in general with deliveries of daily food rations to local people, some of them called *kittim* and normally understood to be mercenaries of Greek origin in the service of the Judean king and stationed at the small fortress of Arad.[55] The Lachish letters for their part are exceptional texts, containing reports from a local military commander to his superior officer. They have sometimes been overly dramatized, not least because of the mentioning in one of the letters of an official named Shallum the son of Jaddua, in the same line as an unnamed prophet. Because of this scholars believe them to refer to events at the very end of the history of the Judean kingdom. However, a more likely interpretation is that they simply reflect—as did the Arad ostraca—the daily life of a small military detachment, this time in the Shephelah some thirty miles southwest of Jerusalem.[56]

Written documentation pertaining to the religious life of the inhabitants of this area are found mostly in the form of indirect references to religious practices and beliefs and as theophoric elements in personal names. A few years ago, the North American scholar Jeffrey Tigay published a study on the names found in inscriptions from Palestine in the Iron Age and in the Old Testament.[57] His study has been the subject of severe but justified criticism, not least because of its indiscriminate blend of biblical evidence with the evidence recorded in inscriptions.[58] It is, however, important for one reason only, that it has shown the religion of at least official Judah in the seventh century B.C.E. to be highly concentrated around Yahweh as its key figure. This must be seen in the light of Semitic name-giving in ancient times, when a personal name contained a kind of confession by mentioning a god most likely thought to be the protector of the child bearing the god's name. So the Hebrew name of the prophet Isaiah, *Yeša'yahû,* means "Yahweh will save [the child or through the child]," and the one of the son of Saul, Eshbaal, in Hebrew *'îšba'al,* "the man of [the god] Ba'al."[59] Thus the name Absalom—the unhappy son of David—is probably understood in its present context in the Old Testament narrative as "the father of Peace," but the original meaning of the name was probably "the [god] Shalem is the father."[60]

Thus the Lachish letter 1 contains a list of ten names, five of which are patronymics, leaving five persons active seen from the horizon of the writer of this letter: Gemariah, Jaazaniah, Hagab, Mibtachjahu, and Mattaniah. The patronymics are Hissilyahu, Tobshalom, Jaazaniah, Jeremiah, and Neriah.[61] Of the ten names (one of which appears twice), eight contain the name of Yahweh as their theophoric element, one has Shalom or Shalem, and one has no theophoric element at all. Translated into statistical terms, it means that 80 percent of the names in this small sample are "Yahwistic" names, which compares well with Tigay's other results. The conclusion must therefore be that Yahweh was by far the most important deity to invoke when naming male children (we know from inscription far less about female names in this period) in Judah in the seventh century B.C.E. There is no reason to assume that the persons mentioned are important people belonging to the elite of the society. They constitute, rather, names of ordinary persons, either the members of a group of workers or a military section or patrol. This short list may therefore be representative of the religious outlook of the average male of the kingdom of Judah approaching its end.[62]

It will, on the other hand, be interesting to compare this evidence to a similar collection of names in a source from, say, Israel before the destruction of that kingdom in 722 B.C.E. Although we do not possess a short list like Lachish letter 1, we can make use of the earlier-mentioned Samaria ostraca, dating from the eighth century. A casual glimpse through these rather insignificant inscriptions says that a fair share of names include references to Yahweh, but this time also other divine names are represented in statistically more substantial numbers. Whereas nine names occur with Yahweh (in the ostraca normally written in its short form yw) as their theophoric element, among which Yedayaw, Gaddiyaw, and perhaps Egliyaw—from a religious point of view a highly interesting name,[63] six names include the deity Ba'al, such as Abiba'al, Meribba'al, not to speak of a person called simply Ba'ala. Other deities present in these ostraca inscriptions are El, as Elisha, and Eliba, and probably "Elyon," in the Old Testament normally understood to be an epithet attached to Yahweh, but in the west Semitic pantheon shown to be an independent figure.[64] The god Gad, many years ago recognized to lie behind the biblical tribe of Gad,[65] seems also to be present in the name of Gaddiyaw, meaning "Yahweh is my Gad," which tells us that the two gods have amalgamated at least in the conscience of the name giver.

Again in the case of the Samaria Ostraca, the names exclusively refer to males. We know next to nothing from inscriptions about the naming of females. We can only say that when the personal names of the Lachish ostraca of the seventh century are compared to the Samaria Ostraca of the eighth century, the difference in usage is conspicuous. The almost exclusive character of the names with Yahweh as their theophoric element in the Lachish letters more than indicates a concentration among the male population of Judah around this deity, whereas in Israel a hundred years before this was not the case. The Samaria Ostraca provide only a small sample of names. A

difference in the ratio between names with Yahweh and Ba'al of three to
two may therefore be casual, and we only know that these two gods were
highly popular in the kingdom of Israel right down to the fall of that state
at the end of the eighth century.

Does this lack of presence of female deities indicate that they were unknown to the population of Palestine in the Iron Age? A discussion of the
religious iconography of female deities that is found in the comprehensive
monograph on this imagery by the Swiss scholar Urs Winter and in other
contributions from the same school of research[66] tells us another story. Female deities seem to have been richly represented in iconography, but not
in writing. Exceptions are a couple of very important inscriptions from the
southern part of Palestine, from Kuntillet 'Ajrud in northeastern Sinai, probably dating from c. 800 B.C.E.[67] Other inscriptions come from Khirbet el-
Qom, close to Hebron in the Judean hills, probably half a century or more
later than the one from Kuntillet 'Ajrud.[68]

Whereas the Khirbet el-Qom inscriptions have been put together in different ways and may or may not mention Yahweh and his Asherah (probably the most likely reading of the text),[69] the inscriptions from Kuntillet
'Ajrud are rather unequivocal as far as the interpretation of the following
lines is concerned:

> *'mr'[šy] hm[..]k'mr lyhl[ ]wlyw 'šh wl[ ] brkt(y) 'tkm lyhwh šmrn 'wl 'šrth*

> "A[shy]o the king said: Tell x, y and z, may you be blessed by YHWH
> of Shomeron (Samaria) and his ASHERAH."

> *'mr'mryw'mr l'd(w)ny h[š]l[m] 't(h) brkt lyhwh t(y)mn*
> *wl'šrth ybrkk wyšmrk wyhy'm'd(w)ny[-]*

> "Amaryo said: Tell my lord, may you be well and be blessed by YHWH
> of Teman and his ASHERAH. May he bless and keep you and be with
> you."[70]

Both texts put a Yahweh together with "his Asherah," which cannot for the
reason already mentioned above in connection with the *dwdh* of the Mesha
stele be a personal name. Somehow it must have been understood by the
scribe as indicating something belonging to Yahweh, the character of which
being so far unknown, although a reference to the Asherah-poles or groves
mentioned in the Old Testament seems obvious. In the Old Testament it is
mentioned a number of times how the holy stones of Ba'al—the *massebôt*—
are destroyed together with the symbols of Asherah.[71] However, this is secondary evidence. More correct would it be to compare the Kuntillet 'Ajrud
inscriptions to evidence from western Asia in the Bronze and Iron Ages of

the goddess called in Ugaritic *Athiratu,* in names in the Amarna tablets Ashirta.[72] In the Ugaritic pantheon this goddess is the consort of Ilu (El). It would be natural to see this also to have been originally the role of the Asherah of Yahweh. Her identity might, however, have changed at a point or have been different in different places. In Palestine in the first millennium B.C.E. her name was probably not understood to be a personal name. It was probably so that she had lost her quality as a personalized deity, although still attached to Yahweh as a holy object or symbol of some sort. This could very well be a step in the process of the ongoing divorce of Yahweh from his consort. In the later Old Testament tradition this process has been modified so that—apart from one conspicuous instance in connection with the narrative about King Josiah's purging of the Temple in Jerusalem, whereby he closed the part of the Temple devoted to Asherah (2 Kings 23:6–7)[73]—any trace of the original position of Asherah as the consort of Yahweh, understood to be head of the pantheon, has been erased.

An overview of the religious part of the life of the Israelites and Judeans therefore confirms the impression of many independent sources. This religion in its various forms and expressions compares well with the standards of religion found in other places such as Moab. It says that it is too early to speak about monotheism in any form. There is, however, certainly a strong tendency toward a strengthening of the position of the chief god of the pantheon, to the cost of his minor colleagues, male as well as female deities. This process towards monotheism was working in other places as well. It may even be possible to speak about a definite religious trend, which was in the Persian and Hellenistic-Roman period to develop into a monotheism of the kind understood by posterity as the belief in one god only. The decisive steps in that development have, however, not much to do with the Israelites and Judeans of the Iron Age.[74]

ISRAEL AND JUDAH
IN MESOPOTAMIAN TEXTS

Not a single document from the rich treasures of Assyrian and Babylonian inscriptions ever refers to the kingdom of Israel as Israel. On the other hand, the Assyrian and Babylonian historical texts normally refer to the kingdom of Judah as exactly that, Judah (in Akkadian normally *Yauda*). None of them ever, however, refers to the Kingdom of Judah as the House of David. In contrast to this, Israel is in Assyrian inscriptions normally called either "the House of Omri" (in Akkadian, *Bît Humriya*) or Samaria (normally in the form of *Samarina*). Only one inscription may be understood as containing a corrupted form of Israel, an inscription that is at the same time the earliest Assyrian reference to Israel.

In his annals, King Shalmaneser III of Assyria (858–823) describes his battle against a coalition of kings from Syria and Palestine, including among them an *A-ḫa-ab-bu^{KUR} sir-'i-la-a-a,* who contributed to the hostile coalition with 2,000 chariots and 10,000 foot soldiers.[75] This is a display of power, as only one among the other allies could muster a force even bigger than that, Adad-'idri (Hadadezer) of Damascus, who contributed with 1,200 chariots, 1,000 horsemen, and 20,000 foot soldiers. The king of Hamath mustered for his part 700 chariots, 700 horsemen, and 10,000 foot soldiers. Although there can be little doubt about these numbers being exaggerated by the Assyrian narrators, the place of Ahab, because it cannot be anybody else than this king of Israel, as the second strongest participant in the anti-Assyrian coalition remains. This place of honor is evidence of the importance and strength of his kingdom around the middle of the ninth century. The battle was being fought in 853 B.C.E., a date secured by a reference in another Assyrian inscription of the same year to a solar eclipse that can astronomically be calculated to have taken place in that year.[76] The rendering of Israel as Sirila— because this is the most likely "restoration" of this name otherwise unknown—is at the same time important. It confirms the Tel Dan and the Mesha inscriptions insofar as this name's being au courant as a name of the kingdom that according to the Old Testament had Samaria as its capital. It is at the same time a name otherwise unknown to the Assyrians, something that can be deduced from the corrupted rendering of it in this inscription. This also compares well with the fact that although Shalmanaser III refers repeatedly to this event in other inscriptions, and may at the same time also be referring to other encounters with the same coalition, no further reference to Israel or a king of Israel is found in this connection.

Dating from a later part of his reign, from c. 830, Shalmaneser's "Black Obelisk" inscriptions contain a highly interesting reference to Israel, or rather, it mentions how Jehu, in Akkadian *Ya-ú-a mar Ḫu-um-ri,* Jehu the son of Omri, paid tribute to the Assyrians.[77] Evidently the coalition of Syro-Palestinian kings broke shortly after Ahab's death, after which nobody could stop the Assyrian advance toward the Mediterranean. The local kings had to surrender and accept a position as vassals or they vanished in front of the Assyrian onslaught. Jehu evidently chose the first option and surrendered. His title as formulated by the Assyrians is imprecise if it was understood to include his patronymic, as Jehu was certainly no son of Omri. He was—according to the Old Testament narrative—of the family of Nimshi and the usurper who physically destroyed the House of Omri (2 Kings 9–10). The

Assyrians, nevertheless, called him a son of Omri. This is hardly a contemptuous reference to Jehu, not mentioning his own patronymic but the dynasty he substituted with his own family; it was, rather, an acknowledgment that the official name of his state is "the House of Omri." This is confirmed by the fact that a number of Assyrian inscriptions subsequently followed this practice and called the kingdom, the capital of which was Samaria, "the House of Omri" without any indication of this being anything but the name of the state.

Thus Adadnirari III (810–783) in his annals describes "the House of Omri" as a part of his kingdom, together with Tyre, Sidon, Edom, and Palestine.[78] In another inscription, however, he also mentions that he has received tribute from Joash of Samaria,[79] whereas the great Tiglath-pileser III (744–727 B.C.E.) in his inscriptions refers to Menahem as from the city of Samaria.[80] In another account the Assyrian king explains how he reinstalled Menahem[81] after having subdued him and how he extracted tribute from his country. Tiglath-pileser mentions a deportation from "the land (of) the House of Omri" in the same text. He continues his report by telling how he ousted Pekah (*Pa-qa-ḫa*) and installed a new king, Hoshea (*A-ú-si-'*). At the same time the Assyrians changed the political status quo in Palestine by reducing the kingdom of Israel/the House of Omri to the environments of Samaria.[82] The Old Testament narrators also mention a number of these events, thus Menahem's tribute to Tiglath-pileser (2 Kings 15:19–20), Tiglath-pileser's territorial "rearrangements," and the overthrow of Pekah and the installation of Hoshea (2 Kings 15:27–30).

After these territorial changes it becomes more normal to refer to the northern kingdom as "Samaria," although Sargon II (721–705) more than once makes a distinction between Samaria and "all of the House of Omri."[83] However, when the end comes to the kingdom of Israel with the destruction of its capital, Samaria, in 722 or 721 B.C.E.,[84] it is simply Samaria that is used as the name of the country from which, according to Sargon II, 27,290 inhabitants are deported.[85]

Thus there can be no doubt that in the eyes of the Assyrians, after they obtained a firsthand knowledge of the territories of Palestine, Israel was not the name of the Northern Kingdom. They almost exclusively used the term "the House of Omri" or "the land of the House of Omri." This indicates not that it was Omri's dynasty that governed that country, but that it was the official name—although maybe originally only the dynastic one—of the country, like the official names of the Aramaean kingdoms of Syria and Mesopotamia, also carrying the same type of dynastic names. Samaria was the name of the capital of "the land of the House of Omri." However, after only a section of the country previously ruled by the kings of Samaria was left around the city after the Assyrian rearrangements of the territory, the kingdom was reckoned no more than a city-state of limited extend and power.

We cannot of course say whether this was a reflection of local practices as well. There is, however, reason to understand the reference to the anonymous king of Israel, the "son of Omri" in the Mesha inscription, in this light, although Mesha knows of the other name of the country, Israel. It also says as already indicated above that we have no idea of who this anonymous king of Israel really was; as a matter of fact, we cannot even be sure that the Mesha inscription goes back to the middle of the ninth century (or just after), as normally assumed. A son of Omri as king of Israel was understandable right down to the fall of Samaria.[86]

The situation is very different when we come to the Assyrian references to the kingdom of Judah, which opens with references in Tiglath-pileser III's inscriptions to Jehoahaz and Azariah of Judah. The first (*ia-á-ḫa-zi ia-ú-da-a-a*) is found in a listing together with kings from Syria, Cilicia, Phoenicia, Palestine, and Transjordan,[87] the second ([*A*]*zriau ia-ú-da-a-a*) appears in connection with the payment of a tribute to Assyria.[88] Over a period of more than a hundred years there are frequent references to Judah and its rulers. These include the description of Sennacherib's campaign that led to the virtual destruction of Hezekiah's kingdom and the siege of Jerusalem in 701 B.C.E. At this time Hezekiah, the man of Judah (*[LÚ]Ia-ú-da-ai*)—quoting Sennacherib—was shut up in his city, known by name to the Assyrians as Ursalimmu, "like a bird in its cage."[89]

Thus Sargon II, the conqueror of Samaria, also boast of having subdued the country Judah and lists the ruler of Judah among the people who have been persuaded by the king of Ashdod into a rebellion against Assur.[90] Asarhaddon (680–669) for his part, evidently respectful of his loyalty, refers to Manasse as king of Judah, in one text placed alongside the kings of Tyre, Edom, Musuri, Moab, Gaza, Ashkelon, Ekron, Byblos, Arvad, Samsimuruna, Beth Ammon, and Ashdod.[91] Furthermore, also Ashurbanipal in the beginning of his reign refers to Manasse of Judah as one of his faithful vassals, in a long list of names of kings from the Levant.[92] Finally, an anonymous textual fragment, probably from the beginning of the Assyrian rule over Judah, mentions a comprehensive tribute paid by the inhabitants of the land of Judah.[93]

The final references to Judah come from Neo-Babylonian documents. Thus the Babylonian Chronicle relates how Nebuchadnezzar in his seventh year laid siege to the "city of Judah," conquered it, looted it, and installed a new king "after his own liking."[94] Finally an administrative document from the latter part of the reign of Nebuchadnezzar records deliveries to various persons, to people from Byblos, Tyre, Arvad, and Jehoiachin, called the son of the king of Judah, and five unnamed sons of the king of Judah.[95]

In conclusion, it is obvious that Judah only at a late date came within the horizon of the Assyrians. Before Tiglath-pileser III, there is no evidence that the Assyrians knew of this tiny place, whereas Judah's northern neighbor was known to the Assyrians at least from 853 B.C.E., although on a regular basis only from the reign of Jehu down to the fall of Samaria. The Assyrian and Babylonian texts have little to contribute to our understanding of these two states of Palestine, except that they belonged among a series of Palestinian states, among whom we should mention Ashdod, Ashkelon, Gaza, and Ekron.[96] There is, however, very little in the Assyrian phraseology to distinguish Judah from these states at the coast—in fact, Asarhaddon's inscriptions reckon Judah to be along the coast, that is, among the states of Palestine. Israel, "the House of Omri," for its part is treated a bit differently as Assyrians texts—at least in the latter part of the Assyro-Israelite relationship—are able to distinguish between the capital and the country. Evidently "the House of Omri" was thought to be a more comprehensive and territorially important political structure than the petty states that surrounded it. It should finally be stressed that the Assyrian and Neo-Babylonian texts say nothing about the ethnic composition of the Palestinian states. On this subject their evidence is 100 percent neutral, although it should be mentioned that the authors of the Assyrian texts were able to make such distinctions when necessary. One such example is the Greek mentioned by the Assyrians a number of times. In the days of Sargon II, this "Greek" is accused of being a rebel against the Assyrian overlords.[97]

EGYPTIAN EVIDENCE

Egypt's position was close to the borders of Palestine. There has also in the past existed a close relationship between Egypt and Palestine. Palestine was in the Late Bronze Age part of the Egyptian empire in western Asia, and this relationship may not have ended before the Early Iron Age. Assyrian inscriptions also mention Egyptian activities in Palestine. Archaeology testifies to trade relations between Egypt and Palestine that also included the Iron Age. In spite of all this evidence, neither Israel nor Judah is mentioned as much as a single time by name in an Egyptian document from the Iron Age.

The most important Egyptian inscription of this period that can be related to Egyptian military activity in Palestine is the list of conquered cities in Asia in a commemorative inscription of Pharaoh Shoshenq (c. 945–924 B.C.E.),[98] the founder of the Egyptian Twenty-second Dynasty, a dynasty of Libyan origin.[99] According to this inscription Shoshenq led a campaign into Asia which took him to Megiddo and Ta'anakh at the entrance to the Jezreel valley, and from there down to Beth-shean and across the Jordan to Mahanaim. From here he seems to have returned right through the central Palestinian highlands, following the descent to the coastal valley at Bet Horon, and after that to have turned against the Negev. None of the places mentioned by Shoshenq in his list, however, refer to the central part of either Israel or Judah.[100]

Many theories and explanations are put forward to explain the motives behind this campaign, which is formally embedded in traditional Egyptian iconography dating back to similar lists ranging from Thutmose III in the fifteenth century B.C.E. to Ramses III in the twelfth century. Thus scholars have seen Jeroboam I's shift of capital from Shechem to Penuel to Tirzah (1 Kings 12:25; 14:17) as a consequence of Shoshenq's military activities, although the inscription itself mentions none of these places.[101]

The date of this expedition has been calculated on the basis of the biblical chronology, which places it in the fifth year of Rehoboam (1 Kings 14:25), to have happened around 926 B.C.E.—some scholars would even maintain c. 921 B.C.E.[102] However, if Shoshenq had died probably already in 924 B.C.E., the last date seems impossible, and in any case even 926 B.C.E. seems, although not in itself impossible, then at least a bit late. However, to change the date would create even more problems with the usual chronologies of the kings of Israel and Judah. It may serve as another warning of the problems that may arise when a too-narrow link is sought between biblical information and ancient Near Eastern sources. This becomes even clearer when we move to the biblical evidence about the campaign of Shoshenq in Palestine.

According to the note in 1 Kings 14:25–26, "Shishak" went against Rehoboam's Jerusalem and carried away the gold treasures from the temple and the palace, everything prepared by Solomon, which had to be replaced by things made of bronze. Scholars are probably correct that his note may be a reflection of the same tradition as in Shoshenq's own commemorative inscription. The same scholars, however, often maintain that the biblical version says that Rehoboam paid Shoshenq to keep him away from conquering Jerusalem. They take the phrase "And he took away the treasures of the house of the LORD and the treasures of the king's house" (1 Kings 14:26) to mean that Rehoboam took them and delivered them to Shoshenq, just as Hezekiah did when confronted by Sennacherib's army (2 Kings 18:14–15).[103]

The same scholars do, however, forget that Sennacherib practically destroyed every urban settlement in the kingdom of Hezekiah (and Sennacherib is not silent about this havoc!), whereas Shoshenq's army did not touch any named Judean settlement—at least not a single one is included in his list. In short, every kind of ingenuity has been used to explain how all of this happened, and none of it is necessary if it is only assumed that the biblical tradition of Shoshenq's campaign in Judah is not history but fiction. It could, however, be based on the Egyptian tradition of this pharaoh's campaign in Palestine.

It will accordingly have to be concluded that in Egyptian tradition there is—apart from the victory inscription of Pharaoh Merneptah from around 1200 B.C.E.—absolute silence about Israel and Judah as far as the Iron Age is concerned. Although Egypt and Judah and Israel were almost neighbors, Egyptian sources have nothing to contribute. This does not mean that Israel and Judah did not exist. Assyrian documents say they do, very clearly. It is more a consequence of the state of internal affairs in Egypt. Egypt was changing its role from an imperial power to become a victim of other imperial powers in antiquity, such as at first the Assyrians, who were followed by the Persians, and after them the Greeks and the Romans.

EXCURSUS: THE HEBREWS

At this point the direct references to Israel in inscriptions from the ancient Near East seem to be exhausted. This does not at the same time mean that any other written contemporary document is indifferent and not able to throw any light on the subject. It can be argued that other types of documents are equally important, although for other reasons. These may include law codes from Mesopotamia that can be compared to biblical law collections. Not least, the first secular part of the so-called "Book of the Covenant" (Ex. 21:2–23:6) seems firmly embedded in the Mesopotamian law tradition.[104] It can also be religious texts such as the epic literature from Ugarit,[105] or Babylonian literature like the epic of Gilgamesh or Atra-ḥasis, both containing versions of the story of the Flood closely related to the version found in Genesis 6–8.[106] Interesting information can also be found occasionally in Egyptian tales such as "The Two Brothers," which seems closely related to the narrative about Joseph and the wife of Potiphar (Genesis 39).[107] Finally also private documents such as letters and contracts can provide important information. All of this is relevant to the study of the Old Testament, but none of this is specific to Israel understood to form a special and identifiable ethnic unit. Such evidence will tell us that the literature of the Old Testament is a part of the ancient Near Eastern heritage that was common to "all" of western Asia. This heritage had no fixed and ethnically defined boundaries. It was current in the second as well as in the first millennium B.C.E., and partly survived into the first millennium C.E.

It would of course be very important if, for example, it could be shown that the version of the story of the Flood in Genesis 6–8 was closely related to one of the Babylonian versions, which could be dated more precisely. If the relationship between this narrative in Genesis and the version in the neo-Babylonian version could be established, this could provide us with a clue to the date of the biblical story which could in that case not predate the neo-Babylonian original. It must, on the other hand be said that such links are very difficult if not impossible to establish.

We will leave the subject at this point in order to return to it in the following chapter. Here another problem, which may according to some scholars belong in the same category, remains to be discussed. This concerns the acceptance in the biblical narrative of traditions belonging to a distant past, which has been lost except from fragments that have been adopted into a new, much later, framework by biblical writers. In this place we have to discuss the "second" name, which is occasionally used of the biblical Israelites in the Old Testament, the term "Hebrew." This term gave name to the Hebrew language of the Old Testament, which is often, out of respect for its Jewish origin, called the "Hebrew Bible" also by writers with a Christian background.[108] Later in the Christian tradition it became the name of the Jewish people.

Around the turn of the twentieth century, the study of the Old Testament and the history of Israel had passed through a highly interesting and diversified phase of discussion between a conservative string of scholarship and its more radical counterpart. This subject will be addressed below. Here is only to say that while the so-called radical ideas mostly originated among German scholars, a much more radical French direction placed the Old Testament within a very late historical framework, in the late Israelite, if not the Hellenistic period. At the beginning of this century these radical ideas, whether German or French, were revised and transformed into a much more conservative paradigm for biblical studies. The change in scholarly direction should be seen in light of the ever-growing and diversified amount of external "evidence" showing the antiquity of several concepts formerly believed to be late. Scholars were hunting for traces of the Israelites in historical sources to prove the truth of the Bible, however combined with an increasingly sophisticated methodology.

The Amarna tablets should be included among the more important discoveries of documents from the ancient Near East at the end of the nineteenth century. This is a collection of some 350-odd cuneiform tablets, mostly letters sent from Syria, Phoenicia, and Palestine to the Egyptian court around the middle of the fourteenth century B.C.E.,[109] at a time when the petty kings and administrators who wrote the letters were Egyptian subjects. Only a minor number of the tablets include letters exchanged between the rulers of the leading powers of the time. Apart from Egypt, this involves Babylonia—at that time called Karaduniash and ruled by a dynasty of foreign origin; Mitanni, a Hurrian kingdom in northern Syria and Mesopotamia; Hatti—the expanding empire of the Hittites; and Assyria, then at the very beginning of a new era of greatness.[110]

As already mentioned, these letters contain not a single reference to Israel either in Egypt, in the desert, or in Palestine. However, in the letters from the ruler of Jerusalem, ÌR-Ḫeba, there are some references to a people called in Akkadian *ḫa-bi-ru*. They are said to constitute a danger to the regents of that region and are sometimes mentioned in association with a certain Labayu from Shechem.[111] It was inevitable that the *ḫabiru* should be compared to the term "Hebrew" in the Old Testament. They were soon put in connection with the appearance of an element evidently of Asiatic origin, which had been known for some time from Egypt in the form of '*pr.w*. They appear in Egyptian texts dating from the time of the New Kingdom, that is, the second half of the second millennium B.C.E. The '*pr.w* was found in low occupational positions, such as wine production.[112] These '*pr.w* had already for some time been understood as synonymous with the Hebrews, or Israelites, in Egypt and thought to confirm the biblical evidence of the Israelites' slaving for the Egyptians.[113]

The philological problems involved in relating, on one hand, the '*pr.w* to the Hebrews or to the *ḫabiru,* and on the other the Hebrews to the *ḫabiru* are not overly difficult to solve.[114] The only problem as far as the Amarna tablets are concerned is that the *ḫabiru* turned up only in the letters from Jerusalem. Exactly this part of Palestine was—at least according to the Old Testament—only conquered by the Israelites during the reign of King David, several hundred years later.

This problem was soon solved when it was proposed that the frequent mentioning in the Amarna tablets of an element, written SA.GAZ, SAG.GAZ, or just GAZ, should be understood as additional references to the activities of the *ḫabiru*. These people appear in a context almost identical to the one found about the *ḫabiru* in ÌR-Ḫeba's letters from Jerusalem. The hypothesis was later confirmed by evidence from the Hittite archives at Boghazköy/Hattushash.[115]

Now, the problem of too few and too locally limited references to the "Hebrew" was solved, only to be substituted, however, with another one, the ubiquity of these "Hebrew." As already mentioned, the "Hebrews" turned up not only in Egyptian inscriptions, in the Amarna letters now covering all of the territory of Egypt's empire in Asia in the Late Bronze Age, but also in the Hittite archives from Asia Minor. Many other references to them have subsequently been found not limited in time to the fourteenth century B.C.E., but in fact covering most of the second millennium B.C.E. Furthermore, they also appear in documents that take us from Egypt in the southwest to Susa in Persia in the east and Hattushash in the north.[116] Instead of too few "Hebrew" there were now too many to facilitate an equation with the "Hebrews," alias the Israelites, of the Old Testament. What from the beginning looked like an easy ethnic identification—the Hebrew being Israelites—at the end turned out to be something quite different.

This is not the place to survey the discussion about the identity of the *ḫabiru* in its totality. It should be enough to say that the *status quaestionis* still remains the verdict of the Assyriologist Benno Landsberger from 1954. In his opinion, *ḫabiru* in the documents of the second millennium B.C.E. is not an ethnic term. It is a sociological term that means "refugees," and no *ḫabiru* is ever said to be "at home." Whenever the sources have anything particular to say about a *ḫabiru,* he invariably comes from some other place.[117] The frequency of the references to the *ḫabiru* and their dispersal over almost all of the ancient Near East in the second millennium is an indicator of the magnitude of the problem of the refugees. Another testimony of its importance is provided by the international treaties of the Late Bronze Age, where paragraphs concerning reciprocal extradition of refugees are common, including at the end the great treaty between Ramses II of Egypt and Hattushilish III of Hatti (c. 1259). This treaty brought to an end more than two generations of bitter struggle between these two great powers.[118]

The only correction after Landsberger settled the matter of the identity of the *ḫabiru* concerns the references to the *ḫabiru* in the Amarna tablets. In these letters the term is often used not as a social designation but as a pejorative term, in order to describe the enemies of the public order, that is, the enemies of the Egyptian overlords and their local vassals.[119] This secondary use of the term is obvious in cases where a petty king of one of the small Syro-Palestinian city-states calls his colleague in the city next to him a *ḫabiru,* simply in order to defame the person in the eyes of his master. Thus there are frequent references to cases where a named regent is said to have given his land to the *ḫabiru.* This does not mean that he has in fact done so, only that he—according to the not too trustworthy testimonial of the person who formulated the accusation—has stirred up rebellion against his overlord.[120]

This does not say, however, that there was not a *ḫabiru*/refugee problem in Palestine at all. Not all documentation belongs in this category; furthermore, such a secondary use of the term only makes sense if it has as its presupposition that it is understood also in its original sense,—the problem must have been alive and real also in Palestine. This is indirectly confirmed by the mentioning of the *ḫabiru* in an Egyptian inscription from Beth-shean, which dates to a period half a century after the Amarna tablets and informs us about Egyptian troops fighting, among others, *ḫabiru* in the vicinity of Beth-shean.[121] Most likely the other enemies mentioned in this text are tribal units, though none of them are known from the Old Testament.[122]

In the first millennium B.C.E., documents mentioning the *ḫabiru* are almost totally absent. Only a very late Egyptian papyrus includes a reference, which can be interpreted in this light as a late and secondary application of the term.[123]

The possibility thus still exists that there could be some kind of relationship between the Israelites of the Old Testament sometimes called "Hebrew" and the evidence of the documents from the second millennium. It might no longer have been understood as having anything to do with a specific ethnic identity. However, the tradition about the *ḫabiru* in Palestine in the Bronze Age could still also, after the refugee problem itself had been solved or the term *ḫabiru* gone out of use, have survived to be taken up again by later biblical writers. If this is true, it does not say that there was a direct line from the *ḫabiru* of the Bronze Age to the later Hebrews or Israelites; it is enough that the term was transferred and reused in a different meaning. The question is only when this happened and what meaning the term got in the Old Testament. It could also be the case, however, that biblical writers borrowed the term from a different context, if it could be demonstrated or made a reasonable assumption that late documents from the ancient Near East might have contained references to the *ḫabiru.*

In order to answer these questions it is necessary to understand that the term "Hebrew" in the Old Testament is rarely used out of a context that somehow relates it to the semantic field of the *ḫabiru.* Most of the evidence in the Old Testament can be found in three narrative contexts. The first one is the Joseph novel (Genesis 37–50), the second the story about the Israelites' being oppressed in Egypt (Exodus 1–15), and the third the narratives dealing with the struggles between the Israelites and the Philistines (1 Samuel 13; 29).[124] In the Joseph novel, the term is used about Joseph in Egypt, who from the perspective of the Egyptians could be considered a refugee, although he obtained a very high position in the Egyptian society. He also came from "the land of the Hebrews" (Gen. 40:15). In the Exodus narrative, of course, the Israelites had stayed in Egypt for generations, although they were never treated as Egyptian citizens, but more like foreign refugees without rights of their own. Finally, in the narrative in 1 Samuel, the references are found in a context where the "Hebrews" are considered to be rebels against their overlords. These overlords are supposed to be the Philistines, who reckon young David and his attendants to be "Hebrews," because David had rebelled against his overlord, Saul (1 Sam. 29:3). In all these cases the Hebrews mentioned by the text of the Old Testament are at the same time Hebrews and Israelites, or the forefathers of the Israelites. It can therefore be concluded that the term Hebrew as used by the Old Testament writers is at the same time endowed with at least traces of its original social content and function and an ethnic designation, meaning Israelite or even Jew (the later derived meaning of the term). Even in the few instances where the term is used outside of these narratives, the term still keeps its meaning as a name of a person not at home in his own country and at the same time a member of the Israelite nation. Thus Abraham is called a Hebrew (Gen. 14:13), and the prophet Jonah, running away from Yahweh, describes himself as a Hebrew (Jonah 1:9).

Only one string of texts shows a different picture. This string involves the introductory paragraph to the Book of the Covenant in Exodus 21:2–6, concerning the purchase of a Hebrew slave, who will have to be—according to the usual interpretation—set free after having served for seven years.[125] This law is accompanied by the related rules of the Sabbath year in Deuteronomy 15 and Zedekiah's freeing of the slaves during the Babylonian siege of Jerusalem (Jer. 34:8–17).[126] The reference in Exodus 21:2–6 to the Hebrew slave is the only one in the Old Testament where there is no trace of a national meaning to the term. In the two texts, which are dependent on Exodus 21:2–6, the national meaning is already there.

This goes against Oswald Loretz who opts for the law in Exodus's being secondary in comparison to, for example, the passages in 1 Samuel, which he already considers being late. It does, however, not mean that the law of Exodus 21:2–6 is very old.[127] As already indicated above, the corpus of laws found in the first, secular, part of the Book of the Covenant is seemingly very closely related to the Mesopotamian law tradition, which means that it belongs in a learned tradition, not in the courts of law. As is now clear from the discussion among Assyriologists, the Mesopotamian law codes were never compiled in order to provide guidelines for the courts; they belonged to an academic enterprise, which carried on without regard for the world outside the academia.[128] It is difficult to state precisely when this academic law tradition was adopted into the Old Testament. The life at courts in ancient Palestine hardly needed any written laws, but followed other rules and practices.[129] The adoption of the Mesopotamian law tradition seems already to presuppose a close acquaintance with Babylonian society, a thing that—in spite of the short Babylonian supremacy over Judah at the beginning of the sixth century B.C.E.—could hardly predate the Babylonian conquest of Jerusalem.

The conclusion must be that although the precise date of the references to the Hebrews in the Old Testament cannot be settled with certainty, they are probably all representative of a very late secondary development of the term. This development may have been facilitated by the self-consciousness of the biblical authors of belonging to a nation of refugees—to the exiled from Palestine or to the people who considered themselves to be descendants of such people in exile.

The weak part of this argument is that it is difficult to bridge the gap from the Late Bronze Age to the neo-Babylonian and even Persian periods, to show that the tradition of the Hebrews continued down to late times. If it is true that the late Egyptian reference to the land of the Hebrews mentioned by Loretz goes back to an older Babylonian text, this is of course a link, the only one we possess, but it is still a weak one.

CONCLUSIONS

The name of Israel was found in only a very limited number of inscriptions, one from Egypt, another separated by at least 250 years from the first, in Transjordan. A third reference is found in the stele from Tel Dan—if it is genuine, a question not yet settled. The Assyrian and Mesopotamian sources only once mentioned a king of Israel, Ahab, in a spurious rendering of the name. Otherwise they made use of the dynastic name, *Bît Ḫumriya,* or the city name of Samaria. Judah is in the documents from Mesopotamia always called Judah; its dynastic name (if it ever had one), "the House of David," is unknown to the Assyrians and Babylonians. Inscriptions from Palestine never refer to a political entity called Israel, nor to Judah as a political name.

Some of the kings of Israel and Judah known from the Old Testament, from Ahab to Hosea in the north, and from Azariah to Jehoiachin in the south, turns up in Assyrian and Babylonian documents, but never a person below the kingly level. Omri is mentioned in the Mesha inscription from Moab, but in a context that makes it possible that it is not a reference to the king but to his dynasty or even state, "the House of Omri."

Although most of the references found in these inscriptions are highly interesting, they are not telling us anything particular about the ethnic composition of the two states of Israel and Judah. There never is a reference to anything like the *Benê Yisra'el,* known from the Old Testament. References to these states are in Mesopotamian documents kept in a style that does not separate them or mark them out in comparison to other states in the west. The Assyrians, although they had at that time had relations with the country for more than a hundred years, were able as late as during the reign of Asarhaddon to lump the Judean state together with the coastal city-states of Palestine.

The fact is that the written documents originating in Palestine itself are absolutely mute as to the question of ethnicity. There has never been found any inscriptions referring to the inhabitants of the state of Israel/*Bêt Omri*/ Samaria as Israelites, not even in a political sense. As a matter of fact, there is absolutely no reference that can be interpreted as a national or religious name of a special group of people living in these quarters and having some of the particular traits attached to them by the Old Testament tradition.

The major deity of the state of Judah was at least from the seventh century B.C.E. down to the fall of the state, Yahweh, although this god seems to carry some characteristics not combined with the figure of Yahweh in the Old Testament, such as a "consort" of some kind. This could be seen as an indication of ethnicity, a special god for a special people. This might be so, but in that case the inhabitants of Judah first of all shared this characteristic with the citizens of the state of Samaria, a fact not denied by biblical writers. In other countries as well, Moab, Ammon, Edom, and probably many more, the same thing happened. This says that religious diversities mainly consisted in different names of the chief god of the state religion in these countries. Such a diversity of names may be one of the sources for ethnic difference, but it is impossible on the basis of the documentation in inscriptions to say when this happened, whether such a difference was understood already in the first half of the first millennium B.C.E.

The situation in the north is much more complicated as far as the written evidence goes. Here it is impossible to say that the inscriptions support the picture of a fanatic Yahwism as painted by the biblical storytellers, connected with the whereabouts of the prophets Elijah and Elisha (1 Kings 16–2 Kings 9). On the contrary, the inscriptions tell us nothing about a national or nationalistic religious self-consciousness; rather they testify to a religious situation where Yahweh may be a major deity but where the characteristics attached to this Yahweh in comparison to other deities may be quite confused. The name material at least points to Yahweh's being connected with "baalistic" traits as well as with other named deities.

It is true that the written documentation from the ancient Near East has nothing to contribute to the question of the existence of a specific Israelite *ethnos* that could be identified and separated on the basis of ethnic distinctions from its neighbors. It must at the same time be said that this evidence is not in itself conclusive. There are simply too many empty spaces not covered by material in the form of inscriptions, such as large stretches of the history of the country. The Mesha inscription may date from the ninth century B.C.E., the Assyrian evidence ranges from the middle of the ninth century B.C.E. down to the middle of the seventh century B.C.E. but provides us with only a very patchy picture. The Babylonian evidence is limited to Judah at the very end of its history. Egyptian sources are absent except from the confusing testimony of Pharaoh Shoshenq, who probably campaigned in Palestine and Transjordan sometime during the second half of the tenth century, but who in his commemorative inscription never refers to anything that had to do with either Israel or Judah. The inscription from Palestine itself is generally concerned with other things, such as deliveries from royal farms, reports from officers in the field—often dramatized by scholars who always want their source material to say more than it actually contains—the distributions of provisions, and such. We are until this very day not in the possession of any major dated official inscription that has anything to contribute as to the political conditions in Israel and Judah.

CHAPTER 3

Archaeology and Israelite Ethnic Identity

Already at the beginning of the first chapter of this book the existence of another set of contemporary sources was mentioned—physical remains from the area in which to look for the Israelites, evidence that is supposed to stand aside, however, when confronted with written evidence. It is in this place not my intention to present anything like a comprehensive survey of this kind of documentation that generally comes from numerous excavations in Palestine and its neighboring countries over a period of more than a hundred years. Scholars like Helga Weippert, Amihai Mazar, Amnon Ben-Tor, and Thomas Levy, to mention only a selection of recent contributors, have already presented most of the evidence in more or less up-to-date archaeological summaries.[1] William G. Dever and Israel Finkelstein, both of whom have devoted much energy to present the material for new syntheses concerning the early history of Israel, have evaluated the material, among others.[2]

It is in this connection true to say that especially Finkelstein's studies have revolutionized the study of the archaeology of Palestine in the transition period, c. 1250–850 B.C.E., because of the interest in regional analysis that is characteristic of his approach. By mapping the distribution of settlements in the different parts of Palestine in different periods, it is possible at least to create a general picture of the major demographic shifts that may have happened and to reach a kind of *la longue durée* model[3] for the development of the territory.

THE LATE BRONZE–IRON AGE TRANSITION

The "Late Bronze–Iron Age transition" is a new kind of terminology, partly substituted for the old one, (the end of) the Late Bronze Age and Iron Age I (and partly II), simply because the appearance of iron, which gives name to the Iron Age, did not happen suddenly. It was never so that one morning people woke up and told themselves: "Welcome to the Iron Age!" as modern people are already preparing for the "Welcome to the third millennium!" On the contrary, the Iron Age developed in many ways out of the world of the Bronze Age, culturally, demographically, ethnically, and politically.[4]

The concept of an Iron Age was created on the basis of North European archaeology by the Danish archaeologist Christian Jürgensen Thomsen in the first half of the nineteenth century. He divided the distant past into three ages—the Stone Age, the Bronze Age, and the Iron Age[5]—which were subsequently and by other scholars subdivided into, respectively, the Paleolithic, the Mesolithic, and the Neolithic periods; and the Early Bronze Age, the Middle Bronze Age, and the Late Bronze Age. The Iron Age created more problems because this period already in Scandinavian archaeology took us down into the historical period. So, for example, the Danish Iron Age was divided into three periods, the Celtic Iron Age, the Roman Iron Age, and the Germanic Iron Age.

All of this looks very artificial. Although these terms are still in general use, they have sometimes been modified and are still undergoing changes. An example of this is the introduction of the concept of the Chalcolithicum as an intermediary period between the Neolithicum and the Early Bronze Age, in Palestine roughly to be dated to the period between, say, 4300 and 3500 B.C.E. The same choice of an intermediate term would suit the archaeological situation of the Levant excellently at the end of the Bronze Age. First of all, the introduction of the concept of "the Late Bronze Age" is not so much an archaeological as a political device, roughly dependent on the date of the Egyptian conquest of Syria and Palestine, which occurred around 1500 B.C.E. The end of the Late Bronze Age was originally also brought into connection with the supposed date of the Egyptian departure from these areas and the coming of the so-called "dark ages." This period is considered to experience more primitive political structures when compared to the Late Bronze Age. The standard of culture was also considerably lower than that of the sophisticated states of the Bronze Age. This changed cultural and political situation was generally considered the work of newcomers, new nations who invaded the Levant. Scholars talked about invaders like the "Sea People" coming across the ocean[6] or overland like the Israelites. Other scholars talked in general terms about the migration of the Aramaeans, who took over after the Amorite (if not Canaanite) civilization of the Bronze Age.[7]

While beguilingly simple, this view of the transition has been demonstrated to be much too superficial to paint a true picture of the situation in Palestine around, say, 1200 B.C.E. First of all it must be noted that iron—which is in fact a metal found all over the place—was known in the Levant already before the coming of the Iron Age. It was, however, not used to produce weapons and utensils for the simple reason that it was brittle and not in any way comparable to weapons and utensils made of bronze, not, at least, before the smiths learned to produce steel. That hardly happened before the beginning of the first millennium B.C.E.[8] Iron was in fact inferior to bronze before steel was invented. The main reason that it appears much more regularly after c. 1200 B.C.E. than before that date is that bronze, being a mixture of mainly copper and tin, was hard to obtain because the materials had to be imported. The production places were situated a long distance from the centers of the world, that is, the ancient Near East. The lifeline of the trade in these products was more or less cut at the end of the Late Bronze Age because of the breakdown of international trade, which was a side effect of the diversified troubles that hit most of the civilized world between 1300 and 1000 B.C.E.[9]

After that time it is also necessary to reconsider the political development and especially the idea of large-scale migrations that were supposed to have destroyed the civilization of the Bronze Age in the Levant. It has to be recognized that although the period around 1200 B.C.E. was characterized by migrations—even major ones—most of these seem to have followed sea routes, whereas it is much more difficult to pinpoint examples of major migrations that used routes over land.

There are simple logistic reasons for this. Transportation over the sea was swift and easy, at least during the summer period (the Mediterranean being notoriously treacherous during the autumn break and not very useful for overseas communication in antiquity during the winter months). Travel overland was possible when people moved in small numbers. The very dry climate made it precarious to travel in numbers for the simple reason that it was impossible to provide food and especially water to drink for hordes of people traveling along the dusty roads.[10] Theories about large-scale migrations are the products of the European academic mind, accustomed to the tradition of the migrations of the German tribes in the time of the Roman Empire. They are simply "armchair" theories, which have never taken into consideration the physical environment of the ancient Near East, which was, around 1200 B.C.E., if anything at least as dry as today.[11] The Amarna archive includes repeated reports from the petty kings of Syria, Lebanon, and Palestine that these regents before the arrival of the soldiers have prepared deliveries for the pharaoh's soldiers themselves.[12] These reports tell us something about how well prepared even a minor military expedition had to be in order to travel without having to be overly occupied with procuring provisions for its soldiers. "Living off the land" was of course a possible option, but invariably guaranteed the destruction of the society through which the soldiers marched and therefore was something not to be recommended in a friendly neighborhood.

A third factor that must be reconsidered when surveying the sociopolitical, economic, and cultural situation during the period from c. 1250 to 850 B.C.E. is that although large stretches of land were affected by the events at the end of the Late Bronze Age, not all were. Especially the Phoenician cities in Lebanon, such as Beirut, Byblos, Tyre, and Sidon were more or less unaffected by the changes and hardly any of them destroyed by foreign invaders.[13] This also is true of the northwestern part of Palestine, where places like Tel Achzib culturally seem to have been closely related to Phoenicia,[14] while the area to the south of Achzib had a more complicated and diversified history in this period.[15]

All this does not exclude the arrival of any new people. It was not so that anything like fixed borders existed in the Near East in antiquity. A border of one sort constituted a kind of mental lines of division that enabled people to make a distinction between themselves and their neighbors. This could be the village across the stream, or it could be a nomadic group traveling around along the fringe of the land belonging to the village; it could in fact be any person not belonging to the village, irrespective of his place of origin. On another side, the economic-political side, the border functioned as a guideline for the taxation: one village paying taxes to the king of this town, its neighboring village paying taxes to a king from another town.

As a matter of fact, ancient borderlines were of an osmotic kind, allowing for the passage of all kinds of people. They were very different from modern borders, which are considered as fixed and guarded lines drawn more or less artificially in the landscape and supposed to keep people not belonging to a specific country away. Although it must at the same time be said that modern borders somehow, and in spite of the intentions of the people who draw them, still possess this osmotic character. This tell us that such borders were always to a certain degree open to potential immigrants who, like the biblical patriarchs, could pass through the borders normally without the road being blocked in front of them by border officials.[16]

The refugee movement could therefore not have grown into such a major issue as it was to become in the Late Bronze Age, if the borders were not relatively safe to pass without permission to do so. Passports were known,[17] however probably reserved for persons on official missions, such as emissaries or merchants, who in Syria in the Bronze Age were also first of all state officials and only after that worked for their own benefit.[18] But apart from this kind of business, few ordinary people traveled if not forced to do so.

Nomads were around in numbers that changed according to the local circumstances, whether political or environmental, and depending on a number of choices made by the population involved in this kind of migratory life. Nomads are frequently referred to in the documents of the Late Bronze Age, in Akkadian documents often named *Sutu,* in Egyptians texts called *shasu.*[19] There are, however, very few documents that say that they constituted a serious threat to the established political systems such as the Egyptian empire in Asia. Nomadism is a style of life that needs space, and space is in short supply in most of the cultivated areas of the Near East. Nomads will accordingly in such areas tend to form a minority. They are, however, known from history sometimes to be a very troublesome demographic element. In areas and periods without strong and sound states determined to keep their territory under control, the nomads were often able to develop into a scourge of the settled population, sometimes leading to desertion of villages and cities.[20] In areas not cultivated they would always constitute the majority, but here nobody else would be able to survive and competition for land and water rights would normally come from within the nomadic society itself.

In the Late Bronze Age, Palestine was characterized, in comparison with the preceding period during the first half of the second millennium B.C.E., by a considerable reduction in settled civilization. This was especially felt in the highlands in the northern and central parts of the country, and in the Negev. Here only a few major settlements existed, such as Hazor in northern Galilee, which was still a mighty city with probably about twenty-five thousand or more inhabitants,[21] or in the central part, Shechem. The status of Jerusalem is difficult to access, since so far no traces have been found of a city in this place that dates from the Late Bronze Age, which is an extraordinary fact in light of the five odd letters from the king of Jerusalem found among the Amarna tablets.[22]

The reduction of settlements and the practical disappearance of village culture can be attributed to a number of factors such as an increasingly felt and prolonged drought, which according to some climatologists characterized the period from 1500 to 1200 B.C.E. Drought alone, however, is not able to explain the total disappearance of village culture and the reduction of agriculture that have been part of this process. Political circumstances may also have favored this negative movement away from settled life, or from undefended small settlements into major fortresses, almost small towns. Although Palestine was in the Late Bronze Age a part of the Egyptian empire, more than half of this period was characterized by a lack of interest on the part of the Egyptians in securing the area for its local inhabitants. If local troubles arose, mostly in connection with internecine fights between the petty rulers of the country such as those mentioned in the Amarna letters, the Egyptian overlords had no intention of getting involved. The only exception was when their own interests—mostly of an economic sort—became jeopardized by a development in their provinces. The local chieftains probably understood this very well, and some of them saw here a chance to take personal advantage, to amplify their territories to the deficit of their neighbors. It is clear, however, from the Amarna letters that that kind of local political power play was limited to certain areas of the Egyptian empire, such as the territories in Syria bordering the Hittite empire, or in the highlands of Palestine. Here local developments could hardly constitute a threat to the Egyptians, who were mostly staying in the lowlands.[23]

The Egyptians created a kind of power vacuum, so to speak, in the highlands by not getting themselves involved in any serious way. Together with the generally worsened natural conditions, this made the life of the peasant population overly difficult, with a serious reduction of this vital part of the population as its consequence. Safety will always have the first priority, and to the ordinary peasant safety at that time consisted either in joining the migratory part of the population, which always could get away from trouble (if not itself causing it), or in choosing a life in heavily fortified urban centers.

The Amarna letters were formerly often understood to provide evidence about an extraordinary period of Egyptian history characterized by the so-called religious revolution of the heretic Pharaoh Akhenaton (c. 1353–1336 B.C.E.).[24] In this connection there was no spare time left to speculate about the foreign possessions. The orientation of the Egyptian court was exclusively directed toward the religious struggles in their homeland. Thus the chaotic situation of which the Amarna letters provide such a vivid impression was extraordinary and not reflecting Egyptian practice in general.[25] As a consequence of their neglect, the Egyptians lost large stretches of their empire to the great Hittite king Shuppiluliumash I (1344–1322 B.C.E.).[26] After the Amarna period the Egyptians consolidated their sway over what was left of their empire in Asia, and local affairs returned to a more peaceful kind of normality.

This interpretation of the Amarna period and of the evidence of the Amarna letters is not only too simplistic, it is probably totally wrong. Also in this period the Egyptians cared about their possessions in Asia. If we forget the relatively minor number of regents in Asia who in their letters to the Pharaoh delivered the ammunition to this interpretation and concentrate on the many letters answering Egyptian requests with a "Yes, sir, we obey!" our impression will be quite different. It will show that the Egyptians were heavily engaged in Asia, although fighting a losing battle against the Hittites. It is true that they lost the northern part of their empire to the Hittites, but it was not because they were indifferent, but rather because they were "outgunned" by the Hittites and their Syrian allies.[27]

During the Ramesside period covering the Nineteenth and Twentieth dynasties (c. 1292–1075 B.C.E.), the Egyptians truly reorganized their remaining possessions in Asia. They created a fixed system of provinces and especially a network of Egyptian strongholds garrisoned with troops from Egypt or mercenaries from other places, some of them related to the Sea People.[28] This system proved its worth, and in spite of an international political and economic situation that deteriorated constantly over the next couple of centuries, they remained firm in Palestine and probably also in southern Lebanon. Information is sparse, and as far as Syria and Transjordan go it is generally missing except from the beginning of this period, when the Egyptians were very active also in these regions. However, Palestine remained in Egyptian hands well into the first part of the Iron Age. When exactly the Egyptian dominance ceased in Palestine is difficult to say, but there are traces of their presence at least until the latter part of the Twentieth Dynasty (probably down to c. 1100 B.C.E.).

The Ramesside period covers the first part of what was already described as the transitional period, which in Palestine is not characterized by dramatic and radical changes that brought about a totally new civilization to be connected with the arrival of the Israelite nation. This is an image painted with the help of, on one side, the biblical description of the Israelite conquest of Canaan and, on another, the fantasies of scholars paraphrasing this narrative. Instead of this, a gradual development began in the highlands of central and northern Palestine as well as in southern Lebanon in the Beqa valley. In these places villages started to reappear shortly before 1200 B.C.E. and to multiply over the next century and a half.[29] Thus this period was witnessing a process of settlement in undefended agrarian homesteads, hamlets, and villages.[30]

Who participated in this development? Without doubt many scholars would still entertain the hope here to see the traces of Israelite newcomers to the Canaanite scene. Although they would have to give up the idea of an Israelite conquest of Palestine so beloved not least by North American and Israeli scholars of the past, they would try to save what can be saved. They will adopt the alternative theory of the past about the Israelite settlement in Palestine that the German Old Testament scholar Albrecht Alt formulated early in this century. According to Alt, the Israelites came to Palestine as small-cattle nomads looking for grazing for their animals, and only settled during a later and secondary part of their immigration movement.[31]

In order to maintain any of the early hypotheses about the historical origin of Israel it will be necessarily to find at least some traces of Israelite civilization that might indicate that this people was a newcomer to the Palestinian scene. As already mentioned, such traces were believed to exist in the form of a special type of pottery, the collared-rim jars, and as a special house type. Without having to repeat myself, it has to be said that none of this would match the archaeological findings. Such items are not exclusive to areas supposed to have been settled by Israelites. As it turned out, the verdict had to be that at least the majority of the villagers were peasants coming out of a peasant society and trained to employ as sophisticated agricultural techniques as were known at that time and place. These techniques included the terracing of the mountain slopes and the construction of waterproof cisterns.[32] What scholars ask early Israelite ingenuity to have produced is simply amazing: first of all they, being nomads, should have introduced a new style of housing. Second, they should have started producing rather cumbersome types of pottery such as the collared-rim jars, quite unsuitable for nomads on the move, and, finally, they should almost at once have become engaged in technical highland agriculture. The Italian Assyriologist Mario Liverani once remarked that the early Israelites were regarded to be almost like people who move into a flat already complete with furniture and everything and have only to continue where the former inhabitants left.[33]

It is for many reasons obvious that the village civilization of the early transitional period did not represent anything new from a cultural point of view. Their majority without doubt came from the settled population of the Late Bronze Age, which had, however, for centuries been living inside walled cities looking for protection in unruly times. They were certainly not alone, as there is reason to believe that at least some parts of the former population on the fringe of the Bronze Age society participated, among which previous nomads, outlaws, or bandits could be found.[34] However, the place of origin of the village population must be sought among the inhabitants of the cities of Palestine in the Late Bronze Age. As a matter of fact this linkage would make sense in that at least some of the cities of the Late Bronze Age went through a rather problematic stage of their existence, in combination with occasional destruction and desertions. The case of Hazor is highly illustrative, supposing that the Israeli scholar Yigael Yadin was correct when he proposed a connection between the appearance of villages in the mountains of northern Galilee and the destruction of Late Bronze Age Hazor.[35] In the Iron Age, Hazor continued to be settled, but only a tiny fraction of the area covered by the Bronze Age city was rebuilt. The majority of the population of the earlier great city of Hazor never returned to their city after its destruction. Some probably did, other people stayed away and settled in villages, and of course some were killed when the city was destroyed. His colleague Yohanan Aharoni also saw a connection, but believed the village culture to have appeared before the fall of Hazor.[36] Both theories can only be considered preliminary, and modern investigations have revealed a much more complex picture than the one envisaged by these pioneers, among other things a much more complicated archaeological situation among the villages in the north Galilean mountains.[37]

Now a number of theories have been proposed in order to explain this change of settlement style from heavily fortified cities to scattered villages in the mountains without fortifications. Among the more exotic explanations we have to reckon the one by George Mendenhall. He talks about a Hebrew conquest of Palestine as the consequence not of an invasion from the desert but as the result of a rebellion among the peasants of the Late Bronze Age Canaanite almost totally urbanized societies. The poor peasants turned against their former masters in order to create a new society.[38] Although Mendenhall's theories have subsequently been modified and presented in a more sophisticated form by other scholars, among whom we especially have to mention Norman K. Gottwald,[39] they have little that speaks in their favor. First of all there is no contemporary—or for that matter later—source that supports the idea of a rebellion. Second, this theory is built on a comprehensive series of social models that partly belong among the already mentioned armchair theories often not supported by social-anthropological "hard facts" that may have a different story to tell.[40] The explanation finally relies on a number of romantic stereotypes about "the society of the poor and destitute," about the readiness of such people to engage themselves in revolutions. It doesn't take into account that most revolutions of this world have been initiated "from the top," so to speak, and not "from the bottom." It has more often than not been members of the elite, officers in the army or intellectuals, who have arisen to the situation and used public discontent—often with the best of all intentions—to create a power position of their own.[41]

Mendenhall wanted to place Moses in this role as the originator of the revolution. This is, in the light of the biblical narrative, not a bad idea. The book of Exodus evidently describes Moses as a member of the (Egyptian) elite before he turned into a "revolutionary." Also Gottwald plays with this idea of a prime mover different from the multitude of Canaanite peasants.[42] To both of them, and in spite of their differences, the idea of Israel as from its very beginning a society kept together by their Yahwistic faith is fundamental to their revolutionary theories about the origin of Israel. The problem is that they in their reconstruction of the early Israelite society reproduce the monotheistic Israel of the Old Testament as if it was identical with the central Palestinian society of the transitional period. They consider Israel to be born as a nation fundamentally different from its surrounding nations. It may be possible by combining a rationalized version of the biblical narrative with material remains and mute artifacts as well as written documents to construct a model of the development of Israel, allowing for the idea of a growing syncretism between Israel and its Canaanite neighbors. This model can, however, never be anything except a postulate that certainly needs solid evidence of a monotheistic Yahwism in, say, the twelfth to the eighth centuries B.C.E., and such evidence is conspicuous by its absence.

The alternative has been a kind of "evolutionary" model in favor of which this writer has formerly spoken, assuming the growth of a village culture to be a natural development as the conditions of life in the cities of Palestine deteriorated during the latter part of the Late Bronze Age.[43] This theory is based on solid facts in that it takes into account the lack of ethnic markers showing different people to be involved in the transition from urban to village lifestyle. According to this explanation, ethnic differences were expected to appear only as time went by because of the differentiation of interest—economical, political, regional, and not least religious (mental)— that might appear as villagers joined together in kinship groups, lineages, and at the end of this development, tribes.

The force of this model is that it does not rely on secondary sources such as the Old Testament; it is based on a reasonable interpretation of the physical remains dating from the period in which this development is supposed to have taken place. It has, however, its share of problems.

It is the opinion of most of its adherents that this development was gradual and did not involve any kind of force from the authorities of the country. This happened in a power vacuum, which allowed citizens in the cities to escape from whatever burden the society used to place on their shoulders in the form of taxation, forced labor, and the like. The assumed early decline of the Egyptian empire combined with a general deteriorated economic situation weakened the cities and made it increasingly unproductive to live in urban settlements partly paid for by the income from trade. As a consequence, the inhabitants of the cities simply moved to the countryside, not as a protest against their former masters but simply because it was seen to be more practical, to provide a better chance of survival. At the same time, and this has especially been Israel Finkelstein's part of the hypothesis, a reciprocal movement among the migratory part of the Palestinian population chose to settle probably sometimes in settlements combining former urban dwellers with nomads, or sometimes in villages of their own.[44]

However, the breakdown of Egyptian power did not, as already indicated, coincide with the appearance of villages in the mountains of Palestine. On the contrary, the beginning of the transitional period saw a consolidation of Egyptian presence. If the inhabitants moved into open and undefended villages in the mountains, this movement must in one way or another presuppose a political development that made such a movement possible or profitable.

One way to look at the development would be to see the movement out from the cities as a negative reaction to the strengthening of the Egyptian sway over the country in the Ramesside period. It was not the local regents who created the problems—it was the Egyptians who forced more taxes and labor service on the inhabitants of Palestine. In this way they sought to make up for the loss of income from international trade. Here they found payment for their efforts in maintaining the empire and to keep up an economy at home that was also weakened by the deterioration of the international trade.

Such a theory would be able to explain the increasing presence of the village culture in the fringe areas of Palestine. It will not, however, provide an answer to Finkelstein's claim that nomads also participated in numbers in this process. It is one of the results of this writer's study of nomadism that nomads, once they have chosen this way of lifestyle, are difficult to induce into taking up a settled form of life again, nomadism providing them with more options than the life as settled peasants. Nomadism is to the surprise of the casual European observer a highly capitalistic enterprise, allowing for, in theory, an unlimited growth of the herds. It is also healthier, because nomads during their shift from summer to winter pasturage and back again follow the optimal ecological possibilities of their territory. It finally provides the nomads with another option: enabling them to assemble and move much faster than most settled people. This has traditionally in the Near East given the nomads the possibility to exploit the resources of the other parts of the society. They have been acting as highwaymen or they simply established some sort of military supremacy over the settled population (as well as over the less mobile part of the nomadic society).[45] Only determined efforts from the side of the established authorities, such as an army run by a centralized government with ample resources, have at times been able to blockade the negative effects of nomadism and to make life safe in other sectors of the country.[46]

The evolutionary model for the development of settled life in unprotected villages has not provided any answer to this view of nomadism. It has not explained at all why a nomadic element should be present in these villages. Nomadic presence is a reasonable assumption, as different forms of nomadism certainly played their role in the societal development in this period (as in any other period up to the present time, when the problem has been settled at least in Palestine).[47]

Another theory about the origin of the village culture in the transitional period takes account of these circumstances pertaining to the role of nomads in Near Eastern society. This theory points at conditions that would on one side allow a safe life in settlements without elaborate fortifications of their own and on the other induce, if not force, migratory elements to settle down. In light of the present state of knowledge of the political development, there must be a centralized power behind the considerable efforts conditioning such a demographic change, which started to manifest itself in Palestine shortly before 1200 B.C.E. It would be foolish to leave out of consideration the consolidation of Egyptian imperial power in the same period. As a matter of fact, it would make sense if the appearance of villages should be understood as the result of a deliberate policy from the side of the Egyptians. In this way they sought to consolidate their sway over the territory, in order to improve its economic potential by moving a part of the urbanized population out of the more and more unproductive cities into the countryside, to till the land and provide revenues for their overlords.[48]

To do so would, as already indicated, make necessary the use of extensive force to keep down unrest and to keep away elements not part of this venture. It is therefore extremely important that as early as during the reign of Sety I (c. 1290–1279) the Egyptians were highly active around their stronghold at Beth-shean, conducting a "peacekeeping" mission among unruly elements. These included the *ḫabiru,* and some other named groups, the Tayar and Rahamu, possibly tribal units living in the vicinity of Beth-shean.[49] There are no parallels to this text, and we are therefore ignorant of other attempts of the same sort. However, the military efforts that followed to wrestle Syria from the Hittites, during the reign of Ramses II (c. 1279–1213) probably, presupposed the establishment of a safe base in the remaining part of the Egyptian empire. Finally also the campaign of Merneptah, which included among other events the "pacification" of Israel, could be understood as such a venture on the Egyptian part against unsettled or discontented demographic elements in the central highlands of Palestine.

Finally, the reciprocal movement during the eleventh century toward more centralized types of settlements, which is certainly in evidence in the northern Negev,[50] might be a reaction to—among other things—the reduction of Egyptian interest in the area at the very end of their presence in Palestine. This would cause villagers to again seek protection within walled settlements against the nonsettled population threatening their survival either directly or through "taxation" in the form of protection money.[51] This change is certainly part of a process leading toward a more centralized political system among the settled population as a local kind of answer to the challenge caused by the disappearance of the hitherto central authorities of the Egyptian empire in Asia.

THE FIRST MILLENNIUM

According to the Old Testament, the history of Palestine in the Iron Age opened with its greatest historical moment when it became the center of a great empire. This empire is supposed to have stretched from, in the north, the Euphrates and reached as far south as the Brook of Egypt, most likely present-day *Wadi el-Arish* in northern Sinai. This huge empire was ruled by two mighty kings, David and Solomon, residing in their great capital, Jerusalem, where especially Solomon carried out great building projects such as the Temple of Yahweh, the royal palace compound, and the Millo.[52]

The biblical evidence goes as far as this. Now we will turn to the material remains from the center of this empire, Jerusalem. In the tenth century B.C.E. the center of this empire is supposed to be the Jerusalem situated on the southeastern hill, the Ophel, to the south of the present *Haram eš-Šarif,* the Temple Mount, with an extension to the north including the southern part of the Temple Mount. The core of this Jerusalem was a small fortified town the size of a few hectares and with a population of hardly more than a couple of thousand persons, including women and children, that is, with an adult male population of about three to four hundred men.[53] The extension to the north was supposed to have housed public buildings of different sorts, such as the centers of administration, the palace, and the Temple compound.

Biblical scholars on the basis of the information contained in the Old Testament have constructed the chronology of this period. As soon as this chronology is left out of consideration, the date of the extension to the north of the original settlement and also that of the settlement itself on the southeastern hill of Jerusalem can only be settled on the basis of another chronological system. This system has been (or has to be) constructed on the basis of pottery found during several excavations which have been conducted in many parts of Jerusalem. This problem has probably all too seldom been acknowledged by historians of ancient Israel. The reason is the dearth of written documents in the shape of inscriptions, as next to nothing has been found from the tenth century B.C.E. No inscription exists that can be used to anchor the ceramic chronology. Therefore few archaeologists are likely to claim that any dating of the ceramics of the tenth or ninth century B.C.E. is more precise than, say, half a century. This has partly to do with the fact that this pottery was rather uniform in character, from an artistic point of view rather monotonous, and mostly consisting of a rather course monochrome ware that developed only very slowly. It should therefore not be a surprise that some scholars of the present such as the Israeli archaeologist Israel Finkelstein attempt to lower the ceramic chronology.[54] By doing so, they are at the same time disputing the claims that Jerusalem had already developed into a royal center before the end of the tenth century. According to the ceramic chronology recently proposed, there would probably not have been a city at all called Jerusalem situated in central Palestine in the tenth century B.C.E.[55]

The dating of pottery will not have to stand alone, as other means of measuring time are available, for example the vaunted C-14 system of dating and more refined modern methods. None of these, however, when we speak about dating something that is about three thousand years old, are more precise than the already mentioned dates based on analyses of the pottery available. It might well be that future developments in physics would settle the matter and allow a more safe system of dating to be established. So far this has not been the case. At this point we will have to say that even if at some time a royal establishment was constructed on the site of Jerusalem, it might not be before, at the earliest, the first part of the ninth century B.C.E. Even in this case this establishment was limited in extent and only allowed for a tiny population to live there. It might have been little more than a fortress with a villagelike settlement attached to it.

Broadening the circle around Jerusalem, a similar situation seems characteristic of the tenth century B.C.E. south Palestinian landscape. Here little may have happened as far as a political concentration around only one major center is concerned, although regional developments such as those already mentioned in connection with the northern Negev perhaps already in the tenth century can be shown to have occurred.

In this connection a systemic approach to the archaeological remains is recommended, trying to review the region as a whole. The importance of such an approach has already been proved in connection with the situation, not least in central Palestine at the beginning of the transitional period. Here the surveys conducted by a number of archaeologists mapping the demographic changes that occurred in this territory in the period preceding the tenth century B.C.E. have led to important conclusions. A similar comprehensive study of developments that took place in the first part of the first millennium has not been published, but the available material has been statistically analyzed and systematized a few years ago in a study by the American scholar David Jamieson-Drake.[56]

The title of Jamieson-Drake's study is beguiling, as it is certainly not the limited aim of the author only to show the extension of literacy in Palestine around the turn of the first millennium B.C.E.[57] Instead of this, he questions the well-established idea about the existence of a Judean state as early as the tenth and ninth centuries. Although a concentration of the population around fewer major settlements can be demonstrated, the settled area remained almost constant at the beginning of this period, and only in the latter part started to show any significant increase.[58] The concentration of settlements may simply tell us about more unruly political and economic circumstances. Only if at the same time it can be shown that these fortified structures were systematically interrelated, for example in the form of a hierarchical system with local deputies of a major royal center, can they be seen as pointing toward the establishment of a major centralized state.

One such element has been proposed by referring to the construction of fortifications around the new "urban" centers of the early first millennium. These examples include Hazor, Megiddo, Gezer, and Beersheba. One characteristic feature of this time is the development of the gate from a normal four-chamber gate to a new six-chamber type, combined either with a massive wall or with a so-called "casemate-wall."[59] Also in this case the introduction of a biblical argument that it was Solomon who constructed these cities (1 Kings 9:15) led to a confused situation. It was assumed that this kind of fortifications was evidence of a centralized political system. The argument did not pay attention to the wide differences that exist between the different gate systems. We should mention the different forms of the gates and stress the fact that the six-chamber gate is not confined to places supposed to have been Israelite (or Judean) territory. The city gate of Ashdod was constructed according to the same pattern, and Ashdod is supposed to have been a Philistine city.[60] The fortifications and the connected construction of cities were in this way not restricted to so-called Israelite and Judean territory but were also seen in other parts of Palestine, and they cannot for that reason be taken as a proof of a centralized political structure embracing most of the country. From a political point of view, the building of cities and fortresses shows only that people in those days needed protection in the form of more or less solid walls. From an ethnical point of view, these constructions are of no importance at all, and from an architectural one they simply tell us that we here have a natural development based on systems of fortification already known before this building activity started.

The same will have to be said about other types of constructions, such as the so-called palaces of the Iron Age[61] or the Temple constructions. The specimens of, not least, the temples from this period that have until now been excavated in Palestine are rather insignificant structures showing little in the direction of ingenuity on the part of the inhabitants of Palestine.[62]

Now returning to Jamieson-Drake's analysis of the archaeological remains, his final argument is that the establishment of centralized political structures like kingdoms would as a by-product lead to the production of luxury items.[63] This may not at first sound like a convincing argument. It is nevertheless a very important one. It is a truism of the ancient world that the economy as soon as it developed beyond the most basic level (which was always the level of the ordinary population—say 95 percent of the demographic total) presupposed centralized authorities that could guarantee the free movement of persons and merchandise. In fact, the common *local* political system of Palestine and Syria in the Late Bronze Age was the "palace-state." In this organization, the palace, that is, the royal administration, organized the production of luxury goods to be traded for items to be obtained from other quarters. Thereby the "state" increasing the wealth and especially the prestige of the inhabitants of the palace, first of all the king himself, and thereby also the self-esteem of the ruling elite which probably saw their own importance reflected by the status of their king.[64] We cannot say with certainty that an economic system as centralized as the one in the Late Bronze Age reappeared in Palestine and Syria in the Iron Age. However, a significant increase in the presence of luxury items would in ancient economies point to a development toward more centralized political structures such as the state. According to Jamieson-Drake such a development occurred very late in Judah, showing a centralized state probably not to have been established here before the late ninth or the eighth century B.C.E.[65]

The size and character of this state as well as its ethnical identity as a Judean state based, for example, on the existence of a tribe of the same name, cannot be decided on the basis of archaeology. It can be said that it did not carry any markers that point at a specific and discrete ethnic situation within the confines of this state and that made it different from its neighbors in any significant way. The small and local differences that exist may owe their existence to the establishment of a single political system covering at least the southern part of the central highlands and bordering a series of major city-states in the west. It is difficult to say how far it was able to control the Negev. The presence of fortresses such as the one at Arad, including what may have been a small a sanctuary for Yahweh, may tell us about at least a military kind of presence in the northern part of this landscape.[66]

Other items, which testify to the regional importance of this state, are the so-called *le-melek* stamps on handles from jars, which are supposed to have contained either the income from royal estates or tax revenues.[67] These stamps are quite common in contexts normally dated to the eighth century B.C.E. They seem to agree with other kinds of evidence pointing to the creation of a centralized state in the form of a kingdom in the southern part of the central highlands in this period, and thus suit the results of Jamieson-Drake very well. They seem to disappear, on the other hand, during the following century, being probably replaced by a new kind of official stamp on jars, which, however, turns up far more infrequently than the *le-melek* stamps.[68]

Such a situation may point to a diminished importance of the royal administration or to a breakdown of its influence. This is a situation that is also discussed by Jamieson-Drake and reflected by the archaeological remains of the seventh century, which indicate a serious disturbance of the economic infrastructure of the country in connection with a widespread and massive destruction of the cities.[69] We know from experience that the presence of such evidence of "universal" destruction may lead the archaeologists astray when they try to translate their evidence into history.[70] This destruction of Judean sites, however, fits the written evidence dating from around 700 B.C.E., according to which the Assyrian king Sennacherib boasts of having destroyed Hezekiah's entire kingdom, except its capital, Jerusalem.[71] There are reasons to treat such a coincidence with caution. The material remains, however, may confirm Sennacherib's claim, which is evidently not quite wrong when it says that he in fact destroyed the Judean state and left only what would best be considered a city-state of a very small extent in the hands of Hezekiah. Although some reconstruction took place over the next century, lasting until the Babylonian conquest, it might be correct to say that the country never really recovered before it came under Persian control at the end of the sixth century B.C.E. and probably was only fully restored in the Hellenistic period. As a matter of fact, Jamieson-Drake talks about a total societal collapse at the beginning of the sixth century.[72]

As a result of this investigation it seems that the Judean state as a comprehensive political construction, perhaps a territorial state in contrast to the system of city-states which was the normal kind of political arrangement in Palestine in antiquity,[73] hardly survived for more than a few generations. This short period would not have allowed Judah to develop ethnic peculiarities not already present before the formation of the state. This goes well with the evidence already presented, which does not speak in favor of such an ethnic discreteness in this part of Palestine. As a matter of fact, from the material remains there is absolutely no reason to assume the presence in southern Palestine of anything like a state ruling a comprehensive territory and with a common and exclusive ethnic background, not to say identity and conscience. Small local traditions that may be discerned in the material remains do not contradict this, as they hardly go beyond what is to be expected inside any comprehensive political and geographical structure.

Now, a study like the one by Jamieson-Drake is certainly not a flawless one, although it by far surpasses other attempts at "social archaeology" of the Iron Age, such as the one by John Holladay published in a recent "social archaeology" of ancient Israel.[74] The starting point in Holladay's version of social archaeology is obviously the biblical narrative, and he takes much of this to be historical fact, including such questionable subjects as the existence of an Israelite empire in the tenth century. By mixing Bible with archaeology his study is severely compromised, and in spite of its social approach not very different from traditional biblical archaeology as it used to be in the days of archaeologists like William F. Albright and George E. Wright.

When we turn to Jamieson-Drake's study again, his data base has been criticized as being insufficient and his reconstruction accordingly imprecise.[75] This is at the same time correct and misleading. Hardly any territory of this world has been so extensively excavated as Palestine, and the amount of material remains unearthed from this place surpasses most of what can be found in any other country. However, a comprehensive amount of this derives from excavations conducted by techniques now considered obsolete. This, of course, compromises any thesis that is based on this material and makes the use of it in a synthetic analysis like the one by Jamieson-Drake problematic if this factor is not properly acknowledged by the researcher, and it is probably here that Jamieson-Drake should be criticized.[76] He should in his statistics have included a factor of error when it came to material and results deriving from excavations from more than, say, ten years ago, and have multiplied this factor as he went even farther back in time. That is the reason why a certain place may need to be reopened time and again. The best example of this is ancient Jericho, which was excavated by the German archaeologists Johannes Watzinger and Ernst Sellin at the beginning of this century. Excavations were resumed by the British archaeologist John Garstang in the 1930s and again by Kathleen Kenyon in the 1950s. Now, in 1997, excavations on Jericho are again taking place conducted by a mixed Italian-Palestinian team.[77] In this way, results from an excavation like that of W. F. Badè of Tell en-Nasbeh (probably ancient Mizpah) between 1926 and 1935, which effectively removed the site from the surface of the earth, cannot carry the same weight in a statistic analysis as Jamieson-

Drake's, or as successively and with increasing weight, J. W. Crowfoot's at Samaria between 1931 and 1935, Kenyon's at Jericho between 1952 and 1959, William B. Dever's at Gezer between 1964 and 1973, or the present ones at Megiddo by David Ussishkin and Israel Finkelstein.

In this way several of Jamieson-Drake's statistics may have to be revised. It is a question whether this will change his general results that the appearance of the kingdom of Judah as a fully developed early state happened rather late in comparison to the usual estimate, which on the basis of the Old Testament placed this event in the tenth century B.C.E. Judah as an autonomous political structure survived for a very short span of time and may never have developed anything like a consistent "national" identity, not to say ideology. It is perhaps absolutely correct when an Assyrian source from the seventh century places Judah among the Philistine states on the coast. To the Assyrians who were now acquainted with this territory for more than a hundred years, there were probably few things that separated the "Judeans" from the Philistines.

The territory of the Judean state is, however, only one among a number of regions and subregions in ancient Palestine, which have to be studied in the same way as has happened to the Judean area. Little in the way of comprehensive synthesis on a regional scale has so far been done. Israel Finkelstein has, however, published the first part of a series devoted to the three main regions of the country—the Negev, the central highlands, and the north.[78] It would probably be just as important to collect the evidence from the Mediterranean coast, on one hand to the south of the Carmel range and on the other on the plain of Acco, in the first part of the first millennium B.C.E., most likely in the hands of former Sea People.[79] It will also be necessary to deal separately with the Valley of Jezreel and the north Galilean mountains and with the Huleh Valley farther to the northeast. Such a study should also include the different regions of Transjordan and southwestern Syria, such as the Golan Heights, Gilead, and the plain of Moab.

First it is necessary to carry such comparable studies farther. Only then will it be possible with certainty to decide the amount of regional differences within a common cultural framework with no marked ethnic differences between neighboring regions, although allowing for such differences to grow as the distance widens. It might well be that we have to recognize that certain regions show peculiarities of an extent and importance that say we are also confronting ethnic differences of a supraregional character, indicating the existence of ethnic differences that were felt and acknowledged by the people living in these regions. Whether such analyses of the material remains will be able also to discover major ethnic or even "national" diversity has still to be seen.

A study comparable to the one by Jamieson-Drake of the developments in the territory that was dominated by the state of Israel, in the Iron Age identical with "the House of Omri" known from ancient documents, has not been published. Pending the results of such a study, it is likely that evidence may speak in favor of a political and demographic development in this territory that predated the developments in the south by probably a hundred years. It is likely that a marked increase will show up in the form of centralized fortified settlements from at least the end of the tenth or the beginning of the ninth century at such as Hazor, Jezreel, and Samaria.[80] The situation is otherwise very much the same as the one found in later Judean territory: a number of regional diversities developed through the centuries squarely belonging within one and the same culture, not fundamentally different from the one found in the southern part of the central highlands. This fundamental uniformity embraces all kinds of material remains—art, burial customs, and buildings. When serious deviations occurred, these are more often than not attributable to foreign import and inspiration rather than to local inventiveness, as is the case with the ivory decoration found in the remains of the royal palace of Samaria showing definite relationship to the art of Syria.[81] It might in fact be true that such new elements were limited to the upper stratum of the society and therefore not markers of ethnic differentiation, only of the more refined "international" taste of the societal elite, which could afford such luxury.[82]

One such regional development may be the so-called Samaria ware (incidentally dubbed so because it first appeared during the excavations of Samaria), which can be subdivided into at least two groups of pottery, one of which being extremely fine and delicate, the other rather course. This last mentioned ware has mostly appeared in major places like Samaria, Hazor, and Jezreel. It should probably be considered a kind of "palatial" pottery, either distributed among the governmental centers of Israel or traded by production facilities attached to the royal economic setup, if it is not simply imported from Phoenicia, as most archaeologists will now argue.[83]

The character of settlements like Hazor and Megiddo, similar to fortresses, or the official character of the palatial complex at Samaria, as well as of the so far mysterious structure at Jezreel[84] may not in themselves indicate a centralized territorial state. However, in this case the date of the appearance of these architectural structures more or less concurs with the evidence from contemporary inscriptions speaking about an important political organization known as Israel or the House of Omri. It is therefore difficult to escape the conclusion that these fortresses belonged to the kingdom of Israel and are evidence of its potential as a territorial state of some circumstances as early as in the ninth century. It cannot be demonstrated whether it was at the same time also a "national" state with a national identity and ideology of its own. It is, however, a reasonable assumption that the kings of this state, in order to pay for their building activities as well as for the expenses connected with an active foreign policy, would have employed the age-old means of rewarding taxpayers with extensive royalist propaganda. In this way they could increase the prestige of the dynasty and the kingdom and thus make the burdens placed on the shoulders of common persons the more endurable.[85]

CONCLUSION

For at least one and a half centuries the state of Israel played its part in the international power game. After the middle of the eighth century, the rise of the neo-Assyrian empire spelled an end to its independent existence. Then the Assyrians split its territory into several minor units. Soon after its capital was also destroyed (722 B.C.E.). Biblical sources as well as Assyrian ones speak about a massive deportation from Samaria (27,290 according to Sargon's annals[86]) and a later massive forced settlement of foreign elements deported from other quarters of the Assyrian empire (2 Kings 17:6,24). This is in accordance with Assyrian and later Babylonian practice. In this way they broke the local power structure that had existed before their conquest in order to create a new one in which they themselves or people directly dependent on the support from their Assyrian overlords played the role of the former masters of the country.[87] The area of the former state of Israel never again obtained an independent political status, although local potentates, governors, and officials sometimes assumed what could be called a semi-autonomous status. The local population might have received a massive contribution of foreigners in the Assyrian period, something that should be reflected in the material remains, but most of it remained stable, tilling their farmland, breeding children, and living a peasant's uneventful life. There isn't any evidence of resistance from common people against the foreign intruders. There are no vestiges of an ethnic background that led to the rejection of foreigners in this part of Palestine. There is, as a matter of fact, nothing that may look like a national consciousness.

CHAPTER 4

The People of God

The Two Israels in the Old Testament

THE EXILE AS A
FOUNDATION MYTH

The image of Israel in the Old Testament is ambivalent. On one hand it is the people of God, the elected one, God's own possession, the light to the nations. On the other, it is a depraved people, a people who cannot understand, who have been warned, but nevertheless are following in the footsteps of their fathers, forgetting their God, a people to be swept away and punished. Before the Babylonian exile we see a people of sinners and transgressors, but after the exile a purified community of believers, never more clearly expressed than in the description of the new Israel after the purge in Isaiah 4:

And in that day seven women shall take hold of one man, saying, We will eat our own bread, and wear our own apparel: only let us be called by thy name, to take away our reproach.
In that day shall the branch of the LORD be beautiful and glorious, and the fruit of the earth shall be excellent and comely for them that are escaped of Israel.
And it shall come to pass, that he that is left in Zion, and he that remaineth in Jerusalem, shall be called holy, even every one that is written among the living in Jerusalem:
When the LORD shall have washed away the filth of the daughters of Zion, and shall have purged the blood of Jerusalem from the midst thereof by the spirit of judgment, and by the spirit of burning.
And the LORD will create upon every dwelling place of mount Zion, and upon her assemblies, a cloud and smoke by day, and the shining of a flaming fire by night: for upon all the glory shall be a defence.
And there shall be a tabernacle for a shadow in the daytime from the heat, and for a place of refuge, and for a covert from storm and from rain.

This place goes with several others in the first part of the book of Isaiah—the so-called "proto-Isaiah"—supposed by traditional scholarship to represent the prophecies of a prophet who lived in the eighth century B.C.E.[1] One such text is the final part of chapter 6, which describes the end of the unfaithful Israel, of which only one in ten people will be spared. The multitude will be killed or deported far away to foreign countries. Only a remnant shall return after the punishment (Isa. 6:11–13). This "gospel" says that because of their idolatry the prophets frequently warned the Israelites of ancient times. These prophets had spelled out the coming doom to their people, only to be mocked and persecuted because of their preaching (Jer. 7:25; 2 Kings 17:13). In spite of all the warnings, the people refused to bow before Yahweh, and at the end catastrophe struck just as prophesied and the people had to go into exile for seventy years (Jer. 29:10[2]), and the country could have its rest (2 Chron. 36:21, with a reference to Jeremiah). After the exile, the people, now understood to be the children of the generation that was carried away, were allowed to return to the country of their fathers, now with the firm intention that another exile should never happen as long as the world exists (Jer. 31:36–37).

The exile in this way has two roles to play. It at one and the same time disconnects and unites the present and the past. It is also the instrument that guarantees that the transgressors are punished because of their sins and never allowed to return, and that their country is cleansed of their sins. The generation that returns to the land of their fathers will at the same time understand that it is their land. It belonged to their fathers and was left without inhabitants as long as the exile lasted, which says that nobody except the generation that returned should be allowed to stay in the land. As the true heirs of the fathers, the sons will take up and fulfill their obligation to Yahweh and the land in the place where their fathers failed. The exile is in this way clearly seen as a foundation myth of the Jewish people that arose sometime in the latter part of the first millennium B.C.E.[3] Without the idea of an exile there could be nothing like the purified remnant of Isaiah, residing on Mount Zion under the palladium of their God.

The disconnection between the generations had to be established, because without the exile which person would have been able to tell the son from his father? Who could say, "This person, the son, is doing his duties to the Lord, while his father has sinned and will be punished"? Without an exile, how could it be established who was punished and who was saved from it, who was cursed and who was blessed? It would be like Proverbs, where the transgressor will always be punished, while the pious person will survive and prosper. Without an exile there would be no differentiation between

sinner and righteous, and no prospect of the people of God liberating itself
from its sinful past. If there had been no exile, it would have had to be invented! And some will certainly say, "And so they [i.e., the narrators of the
tales of the exile in the Old Testament] truly did!"

The exile is, however, just as important as the instrument that connects the
generations, for without an exile the sons could claim no right to inherit the
land of God. The fathers were condemned because of their transgressions,
and thereby forfeited their claims to the land that was, after all, a gift from
God which could be reclaimed anytime. If there was no exile, who could tell
the sinner from the righteous, thereby deciding who would be the person to
inherit the land and who to walk away from it to a place of condemnation?
The exile creates a legitimate right to the land; without an exile the sons
would have no claims to their land. Thus the people who lived in the land
when the sons returned from the exile—something that is not forgotten by
the authors of Ezra-Nehemiah—were intruders, as all of Israel was carried
away into exile. Such persons could have no claim on the land and no right
to be there; they were not the sons of the fathers and could be removed, having no share in the country together with the true heirs of the past.[4]

It is obvious that irrespective of the historical content of the tradition of
the exile—after all Jerusalem was sacked at the beginning of the sixth century B.C.E. and some people carried away to Babylonia—it has been turned
into a foundation myth. We may ask for the identity of the people who created this myth. Although no airtight answer can be given, it should not be
too difficult at least to indicate who they were: members of the early Jewish
community, probably staying in "exile," in the *golah,* most likely in
Mesopotamia. The myth of the exile was therefore created as a program for
the return to the country of God, where a new and ideal nation of God should
be established. This new nation should consist of the holy ones, the purified
remnant. They had no part in the abominations of the past. They were the
people of God. If they had not created such a myth of the exile, there would
have been no Jewish people, no Jewish society in Palestine, nothing that distinguished a Jew from other people, and no relationship in the form of a new
covenant (cf. Jer. 31:31–34) to the God of the land of Israel.

THE EXODUS
AS A FOUNDATION MYTH

It is certainly not unusual for people to possess their own foundation myth.
It is as a matter of fact a quite common, almost universal phenomenon, that
any group—ethnic, national, political, religious, and occupational—will be

in possession of a narrative about its foundation known to and accepted by its membership. Among the more famous myths belonging to this genre is from ancient times the tale of the founder of Rome, Romulus. Romulus was brought up, together with his brother Remus, by a wolf, which in the version of Livy saved the twins from the Tiber where they were to be drowned.[5] Another example is the legend of Sargon of Akkad, who was exposed on the river but saved and brought up by a fisherman in a way closely resembling the myth of the birth of Moses. This Sargon was to become the creator of a mighty empire.[6]

Sometimes such origin myths may change, being replaced by other tales, or the old and the new myth may blend together to form one narrative. This happened when the myth that the Romans descended from Trojans was made famous by Virgil's epic *The Aeneid,* then combined with the Romulus legend in Livy's history.

The peculiar thing about the foundation myth of Judaism, however, is that it is not the only one. As a matter of fact, it is closely paralleled in another foundation myth, the myth of the origin of the fathers, a myth that follows a course that is almost identical with the one belonging to the sons. This myth can be identified as the myth about the miraculous salvation of the Israelite people from their oppressors in Egypt and the covenant with Yahweh, who through a human agent, Moses, saved his chosen people from serfdom in a foreign country. A period of many generations, in all 430 years (Ex. 12:40), preceded this liberation. During this time Israel stayed in Egypt after its forefather Jacob, the first Israel (Gen. 32:29) and thus the apical ancestor of the people, had first traveled there from the land of Canaan during a season of famine (Genesis 46).

We therefore have two parallel lines of narrative. The first one includes the initial settlement of the patriarchs in Canaan after Abraham had been ordered by God to leave Haran (Genesis 12). Abraham settles in Canaan and after him his son, Isaac. Their settlement is, however, never understood to be a stable one, fixed for eternity. It is always seen as under the perspective of the future exile in Egypt[7]—probably also with a side view to the future one of Mesopotamia[8]— where the patriarch has to travel in order to become the forefather of a great nation. Being only a handful of persons when they left Canaan, the Israelites came out of Egypt as a mighty nation. In this way Egypt became the cradle of the Israelite people, but would have turned out to become their grave if they had not been liberated from this place in time by the intervention of the God of their fathers, here Abraham, Isaac, and Jacob.[9]

After the escape from Egypt there follows the constitution of the people

at Sinai, when Moses on behalf of the people entered the covenant with Yahweh (Exodus 19–24), and again after this event the forty years in the desert.
From its very beginning, the Israelite people proved unworthy of the divine
grace bestowed on them by at first grumbling over their hard fate in the
desert (e.g., Ex. 16:3). Thereafter they declined to enter the land of their fathers because of fear of the inhabitants of the country (Numbers 14). Because of their lack of faith in Yahweh, they were punished so that no one
who left Egypt should survive in order to enter the Promised Land. Only two
persons should see the land—Joshua, whose task was to accomplish the
conquest of Canaan, and Caleb, who had vouched for an early entry into
the country (Num. 14:38).

The occupation of the country is accomplished, as narrated in the book
of Joshua, in the form of a sweeping military campaign during which most
of the country is subdued. What is left is kept in a state of bondage to Israel
(Joshua 9). After the settlement the country is distributed among the tribes
of Israel (Joshua 13–19). The conclusion is achieved when the people—not
only their leaders—swear to keep the covenant with Yahweh (Joshua 24).
Before that goes a warning that residence in their country can soon be forfeited if they should break the covenant with God (Josh. 23:16).

The second part of the narrative begins exactly at this point when Joshua
has died (Josh. 24:29–30, and repeated in Judg. 2:8–9). This part of Israel's
history is introduced by a sermon from the angel of Yahweh. This sermon
surprisingly talks about the sins of Israel, that they had forsaken their God
to worship other gods. For this reason they are going to be punished. This
sermon may seem a bit premature, as the narratives about these transgressions follow only in the next few chapters in the book of Judges, after Joshua
had died and the people started worshiping other gods[10]—only to get punished and saved again time after time until the time when the people chose
a king to rule over them instead of judges appointed by Yahweh as saviors
of Israel.[11] At this crucial point another warning follows against the worship
of foreign gods. This time the warning is formulated by the prophet Samuel:
If they sin, they and their king will lose their lives (1 Samuel 12).

These warnings are repeated several times, in the forms of oracles. One
such concerns the continuation of the royal house of David (2 Samuel 7).
Another is included in Solomon's prayer to God at the dedication of his Temple in Jerusalem. Here the perspective of a coming exile is expressed in
Solomon's address to God that he will pardon the transgressors who have
been sent into exile (1 Kings 8:46–51). The future disaster becomes even
clearer in the following chapter, when God directly addresses Solomon and
warns him against breaking the covenant and worshiping other gods. This

will have fatal consequences for Israel and its royal house, which will be destroyed while Israel will be "cut off . . . out of the land which I have given them" (1 Kings 9:7).

In the following sections dealing with the history of the divided kingdom, the perspective is unfaithful Israel against a Judah that is only slightly better. These narratives show to the people of God the fate of the unfaithful. They are at the end of Israel's history, when the Assyrians conquer Samaria, dragged away into an exile without return, only to be replaced by foreign peoples deported to the territory of the former kingdom of Israel, where they are still living (2 Kings 17).

In spite of this warning and in spite of some kings of good intentions like Hezekiah and Josiah "following in the path of David," Judah never understood what was in preparation. The Judeans take up the abominations of their northern brethren, only to be promised not redemption but utter destruction (2 Kings 21), something that became true when Nebuchadnezzar conquered and destroyed Jerusalem and its Temple and carried its inhabitants away into exile in Babylonia.

This part of the narrative ends at this point, although with an end note about the release of King Jehoiachin from prison in Babylon after the death of Nebuchadnezzar (562 B.C.E.; see 2 Kings 25:27–30). This note is most likely included in order to tell the reader that the house of David was not annihilated at the destruction of the Judean kingdom. Also in the future there will be hope for a king of the house of David to restore his kingdom. The exile was not the end in spite of the repeated warnings; it carried in it the future for the people of God and their Davidic king, that a new Israel should arise on the ruins of the old.

If we try to reduce this narrative into its main parts, we might arrive at the following:

> *Prologue:* Reaching from the creation of the world to the dispersal of human beings. This introduces the election of Abraham.
> *First part:* Abraham moves to Canaan, then to Egypt, and finally back to Canaan.
> *Second part:* Israel (Jacob) moves from Canaan to Mesopotamia, then from Mesopotamia to Canaan and finally to Egypt. Israel stays in Egypt for 430 years. Then Israel leaves Egypt and moves to Canaan.
> *Third part:* Israel lives in Canaan for many hundreds of years, then moves out of Canaan to Babylonia (Mesopotamia), and stays there for many (seventy) years.

> *Epilogue:* Israel moves to Canaan to become the new Israel, in
> contrast to the old Israel of the past. Thus the narrative reaches
> an end when it arrives at a situation of everlasting peace and
> blessing ("and they lived happily ever after"!).

The first narrative about the preexilic Israelites is a story of hope and despair. Israel is a great people with great promises. It is saved from Egypt
when Yahweh intervenes and fights the pharaoh to liberate his people. Then
Israel can receive Yahweh's covenant and law book. As the people of God,
Israel is destined to have a great future as a people blessed by God. Israel
is, however, punished and destroyed by God because of lack of faith in its
God, however much this is against the plans of God.[12]

As a contrast, the new Israel starts out without much prospect of success,
out of the ruins of Jerusalem destroyed by the Babylonians, only hoping for
the grace of God to liberate it from servitude and bring it back to the land
of the fathers. A new Temple is constructed on the ruins of the old, but the
accomplishment of this building project is reached only by the help of direct interventions from foreign kings—first Cyrus, then Darius (Ezra 5).

The exodus myth describes how the Israelites were led out of Egypt into
Sinai, where, through Moses as caretaker, they were given the covenant and
the Torah. The myth of the exile and return has a similar story to tell. It is a
story about getting out of the house of servitude, about returning to Israel's
own country, and about the Law, which was this time given to it by the
hands of Ezra the scribe (Nehemiah 8). The last act was completed in the
form of a new contract between God and the people, whereby Ezra sur-
passed both Moses and Joshua, so to speak, by combining the achievement
of both the ancestral heroes in one act (Nehemiah 10).[13] Both parts agree
that the constitution of Israel—of the preexilic treacherous as well as of the
postexilic "holy" Israel—was identical with the Torah, the law of God. This
law obliged Israel to worship God and only this one God and to forsake the
abominable habits of their parents, something that was connected, however,
with the settlement in God's own land.[14] In this way the myth brings together
the idea of a people with a special constitution, the covenant with God, with
only one God to worship, and with a country to stay in as its own country.
The promise says that Israel will remain in its land as long as the first two
requisites are fulfilled, as long as they do not break the covenant and do not
establish relations with foreign gods.

As a foundation myth, the exodus myth therefore constitutes the Israelite people not as a normal people like any other around, but as a separate, elected people of God. The origin myth is simply that of a religious

community, whether people or congregation. It is not a normal myth of origin of a secular entity; it is the kind of mythology that follows other religious communities of this world, including Christianity. It is not history but beyond history, phrased in historical terms; it is the origin myth of a religious history of the chosen people, the holy congregation of God, who having sinned passed the judgment in order to reclaim their land and their God.

HISTORY AS THE EXTENSION
OF THE FOUNDATION MYTH

So far it is obvious that also when compared with other forms of history writing from the ancient Near East, or from the Greek and Roman world, the history of the Israelite people as told by the biblical writers is not a history about a secular people—as secular as a people could be in ancient times. It is the history of a selected community always seen in the perspective of its divine constitution. Also in the context of antique history writing it is a kind of metahistory, or for that matter myth that is uniquely focused on one element, the religious part of Israel's existence. The only thing that marks Israel out in contrast to the surrounding nations is its special relationship with its God and the way this relationship decides its destiny. Everything else told by the history writers is to be considered a kind of requisite introduced to the scene of biblical Israel in order to illustrate its religious history to its very end. Thus the foreign nations mentioned by the Old Testament are not foreign nations in the usual sense of the word, they are the instruments of Yahweh's wrath when they are attacking Israel, and they are the victims of his anger whenever he wants to show grace to his chosen people. The king of Assyria is the "rod of mine anger," but Yahweh will nevertheless punish him because of his arrogance (Isa. 10:5–12). The Canaanites and all the other pre-Israelite people of the Holy Land, the Hivites, the Jebusites, the Perizzites, or whatever their names are, are here only to populate the Promised Land and to be exterminated by the Israelites when they arrive. They have no history of their own.[15] The Moabites, the Midianites, the Philistines are around to punish Israel on Yahweh's behalf whenever the Israelites start worshiping other gods after the death of one of their judges, or in turn to be conquered by the Israelite kings whenever it suits the will of the Lord. In short, the biblical history is one that follows no historical laws—political, economical, or human. It is a history totally dominated by Yahweh, who is much more than the God of history. He is the God who himself creates the history and directs it as he wishes until the bitter end, when everything is destroyed, including God's own Temple; we could say when God bids the world of biblical Israel farewell.[16]

As such, the narrative about Israel history is created by its authors to connect the two foundations myths, the one about the exodus and the treacherous fathers who had to be punished, the other about the Babylonian exile and the restoration to please the Jews of later times. It has a content that is exclusively adapted to the task of proving Israel's guilt and Yahweh's innocence in spite of the dreadful destiny he measured out for his chosen people. From the beginning the people were promised doom and despair should they forsake their God and follow foreign idols. Every true prophet spoke about it. Nobody could later come and plead "Not guilty!" because of lack of knowledge. And should any be in doubt as to the justice of God, they should only look for themselves in the prophetic literature so full of these warnings against the consequences of betraying Yahweh, Israel's God.

The prophetic literature, so often considered representative of ancient Israel's Yahwistic monotheistic religion, has very much the same story to tell as the so-called historical books in the Old Testament. It is a history about deserting God and being rejected by him in turn. It is, however, transposed back in time in such a way that the prophets are made the eyewitnesses of the events described in the historical books. In this way the prophets are involved in a kind of circular argument. They provide the evidence for the claim of the history writers that Israel was warned in such a way that no normal person could be in doubt of the consequence of its rejection of Yahweh. These warnings followed at decisive moments in Israel's history, known from the historical narrative especially in the two books of Kings.

Sometimes this is done in a very direct way. This happens, for example, when a redactor of a prophetic book—because it is a misunderstanding that the prophets should themselves have published their own books; they hardly even created anything like a collection of prophecies[17]—places the prophecies of a named prophet like Isaiah or Jeremiah in a context that is partly based—sometimes verbatim—on the narrative in Kings. An exquisite example of this technique is found in Isaiah 7 in the case of the famous "Immanuel prophecy" (Isa. 7:14), with an introduction, however, also found in 2 Kings 16:5. The introduction to the following story about Isaiah's encounter with Ahaz opens with a very precise (probably too precise, and borrowed from the place of the encounter between Rab-shakeh, the Assyrian general, and the inhabitants of Jerusalem, 2 Kings 18:17) description of the place of this confrontation between prophet and king (Isa. 7:3). In itself this confrontation makes little sense except if seen in the light of 2 Kings 16's story about Ahaz pleading for help from Assyria. Every person who read the following assurance about the fate of Damascus and Samaria would only have to look up in 2 Kings to see that it really happened. The two versions of the same event in the prophetic book and in 2 Kings 16 are like the two sides of a coin, not absolute identical but belonging to the same literary production of Israel's religious history.

Another example, this time not so direct, of this literary creation of a kind of intertextuality between prophetic and historical literature could be the case of the temple in Shiloh. Jeremiah asks people to travel to Shiloh in order to see what is going to happen to the Temple of Yahweh in Jerusalem (Jer. 7:12). This temple in Shiloh is well known from the biblical historical narrative as the sanctuary where the prophet Samuel grew up (1 Samuel 1–3). It was the home of the priest Eli and his wanton sons, the place where the holy ark stood before it was lost to the Philistines; in short, the sanctuary of Yahweh that truly preceded the establishment of Jerusalem's Temple. From a literary point of view there is plenty of evidence of the presence of a temple at Shiloh.

For more than two generations, archaeologists have been looking for this temple without finding so much as a trace of it.[18] The reason for the search is, of course, that there must be a temple in Shiloh since the Bible says so. The possibility exists, however, that there never was a temple at the historical site of Shiloh in Israelite times. Everybody could go and see for himself or herself what Yahweh will do to his Temple in Jerusalem: he will totally remove his Temple from the surface of the earth, just as happened to the temple in Shiloh. At the time when the sermon against Jerusalem's Temple of Jeremiah 7 was first formulated there was just as little evidence of a temple here as has shown up in modern excavations. Maybe the author of Jeremiah 7 asks his reader to travel to Shiloh to find a temple that is not there and never was there, except in the biblical narrative. If the reader really wishes to see what kind of temple there was in Shiloh, he would have to look for himself, however, in the biblical narrative of 1 Samuel.[19]

This is not the place to dwell on the relationship between the prophetic literature and the historical narrative in the Old Testament. Although an overwhelming majority of biblical scholars will still be of the opinion that this prophetic literature contains prophetic sayings that originated in the Israel of the monarchical period, it has to be said that they are involved in a kind of ghost hunting. The prophecies of the Israelite prophets owe their existence to literary creations of a much later period, and it was the editors, the collectors of this literature, and not the ancient prophets who decided who was the prophet who authored what prophecy at which occasion.[20] The collectors, however, lived in the same society as the authors of the historical literature. They entertained the same ideas about Israel's sad past history. They knew just as well as the history writers what happened, when it happened, and why it happened, and played their part in creating an image of the Israel of the fathers, the Israel that was condemned because of lack of faith in God.

History is one of the remedies open to the creators of ethnicity, and as has become conspicuous recently, it is of little importance whether this history is a real history or an invented one. History is written in order to create identity among the members of a certain society, congregation, or whatever ethnic group we may speak about. The only important thing seen in the perspective of the author, who created this history, would be that it must be acceptable for its readership; its readers must be able to identify with the history as it has been told to them. Acceptance or nonacceptance is the only necessary condition, and here it is immaterial whether we speak about a community of learned historians in modern times, about the citizens in an old nation-state like Denmark,[21] or the members of a religious community like the Mormons. There is, of course, a vast difference between what is acceptable to the community of professional historians and what is believed by a religious sectarian group, but this difference does not say that one way is better than the other, only that the people involved belong to different cultural environments.

The biblical history about Israel in its double form as preserved in the historical books of the Old Testament and as commented on by the prophetic literature is a history that has been accepted by its audience; otherwise it would not have been preserved. It is told in such a way as to persuade its readership into believing that this is a true history. It is therefore firsthand evidence for the type of readership that accepted this history as a true one; it is simply a reflection of the self-understanding of the people who created this history and for whom it was created. This community will have to be understood as a religious community, not an ordinary living organism such as a normal people; it is the people of God, now past its punishment and redeemed by its God. It is a community with a firm conviction of belonging to a specific place, which it alone is entitled to possess because it is the gift of its God, and because its membership are all one and the same family, the descendants of the patriarchs, Abraham, Isaac, and Jacob. It is also a community on which rests the obligation to keep itself clean, to escape intercourse with other nations, and it is a congregation held together by the same old constitution as was given to the fathers on Mount Sinai at the birth of the nation. The image of Israel as found in the historical books and in the prophetic literature in the Old Testament is therefore the image of Israel created by this religious community—it is a theory or a metaphor about an Israel that never was.

THE TWELVE-TRIBE SYSTEM

Official Judaistic monotheism centered on its Temple, the abode of the mighty creator of the earth, the universal Yahweh. This was, according to the way it understood itself, not a recent development but part of an old history, which started even before the covenant on Mount Sinai, with the election of Abraham and the establishment of an Israel consisting of twelve tribes, the descendants of the third patriarch, Jacob. This was the golden past, still in force when Solomon founded his magnificent Temple and divided his kingdom into twelve districts (1 Kings 4:7–19), which did not—this has to be admitted—absolutely concur with the tribal division as told by the book of Joshua (Joshua 13–19). The new Temple was much more modest and only a remnant of the tribes of Judah and Benjamin was spared, whereas the ten other tribes were doomed to wander into exile from which they—according to the official ideology—never returned.

The idea of human groups—whatever their character—having apical ancestors, whether in the form of human beings, divinities, or animals (or as combinations of these: especially human plus animal, human plus divine) is widely known from many parts of the world. The idea of the people or the *ethnos* consisting of twelve named units is something more specific, however, still, it is not peculiar to the tradition in the Old Testament about ancient Israel. The idea of a party of human beings split into twelve units was certainly not unknown in the ancient Near East.[22] Nowhere, though, was it so exclusive as in the Old Testament, where the assumption of an Israel consisting of twelve tribes all related by blood seems connected not least to the Greek idea about the origin of the Greek nation.[23] Thus it was a basic assumption to the Greek mind that the Hellenic nation was divided into twelve *ethne*—people with a common language, blood, and religion. The center of this aggregation of people in the Greek tradition was a sanctuary, the one of Apollo in Delphi in central Greece, around which was formed a so-called "holy league," an *amphictyony*. This organization was a sacral institution intended to keep its unruly membership in check and create peace within the group. It never succeeded in this, except that it functioned as the common bank of all its membership. The only time the holy league became operative was when one of its members occupied the sanctuary (and thus robbed the bank). This was the so-called "holy war" of the amphictyony.[24]

Almost sixty years ago, the German Old Testament scholar Martin Noth published a small study in which he argued that the Israelite society before the introduction of the monarchy was organized in the same way as an amphictyony consisting of twelve members. It had its central administration at one of the major sanctuaries of the country, with a small administrative staff of its own. To this staff belonged the "judge," the principal arbiter of the country, who could step in and mediate between any part of the membership group should disorder and discontent arise.[25]

According to Noth, the amphictyony was all-important, as it also became the center of the early Israelite tradition. Here the traditions about the patriarchs were told and held in esteem,[26] and here the traditions of the exodus and the wanderings in the desert developed into a national foundation myth. Here was the center of Israelite monotheistic Yahwism. In short, without the amphictyony there would not have been any Israelite nation or national identity—according to Noth.

It goes without saying that scholars of all denominations and convictions almost universally accepted Noth's hypothesis. The reason was that it provided an answer to most problems created by the biblical tradition. Everybody agreed at the same time that it couldn't be anything but a theory. No solid evidence of its existence could be offered or was presented by Noth and his followers. Conversely, something more important was achieved. Noth moved the creation of the biblical tradition to the earliest possible moment in Israel's history and placed it at a common sanctuary devoted to Yahweh. Therefore the central parts of Israel's early self-interpretation, the idea of the covenant,[27] the monotheistic God,[28] the consciousness of being an elected people,[29] the people of God, was not the outcome of a long and difficult history of the tradition. It predated the establishment of the tradition itself; the tradition did not develop, but was manifest and decided in advance. Few Christian theologians or scholars of Jewish extraction had difficulties in accepting this view, which from a conservative theological point of view became a reassurance of the unchanging nature of God from the very beginning to the present.[30] At the end, the amphictyony became a kind of a black box where explanations of everything peculiar to the Israelite tradition could be found, while at the same time it developed into a major, overarching hypothesis that encompassed any element in Israel's early history, religious as well as administrative. The wars of early Israel were conducted as "holy wars" to defend the sacred league against intruders,[31] but once eleven members of the amphictyony had to convene in order to defend it against a serious infringement on it done by one of its own membership (Judges 19–21).

As happens to all such theories, they break at one point because of their own weight, because they are believed to be able to explain more than is possible. Once some part of a hypothesis has proved to be wrong, the dismissal of this part is often soon followed by the refusal of the hypothesis as a whole.

This happened to the amphictyonic hypothesis after it had dominated for forty years historical investigations devoted to early Israel, that is, Israel before the introduction of the monarchy. In the 1970s, almost simultaneously a number of studies appeared taking it to pieces. Thus Andrew Mayes criticized Noth's theory on several points, including his use of the lists of the twelve tribes in the Old Testament, his ideas of the central sanctuary, his concept of the judges of Israel. Mayes was expounding a different view of the system of tribal borders in the Old Testament, and finally shared another idea of holy wars in ancient Israel.[32] Postdating Mayes's study by a couple of years, the Dutch scholar Cornelius H. J. de Geus directed his fire against the system of the twelve tribes, which is in the Old Testament not limited to one system but involves at least two systems.[33] He also devoted much energy to a discussion of the social structure, including the issue of ethnicity in ancient Israel, thereby opening what was to develop over the next ten to fifteen years in this respect.[34] Finally, he also touched on issues such as the central sanctuary, the holy war, and the judges.[35]

Both these volumes were preceded by a study on the amphictyony in Danish by this author. It took up most of the same issues as Mayes and de Geus:[36] the central sanctuary and the Israelite priesthood, the role of the judges—whether rulers of Israel or local chieftains—the kings seen in contrast to the chieftains, the issue of the holy war in Judges 19–21, the relationship between Israel and Judah before David, the wars between the Israelites and the Philistines, and the twelve-tribe lists. This study, however, also contained a special chapter devoted to the so-called model of the Israelite amphictyony, its Greek parallels, which were all seen to be much later than the Israelite league and not always consisting of a membership of twelve people.[37] The Swiss scholar Otto Bächli in 1976, who although still in favor of maintaining the hypothesis as such, could only put up a vague defense of its merits, adeptly reviewed the discussion (minus de Geus).[38]

It was characteristic of most of these studies that they based their deconstruction of the hypothesis on historical matters. Whereas the Greek amphictyony possessed a single central sanctuary (the one in Delphi—in fact, two), which was well known, recognizable, and always a real sanctuary of ancient Greece or Asia Minor, no place in ancient Palestine could claim to have been a central Israelite sanctuary before David turned Jerusalem into the capital of all Israel and Solomon built his Temple in this place. This does not say that there is not a plethora of sanctuaries in the pages of the Old Testament, such as Shechem, Shiloh, and Bethel, to mention only a few in central Palestine. Another questionable issue was the position of the judges, the heroes of premonarchic Israel, who are said by the biblical writers to have ruled all Israel. The historical analysis of the narratives of the book of Judges, however, showed that they were probably limited to only a minor part of the country, and that they never commanded an army consisting of "all" Israelites, with participants coming from every single Israelite tribe. The idea of all Israel working and functioning together was attacked from different sides. Serious criticism arose as a result of the analysis of the Song of Deborah (Judges 5). This text was generally understood to date from the premonarchic period,[39] and showed the tribes of Israel not to act in unison. It also mentions a tribe that is not otherwise in the Old Testament reckoned an independent tribe.[40]

A few scholars, however, included in their general attacks, or launched a criticism against parts of, the amphictyonic hypothesis that was of an ideological nature and had to do not with history but with tradition history and literature. Thus the Swiss scholar Fritz Stolz showed the idea of a holy war as expressed in Judges to be a reflection of Deuteronomistic war ideology and not an old concept in ancient Israel.[41] The same happened to the covenant theology of the Old Testament. Although scholars assumed this covenant ideology to have a central position in the tribal league, and although many scholars wanted to prove that it belonged to premonarchic Israel,[42] it never really became an integrated part of the amphictyonic hypothesis.[43] Now Lothar Perlitt of Göttingen had already, before the attacks started on the amphictyonic hypothesis, removed this part of the construction. He showed that the covenant theology should be seen as the result of Deuteronomistic thinking and concepts. He thereby put an effective end to a very long discussion about the origin of the covenant in the Old Testament.[44] In Perlitt's opinion, most likely inspired by his spiritual forefather, Julius Wellhausen,[45] the covenant theology is not developed in the prophetic literature, which he traditionally considers to be preexilic. Only in the presumably exilic Deuteronomistic rethinking of Israel's religion, and in literature postdating the Deuteronomists such as the Priestly writer in the Pentateuch, this has changed into the solid block of covenant theology that dominates the idea of Israelite religion as expressed by the Old Testament writers. Anyone conversant with the history of Old Testament scholarship will here recognize Wellhausen's famous statement, that the prophets predate the Law, the Torah of later Judaism.[46] It goes without saying that if Perlitt is right, ancient Israel did not know the covenant. Therefore this vital part of the theology of the Old Testament has vanished, and with it the idea of Israel as a people that was contracted by God. Only a vague idea of religious relationship would remain, probably not enough to keep a sacral league together as envisaged by Noth and his followers.

Lesser ideological matters that were identified by the early criticism of the amphictyony concerned the course of history as described in the book of Judges. This history, in my opinion, did not present a report of the wars between premonarchic Israel and its neighbors, the Philistines, the Moabites, and the Canaanites, but rather functioned as a literary device which had nothing to do with Israel's early history. It was a literary product employing the traditional enemies of Israel as found in the books of Samuel and Kings. In this way the story of the judges and their wars reflected the descriptions of Israel's history as found in the later historical parts of the Old Testament. It had no existence of its own. Also, in the past Israel fought the same cruel enemies as it was destined to fight in its later life. When Israel under its kings became involved in warfare against these foreign nations, the reason was the same as in the period of the Judges—that Israel had forsaken its God and was punished by God because of this.[47]

A literary solution was also the only feasible one to the old intriguing problem of membership in the amphictyony. We may disregard the evidence of the Song of Deborah's counting no more than ten tribes, and the issue once debated about a sequence of amphictyonies, one consisting of six tribes, another of ten, and a third of twelve tribes.[48] Instead we should remain with the list of tribal members found in different places in the Pentateuch. Here the list of the twelve tribes appears in the form of two main types. One includes the priestly tribe of Levi and the oldest son of Jacob and Rachel, Joseph. The second leaves out Levi but substitutes for Joseph his two sons, Ephraim and Manasseh.[49] These lists were sometimes believed to represent the development of the twelve-tribe league at two different periods of its existence. The discussion mostly addressed the question about which of the two lists should be considered the older one. It is, however, obvious that there are no historical reasons for the existence of two different lists in the Pentateuch as long as we do not accept the general outline of the biblical history as history. Few critical scholars of the days of Martin Noth and his amphictyonic hypothesis were ready to do so. The change between the two forms of the list occurs in the moment when the tribe of Levi is excluded from the number of ordinary tribes and turned into a tribe of priests (Ex. 32:29). This makes them different from their brothers, and Ephraim and Manasseh therefore substitute for them in the list (Joseph is split into two tribes, following the note about the birth of Joseph's two sons in Gen. 41:50–52).

There are no historical, only literary, reasons behind the change of the list. The form and time of appearance simply reflects the course of the narrative and presupposes events narrated in the books of Genesis and Exodus. The lists have no independent life outside this literary framework. Therefore whenever they appear in the biblical literature about early Israel, it is a textual reference, and not a historical one.[50] Moreover, it is equally obvious that the order in which the tribes appear in these lists, at least so far as their two main forms are concerned, is also an artificial one not originating in the real world but inside the framework of the religious world of the biblical narrators.

EXCURSUS: THE DEVELOPMENT OF
THE LISTS OF THE TWELVE TRIBES

It has always been a problem that Judah is normally situated in a rather inferior position in the lists, while insignificant tribes like Reuben and Simeon take the places of pride at the beginning of the lists. The position of Judah may, however, be the result of a narrative-theological speculation, which makes Judah the head of a section consisting of three tribes taking up their position in relationship to the holy ark of Yahweh. The key biblical passage as to this relationship is found in Numbers 2:3–31. Here we find a description of the position of the twelve tribes around the ark, starting with Judah in the pole position, leading a section of three tribes (Judah, Issachar, and Zebulun) covering the eastern side of the sanctuary. Moving clockwise, the southern side is occupied by Reuben, Simeon, and Gad; the western side by Ephraim, Manasseh, and Benjamin (the Rachel tribes); and the northern one by Dan, Asher, and Naphtali.

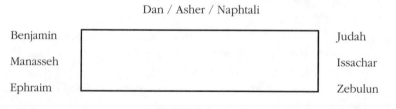

Dan / Asher / Naphtali

Benjamin	Judah
Manasseh	Issachar
Ephraim	Zebulun

Gad / Simeon / Reuben

The order of tribes in this list is unusual: Judah, Issachar, Zebulun, Reuben, Simeon, Gad, Ephraim, Manasseh, Benjamin, Dan, Asher, and Naphtali. The primary order is found in the story of the birth of the sons of Jacob (Gen. 29:31–30:24 with an appendix 35:16–18; cf. Ex. 2:2–4): Reuben, Simeon, Levi, Judah, Dan, Naphtali, Gad, Asher, Issachar, Zebulun, Joseph, and Benjamin. The second list (Num. 1:5–16) has in its first edition Reuben, Simeon, Judah, Issachar, Zebulun, Ephraim, Manasseh, Benjamin, Dan, Asher, Gad, Naphtali, but immediately afterward the second list is corrected (Num. 1:20–43) to: Reuben, Simeon, Gad, Judah, Issachar, Zebulun, Ephraim, Manasseh, Benjamin, Dan, Asher, Naphtali. The moment we substitute the list in Numbers 2 with the one in Num. 1:5–16 it is quite easy to see what may have happened to the order of the tribes (now reading counter-clockwise:

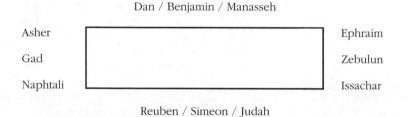

Dan / Benjamin / Manasseh

Asher		Ephraim
Gad		Zebulun
Naphtali		Issachar

Reuben / Simeon / Judah

This order is obviously absolutely impossible, subordinating Judah under Reuben, and Ephraim under Issachar. The two most important tribes in Israel's history have been removed from the place of honor. They have been placed in subordinate positions under the heading of quite insignificant entities, as with Judah in the third place after Reuben, preceded in the second place by the just as insignificant Simeon, or in the case of Ephraim in the third place after just as insignificant Issachar and Zebulun. Something had to be done before the author of Numbers could present his "diagram" of the sanctuary before his audience, something that led to the reposition in the corrected form of the list in Numbers 1:20–43. Now we get the following listing (still reading counter-clockwise):

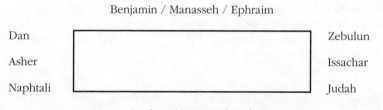

Benjamin / Manasseh / Ephraim

Dan		Zebulun
Asher		Issachar
Naphtali		Judah

Reuben / Simeon / Gad

Now everything is as it should be. Both Judah and Ephraim are put in front of their own sections of three tribes, and the three tribes of Rachel are placed together. The trick was only to move Gad to the former place of Levi, not a great change. Although Gad is not considered a full son of Lea, he was born by her maid Zilpah (Gen. 30:10–11).

The system of the twelve tribes is absolutely artificial, and the individual steps in its development can be seen as literary responses to problems presented by the main course of the narrative. Levi is originally the third full son of Lea. However, because he stands apart from his brothers on the issue of the golden calf (Ex. 32:25–29), he is made a tribe of priests and therefore no longer to be included among the ordinary people of God, which must perforce consist of twelve tribes. Another tribe has to take up his place, and the choice is Joseph's second son, Ephraim (who had, like his grandfather, obtained the paternal blessing to the deficit of his older brother, Manasseh: Genesis 48). As carrier of the blessing of the patriarchs, Ephraim cannot be left out when the list is reshaped in Numbers 1:2–16. Now the author is presented with a new a problem, since he could of course not work with a list consisting of Ephraim and Joseph at one and the same time. Therefore Joseph would have to be replaced by Manasseh, his first son, which was truly done in order to keep the number of tribes belonging to the people of God. A new problem arose again when our author wanted to make up his order of the sanctuary of the Lord in the desert. Now his corrected list would have created some intolerable problems, placing the two most important tribes of the Old Testament narrative about the history of Israel in secondary position. The solution to this dilemma was, as already explained, to make a small "improvement," taking the tribe of Gad from its position in the middle part of the list and moving him forward to the third position. No harm was done to the hierarchy of Israelite tribes, as Gad was never placed in an important position in any edition of the lists. The only change between Numbers 1:20–43 and Numbers 2 is that the description of the sanctuary in Numbers 2 starts with the placing of Judah in relation to the ark, instead of in the fourth place. Judah has to have this position in light of the later "history," according to which Judah was predestined to provide the home of the ark in the Temple in Jerusalem.

The system of the twelve tribes as presented by the biblical narratives is therefore a highly artificial one, elaborated on and changed, not according to historical circumstances but because of literary motives and religious concerns. The lists do not predate the narrative in the course of which they are presented. They are themselves parts of this narrative and dependent on its course. The lists are literary products of another literary product and have no life of their own, but they testify to the artificiality of the whole construct of the people of God as narrated by the biblical writers.[51]

REESTABLISHING THE AMPHICTYONY

The description of the tabernacle sanctuary in the desert is a vital and a central part of the narrative about Israel's early history in the Old Testament. The tabernacle is the first result of the new relationship between Yahweh and Israel established at Sinai, and therefore a center of this Israel. Seen in this light, a chapter like Numbers 2 describing the position of the individual tribes in relation to the tabernacle is most important, because we here have a description of the central sanctuary of this nation.

In the old days of historical investigation, scholars were desperately look-ing for a central sanctuary of early Israel, but in vain: too many candidates and none of them fulfilling the requirements for being a central sanctuary before Jerusalem was, in the biblical tradition about Solomon, accorded this position. None of these scholars, however, recognized that the central shrine was always there, in the desert in the form of the tabernacle erected around the holy ark of God. Or better than that: the ark itself was understood to be the only sacral center in the midst of Israelite life. The biblical writers con-structed the nation of Israel as a twelve-tribe people with the ark in its mid-dle. This ark formed the center of Israel's religious activities right down to its solemn installment in the Temple, when the Temple itself became the center (or should have been this, if not for Jeroboam's sin, the establishment of the bull sanctuaries at Dan and Bethel; 1 Kings 12:26–33). It is described as a sanctuary always on the move—therefore it was in itself contradictory and against the tune of the narrative to look for historical stable sanctuaries as the home of the Israelite religion before Solomon's Temple. Scholars were chasing a mirage that never existed except in the minds of the biblical writ-ers. Instead they should have concentrated on the item that was the real cen-ter—the ark always on the move and always to be protected, until it was lost to the Philistines and the hope for an Israelite future temporarily quashed.[52]

From the point of the narrator the shrine of the ark, therefore, should be understood to form the center of Israel, a central shrine as good as any shrine in any Greek amphictyony. As a matter of fact, Noth was absolutely right: the Old Testament historians wanted Israel to be organized like a sacral league consisting of twelve entities, tribes, around a central shrine, the taber-nacle, seen as always on the move. In contrast to the central shrine of a Greek amphictyony, the ark rested only temporarily, at different places, in-cluding at the end Jerusalem, from where it was destined one day to be car-ried away into exile like the people surrounding it.

Most elements belonging to Noth's amphictyonic model work as soon as its existence is moved from the historical level to the literary level. The Is-raelite amphictyony has a central shrine. Its membership consists of the twelve tribes of Israel. It has a name, Israel, and a constitution, the covenant, concluded at Mount Sinai. The constitution also includes a law book dic-tated (or donated as a gift; cf. Deuteronomy 4), given to it by God himself. The shrine has its priesthood, the Levites, and there are secular judges, in-stalled by Moses himself to relieve him from his work (Ex. 18:13–26). The league can fight its own wars against foreign enemies such as Sihon, the king of Heshbon (Num. 21:21–31), and it can through its officers distribute

justice amongst its membership as in the case of the sinful acts of the Israelites at Baal-peor (Numbers 25).

On the historical level, there is no foundation for the hypothesis. So much
was made clear by the discussion of the late 1960s and early 1970s. However, as a literary device invented to explain the nationality of the Israelites
the authors succeeded in creating a model of a society that never existed.
They based their "nation" on a common foundation myth, the exodus event,
and a common religious organization with a common shrine, the tabernacle. Nevertheless, the Israelites should be understood as constituting a special ethnos, free from foreign interference although always ready to seek
such relations, thereby breaking the law of its God.

The historical narrative that follows after the conclusion of the migrations
in the desert has as its aim to transform this mobile "amphictyony" of the Israelites into a settled society. The governing thesis is that the Israel of Palestine's past constituted a holy league ruled by God, and with a long history
preceding its entry into the Promised Land. The model of the society of the
past helped to convince that Israel in every aspect possessed its own ethnic
identity also when it became the people of God in God's own country. It
broke down, however, because it was not possible to maintain this identity
in relation to the other inhabitants of the country. The Levite Pinehas could
easily kill the Israelite who brought with him a Midianite woman (Num.
25:6–8). It was far more difficult to prevent King Solomon from being let
astray by his many foreign wives (1 Kings 11:1–13). This happened even
though Solomon had tried to copy the original distribution of the country
into twelve tribal units in the form of a royal institution of twelve provinces
(1 Kings 4), and most of all, in spite of the fact that he had built a lasting
abode for his God.

The amphictyony is a metaphor. It can never be considered more than,
or at the same time less than, a metaphor, since it is not reflecting a reality
outside the text where it can be found and where its history develops. This
metaphor of the amphictyony is decisive when the new Israel, although no
longer a people of twelve tribes, returns home under the leadership of
twelve men (Neh. 7:7[53]). In this way Israel was reestablished after the exile,
when a new (i.e., at the same time old: Nehemiah 8) constitution is given to
it, and the Jews are forced to divorce their foreign wives (Ezra 10). We are
back at the place from where we set out: the notion of the purified remnant,
resting on Mount Zion under the protection of Yahweh, free from foreign
elements, a holy people of God. A narrative contained the metaphorical expression of this people as a people of old, with a pedigree reaching back to
the twelve-tribe sacral league, installed by God and his loyal servant Moses.

Martin Noth placed his *Grundschrift,* that is, the earliest version of the Is-raelite tradition, in the context of the amphictyony as he saw it,[54] and was followed here explicitly or implicitly by almost every Old Testament scholar of his own time. The consequence of the dissolution of the historical part of his argument is that his idea of the original historical place of the Israelite tradition has disappeared. There is no longer any historical *Sitz im Leben,* original home, of this tradition in Israel's past history. Noth was evidently right in assuming that the idea of the twelve-tribe people was central to the notion of the Israelite nation as expressed by the Old Testament writers. Without this institution there would have been no reason for the claim that Israel was a special people, with a special history and with special claims that made it different from (and preferable to) any other people of this world. Israel would not have had a history of its own but would have been just one among many other ethnic groups or entities of ancient Palestine. The amphictyony transformed the tradition of a kingdom of the name of Is-rael—one state among many others in Palestine in the Iron Age—into a spe-cial nation. This nation was different from any other ethnic group present in the country, and thereby allowed for any "new Israel" to assume the right to claim the land for itself.

In this way the amphictyony is removed from the historical scene, al-though at the same time retained as an ideological, or literary, construct. This operation destroys any idea of an old unifying Israelite tradition that existed before, at the earliest, the creation of the political units of Israel and later Ju-dah in Palestine in the ninth and eighth centuries B.C.E.[55] This "biblical" Is-rael was no more than the creation of the biblical writers, and their basis was not the Israel of past history, but the institution of the twelve-tribe league. In this way, the tale of the Israelite twelve-tribe people is the prod-uct of a literary mind. This mind works on literary premises, incorporating whatever information the narrator thought fit to promote his own ideas, ir-respective of whether his traditions came from Palestine or from some other source.

BIBLICAL ISRAELITE "NATIONALITY"

Having established the Israelite people as an amphictyony consisting of twelve tribes surrounding its central shrine, the ark of God, the next step will be to see how this twelve-tribe people is defined by the biblical tradi-tion as different from other people. We have already presented the origin myths of this Israelite people, and the parallel lines between the first part of the history, the center of which is the exodus and the Sinai covenant, and the second, which centers around the exile and redemption from exile, have been underlined. Now remains to be seen what particular elements the biblical writers believed to constitute a people or a nation, particularly in the light of the classic definition of ethnicity as found in ancient sources, which is that an ethnos will share common "blood," "language," and "religion."[56]

Common Blood

Probably no ancient tradition paid an attention to the requirement of common blood for membership of a specific people that can be compared to the emphasis placed on this in the Old Testament. The Israelite people is seen as the descendants of one man and one woman, Abraham and Sarah, said to be half-sister and -brother (Gen. 20:12). The outcome of this marriage is a son, Isaac, who marries his paternal cousin from Haran, Rebekah (Genesis 24).[57] Abraham, however, was accompanied by his nephew Lot, who departed and settled among the inhabitants of the land, that is, in Sodom. Thus he became part of the local society (his daughters became engaged to marry local people, Gen. 19:14). Although he escapes from Sodom without this misalliance having come to pass, his destiny is fixed as he is going to become the apical ancestor not of Israel, but of the nations of Transjordan, the Moabites and the Ammonites. In order to become this, another misalliance, between him and his daughters, must happen (Gen. 19:29–38). A second son is born to Abraham, Ismael, whose mother, Hagar, however, is an Egyptian and therefore automatically disqualified as the apical mother of the Israelites.

Isaac, having accomplished the requirement for not mixing the blood, begets two children with Rebekah, Esau and Jacob. Esau marries two of the daughters of the land, Judith, the daughter of the Hittite Beeri, and Basemath, the daughter of the Hittite Elon (Gen. 26:34–35). Thereafter his "career" resembles the one of Lot closely. First he is cheated by Jacob who obtains the paternal blessing—something that is necessary to keep the bloodline clean—and thereafter he leaves, first to ally himself with the Ismaelites to marry a daughter of Ismael (Gen. 28:8–9). Later he is to become the apical ancestor of the Edomites (Genesis 36).

Jacob is sent away to his maternal family in Haran in order not to marry a Canaanite woman. In Haran he marries two daughters of his maternal uncle Laban, Rachel and Leah, who at the same time—since the Abraham family is strictly adhering to the rule of the preferred marriage (the father's brother's daughter being the preferred spouse)—are members of his paternal family. Jacob is therefore to keep the bloodline clean, although he at one point is forgetting himself by allowing his raped daughter Dinah to become engaged to her rapist, Shechem, the Hivite (Genesis 34). This time the two brothers of Dinah, Simeon and Levi, defend the purity of the selected family. They kill Shechem and all his family to expurgate the intrusion of foreign blood in the veins of the Abraham-Isaac-Jacob line. Jacob and his wives and their maidservants beget twelve sons, each of them apical ancestors of one of the Israelite tribes.

Having stated his point, the author becomes more relaxed on the topic of foreign marriages as the story proceeds. The distance to mixed marriages, however, is still operative when it comes to Judah's marriage with Shuah, a Canaanite woman (Gen. 38:2). This mixed marriage carries no blessing with it. They beget three sons, Er, Onan, and Shelah. Yahweh disapproves of Er and lets him die. Onan becomes the apical ancestor of an abominable practice and dies because of this. Only Shelah is spared. The end becomes more bright, when Er's widow Tamar begets twins with her father-in-law, Judah, and one of these, Perez, is destined to become the apical ancestor of the Davidic dynasty (Gen. 38:12–30).

The following mixed marriages generally include liaisons between descendants of Jacob and Egyptian women. Jacob's preferred son, Joseph marries the Egyptian Asenath, the daughter of the priest in On (Gen. 41:45), which results in the birth of Ephraim and Manasseh, who is going to obtain a central position among the twelve Israelite tribes. Moses, the hero of the Exodus and himself a descendant of Levi, marries Zipporah, the daughter of the priest Jethro in Midian, which results in the birth of two sons, Gershom (Ex. 2:21–22), and Eliezer (Ex. 18:3–4). The prohibition against marrying women from Canaan thus finds no parallel when it comes to the issue of accepting Egyptian or Midianite women in marriage, although at a later date an Israelite is killed because of a planned marriage with a Midianite woman (Num. 25:6–8).[58]

The dangers connected with engagement with foreign and especially Canaanite women are directly addressed in the outspoken prohibition against marrying the daughters of Canaan in Exodus 34. The reason given in this place is that these women will persuade their husbands to worship foreign, that is, Canaanite gods. Thereby they will forsake the God of their fathers, Israel's Yahweh (Ex. 34:16). This warning is repeated in Deuteronomy (Deut. 7:3–4), and the same reason is given. In both cases the prohibition is presented in connection with a warning against breaking the covenant by establishing a covenant relationship to the Canaanites (Ex. 34:15; Deut. 7:2). This covenant was broken, however, not because the Israelites wanted it so, but because of the treacherousness of the Gibeonites, who saved their lives by pretending not to be Canaanites (Joshua 9). No

wonder that the Israelites soon after Joshua's death are said to have inter-
married with Canaanite women (Judg. 3:6). After all, they had allowed the
Canaanites to live in the country, and the result is well known that they worshiped the gods of Canaan.

The fatal influence of the foreign women is epitomized in the shape of
Delilah, who brings Samson to his fall (Judg. 16:4–22). Another example is
Jezebel, the Phoenician queen of King Ahab, who almost ruins the kingdom
of Israel and causes the fall of the dynasty of Omri (1 Kings 21; cf. 2 Kings
9:30–37). Their corrupting influence is spelled out in the note on Solomon's
many foreign wives who turned him away from the Lord, with disastrous
consequences for the survival of his kingdom.

Intermingling with foreign women means playing with foreign gods,
which is the same as breaking the covenant relationship. The importance of
keeping the blood clean from foreign influence therefore means at one and
the same time to keep the covenant with Yahweh. Only if the bloodline is
kept free of foreigners will Israel be able to survive. This says that in the biblical context the classical idea about common blood has been extended to
include also the religion. The question of the correct relationship with Israel's God is the same as keeping the pedigree immaculate. The blood as an
element that keeps an ethnos together is not a quality in its own but always
carry the connotation that it is part of the special relationship between Israel and its God. Not even after ten generations are the offspring of mixed
alliances between Israelites and foreigners allowed entrance to the congregation of the Lord (Deut. 23:3). No wonder that Ezra had to clean the foreign element out of his Israel before the new Israel could have any hope of
survival (Ezra 10).

This does not mean that the Old Testament does not contain sections that
seem to go against this general *theological* line. We have already touched
on a couple of such examples, such as the case of Ruth, the ancestress of
David, and Jael, the Kenite woman (Judg. 4:17). Also in practical ordinances
examples can be found showing a reality behind the official facade which
was quite different from it, as we must expect it to be in a living society.
One such example is the law concerning women taken as prisoners of war,
and their rights when they become members of the household (Deut.
21:10–14). Other examples could be the repeated obligation to allow foreigners, the *gerîm,* to live among the Israelites, to offer them a refuge from
their enemies (Ex. 22:20; 23:9; Lev. 19:33–34; Deut. 10:19). We should also
include the prohibition against the extradition of slaves who have escaped
from foreign masters (Deut. 23:16–17)—normally with a reference to the status of the Israelites as *gerîm* in Egypt.

Common Language

To the Greeks, the language was one of the most important elements that marked them out as a special ethnos. It was, however, not so that they did not acknowledge the existence of several different Greek dialects, such as Attic, Ionian, Dorian, Aeolian, or even literary dialects—Homer's probably artificially antique Greek, for example. These dialects were at least in theory understood by every Greek in every part of the Greek commonwealth and marked them off over against the barbarians.

The biblical writer also accepted the importance of languages. Otherwise the story of the Tower of Babel and the desertion of that great city (Gen. 11:1–9) would make no sense at all. This story, which is somehow a variant to Genesis 10's "table of nations," explains why all the different nations appeared, each with its own language, out of an originally single nation with only one language—a thought also shared, incidentally, by the Greeks.[59] This theme had already been an integral part of the distribution of nations in Genesis 10. In this list the sons of Japheth lived in their islands, each with its own language (Gen. 10:5). Here also the sons of Ham and Shem were identifiable because of their own language (Gen. 10:20, 31). The profusion of nations enabled God to choose one for himself, as formulated by Deuteronomy 32,[60] an act that in the narrative version of the election is presented as the election of a single person, Abraham, who was to become the progenitor of a great nation (Gen. 12:1–2).

So far language could be considered a reason for the ethnicity of the descendants of Abraham. The fact is, however, that it is never stressed by the biblical tradition that language was something special to the Israelites, something only members of the Israelite people shared and which set them apart from the neighboring countries. In the world of fairy tales of the patriarchs,[61] language is never seen as something that creates a distinction between these figures and their environment. To the contrary, everybody around seems to be speaking the same language—Philistines, Egyptians, and Aramaeans. Nowhere is it said that an interpreter was needed in order to establish a link of communication between, say, the Egyptian pharaoh and Abraham and his descendants. Interpreters are known. Aaron, who is installed as the interpreter of Moses vis-à-vis the Egyptian court, is a well-known example. He, however, obtained his position not because of language problems (the author does not even refer to Moses' upbringing at the Egyptian court as something that should make him able to communicate directly with the Egyptians), but because of Moses' lack of ability to express himself in words (Ex. 4:10–16).

This situation does not change as the narrative proceeds, not before the Assyrian general Rab-shakeh addresses the inhabitants of Jerusalem in their own tongue and is asked to speak Aramaic. The officers of King Hezekiah understand Aramaic, not the ordinary people. This should prevent Rab-shakeh from addressing his audience in Judaic (2 Kings 18:26–28; Isa. 36:11–13; cf. 2 Chron. 32:18).[62] The only other example of Judaic used as the designation of the language of the people of God is found in Nehemiah 13. Here a part of the community is accused because they are not able to speak Judaic because of mixed marriages between Judeans and women from Ashdod, Ammon, or Moab. Because of this half the children speak Ashdodite or some other language, but not Judaic (Neh. 13:23–27).[63] This is the closest passage in the Old Testament to the Greek understanding of the language. Here the language creates a line of division between Judaeans ("Israelites") and foreigners. It is in this place seen as a consequence of the prohibited marriages with foreign women. A warning is issued according to which the mixed marriage is in itself understood to constitute a transgression against the will of God, and not explicitly as leading to the worshiping of foreign Gods.

As such this warning is related to a number of other instances when a distinction is made between the local language and foreign ones. In Deuteronomy one of the curses to fall on the head of the unfaithful has to do with a foreign invader with a language that "you" do not understand (Deut. 28:49).[64] Isaiah warns the drunken people of Ephraim against prophets and leaders stuttering when talking a foreign language (Isa. 28:11).[65] Zechariah says in a prophecy about times to come, "Ten men shall take hold out of all languages of the nations" (Zech. 8:23),[66] while according to Isaiah God will collect "all nations and tongues" at the end of the days (Isa. 66:18).[67] In one passage in Isaiah we find a mysterious reference to five cities in Egypt that one day will be speaking the language of Canaan, which is normally understood to be a reference to Hebrew (Isa. 19:18).[68] Three times in Esther there are references in connection with the Persian provincial administration that all people were allowed to retain their own languages, the third time with a special reference to the Jews and their language (Esth. 1:22; 3:12; 8:9).

Although some of these examples are expressing the opinion that every people has its special language, that is, that the language is a marker of ethnicity, it is remarkable that there is no specific theological importance attached to this notion. The people of God is never characterized as something special because it was supposed to have its own language. The references to language differences are in this respect absolutely neutral, and it is never said that in order to be part of the people of God, you must speak one and the same language (although the passage Neh. 13:23–27 is close enough).

We may ask why the language plays such a secondary role, and the answer will depend on the dating decided in advance of the biblical tradition. If we assume that this tradition is old, going back to preexilic times, the lack of linguistic differentiation between Israel and its neighbors could be explained as a reflection of the status of the Hebrew dialects spoken in Palestine at that time. These dialects were, in spite of occasional "shibbolets,"[69] more or less one and the same language. This also applied to the linguistic situation among the Philistines, which the recently found inscription from Ekron shows.[70] The neighboring people in Transjordan and in Phoenicia spoke dialects closely resembling the archaic Hebrew of Palestine in the Iron Age. It can be assumed that any person coming from Rabbath Ammon, for example, would be able to understand the dialect spoken in, say, Jerusalem, and vice versa. Only in the case of the Syrians speaking Aramaic would this situation change, Aramaic having developed into an independent language with so many peculiarities in comparison to the older Amorite dialects that it would have required special knowledge to interpret this language. However, apart from the Rabshakeh incident already mentioned above, there is no indication of language problems created by Aramaic-speaking persons. Neither are their any references in the Old Testament narratives to the, already in the Iron Age, more and more dominating role of Aramaic in northern Palestine.

In a postexilic context this lack of interest in language may sound peculiar only if the perspective is strictly Palestinian, and even here a multitude of languages would have been known—Hebrew, Aramaic, Persian, and also before the Hellenistic period Greek—narrowing the perspective down to being probably "Jerusalemite." There is, on the other hand, a more reasonable explanation for this lack when seen in the perspective of the Persian, and especially of the Hellenistic, period. At that time the members of the people of God could be found in many different places speaking a plethora of foreign languages. It would therefore in practice be extremely difficult to tell a Jew from a heathen on the basis of language only. Language therefore became a minor issue, and in fact continued to be so until modern times, Hebrew normally taking the place of honor in Jewish tradition, but closely followed by Aramaic.

Common Religion

As the third element in the classical definition of ethnicity, religion appears. It goes without saying that religion according to the biblical narrators did really decide who was and who was not an Israelite. Everything said so far convenes on this theme, the exclusivity of the Israelite religion. As such, a major monograph could be written on the subject of Israel's religious self-definition. It would more or less be a restatement of the biblical testimony and repetitive without end. It can all be formulated in one short sentence: Without its Yahwistic faith, Israel would never have existed. Religion and ethnos are two sides of the same coin. To be an Israelite says to worship the God of Israel, Yahweh. Not to worship Yahweh means that the person denying the supremacy of Yahweh is either not an Israelite or an apostate to be excluded from the community of Israelites. The Old Testament historical narrative has this story to tell almost from its very beginning, and the theme dominates the narrative until the destruction of Jerusalem and its Temple, and even beyond that. The prophetic literature concurs with this and supports, as should be expected, the view of the history writers, and the book of Psalms finally provides the poetic expression of the same belief in Yahweh as Israel's God and in the fatal consequences of deserting Yahweh.

Still, compared to other religions evidence from antiquity, this idea of a special religion valid for all Israelites is of quite astonishing dimensions. Never in the treasury of ancient Greek and Roman literature do we find anything comparable to such a belief in a mythic coherence between God and humans as is expressed by the Old Testament stories, prophecies, and hymns. The only time when a similar tone was reached was when sectarian religious congregations of various kinds appeared in the Hellenistic-Roman period, such as the Isis mysteries, the cult of Mithra, and not least Christianity, which has, of course, borrowed much of its phraseology from the Old Testament. It is, as a matter of fact, highly likely that the biblical insistence on the peculiar relationship between the Israelite people and Yahweh has little in common with Herodotus's talk about "the temples and religious ritual; the whole way of life we understand and share together."[71] Herodotus is not so much thinking of a specific and exclusive religion as he is talking about "culture." As already mentioned earlier, religion to the peoples of the classical world meant something that at the same time was less precise than the modern word "religion" and more comprehensive. It was almost a synonym for "culture."[72] Herodotus "knew" that his fellow countrymen worshiped many gods and that they did not always agree on which deity was the most important one. He also knew, however, that in spite of this, they shared a common set of religious and cultural norms and habits that distinguished them from foreigners, but it has only little in common with the tight theological system of the Old Testament.

The God of Israel was an exclusive God, the famous, in Hebrew אל קנא, the "jealous God."[73] This has sometimes been taken to express a very old Israelite concept of God, for no particular reason other than that it was an exceptional expression not found in any other ancient text, and therefore perforce original.[74] The five contexts in which this expression is found are, however, revealing. In Ex. 20:5, in the context of the Ten Commandments, the first commandments have to do with Yahweh's exclusivity and with the prohibition against molded images. Yahweh's jealousy is mentioned to put stress on the threats against the transgressor of the prohibition of worshiping other gods. In Exodus 34:14—part of what has sometimes also been understood to represent another "Decalogue"[75]—we have exactly the same sequence of foreign gods and molded images. The reference to Yahweh as the jealous God therefore has exactly the same intention as the one in Exodus 20. In Deuteronomy 4:24, and 6:15, we again find the same theme practically without any variation at all, and, finally, Deuteronomy 5:9 is no more than a repetition of Exodus 20:5.

Far from being an old and original part of the image of God among the early Israelites, this expression is a deliberate theological expression coined by the theologians who in these narratives presented their version of how Yahweh became the God of Israel. There is no reason to see this expression as something special in comparison to other expressions of the uniqueness of Yahweh in the Old Testament. The jealous Yahweh is absolutely in accordance with the general idea of Yahwistic religion as found in the Old Testament. It is part of a religious discourse that is directed against probable transgressors of the first and most important commandment: "Thou shalt have no other gods before me," and it has no existence of its own outside of this context. It is not an old expression of Yahwism; it is a theological reflection of the creator of biblical Yahwism. Only a transgression against one of the most fundamental rules of historical research will allow for such an idea. This rule says that we should never in a late source try to isolate some idiosyncratic part of it and transfer it back in time to the origin of the historical phenomenon under study. We should not use it to explain the development from this assumed origin until the moment the source in question was drafted.[76] Such an argument is of course a false one.

It is certainly not difficult in the Old Testament to find expressions of early religious ideas. They are, as a matter of fact, quite common, too frequent to cite in this place. Theologians have often in a rather helpless way tried to reconcile them with the official notion of God in the Old Testament. According to the main expression of biblical religion, this has nothing to do with religion in the proper sense of the word. It is theology. In this way the religion of Israel is not religion but theology. It is monolithic from its very beginning, showing no development. Yahweh is one and the same God from the first moment when he is presented to the readership of the biblical text, and he never changes. The faith, credos, in fact everything that has to do with this deity remains stable. It is not possible to write a history of the religion of ancient Israel—although it has certainly been done several times—taking us from, say, the tenth century B.C.E. down to the ninth century B.C.E., and farther down to the eighth century B.C.E.[77] This is an illusion created by the biblical writers and paraphrased by modern scholars.

The only thing that is possible is to trace elements that do not concur with the official version of "Israelite" religion expressed by the authors of the biblical narrative. Thereafter such elements should be compared with the official theology of the Old Testament in order that we should catch a glimpse of the religious background of the writers who formulated the theological doctrine. Such elements may show up to be of Palestinian origin, or Egyptian, or they may derive from Mesopotamian religion in some of its many forms. Other elements may come from different parts of Syria. Some may be old, with a background for example in the Late Bronze Age; some may be recent, having a Persian or even Greek-Hellenistic origin. The biblical writers have effectively demonstrated that they were well acquainted with a huge treasure of traditions coming from many places in the ancient world, but also that they cared to include only what they thought would forward their own "gospel" about Yahweh, the God of Israel, and his people.

It is thus characteristic of the Old Testament idea of the relationship between Israel and its God that Israel did not choose its God, it was chosen by God himself. This idea of being an elected people, a religious elite, always surrounded and threatened by the Gentiles is another part of the theological world of the biblical writers, although, as should be expected, it has for long been considered one of the original elements of the Israelite religion.[78] It is in itself not a very comforting piece of religious thinking, especially if one does not belong among the elected ones; it is, however, moderated by the tragic side of this quality of being elected. As Flemming Nielsen has recently demonstrated, the Old Testament historical narrative is a tragedy, or kept in the tragic mode;[79] Israel's history as the elected people became the history of a doomed nation of God, rescued at the uttermost brink of total disaster by its God. And, seen in retrospect, even this restoration showed itself to be nothing except another tragic history leading to another catastrophe. This tragic dimension creates the greatness of the story that has been conveyed to us by the writers of the biblical narrative and has made it a very convincing one—clearly to such a degree that critical scholars themselves became part of this history.

The people of God, that is, the Israelite nation, is truly an elected people, different from all other nations of the world. There is no reason to question this edifice created by theologians and put into writing by authors in a most delicate style and with great conviction. It is, however, a question whether this people of God is a nation of this world or a holy theory, impossible to transfer into the world of real human beings. The Old Testament in many parts discloses traces of this conflict between what is ideology and what is practically realizable. One way of reconciling the extremes is to identify the tragedy of Israel's past with the present. In this fashion the story about the past becomes a huge sermon directed to the people of the present, in order to convince them that following Yahweh in the sense laid out by the biblical story is the only means to salvation, and no other course is open. It is a story with a double edge. On one side it says that it is a blessing to be the people of God. It is, on the other side, impossible to escape this fate once it has been accepted. There is no way to get rid of Yahweh. Every member of this people is bound to Yahweh by his covenant that cannot be broken without the direst consequences for the transgressor. The Israelite people, the fathers, once subscribed to this law of Yahweh with acclamation in spite of all the warnings (see Joshua 24). Thereafter the only course was to obey and follow orders or to die ignominiously far away from the land of God.

THE PROMISED LAND

Of the three criteria mentioned by Herodotus in describing the ethnicity of the Greek nation, the biblical Israelites passed on two, common blood and common religion, but failed as far as the third one, common language, is concerned. However, the way the common blood was defined in the Old Testament showed it to be subordinated under the religion. The concept of religion for its part meant something different, and in a way much more restrained, than intended by the father of history, being narrowed down to the faith in Yahweh exclusively. Every single part of an Israelite's life should in theory be organized according to this faith. The demand put on the Israelites by the jealous God left nothing untouched. The history of the Israelite people as told by the Old Testament historians, however, showed the breakdown of this special relationship owing on one side to human, or Israelite, failure and on another side to the unhealthy influence of foreigners, especially foreign women.

One element belonging to the definition of Israelite ethnicity as presented by the Old Testament is peculiar to the biblical tradition. That is the special role attributed to the land of the Israelites, understood not only to be the land of promise and hope but also the gift of God. In the Greek tradition the notion of a country specially designed for the Greeks, where only Greek could live and where in theory at least every Greek ought to live and die, was absolutely unknown, and for good reasons. The Greek literature abounds in tales about Greek heroes going home and experiencing all kinds of tribulations during their travels. Homer's *Odyssey* is only the best known among several other examples.[80] The theme is more complex, however, than just one of return, of getting back to the place where the journey started.

Odysseus, the hero of Homer, set out for the siege of Troy, after which he returns home, although it takes him many years to achieve his goal. At home his faithful wife, Penelope, his young son, Telemachus, his father, Laertes, and his dog are waiting for him, the dog dying as soon as it recognizes him in the disguise of a beggar.[81] Several times Odysseus is delayed on the way home, or he is seduced into staying, for example on Calypso's island. It is the longing for the family at home that forces him to carry on with the journey. His travels do not end with the reunion with his wife, but only when he arrives in his father's home.

In the same way the heroes of Apollonius's elaboration of this theme, *The Argonauts,* set out to experience the world, but at the end the goal is only reached when they—or most of them, having lost some of their company including Heracles during their journeys—return home again.[82] This is the normal version of the story, although one conspicuous example, Virgil's *Aeneid,* is structured in a different way. Virgil's epic contains the story of a company of refugees from Troy who under the leadership of the surviving Trojan hero, Aeneas, travel around in the Mediterranean. Here they are met by all kinds of adventure and temptation, very much like Odysseus and his men. They never come back again, but settle in a foreign and unknown country, different from the one from which they set out. Here they are to find a new home, found a new society, and in the end become the ancestors of a great nation, Rome.[83]

The biblical story of Israel and its land is at one and the same time very close to and very different from the classical tradition of the traveling heroes. The biblical narrative includes several stories about a return. After human beings have been dispersed over the surface of the earth as a consequence of its insolence, when the people of Babel forsook their city,[84] Abraham's father decides to move from Ur of the Chaldees to Haran. Only the direct order of God sends Abraham from Haran to Canaan. This place he immediately leaves in order to go to Egypt (Genesis 12). Lot, Abraham's nephew, departs for Sodom, and will never return to the country of the Israelites (Gen. 13:5–13). Isaac never goes farther away than Gerar, a city of the

Philistines (Genesis 26), but Jacob travels to Mesopotamia to find a wife and to escape Esau (Genesis 28). Esau leaves for Seir and is thus excluded from the story about the Israelites (Gen. 28:8). Jacob's beloved son Joseph is sold off to Egypt (Genesis 37) and will not return except in a coffin (Gen. 50:26; Josh. 24:32), although he is joined by his brothers and his father in Egypt. There they all live for the rest of their lives and die, Jacob to be brought back and reunited with his fathers in the cave of Makhpelah (Gen. 49:4–14).

From Egypt the descendants of Jacob and his twelve sons return to their country after many hundreds of years, and after having been traveling in the desert for forty years. This is the only example of the journey itself being of importance; otherwise the "geography" is set as two places put in opposition to each other: on one hand Canaan, and on the other the foreign countries, either Mesopotamia or Egypt.[85] The story of the journey in the desert is interesting because the reasons for it are close to similar themes among the Greek traditions. The sojourn in the desert is seen as a punishment from God because of Israelite disobedience, now that they were so close to entering their ancient homeland (Numbers 14).[86] The desert is, like the Greek ocean, a dangerous place where every sort of danger can be encountered. Here Israel has to fight its enemies and to escape from the snares of the local people (again the incident at Baal-peor, Numbers 25). They try to divert Israel from returning home by alienating the Israelites from their God. The Israelites have to travel through the desert in the same way the Greek heroes have to cross the sea—after all, water was and is in short supply in the Middle East. The narrative function of the two elements, desert and sea, is exactly the same: the place of tribulation where somebody has to prove his or her worth. As such, these stories are related to the well-known fairy tale of the male hero who in the Scandinavian tradition often goes to the mountains, in the German to the woods, and in the Middle Eastern to the desert to win a kingdom and a princess.[87]

The result has to be that this tradition of traveling, and especially of return, although related to the literary traditions of the ancient Near East,[88] closely resembles the Greek tradition of the *nostoi*—the return of the hero to his paternal home.[89] Virgil adopted this pattern of narrative to create a Roman past to suit the Grecian taste of his audience, a Roman past that, or so we must imagine, would only have earned contempt from a man like Cato the Elder. In the same manner the biblical writers elaborated on a fixed theme of returning home and created their own version, transplanting the setting of the narrative into their own environment, the Near East.

There are, however, other elements in the biblical story about the return of the people of Israel to its land than these, one of them being the problem

of the inhabitants of this land, the Canaanites, the Hivites, Perizzites, and all
the other ancient people of Canaan. In Virgil's poem, the arrival of the Trojans in Latium is followed by a series of military encounters between the Trojans and local heroes like Camilla or Turnus. Now, Virgil's epic was never
finished, or so tradition says, so we do not know the end to these encounters, except in the version told by Virgil's younger contemporary Livy.[90] In
the *Odyssey,* the place of this motif is occupied by the theme of the suitors
whom Odysseus has to kill in order to regain his position in his own house.
In the Old Testament the Canaanites are to be extinguished if Israel will entertain any hope of reclaiming the land and remaining in it forever. In spite
of a promising opening—only the harlot Rahab is spared among the inhabitants of Jericho (Josh. 6:20–25)[91]—disaster is soon spelled to the Israelite
conquest initiative. This enterprise is doomed when the Gibeonites cheat
and enter into a covenant with the Israelites by claiming that they, like the
Israelites, are newcomers to the country (Joshua 9). Once concluded, the
covenant cannot be broken again, but it is in itself a transgression against
the prohibition of Yahweh and should have been avoided if the Israelites
had adhered strictly to the command of the Lord prohibiting Israel from making *any* covenant with foreigners.[92] Although the Gibeonites were made servants to the Temple (another infringement of the holiness of Yahweh) and
woodcutters (Josh. 9:27), they were spared and not given to the sword, the
fate duly meted out for every Canaanite.

There is a clear contrast between the magnificent genocide prepared by
the ideology of the exclusive right of the Israelites to the land of the Canaanites, as epitomized by the solemn conclusion to the book of Joshua (Joshua
24), and the wantonness of the splitting up of the country into twelve (in
fact only ten) tribal territories (Joshua 13–19). The realities of Israelite presence in their country is never so sharply presented as in the first chapter of
the book of Judges, according to which Canaanites were left to live all over
the country, and only later were reduced by the Israelites (although not expressly said to be killed). Far from being an alternative version of the conquest story, this chapter makes very clear what it was all about. The
Canaanites were left to live *in* Israel. They were not extinguished, as they
should have been, but allowed to spread their habits among the Israelites
and to divert the Israelites from their master and God.[93] Shortly after follows
the first foreboding that the Israelites will not remain in their country.

After the exile, when the final (at least according to the biblical historians) return took place, the problem was again the inhabitants of the land,
the people who were never carried into an exile and who had never returned from an exile. The problem was this time not to get the Israelites into

the land. The problem was to get them out again. This means that the inhabitants of the land who were already there when the people in exile returned home were either themselves Israelites who had never been carried into exile, or they were newcomers, people who had annexed the land of Israel while its legitimate inhabitants were somewhere else.

It took four narrative steps to fulfill this requirement, to remove the Israelites from their land. The majority had to go after the fall of Samaria, when Sargon of Assur deported its population, Israel's lost ten tribes. Second Kings states without further ado that "in the ninth year of Hoshea, the king of Assyria took Samaria, and carried Israel away into Assyria, and placed them in Halah and in Habor by the river of Gozan, and in the cities of the Medes" (2 Kings 17:6). The same chapter states that at a later date the king of Assyria replaced the exiled people from Israel with people from many other places, whom he settled in the territory of the former state of Israel (2 Kings 17:24).

The ten tribes put aside, two remained, and here three occasions follow that force Israel to leave its land, the first one being the deportation of ten thousand people, when Nebuchadnezzar for the first time subdued Judah "save the poorest sort of the people of the land" (2 Kings 24:14, KJV). The second exile followed after Nebuchadnezzar finally conquered Jerusalem and destroyed it with its Temple when Nabuzaradan left only "the poor of the land to be vinedressers and husbandmen" (2 Kings 25:12, KJV). In this way "Judah was carried away out of their land" (2 Kings 25:21), which did not prevent Nebuchadnezzar from placing a governor, Gedaliah, to rule in his place over the remaining Judeans. Gedaliah was murdered shortly after, however, at which occasion "all the people, both small and great, and the captains of the armies, arose, and came to Egypt" (2 Kings 25:26, KJV). The country was finally emptied of its inhabitants. The ideology of the "empty land" could take over and direct the construction of the return from the exile. The land of God could now, according to Chronicles, enjoy its Sabbaths for seventy years as prophesied by Jeremiah (2 Chron. 36:21).

The history of the land and of the people of God in this way is bound together so that they cannot again be separated. After Israel has been carried into exile the land is empty until Israel, or its remnant, returns. Any person present in the country must perforce be intruders without any claim to the country, to be removed from it if it is to truly be again the land of God. The books of Ezra and Nehemiah occasionally refer to the presence of persons in the country who did not take part in the exile. The most notable example is the governor in Samaria, Sanballat, and his fellows, who after all according to the official ideology were not genuine Israelites. Ezra and

Nehemiah are, however, most explicit when it comes to the role of the people in exile when they returned home. They had first of all to build the Temple. It is expressly noted that this event had to do with the people from the exile and was supported by Jews still living in Mesopotamia. Nobody else had any part in this enterprise, for as is written at the very end of the book of Zechariah, "and in that day there shall be no more the Canaanite in the house of the LORD" (Zech. 14:21).

THE PEOPLE OF GOD
AND THE "REAL WORLD"

One thing is theory, something else is reality. So far the ethnicity of the Israelites as understood by the writers and editors of Old Testament literature is a highly ideological one: a people elected by God, governed (through the covenant) by God, bound to the exclusive worship of this God, and donated a land of its own. This seems to be a tightly woven texture, as already indicated more adaptable for a religious, even a sectarian, community which fought to establish its identity in contrast to other groups and sects. It is, however, also a kind of texture through which some glimpses of reality glimmer. There are even some serious gaps in this garment, showing serious problems with the real world.

Circumcision

The problem is not the historical narrative as found in the Old Testament. Irrespective of whether we read the Pentateuch or the Deuteronomistic history (the books of Joshua through 2 Kings), or the Chronistic one (1 and 2 Chronicles, Ezra, and Nehemiah), all are in general agreement as to what constituted the Israelite people. The problems arise on individual matters. One such example involves the circumcision, which according to Genesis 17 was instituted as a symbol of adherence to the covenant that includes all male children from eight days old. Circumcision, understood to be a bodily symbol peculiar to male Jews, was in antiquity, however, not exclusively Jewish. On the contrary, the custom was widely practiced, in Egypt and western Asia, apart from Mesopotamia, and by Herodotus was reckoned to be of Egyptian origin.[94]

All of this is indifferent to the biblical narrative, which claims that the circumcision is a sign that the person in question belongs to the people of God. This from a historical point of view would only have made sense in Mesopotamia, or in periods when the people of the Levant were confronted with foreign newcomers who did not practice the custom, such as the Persians and the Greeks. Conversely, the Philistines, who are in the Old Testament continually being defamed for not being circumcised, might have known the practice.[95] Circumcision was probably seen as a sign of difference between the clean and the unclean, which meant that a person not belonging to the people of God could as a definition never be circumcised irrespective of the realities of this world. This also involved the Israelites, who are said to have given up the practice while in the desert and only reassumed it again after having crossed the Jordan River (Josh. 5:2–9).

Related to the question of circumcision we also find problems that have to do with foreigners who are accepted in an Israelite household as slaves, or servants. Abraham circumcised as the first his household, described as "every man child in your generations, he that is born in the house, or bought with money of any stranger, which is not of thy seed" (Gen. 17:12; cf. 17:23). The Hebrew word used for "stranger" is נכר, meaning technically "foreigner" in the sense of "a person from a foreign country." The provision therefore clearly has to do with a foreigner who was adopted into a household as a slave, no matter the origin of this person, and it is expressly mentioned that this person is not an offspring from Abraham.[96] Being circumcised, however, meant to be accepted as a member of the congregation of Yahweh, and this could therefore also include people without blood relationship to descendants of one of the twelve Israelite tribes. This is obviously in conflict with the prohibition against intercourse of any kind with foreigners, including their gods. It tells us that under certain circumstances it was possible also for people of non-Jewish extraction to enter the Jewish community. From an ideological point of view the author of texts like Genesis 17 described a closed society. He was evidently also living in the world of realities, and had to pay attention to the facts of life, including the fact that his community was not the only one around but would include also descendants from other parts of the society.

In the "real world" such things happen, though ideologically impossible. Every traditional society will entertain ideas about the importance of blood relationship and will draft genealogies to demonstrate how true this claim is. However, every social anthropologist worth his salt will also be able to show that the idea of common blood is nothing but a metaphor that describes coherence inside the society and borders between one social group and its neighbors. As an expression of this blood relationship, family trees or genealogies are established to prove the case of common descent. In real life, however, such genealogies have more purposes than just this rather nonproductive one; they are also a kind of roster or who's who, placing the individual members of the society in a hierarchical framework. Genealogies are, on the other hand, highly suited to manipulation and may change according to circumstances, when for example a new branch has been accepted into a community, either in the form of a single person or a whole family. In such cases the newcomers have been grafted onto the family tree of the society that has welcomed them. After some generations nobody ever questions that they were blood relatives and old members of the community. There are also examples of the same society entertaining more versions of their genealogies, one for each major section of the society—one genealogy valid among the ruling elite, other genealogies preserved by members of the lower-ranging groups.[97]

We know from various sources that the Jewish society of the Hellenistic-Roman period was not a closed one. One day it also had to accept an Edomite (Idumaean) as its ruling king. Also the early Christian discussion as reflected by the story of the meeting between the apostles Peter and Paul in Jerusalem is in line with this idea of an open Jewish society. The Jewish-Christian position started with a demand for circumcision, and only when pressed hard did they have to yield to the necessity of throwing the doors of growing Christianity wide open to heathen proselytes (Acts 15). Any society needs such a door to allow for passage in and out of the society, regardless of the ideology of being a closed community based on immaculate pedigrees. The idea of common blood that is central to the ancient understanding of ethnicity was sharpened by the Jewish theologians. These formulated the Old Testament version of the doctrine as one from which no one could escape. Conversely, the biblical writers had to allow for the fact that common blood was by their society at large often understood in the usual sense as a metaphor connoting membership of a certain ethnic group based on blood relationship, whether real or putative.

The artificiality of the biblical understanding of blood relationship, and the very stiff way it is supposed to be maintained (compare Ezra 10), will also be evident in the moment the genealogies themselves are studied. As described above, the Old Testament has an almost fossilized system of genealogies, which only changed because of literary matters, not because of a change in the system. Israel always consisted of the same twelve tribes. One exception is the case of the Levites, who were said once to have been a tribe of their own, though never as long as Israel was in its land, and allowed an independent position including the right to ownership to its share of the land. We will not get involved in this place in the age-old discussion about the possible origins of the Levites, whether there ever was a secular tribe of Levi. It is clear, however, that the distinction we find in the Old Testament is a literary and ideological and not a historical one (Ex. 32:25–29).[98] The tribe is said to trace its origin back to the time before Israel entered its land, so the myth of origin of this priestly caste is embedded in a narrative of which the historical content is probably nil, and it cannot be removed from this narrative. It is not a secondary element herein, but a part of the plot. The genealogical system is therefore artificial and has little in common—except for the idea itself—with genealogies as known from really existing traditional societies of the world of realities.

The Land of Israel

The artful way the theological definition of Israel and its ethnicity is construed by the biblical writers also becomes evident when we turn to the question of the land of Israel, this time not as a theological expression but as a geographical entity. It is astonishing that the Old Testament is very much in doubt about how to define this land of Israel in geographical terms. As a matter of fact, we find more than one definition of the extension of the land, and they are often in mutual conflict.

The most extensive definition of the land of Israel is found in the promise of God to Abraham: "Unto thy seed have I given this land, from the river of Egypt unto the great river, the river Euphrates" (Gen. 15:18). This must in its present formulation in Genesis 15 mean from the Nile to the Euphrates.[99] Also Solomon is ruling over a mighty empire "from the river unto the land of the Philistines, and unto the border of Egypt" (1 Kings 5:1[Heb.]; KJV, 4:21).[100] However, another description of the Promised Land differs from this comprehensive realm of the Israelites. Numbers 34 envisages a future land of the Israelites reaching only from the Brook of Egypt to Lebo-hamath[101] and does not include the parts of Transjordan where, according to Numbers 32, Reuben, Gad, and half of Manasseh settle. This geography is repeated in the vision of the new Israel in Ezekiel 47. Some scholars have been of the opinion that this "map" of the Promised Land is based on ancient realities of the Late Bronze Age reflecting the extension of Canaan in those days.[102] This is just as unrealistic and theoretical if understood to be the historical home of the Israelites in the past as the one found in Genesis 15:18.

The difference in geographical outlook does not end with these two versions of Israel's land. When Moses is allowed from Mount Nebo to overlook the Promised Land, which he was prevented from entering, he surveys its extension from Dan in the north to Zoar in the south and the Mediterranean in the west. Here, however, also Gilead, the Israelite part of Transjordan, is included. This more narrow definition of the land of Israel almost concurs with the repeated summaries that the territory stretches from Dan to Beersheba (Judg. 20:1, including Gilead; 2 Samuel 3:10; and elsewhere), and is generally also the one that is operative in the historical narratives.

Although the Old Testament contains a program for the subjugation of this territory, irrespective of its extension, one thing is certain. The historical state of Israel never ruled over anything like a territory encompassing most of Syria, all of Palestine, the Philistine cities, and Sinai. Only if it is possible to retain the biblical idea of the mighty empire of King David as a historical recollection is it worthwhile discussing the historical content of these territorial claims. As already indicated above, there is little that speaks in favor of the assumption that such an empire ever existed.[103] If this is the case, then the borders of the land of Israel as found in the Old Testament represent the ideological content of a religious program, which has little to do with the political realities of Palestine in ancient times. They function as part of a history that has almost reversed the usual role of this tiny landscape. This history is about a province governed by foreign powers, although sometimes, and for short periods only, allowed to share at least a token independence together with similar small territorial units in the southern Levant.

The "Nations" of the
Land of Israel

Now this land of the Israelites, identified with the small geographical territory known since antiquity as Palestine—or the Palestinian part of Syria, as Herodotus understood it[104]—has in the biblical historical narrative been transformed into a mighty home of the people of God. This is a land blessed by God and flowing with milk and honey, not to mention other things like the enormous grapes, a cluster of which had to carried by no less than two men (Num. 13:23). It was formerly, or so the Bible says, inhabited by many peoples. These are named in one of the more extensive list as the "Kenites, and the Kenizzites, and the Kadmonites, and the Hittites, and the Perizzites, and the Rephaims, and the Amorites, and the Canaanites, and the Girgashites, and the Jebusites" (Gen. 15:19–21).

Although some of these names are known from other sources, not all of them are. There might therefore be reason for the assumption that some are invented as well. This may concern the Hivites, the Girgashites, and the Perizzites, which are known only from the Old Testament. The Hivites are said among other things to be living in Shechem (Gen. 34:2), while the Perizzites may be understood as descendants of Perez, the son of the liaison between Judah and Tamar (Gen. 38:28), and thus technically not a pre-Israelite people of Canaan, but part of Israel. The Girgashites are totally unknown, although references are found to Ugaritic parallels supposed to refer to people from a city somewhere in Syria.[105]

The Kenites, the descendants of Cain, are sometimes (on the basis of Gen.

4:17–22) supposed to have been a gypsy tribe of tinkers and artists,[106] while the Kenizzites are utterly unknown except from the Bible, which makes their ancestor Kenaz, a grandson of Esau (Gen. 36:11). Other information says that Kenaz is related to Caleb (Josh. 15:17) and thus—if he should be understood as the ancestor of the Kenizzites—not one of the original inhabitants in Canaan, but a member of the Israelite community. Although some may argue that we have information about two separate persons, this is hardly likely. The rambling notes about Kenaz and his descendants rather represents conditions in the southern part of the Judean territory, which was dominated by the Edomites from at least the sixth century B.C.E. The biblical authors were evidently in doubt as to the status of the Edomites. How could they, being Edomites and not Israelites, live in a territory that the authors considered being central to the Israelites (Judeans)? The authors therefore in some places, in very much the same fashion as in the case of the Perizzites, reckoned them to be Israelites, while in other places they put them among the pre-Israelite nations of Canaan.

The case of the Rephaim is different, as we may in this case indeed think of people who once lived "in the country." The Rephaim are, however, hardly a living people, but based on Ugaritic material the name of this "people" means the "ghosts of the deceased." The Rephaim were literally the spirits of the ancestors and therefore automatically part of the country's past.[107] If we continue our investigation, the Kadmonites (in Hebrew הקדמני), are simply "the peoples of the East or of the past"[108]—in the last case nice companions to the Rephaim, the ghosts of the ancients.

The Hittites are well known and also appear within the narrative context of Genesis 23, where Abraham obtains his piece of land from the Hittite Ephron. Now, the Hittites are also well known from ancient Near Eastern documents as the name of an Indo-European–speaking people of Asia Minor who in the Late Bronze Age created a mighty empire covering most of Asia Minor and northern Syria. Their south border after the conclusion of the peace treaty between their king Hattushilish III and the Egyptian pharaoh Ramses II lay somewhere between the two Syrian cities Damascus and Homs, and never included Palestine. Apart from being anachronistic, the appearance of the Hittites in the Old Testament has nothing to do with this old empire of the Hittites except for the name. This name lived on into the Iron Age in Assyrian and Babylonian tradition. They used "Hittite" and "land of the Hittites" as a traditional designation of Syria, in the same way as the term "Amorite" was used by them to denote Syria, here, however, following an age-old practice of the Mesopotamian scribes going back to the third millennium B.C.E. The Amorites of the list in Genesis 15, as well as of the narrative contexts in which they appear in the Old Testament,[109] were never a people in its own right. The name represents a Mesopotamian tradition, meaning "westerners," that is, "people from the west" as seen from a Mesopotamian perspective.[110] A state by the name of Amurru existed for a short period at the end of the fourteenth century B.C.E. The name of this state, however, hardly derived from a "western" (i.e., "Amorite") tradition. It was rather a reflection of the Babylonian usage, a name adopted by the first ruler of the part of Syrian territory that belonged to the state of Amurru.[111]

This leaves only the Jebusites and the Canaanites proper. The Jebusites are said to have been the pre-Israelite population of Jerusalem, which should also before the conquest of Jerusalem by David (1 Samuel 5) have been known under the name of Jebus (Josh. 18:28). Outside of the Bible the Jebusites never show up. As far as Jerusalem is concerned, it is always called Jerusalem in ancient documents, from the second millennium.[112] Although the case of the Jebusites is left undecided because of lack of evidence, this "people" might be just as mysterious (or ephemeral) as any other people in the lists of pre-Israelite inhabitants of Canaan.

The Canaanites are for their part better known from ancient as well as biblical sources. Having written a monograph on this people, I can, however, limit the paragraph on them to a short summary of the conclusions to that volume.[113] The land of Canaan might in essence have been a rather vague territorial designation of Phoenicia. It probably included the northwestern part of Palestine, which archaeologically was more a Phoenician than a Palestinian territory.[114] It was in the second millennium used by the inhabitants of Syria, Palestine, and Phoenicia in a not very well defined sense embracing even larger stretches than the ones understood by the Bible to make up the Israelite territory. It is, on the other hand, used in a very precise sense by Babylonian scribes as a reference to the Asian parts of the pharaohs' empire. In the same way, no documents from Palestine or from Phoenicia from this period refer to the inhabitants of this area as Canaanites; only a Ugaritic text makes a distinction between people from Ugarit and people from Canaan. As noted in my aforementioned book, the first Canaanites who are known to have accepted themselves as being Canaanites were North African peasants of Punic origin in Tunisia, in the days of Augustine of Hippo. The reason they considered themselves to be Canaanites was probably the foundation myth of the pre-Roman, Carthaginian society, which Tyrian immigrants had founded.[115]

There was therefore no ethnic identity—let alone a national one—which could be called "Canaanite." There were no Canaanite people. The Canaan of the Old Testament, the archetypal enemy of ancient Israel, is therefore not an enigmatic old nation that once upon a time occupied Palestine. It is more of a literary device created in order to make a distinction between the heroes of the narrative, the biblical Israelites, and the villains, the Canaanites. They came to symbolize the non-Israelite population living in Palestine at any moment of Israel's history, whether understood to be the history of biblical Israel or of postexilic Judaism. In this way "Canaanite" might in fact simply mean the non-Jewish population of the land of Israel, irrespective of the time and circumstances in which the term appears.

The land of God of the Old Testament is therefore a landscape, which in pre-Israelite times was full of people, all of which, however, are products of a literary imagination. They—and especially the Canaanites—have a role to play in a plot, the plot of the history of biblical Israel. They have no "history" outside of this role, no part in the real world. They are at most reflections of demographic circumstances of the Persian and/or the Hellenistic periods that say that Palestine was not exclusively the country of the people of God. The conquest of that country as programmatically explained by the book of Joshua, the elimination of its inhabitants, is therefore not a history that has taken place; it is a history that *must* take place sometime in the future, if the people of God shall survive.

CONCLUSIONS

The Israel(s) of the Old Testament showed itself to be a product of a literary imagination. Its history was not one of the real world, but in its organization was directed by the requirements of the two foundation myths, the first of the Exodus, and the second of the Babylonian exile. Whether or not parts of this history really happened in the "real" world is to the mind that formed this history immaterial. It is true that here and there in the Old Testament we find historical recollections going a long way back in time. Here the Old Testament hardly distinguishes itself in comparison to comparable bodies of historical narrative in the ancient Near East or in the classical world. The historians, however, never display that kind of critical control of their sources which is required in modern historical research. This lack of control means that historical information will be placed in the context where it is required because of ideological and literary reasons, not because it really happened at a certain point in, say, Israel's history. I have in another context mentioned three examples of this "technique" (or lack of control). One involved the immigration of the Benjaminites of the Bible and the Benjaminites of the Middle Bronze Age. The second example is the note in Exodus 1:11 about the Israelites' being forced to work on Pithom and Ramses, a note the historical content of which hardly predates Saite times close to the middle of the first millennium B.C.E. The third referred to the possibility that the tale of the great empire of David and Solomon may reflect the knowledge that there once upon a time existed a major Israelite kingdom, although this was probably nothing else than the one that belonged to the House of Omri.[116]

Instead of a report on what really happened in Palestine in the Bronze through Iron Ages in antiquity, the history writers re-created the past as a tragic drama of Israel, as being under the curse, and at the same time respectively the blessing of God. Every part of the history is seen and should be understood from this perspective, and not as a reflection of the past *as it was*. Every part of the history of Israel in the Bible includes its part of the drama and is related to other parts in an organic way, being organized by writers who had their idée fixe of what constituted the people of God.

Basic to this idea of the people of God is the system of twelve tribes organized around the shrine of Yahweh, as if it was an amphictyonic center in the Greek sense of the word, whether the tabernacle in the desert or the Temple of Solomon in Israel's own land. The orientation around Yahweh's Temple where the ark of covenant was placed is decisive for the definition of the people of God, and removal from this context as happened to the ten tribes of the north after the Assyrian conquest effectively ended their part in "Israel's" history. They never returned, except in the perverse form of a priest who is brought back from the Assyrian exile. He was to educate immigrants from foreign countries in how they should worship Yahweh, the God whom he himself had forsaken, and who had rejected this Israel and thrown it out of his country (2 Kings 17:26–29).[117]

Martin Noth's amphictyony with all its functions—longtime removed from the scholarly discussion—should for these reasons be reinstalled and made operative, although not in the historical context in which Noth placed it. Instead of a historical reality, this amphictyony is an ideological reality, central to the organization of the people of the God in the Old Testament. Noth was absolutely right when he saw his amphictyony as the center of the tradition. It was not, however, of the traditions belonging to the ancient Israelites of the period of the Judges. It was the traditions of the Jewish society that sometime in late Persian and Hellenistic times saw itself as the heir of ancient Israel. The members of this society constructed their own origin myth as a program for taking over a country which they reclaimed for themselves in spite of the inhabitants who already lived there.[118] For this reason the myth of the exile had to be invented, which does not rule out that an exile once took place. Some deportations happened, not only because the Old Testament says so, but also because this was a normal part of the Assyrian and Babylonian practice of subjugating conquered foreign countries.[119]

Having organized their interpretation of the Jewish society as an amphictyony, which, however, survived only in an amputated form after having "returned" from the exile, the writers of the historical narrative set out to give a precise definition of this society understood as the people of God. Historical recollections hardly played any role. The artificial position of the blood was important as being more than a metaphor of ethnic relationship. The notion of common blood told the members of the Jewish society that they were in possession of a heritage that made it possible that any person of Jewish extraction could trace his ancestors back to Abraham. They accordingly reformulated the relationship to Israel's God as a blood relationship, symbolized by the circumcision. It was, however, exactly because of the issue of circumcision that the system was destined to break down under the pressure from a world that was not exclusively Jewish but allowed for the fact that "the Canaanites" were never extinguished. Therefore the community of believers who created the biblical story about Israel was neither in the exile nor in Palestine a majority that commanded all of the country (except for a short time under the Hasmonaeans in the second and first centuries B.C.E.).

Since no person is an isolated island, some kind of osmotic movement will happen between different ethnic groups irrespective of an ideology claiming this to be impossible. Not a single one among even the most fierce and tightly knit religious communities of later times has been able, in spite of often harsh repressive actions taken against transgressors, to prevent members from leaving the community. Therefore rules had to be included that allowed for the fact of proselytes' getting into the community (but hardly the other way round). In the Old Testament this is done in the form (narrative as well as juridical) of accepting foreigners as part of the households and by, in any case, demanding circumcision of males, while women would be accepted when giving birth to the children of Jewish males.

The artificial character of the concept of the people of God found another expression in the lack of a precise definition of the land of this people. At least three different descriptions of its territory can be found in the Old Testament, showing probably that none of them has ever been effective. The land of the people of God was never in ancient times united under a single ruler, except when controlled by foreign powers like Egypt in the Late Bronze Age or Assyria in the Iron Age. After the Assyrians came the Babylonians, followed by the Persians, and in their turn by the Greeks and Romans. Only the Hasmonaeans may have entertained ideas of creating such a national unity (but had to take into consideration the existence of privileged Greek communities in the country)[120] and have tried to achieve this unity.[121]

Finally the artful way the land of the people of God was populated by plenty of "Canaanite" nations, all of them shadowy if not totally spurious entities, has as its corollary the equal artificial nature of the people of God itself. While the Canaanites are to be considered villains of the drama, this drama also needed heroes or there would have been no narrative, and this role was given to the Israelites.

The biblical historical narrative is a story about an exile that somehow never ends. It is a program about a history to come rather than a tale about what happened in Palestine in ancient times. The exile will, according to the biblical writers, exist as long as all of Israel (the sacred remnant of the prophets) has not convened there to form God's own congregation. As time went by, this program was forced to develop into something else, and became part of the idea of a new Israel, also adopted by early Christianity, that should be established at the end of time. This is another story and not part of the discourse of biblical Israel presented here, but it is not to be overlooked if the consequences of establishing this ideology of the people of God is to be followed to its end.

CHAPTER 5

The Scholar's Israel
Hunting a Ghost Society

IMAGES OF ANCIENT ISRAEL

In the final part of this study it is the intention first to present a few samples of the image of ancient Israel created by scholars of the modern age. Second, we will continue with a general discussion of the methods and reasoning behind the creation of the Israel of the scholars of the modern age. It is the intention to show how modern scholars, in spite of the sophistication of their biblical studies, were entangled in a network of biblical concepts and ideas. Only to a certain point had they been able to liberate themselves from the pressure of the biblical tradition. The number of samples has been limited to four, most of all because it would be a hopeless affair to include a comprehensive survey. Such a survey would also be repetitious to a degree that is absolutely intolerable, and would hardly contribute anything of significance to biblical studies as such. Furthermore, it is not the intention to review the scholarly work of the elected four in any comprehensive way; rather, important passages have been isolated and used for a better-focused analysis. In this respect, the following paragraph only has to state a point.

The following examples have not, however, been chosen in a random fashion, since they are all representatives of their time and scholarly environment. The first one will be Julius Wellhausen, by many considered the greatest Old Testament scholar of the nineteenth century, if not of all time. The second will be Martin Noth, the towering figure in continental European Old Testament studies around the middle of this century. Noth was without doubt the brightest star of the German school at the height of its achievement and is still of extreme importance to the study of ancient Israel in most of Europe. As a contrast to Noth, his North American counterpart, John

Bright, has been chosen because Bright was part of a definite anti-Wellhausen tradition in North America, with William F. Albright as its center. Albright deliberately in his approach to biblical studies parted with the German tradition.[1] The revenge of the German tradition followed, when the students of Bright and his generation assumed positions that their teachers would have thought to belong among their German adversaries. At the same time, however, modern German scholars have accepted parts of the ideas of the Albright school, some of them in a rather undiluted form,[2] others in a far more sophisticated form. Rainer Albertz has been included here as the representative of the last-mentioned group. Without doubt his study of ancient Israelite religion represents the most elaborate synthesis of the Alt-Noth school and its American counterparts, including the development of the line of Albright in the works of George Mendenhall and Norman Gottwald. It is the opinion of this author, however, that Albertz's *opus major,* his history of Israelite religion, which is in fact a religious history of the Israelite people, is just as dependent on a paraphrasing of the biblical sources as the images of ancient Israel created by his older colleagues.

The History of the Jewish People: Julius Wellhausen

> *Die Geschichte eines Volkes lässt sich nicht über das Volk selber hinaus-führen, in eine Zeit, wo dasselbe noch gar nicht vorhanden war.*[3]

This sentence opens Julius Wellhausen's discussion of the history of Israel in his *Israelite and Judaean History,* his popular synthesis of his study of ancient Israel.[4] Nobody can disagree with Wellhausen on this point. It is senseless to write a history of Israel before there was an Israel. As a consequence he declines to get involved in a discussion of the patriarchal age, which is according to this criteria not history. At the same time, his reconstruction of the history of Israel, at least until the settlement in Canaan, is limited to a few casual remarks that do not pretend to create anything like a continuous history of the people. At exactly this moment, however, the Old Testament becomes the most important source of information, as Wellhausen reckons the tradition of Israel in Egypt to be historical, although not in the form envisaged by the biblical writers. Instead of an Israelite *nation,* we must reckon with the presence of scattered nomadic groups of many and various origins. The escape, which according to Wellhausen owes its form to "ziemlich boshaften alexandrinischen Legenden,"[5] is part of a later story. This story already sees the Israelite nation as an established fact at the exodus and does not accept that a nation has to grow and develop in a natural form.

Participants in the exodus, which occurred around 1250 B.C.E., were, however, only a limited number of people, a couple of thousand herdsmen, who for a prolonged period sojourned in the desert landscape to the south of Palestine. Starting from the region around the oasis of Kadesh, they in an alliance with the Edomites and Moabites made war on the Amorites, against Sihon and Og, before they were ready to invade the country to the west of the Jordan River.

The basic parts of the history before the immigration can in this way be said to be the stay in Goshen, the sojourn in the desert, and the wars in Transjordan, all of which are memories that were kept alive among the Israelites after the settlement. However, the early Israelites soon forgot all the particulars about their early history. Instead of a keeping a historical picture of the past, the Israelites understood their early history to be the acts of God. This was also necessary because only a part of the early Israelites ever frequented Egypt. Egypt thus concerned only the group of tribes known as "the sons of Rachel," whereas the origins of the other tribes, "the sons of Leah," should be sought in other directions.[6]

The confederation of the Israelite tribes became a fact while the Israelites lived in the desert, probably only in the form of a very loose organization. Such an organization, however, must have existed before the settlement in Canaan. After the settlement the unity of the tribes disappeared.

The following part of Wellhausen's description of the early history of the Israelite people centers on the issues debated in his *Prolegomena to the History of Israel*. This involves the difference between the Jewish law religion, richly represented in the documents of the Pentateuch, and the religion of the prophets. This prophetic religion should be seen as a reaction against earlier Israelite religion.[7] This part of Wellhausen's argumentation is close to the one found in this study. Especially his maxim that "the Law is the product of Israel's spiritual development, not its presupposition"[8] is extremely important, as he sees the present picture of the law-abiding early Israel as the product of late, postexilic Jewish thinking.

The theocratic constitution of Israel which saw Yahweh as the true and only legitimate ruler of Israel was also a secondary product of its history, nothing that was instituted from the very beginning. To the contrary, says Wellhausen: "Israel was a nation like anyone else. Yahweh did not free it from the duty to defend itself against its enemies."[9] Instead of this, early Israel was a loose political organization with a maximum of freedom for its members, reflected in the old adage preserved in the books of Judges and Solomon, "everybody did whatever he wished."[10] Only the loss of political independence "removed the Jews from the political to the spiritual world."[11]

Instead of the artificial imagery of early Israel found in the Old Testament, not everything was chaos; early Israel was founded on the idea of common blood, which was the necessary requisite for every Israelite whose membership in his nation was dependent on his place in his family. "All legitimate relationship is a relationship of blood,"[12] or so Wellhausen may sum up this part of his description of early Israelite social organization.

Although this was the original organization of the Israelites, the period of Moses was a witness to the unification of the Israelite tribes under the banner of the god Yahweh, and from this time onward became the "lasting principle of the ensuing political and religious history."[13] Thus "Yahweh" became the "war cry" of the tribal confederation, and the military camp the first (central) sanctuary of the nation. Everything in this early Israel centered on the religion of Yahweh. The Yahweh religion was controlled by a priesthood, which saw the figure of Moses as its founder. The importance of the religion was summarized in the following sentence: "Israel only became a political unity in the course of time prepared for it through the influence of the religion, as the people of Yahweh."[14] The period of Moses was the truly formative period of early Israel, although Wellhausen declined to see Moses as the founder of a new form of religion, that is, monotheism. The Israelite monotheism was, just like the law, the product of its history and experience.

It is easy to see how many are the lines of scholarship in Wellhausen's description of the emergence of Israel that lead up to the *status quaestionis* of the present day. He perfectly understood the importance of being able to work with a prime mover—in this case the Mosaic period, or even the figure of Moses himself. He also strongly advocated two of the classic criteria of nationality, the common blood and the common religion, although he, like a modern scholar, rejected the foundation myths of both institutions. The idea of common blood as well as that of a common religion was not something that existed in advance of history. These ideas only appeared as part of a historical development that also included the dissolution of the early unity of the Israelite society and its religion as Israel became part of the Canaanite world. The idea of syncretism between Israelite Yahwism and the gods of Canaan, so popular among many Old Testament scholars of the preceding generation, is very much in evidence already in Wellhausen's work.[15]

The level of recounting the history of Israel as told by the biblical writers is reduced to the generalizing level. Wellhausen does not simply paraphrase the biblical narratives, and he is highly critical as to its legendary character and historical value. He reckons large parts of the biblical tradition to belong to the late, postexilic Jewish world. At the same time, he remains faithful to the structure of early Israelite history as presented by the biblical history writers, although the content of this structure has been modified into something that is almost unrecognizable to the casual reader.

It is there, however. Israel developed out of a union between refugees from Egypt and other tribal groups in the desert period. After Egypt followed the desert, then the stay in Transjordan, and, if we were to continue through the rest of Wellhausen history, down through the conquest and settlement of Palestine to the period of the Judges, kings, and so on. Nowhere does he question the general outline of the biblical history except in the case of the patriarchs, when Israel was not yet a people and an Israelite history something unthinkable.

It is therefore easy to detect a kind of dichotomy in Wellhausen's historical reconstruction that sometimes makes it difficult to distinguish between his historical reconstruction and sheer speculation. His hands were bound by the structure of the biblical narrative, and he was never able to leave the biblical story behind him. Therefore in this part of his history we sometimes experience the feeling, from a methodological point of view, of a retrograde movement, maybe in order, as the French would put it, to *reculer pour mieux sauter,* "take one step backward in order to prepare for the leap forward." Wellhausen definitely works with the concept of the early history of Israel's being a late construction. He also understood some part of it to be Jewish-Hellenistic. At the same time—and in spite of a time lapse of a thousand years—he invoked the person of Moses to explain the development of an early Israelite identity, the existence of which is only confirmed, however, by the late tradition.

There might be several reasons for this almost schizophrenic character of the description of early Israel that we encounter in the works of Julius Wellhausen. Only a part of the problem has to do with the stage of knowledge in his own times, that is to say, the lack of solid knowledge of the political situation in the ancient Near East at the time when Israel emerged, at the end of the Bronze Age. Another reason for Wellhausen's obsession with, despite all odds, the reconstruction of a particular Israelite ethnicity in the early part of its history may be his anchorage in the Romantic age. The quest for the original state was an integral part of the Romantic "movement." This obsession with "the original" prevented him from accepting that a secondary development such as the emergence of the Jewish law religion could also have provided the image of early Israel found in the Old Testament. This image must perforce belong to a more pristine stage of Israel's history and therefore have preserved something genuine, something "original." It is a kind of mental matrix from which few historians of the ancient world and its cultures have been able to liberate themselves. A third explanation may be his Christian background, something that—although it is of course nowadays not very politically correct to say—has prevented scholars of a Christian, and here probably more often than not Protestant, orientation from appreciating elements of the Old Testament that are definitely Jewish.[16]

Still, there cannot be doubt that if properly followed, Wellhausen's opening would soon have led to a better understanding not only of the formation of the biblical tradition but also of the development of the Jewish thinking. It can almost be guessed that if Wellhausen had not been censored and turned into something innocent, this present study would have been entirely unnecessary simply because its theses would have been mainstream a long time ago.[17]

"Die grosse Geschichtsschreiberei": Martin Noth and His Circle

In the short section that introduces his history of Israel, simply called "Israel,"[18] Martin Noth presents a sketch of how to identify a historical subject like ancient Israel, because he is in no doubt that Israel is a historical unit. As a matter of fact, his Israel continues its existence in some form until the day the emperor Hadrian banned the Jews from Jerusalem after the revolt of Bar Kochba (132–35 C.E.). Noth also knew, on the other hand, that this Israel had changed identity along the road. He knew that Israel after the Assyrian conquest was something different from the Israel that existed before this date. He also accepts that his Israel in some way or other is related to later-day Judaism, although it should not be confounded with the Jewish society of the postexilic period.

Like Wellhausen, Noth accepts that Israel was the result of a historical development that involved people of different origins and with different historical experiences, and that the unity of the Israelite tribes occurred only after the settlement in Canaan. One precondition, in order that his Israel would be able to emerge as a nation, was a common language. At the same time Noth had to admit that this criterion in the case of Israel is without any value at all, as it shared its language with "its numerous neighbours."[19] The second precondition involved the geographical limitation of Israel to a specific area. This precondition was blurred by that fact that Israel had to share its territory with other groups who had no part in the Israelite confederacy. It was also a problem that this territory did not present any unity with clear and easily definable borders to other territories. The third precondition for Israelite nationality, is according to Noth, a shared history, common to all Israelites, although at this point he does not define it in any precise way.

This description of Israelite ethnicity is interesting for the simple reason that it has little to do with any normally accepted theory of ethnicity, ancient as well as modern. Thus the issue of a common language is hopelessly compromised by the fact that Hebrew was part of a kind of linguistic *Koine*. Everybody in that part of western Asia spoke "Hebrew" in some form or other, and common history is not normally something that precedes the establishment of nationality—it is a remedy to create it where it might not have existed before.[20] The land was shown in this study to constitute a very important part of the definition of Israel as found in the Old Testament. The idea that the possession of the land was the matter of fierce conflicts was not foreign to the biblical writers. In Noth's terminology this probably would say that this is a reflection of the fact that Israel for only a very short period of time was ruling its own territory.

Noth evidently understands the problematic character of his definition of ancient Israel, because he soon after resorts to the old trick of claiming Israel to be something special. In a rather muddled opening to his history, he correctly claims that the history of Israel as told by the Old Testament writers is controlled by an authority that is not the kind of subject to be studied by profane modern historians. Instead of using this knowledge to distance himself from the version of Israel's history found in the Old Testament, however, he immediately confuses the issues. He claims that this kind of supernatural history is found in the traditions of every nation in the world. Thereby he softens up the problem, not of the presence of God as the creator of history in the Old Testament, but of the magnitude of this role of God, which controls every single part of Israel's history down to its last day—which is in history writings something exceptional.

So in Noth's opinion Israel is definitely something special, and not the run-of-the-mill among ancient peoples, and the "proof" of its special status is Judaism, which as already mentioned should not be taken to be ancient Israel, though not totally independent from it either. This part of Noth's argument is particularly weak. It is almost identical with the Old Testament's own concept of the two Israels as at one and the same time two different entities and narrowly related to each other, as a father to his son. Noth at this point clearly turns his argument upside down. The relationship between the Jewish society of the postexilic period and the Israelite one of the Iron Age is not something that can be assumed in advance; it must perforce be the result of investigation. It can be a working hypothesis, but in Noth's argument it is already an established fact. Instead of presenting a decent argument in favor of his hypothesis, he transposes the essentials of Judaism back in time in order to create his image of ancient Israel, thereby disregarding some of the simplest rules of historical investigation.

Although probably the best known and most respected history of Israel from the twentieth century, Noth's textbook is based on an outlook that is directly controlled by the biblical writers, and he does not have the excuse of a Wellhausen who might not have known better. As already described above, Noth founded his reconstruction of Israelite ethnicity on the idea of the sacral league of the twelve Israelite tribes—the amphictyony. In his opinion this is reflected in the biblical tradition of the twelve tribes. As expressed by Noth: Apart from a few isolated spots, the Old Testament always understands Israel as this unity of the twelve tribes, although in history Israelite political unity was an exception rather than the rule. The amphictyony helped to overcome this problem of the dichotomy between the ideology of the twelve tribes' forming a special ethnos, and the historical realities that almost never allowed all of Israel to act together. That he here as elsewhere placed something that belonged at the end of his argument as its opening statement probably never worried him. Israel was something special, a people organized in a league or confederacy of twelve tribes around a common shrine, that is, with a common religion.

Apart from this, Noth's history provided the synthesis of Old Testament historical studies in central Europe, continuing the tradition of Wellhausen, in a much more conservative form, however. To Noth, as to Wellhausen, the patriarchal age was not history but legend, and he did not care much for the historical content of the stories of the Bible about Israel in Egypt or the exodus. Also Moses became much less important to Noth's reconstruction than was usual among his predecessors, partly because he didn't need a Moses to make his version of Israel function. Moses was often seen as the founder of a religion and believed to be necessary—if there had been no Moses, he would have had to be invented, as it is often maintained with a reference to the peculiar Israelite history and religion as told by the Old Testament. On this point Noth was explicitly clear, as he maintained that we do not know anything about Moses except that he may have existed and was buried, without anybody knowing, however, where to look for his grave.[21] The hypothesis of the sacral league of Israelite tribes made Moses expendable.

After the settlement, which in Noth's version closely followed the guidelines laid out by his teacher Albrecht Alt, Noth's history becomes rather conventional and simply follows the Old Testament closely in what can only be called a thoughtful, rationalistic paraphrase of the biblical narrative. The period of the Judges is organized around the amphictyony, as are also its institutions, and the kingdom is more or less considered a natural stage of the development of historical Israel almost as described by the biblical authors.

The Old Testament continued to provide the most important source of historical information. By dating some of the documents found in the Old Testament to very early periods, the scholars belonging to Noth's circle managed to keep them as firsthand sources. This was the case with the story of David, the so-called succession history, which was believed to have been written by an eyewitness to the events described in this gruesome narrative about the tragedy that almost wiped out the family of this great king of Israel.[22]

Following Noth, the majority of histories of Israel were more or less all guided by the image of ancient Israel created by Noth and his teacher, Alt. The spirit of Wellhausen was still known to be around but few read him and understood him to be on a more radical line than the central figures of Alt and Noth. It is the conviction of this author that most scholars of the middle of the twentieth century considered the contributions of Alt and Noth to have modified and improved Wellhausen. They did not realize that the pedigree did not run from Wellhausen to Alt, and finally to Noth, but from Rudolf Kittel, a much more conservative German Old Testament scholar than Wellhausen,[23] to Alt and finally Noth.

The histories of scholars like Martin Metzger, Siegfried Herrmann, Antonius H. J. Gunneweg, Georg Fohrer, and Herbert Donner, to mention only the most important German ones of the generation following Noth[24]—not to forget the Scandinavian and Anglo-Saxon ones[25] as well as the Italian one by J. Alberto Soggin[26]—were all more or less dogmatic paraphrases of the image of ancient Israel originating in Germany. Siegfried Herrmann, however, included a conservative touch that reminds the reader of the opposing position among North American scholars, as exemplified by John Bright.[27] Only one major contribution, this time by the French scholar Roland de Vaux, decided for a more conservative approach promising to create a middle position between Alt and Noth on one hand and Albright on the other. De Vaux evidently saw his history of ancient Israel as a continuation of the tradition of Rudolf Kittel, but did not live to carry his project beyond the initial stages of Israel's history.[28] From a methodological point of view, de Vaux's contribution—the only more recent French one of importance—did not represent any advance in comparison to the earlier German contributions. It was, rather, a retrograde step in a conservative direction, promoting such unlikely ideas from a historian's point of view as the historicity of the patriarchs.[29]

In Defense of the Bible:
John Bright

The complexity of the argument is hardly the first thing that strikes the reader when approaching John Bright's standard textbook of Israelite history, dating from approximately the same time as Martin Noth's German one. It was intended to be an American answer to Noth's history, written in the tradition of the great master of American biblical studies William F. Albright.[30] Although Albright had contributed with several studies on Israel's history, its archaeology, and its religion, he never sat down to write a proper history of Israel—probably because he saw Bright's volume as adequate.[31]

There will be no need to review all of Bright's history, which among its merits may include a clarity of presentation and, for its day, an excellent review of the history of the ancient Near East. It is true that Bright, like his mentor Albright, never doubted the historicity of the patriarchs and defended this vehemently over against their German colleagues, who were sometimes accused of entertaining a negative, even nihilist idea about the biblical tradition.[32] It is also correct that Bright departed from the Alt-Noth reconstruction of the settlement of the Israelites in Palestine and advocated a view on this event much closer to the biblical position. His argument was that there really was a conquest, although never in the absolute way that could be found in contemporary Israeli scholarship like the one by Yehezkel Kaufmann. Kaufmann's version of the Israelite conquest, which slavishly followed the biblical version, could hardly be called a *rationalistic* paraphrase of the Old Testament.[33] In this way, Bright, as well as before him Albright, did not depart from the conservative continental tradition of first and foremost Rudolf Kittel,[34] certainly admired by Albright. It is easy, however, to perceive how close Bright was to Noth—in spite of the rhetoric. This is obvious as Bright proceeds to the period of the Judges, which is in fact just another version of the picture of this period created by Martin Noth, building his description of Israel before the introduction of the monarchy entirely on Noth's amphictyonic model.[35]

Instead we will concentrate on a chapter section titled "The Formation of the People of Israel,"[36] as it should be expected here to find some sort of idea about Israelite ethnicity as it may appear to the members of the group surrounding Albright.

Bright had to admit that Israel's origins were extremely complex. He was not too happy about having to explain why it was so. He at the same time argued that the biblical description of Israel's prehistory was basically correct. Bright, however, accepts that the biblical idea that Israel emerged from a small group of people that grew into a major nation is legendary. He says it is partly contradicted by the Bible itself, which includes another tradition about Israel's origin that is different from the one of the mainstream tradition. However, Bright never says where and in what form this second tradition becomes visible.[37] While this section in Bright's study is particularly rich in biblical references, his postulate about a different biblical tradition on the origin of Israel is not supported by any precise reference to the Old Testament. It is only presented as a casual remark, almost like a lip service to critical scholarship. The reference to the origin of Moses' wife in Midian and especially the role of her family (Num. 10:29–32) hardly contributes much in the way of a sensible explanation to Israel's mixed origins, as this family is not said to be part of Israel, either here or later.

Bright also accepts that not all Israelites took part in the events of the exodus and the sojourn in the desert. The reason is an absolutely rationalistic one, and has been around almost since the beginning of critical scholarship, that Sinai would not be able to house all these people, the multitude of which would fill up the road leading from Egypt to Palestine and back again.[38] This is a typical trick of the most conservative form of biblical interpretation in a rationalistic age, because while claiming the biblical tradition to be true in essence, it at the same time disregards the biblical answers to the problems presented by the narrative itself. The biblical writers knew very well that Sinai would not be able to feed 600,000 Israelite refugees from Egypt. The recurrent theme in the narratives in exodus about the people complaining in the desert is a well-formulated *narrative* reflection on this problem.[39] The biblical writers, however, also knew how to solve the problem by introducing the miracle of the manna, the food Yahweh created to keep the Israelites alive while in the desert. It is of course impossible to use miracles in scientific explanations. This miracle has therefore in other places been rationalized to be a natural phenomenon supposed to be found on the Sinai Peninsula even in modern times, which only shows that the biblical authors when resorting to miracles preferred such ones as would be known in advance, only magnifying their volume.[40]

However, the people who actually participated in the exodus event were, according to Bright, hardly more than a "very few thousand," and this is the reason why we must assume a rather complex origin of historical Israel, that "all of later Israel was scarcely physically descended from them."[41] Instead Israel picked up elements of different origin while in the desert, although these stray persons and groups hardly, according to the biblical narrative, constituted any important addition to the 600,000-odd Israelites out of Egypt.

The following part of this chapter section continues in the same vein, presenting the history as a slight retouching of the biblical narrative, and in this case also the idea of a complex origin of ancient Israel can only be achieved by bending the testimony of the biblical tradition. Thus the episode of the Gibeonites, who by treacherous means obtained a covenant with the Israelites (Joshua 9) and thus were spared, is taken as a historical recollection.

In this way the Gibeonites became part of Israel in spite of the fact that the biblical testimony says that this did not happen. Bright writes, "Though it is said that they were made slaves, and though they remained for some time an alien group in Israel (2 Sam. 21:1–9), they were certainly ultimately absorbed," as if we can be certain of this in light of the biblical tradition distancing itself from the Canaanites. As always, the rationalistic analysis of the Old Testament narrative can achieve its ends only by dissolving the internal logic of the narrative itself. It is impossible to retain the narrative at the same time as we wish to deal rationalistically with its historical "truth."[42]

In the following section Bright accepts much of mainstream German scholarship assuming parts of Israel never to have been in Egypt. According to him such elements were already present in Canaan before the conquest in the shape of the Khapiru (*ḫabiru*), the Hebrews taking Egyptian and other evidence from the Bronze Age to be direct sources of the presence of these elements later to be absorbed by the Israelite tribes. Since he published his history around 1960, it was probably easier to assume such a direct line of contact between the Hebrews and the *ḫabiru*. By doing so, however, he disregarded the new view on the *ḫabiru* that had emerged among Orientalists already some years before the appearance of Bright's history. According to this new view, it was no longer possible to entertain any form of ethnic interpretation of the *ḫabiru*.[43] He also accepts the division between the Rachel and Leah group of tribes. This view had for a long time been popular among German scholars. Bright, however, is so obsessed by his idea of the complex origin that he postulates that there were elements among all the twelve tribes that traced their ancestry back to the Israelites in Egypt.[44]

Summing up his analysis of the exodus and conquest, Bright, however, finds reason to argue that although not all of Israel was in Egypt, all constituent parts of Israel had once been there. Although every single Israelite had not been to Egypt, he or she was in one way or another affiliated to persons who had visited that country. The tradition of Egypt was well alive all over Israel. This tradition of Israel in Egypt could, at the same time, not be separated from the Mosaic tradition, and Bright never doubts the historicity of that. Therefore he resorts to the old theme of the Moses group as the one that really left Egypt at the end of the Bronze Age, concluding the covenant at Sinai before it moved to Kadesh.[45] This also means that the biblical tradition is after all correct and confirms that Israel was a religious community born out of the scattered elements that left Egypt, and held together only by the divine power that all members of the exodus group accepted as their master. In this way it is true to say that John Bright without ever really presenting a critical appraisal of Israel's ethnicity, believed this to be an exclusively religiously defined one, thus at this point siding with the biblical tradition without any serious objections as to its veracity.

With no more review than this, it is obvious that John Bright was here paving the way for the renewed discussion about Israel's origins that followed just a few years after the appearance of the first edition of his history. By stressing the role of the *ḫabiru* in Palestine, but also in Egypt (according to Bright, *ḫabiru* continually walked in and out of Egypt[46]) to be absorbed into the community of the Israelites, there is only a short step to the position of George Mendenhall. Mendenhall simply turns Bright's hierarchical positioning of the Hebrews as subordinated to the Israelites and makes them the forerunners of the Israelite confederation.[47] Instead of being absorbed into an Israel with a theocratic constitution (the Sinai covenant), as is the case in John Bright's vision of the appearance of early Israel, Mendenhall has his Hebrews leaving Egypt under the supervision of Moses and confronting Yahweh at Sinai. These Hebrews were, according to Mendenhall, absorbed not by the Israelites but by the Canaanites, in the process transforming the Canaanites—or their multitudes—into Israelites, according to the principle *Graecia vincta ferocem victorem vixit,* "the conquered Greece conquered its wild conquerors."

Mendenhall's, and especially Norman Gottwald's, reconstruction of the emergence of Israelite nationality included the idea of the exodus group as the only part of Israel that had been to Egypt. In Palestine this group amalgamated with the Canaanites and transformed them into Israelites. We here see the synthesis between the German and North American scholarly traditions, as this was already the position of a scholar like Wellhausen. The essential difference is that the North Americans saw the bulk of Israelites to be former Canaanites, whereas their German predecessors, more in agreement with the biblical tradition, understood the amalgamation between the exodus group and the Israelites to have happened before the Israelite immigration into Palestine. It is the case, however, that to both traditions, and in spite of all their historical considerations, their interpretation of Israelite ethnicity was definitely biblical, seeing Israel as the result of a change of religion from early pagan habits to the monotheistic Yahwistic creed.

"The End of the Line":
Rainer Albertz

Nowhere does this synthesis between North American and central European scholarship become so conspicuous as in the recent history of Israelite religion published (in German) by Rainer Albertz in 1992.[48] In this work we find not only a synthesis between the schools of Albright and of Alt and Noth, but also an incorporation of the revolution hypothesis of George Menden-hall and Norman Gottwald. Albertz, however, also manages to include the so-called evolution model of Israel's origin. Among others, Cornelius de Geus, Lawrence Stager, and this author had worked this out. According to these scholars, Israel did not arise as a society that grew out of a social rev-olution but as the "natural" consequence of a development that embraced large stretches of Palestinian territory and also of neighboring countries. This development included a movement from a centralized form of existence in walled towns to open homesteads and villages in the mountain regions.[49]

Although stated to be a history of Israelite religion, Albertz's work is far more in the way of a proper religious history of the Israelite people, not very far removed from the normal genre of historical textbook dealing with the fate of ancient Israel. As a history of religion it seems, however, to break new ground by its unification of the religious and secular histories of an-cient Israel. Albertz has in a programmatical way expressed this in his "de-fence" of his changing of subject in the study of ancient Israelite religion from a static orientation into a dynamic one, closely comparable to a history of Israelite mentality.[50]

Being a religious history, Albertz's definition of the ethnicity of ancient Is-rael as an originally religious society probably makes more sense than in other cases where the subject was supposed to be the secular history of this people. However, being also a history of Israelite mentality, this difference of approach is more a theoretical than a real one, something that is made clear from the beginning of his chapter dealing with the origins of the reli-gion of the Israelites, that is, before the introduction of the Hebrew monar-chy.[51] The Yahweh religion of Israel was originally in its Israelite disguise the concept that created identity and unity among the exodus group, which under the leadership of Moses liberated itself from the bonds of Egypt.[52]

When speaking about the exodus group Albertz uses very much the same language as before him Mendenhall and Gottwald. This group consisted of Hebrews (*ḫabiru*) enslaved by the Egyptians. It liberated itself from Egypt, and met Yahweh in the desert. The religious experience at Sinai had two consequences. It established the relationship between the exodus group and Yahweh as a historical fact. It also helped to create social unity within the exodus group itself, which had a very different origin. Its members proba-bly had nothing in common except their mutual reaction against the op-pression they had experienced from the hands of the Egyptians.[53] The constitution of this group was therefore from its very beginning antiauthor-itarian and egalitarian, symbolized in its religious imagery. The origin of the group also made an internal "demand for loyalty" necessary among the members of the group, while it at the same time was forced to create boundaries between itself and its environment—something that is also reflected by the special demands made on Israel by its God.[54]

The arrival of this group—now under the leadership of Joshua—in Canaan created a kind of symbiosis. This symbiosis, however, did not create a unity between the former political structures of this country and the newly arrived community. It created liaisons between this community and the peasant society of Canaan, already in the process of liberating itself from its masters in the wake of the dissolution of the Egyptian rule over Palestine. As a matter of fact, Albertz think of the Moses/exodus group as revitalizing a revolutionary movement now already losing its original revolutionary impetus.[55] In religious terms this meant that Yahweh was, in the new synthesis between the two groups, identified with El; in political terms the consequence was the continuous antiauthoritarian attitude of this society against monarchic rule and oppression. The traditional historical reflection of this societal merge between two groups is reflected by the biblical tradition of the Rachel and Leah tribal groups.[56]

The following period of the Judges is characterized by the emergence of the Israelite tribal league, which although not a proper amphictyony in the sense of Martin Noth included most of the religious features associated with this model. Thus the central expression of this league was its wars and the concepts associated with the wars, and the league also was able to create its own system of laws and a priesthood consisting of the Levites to take care of the cult of this society.[57]

Probably the most original part of Albertz's reconstruction of the early Israelite society is his incorporation of the patriarchal tradition. He does not see it as a historical remembrance from the past, something Noth imagined. To Albertz the religion of the patriarchs constitutes a kind of private religion, which existed side by side with the official Yahwistic religion of early Israel. This religion survived the impact of the Yahwistic religion and continued its existence for centuries, creating a religious forum of the families and clans of early and monarchical Israel.

The study under scrutiny in this section is considered to present the end of the line, rather than a new beginning as hoped for by Albertz. This is simply because it constitutes a full-scale synthesis of Old Testament studies at least since the days of Wellhausen, including in its own form almost every major point made by subsequent authors up to this day. It is an all-embracing synthesis which sets out to explain almost everything, but it is at the same time from a methodological point of view a more than questionable enterprise.

The general course of the argument is narrowly bound to the development of Israelite history as told by the Old Testament and modified by German scholars of the modern age. It also, however, pays the kind of attention to "external evidence" that the Albright circle demanded. This "external evidence" was destined at the end to bring Albright's school down, when it was crushed under the weight of contradictory evidence that denied the members of this school the possibility to maintain the (biblical) theory of an Israelite nation that was physically different from the Canaanite one. We might also say that the language—the extensive recourse to the results of higher criticism that is evident in Albertz's study—is different from the one found in, say, John Bright's history. This language, however, covers up the fact that a fundamental agreement exists between the two schools, a general belief in the historicity of biblical Israel.

The number of individual points where Albertz's synthesis could be criticized is great, however, and not part of the debate here. Most of the critical remarks directed in my study on early Israel against Norman Gottwald's idea of a revolutionary and egalitarian Israel will carry the same weight in the context of Albertz's history of Israelite religion, and need not be repeated in this place.[58] Here it is enough to say that the "not-of-this-world" character of Gottwald's reconstruction also lives on in Albertz's reconstructed early Israel. This is probably because he, just as much as any of his predecessors, is governed by the structure of the narrative in the Old Testament. He also accepts the postulate of the Old Testament that Israel, being the people of God, was something unique, something absolutely different from its surrounding nations. Albertz more than most of his colleagues allows for a dynamic development of Israelite religion, and departs from the static impression one gets from the work of, say, an Albright or a Bright or even a Mendenhall. It is, however, the unique character of his ancient Israel that is problematic, as it is only a postulate presented by the biblical authors that this Israel is unparalleled by other societies of ancient times. After all, Albertz's reconstruction is, despite all its sophistication, mostly another example of a rationalistic paraphrase of the biblical text.

RATIONALISTIC PARAPHRASE

Several years ago, in a discussion of the problems involved in studying early Israelite history, I included a section with the title "Rationalising Ancient Historical Sources."[59] At the beginning of this section the following quotation from the work of the Italian Assyriologist Mario Liverani could be found:

> The indolence of the historians is considerable. When they deal with a certain period and they are confronted by a continuous account of the course of events, which has already been included in some sort of "ancient" documentary source (which is perforce not contemporary with the events themselves), they all too happily adopt the account. They confine their work to paraphrasing it or even rationalising it.[60]

Liverani opened an extended discussion of the oldest-known summary of early Hittite history with this "statement." It was his intention to show that the version of this history present in the decree of King Telipinus (c. 1500 B.C.E.),[61] and adopted almost verbatim by most modern histories of the Hittites, had little to do with what really happened before the times of Telipinus. On the contrary, this "history" was a piece of propaganda constructed in such a way that Telipinus—himself an usurper—should be seen as the creator of a durable peace and prosperity in Hatti after a long preceding period of disorder. It is a highly ideological text and not suitable as the foundation of modern historical investigations into the early history of the Hittites.[62]

In few places is Liverani's warning against naively accepting an ancient text as a historical source as relevant as in biblical studies, where the amount of rationalistic paraphrase has in fact been overwhelming. There are many reasons for this, one of the more fundamental being that the historical narrative of the Old Testament has been part of most biblical scholars' first educational experiences in Sunday schools or primary schools. This history has become part of one's cultural heritage in such a way that we automatically subscribe to this history without thinking about it. "We have all been brainwashed by the Deuteronomists," as one of my older colleagues once put it in the classroom, hinting at the circle of authors who according to the usual view created the historical narrative in the Old Testament from the book of Joshua to 2 Kings. Being brainwashed means that we are ready in advance, without reflection, to accept everything that we are told by our biblical source, and only secondary investigation and reflection will eventually persuade us to give up this biblical history of ours. As such, the loyalty that most Old Testament historians feel toward Israel's history as told by the biblical authors is a psychological rather than a scientific fact. It is part of their upbringing and education, not of their historical research.

This may sound like an unfair statement, but the development of historical investigations in biblical studies will tell us that it is correct. Not before the last twenty years has a development started in historical studies that effectively seems to be able to bypass the biblical framework of the history of Israel. This framework includes the following periodization: First came the period of the patriarchs.[63] It was followed by the sojourn of the Israelites in Egypt and the exodus and wanderings in the desert. After the conquest came the period of the Judges. This was in its turn succeeded by the period of the Hebrew monarchy, first the united monarchy under David and Solomon, then the sad history of the two independent kingdoms of Israel and Judah, and finally the exile in Babylonia, the return from the exile, and the post-exilic period. Also a work, advanced in its own time, from the late 1970s, such as the one edited by John H. Hayes and J. Maxwell Miller, follows this biblical course of history; although here—finally (in an American environment)—the historicity of the patriarchal period was seriously questioned.[64]

In the more advanced German discussion, this period had been understood as not being a historical one since Wilhelm Martin Leberecht de Wette at the beginning of the nineteenth century formulated his doubts about its historicity.[65] This view was cemented by Julius Wellhausen at the end of the same century,[66] and perpetuated in Martin Noth's history from the middle of the twentieth century.[67] Only conservative German historians, such as Rudolf Kittel and Ernst Sellin,[68] still nourished the idea of some kind of historicity behind the legends about the figures of Abraham, Isaac, and Jacob. In American historiography, however, the patriarchs were well alive as late as the middle of the twentieth century in the works of William F. Albright and John Bright,[69] only to be challenged in the works of Thomas L. Thompson and John Van Seters in the 1970s.[70]

The next part of the history that had to go—not without a bitter fight—was the exodus and conquest (still with a conservative backlash not least within American scholarship).[71] The exodus was by the critical German school almost completely removed from history. It was described as a tradition that, together with the tradition about the patriarchs, was—in Noth's version—kept alive at the amphictyony;[72] and the conquest was entirely rewritten, whereby the Israelite "conquest" in German scholarship was replaced by the "settlement" of the Israelite tribes.[73] In American scholarship another theory was at the end substituted for the idea of a conquest, claiming early Israel to be the outcome of a social and religious revolution.[74] The scholars who favored this theory, however, for their part kept the idea of an exodus in a reduced version as the escape of an insignificant group of refugees (Hebrews) from Egypt, a thought borrowed from previous German scholarship. This exodus group was the same one that experienced the presence of Yahweh at Mount Sinai, and carried with them the idea of the covenant between God and man, which became their message to the oppressed peasantry of Canaan when they arrived in Palestine.

Already now it is easy to perceive the "mechanisms" of the study of ancient Israelite history. More important than anything, everything has to be defended as long as possible. Old Testament scholarship has been fighting a kind of trench warfare, defending hopeless positions until forced out of its hidings, only to retract to the next line of defense, where the process is repeated for another time. Second, it paraphrased its primary source, the historical narrative of the Old Testament, which is a religious story about God and Israel. Now, God is unsuitable for historical research, and he was therefore at an early date in the history of critical scholarship removed from the biblical history, with the hope that the history that remained could be considered as profane a history as found in other parts of the world. It is of course a highly questionable exercise from the beginning, to remove one of the main characters from the play. The result must be an amputated narrative, and it is hard to see how the other part in the play, Israel, could be left untouched by such developments. However, the next logical step—to remove also biblical Israel from history—was not taken. Instead, the "manuscript" had to be changed so that instead of being a dialogue between God and humanity it could be a monologue only implying the participation of human beings.

The idea of the mass immigration of the Israelites out of Egypt, something that according to the Old Testament involved 600,000 male adults plus their families (Ex. 12:37),[75] had to be modified. Only a tiny group of people was present. It was so tiny that it became invisible to the archaeologists and historians who had been looking for traces of this group either in Egyptian sources (which have nothing to contribute) or in the material remains from the Sinai Peninsula where the Israelites should have sojourned for forty years. Six hundred thousand males with families—that would say above three million people—would, as it was remarked a long time ago, have filled up the whole peninsula, and even if the Israelites marched in broad columns would have meant that the advance guard was well into Syria before the rear guard had left Egypt. Instead of dismissing the narrative as a historical source, it was rationalized into something that to the minds of the historians was acceptable and thereafter transferred into "real" history. It is, however, still a paraphrase of the biblical narrative from which everything supernatural has been removed. At the same time, the recourse to such a tiny group of immigrants as imagined by this kind of research made it possible—in spite of all critical sense that says the opposite—to retain the central parts of the biblical tradition. This included the revelation of the supreme God of Israel, and the originality of the monotheistic credo of the Old Testament. It was not seen as a serious obstacle that neither this group of Moses nor the revelation at Mount Sinai was mentioned in any source except the Old Testament narrative—before it was rationalized. The maintenance of the original monotheism was judged more important than the history of early Israel, and early Israel was accordingly sacrificed on the altar of Yahweh, the Lord of the world.

A similar procedure was chosen when it came to the conquest narratives in the Old Testament. Here it was the unlikely content of the biblical version of the advent of the Israelites into Palestine that forced on the scholars a different view of the "conquest" from the one presented by the biblical narrators. It was not the lack of external evidence in the form of archaeological remains. There were no traces of this new Israel and its activities. A different explanation had to be found, and the one most Europeans subscribed to was the one proposed by Albrecht Alt, who saw the Israelites not as coming out of Egypt but as small-cattle nomads coming out of the Syrian desert tracking for grazing ground for their flocks. At first the encounter between the Israelites and the Canaanites was a peaceful one; the Israelites settled in the mountains and in other places not frequented by the Canaanites, and the Canaanites remained in their cities and valleys. Only at a later date, when a growing Israelite population demanded an expansion of the territory controlled by Israel, the Israelites had to "conquer" their country.[76]

Many objections have during the last generation been raised against Alt's popular reconstruction of the early history of the Israelites. This is not the place to review them, however.[77] More important is the underlying reason for its lasting popularity, in spite of an often-devastating criticism. The theory as such is unsupported by the biblical narrative, although Judges 1 has often been mentioned in support of Alt's reconstruction of the settlement.[78] Nevertheless, it has one major advantage attached to it: it keeps the Israelites together as an ethnic unit different from that of the Canaanites. It helps us maintain one of the major postulates of the Old Testament in very much the same way as the earlier-mentioned reduction of the exodus migration into something insignificant that involved only a small fraction of people. The postulate says that there was and always remained a vast gap between Israelites and Canaanites. It made it possible in spite of all historical considerations to maintain the biblical thesis of Israel as a chosen people. This people "knew" that it had since its very beginning been something special. It goes without saying that the hypothesis about the settlement worked perfectly in combination with the assumption that there once existed a Moses group. In this way the scholars succeeded in transferring the biblical narrative of the election of Israel, of its miraculous escape from Egypt and encounter with Yahweh at Sinai, including the concept of the people of God as the people of the covenant, into something manageable for historians of this world. This was done in spite of the biblical picture's being "not of this world." It remains, however, nothing except another rationalistic paraphrase of the biblical narrative.

It goes without saying that the period of the Judges and the following one of the united monarchy were paraphrased without any further ado. The only difference of approach was that we might probably here and there find a sign of relief that we are now firmly in a historical period and no longer have to deal with sagas and legends. It means that the paraphrase can follow the biblical narrative more slavishly also in evaluation of the events, which is not far away from that of the biblical writers.[79] Whereas in the nineteenth century the historical paraphrase was often done in a rather naive way, it has in this century been dominated by the amphictyonic hypothesis. This hypothesis helped the scholars to create an image of a society that in their eyes was supported by contemporary sources that originated in the amphictyonic assembly of all Israel. The biblical image of a twelve-tribe nation of the *benei Israel* was therefore thought to belong in this period.

It is strange that people may sometimes be so blind that they don't recognize a phenomenon that is familiar because it also turns up in other cultures, including their own. It is a mystery that German scholars of the Romantic period could not see the connection between the heroic tales in the book of Judges and the similar ones found in Norse legends, in Icelandic sagas, in the traditions of King Arthur and the Round Table or of Charlemagne's heroes, or in Greek and Roman tradition. These kinds of tales are common in every place where a "nation" tries to establish a past that reaches back to the darkness of primeval times.[80] The stories in the Old Testament were considered history in spite of the fact that in other places similar stories had to be dismissed.[81] Scholarship developed only as far as its paraphrases of the biblical text became more and more refined. This is evident when we address the work of the latest generation of biblical scholars, including such notables as Gösta W. Ahlström and Herbert Donner, J. Alberto Soggin, J. Maxwell Miller, and John H. Hayes, and for that matter also the English textbook by this writer.[82]

Herbert Donner's history of Israel, which is the latest offspring of the German tradition of writing histories of ancient Israel, follows the tradition from Albrecht Alt and Martin Noth closely but for historical reasons has to give up the idea of an Israelite amphictyony. Apart from that, his reconstruction of the premonarchic period follows the one by his mentors closely.[83] The degree of paraphrase in Ahlström's description of the period of the Judges is considerable. His otherwise sophisticated general approach to historical studies should have enabled him to bypass this problematic procedure. He was evidently caught by another bad habit of early historiographic paraphrase. A couple of generations ago scholars were likely to see behind named persons references to more comprehensive human organizations such as tribes or nations, whose history in a symbolic way was reflected by the fate of the main characters of the biblical narrative.[84]

The famous historian of the ancient world Eduard Meyer had already dismissed the procedure greatly favored by the scholars of the past at the beginning of the twentieth century in the following scornful way:

> Besides, then and now I regard every endeavour to be futile and beyond dispute, which tries to answer these questions or even to translate the Israelite sagas into history according to the very much appreciated fashion. Generally, they deliberately skip—without considering how fantastic the enterprise is—half a millennium and deal with the narratives as suitable historical sources, irrespective of their youth and after they have brushed them up by rationalising means. They even consider these sources to be the imperturbable basis of Israel's nationality and religion.[85]

It would be wrong to say that scholars have paid much attention to Meyer's warnings. Meyer himself was not of much help, as he in fact used the same kind of rationalistic paraphrase as the scholars who were rebuked by him because of bad methodology. The problems connected with the choice of methodology in the study of early Israel have an ironic side. The procedures that turn a patriarch into a tribe are employed by the same kind of scholars who without remorse reduce Israel in Egypt to a few lost souls convening around the figure of Moses. As usual the goal, to retain as much of the biblical narrative as possible as history, is governing the reasoning of scholars also of the present age.

The most advanced histories from a methodological point of view of ancient Israel from the 1980s, the ones by J. Maxwell Miller and John Hayes and by this author, both fail on this point, however, in an infinitely more subtle way (which does not make the failure less serious). Both textbooks accept that we cannot write a history of Israel before the introduction of the monarchy, and that the narratives in Judges are legendary and cannot be used for historical reconstruction. Having stated this, however, both histories of Israel continue with a reconstruction of Israelite tribal society. This reconstruction will at the end of the day and in spite of additional ethnographic evidence have to rely on the same sources that were rejected as historical material. Sometimes it seems as if a social reconstruction has nothing to do with a historical description of the past.[86] These textbooks are therefore perpetuating the tradition of presenting rationalistic paraphrases of the biblical text, though in a new disguise.

Only the most recent major modern reconstruction of the history of Israel, the one by J. Alberto Soggin from 1993, clearly sees how important the removal of the historical amphictyony is for the study of early Israelite history. Soggin has—very much in the style of Martin Noth[87]—reduced the tradition of the judges of Israel to the heritage of a later period, in this case the one of David and Solomon. Noth accepted the traditions of Israel's origins as the legacy of the amphictyony, and with its removal from the historical scene, it is a logical step to move one step forward and consider this period of David and Solomon as decisive for the development of Israelite nationality.

As a matter of fact, this period must be considered the only remaining possibility if we at all intend to speak about an Israelite nationality that has its roots in real history and not in an invented one. The consequence is that the battle between scholars of different observations that is at present being fought on this battleground is particularly fierce. The removal of the united kingdom of David and Solomon including all of Israel will effectively destroy any idea of an Israelite unity that precedes the formation of the biblical tradition, whenever this happened after the mythical episode of the exile and the emptying of the land of Israel. Without a Davidic empire there was no Israel in the biblical sense. The only thing that remains is the tradition of two tiny states of Palestine in the Iron Age, which were long after their disappearance chosen as the basis of a history of a new nation to be established on the soil of Palestine in the postexilic period. The tradition may have been preserved by descendants of the people who were really carried into exile by the Assyrians and Babylonians, or by others, who simply inherited the tradition and re-created it as their own history.

So far the discussion about the empire of David and Solomon has not been brought to an end, although it is this author's firm conviction, following among others Thomas L. Thompson and Giovanni Garbini, that little new can be said in favor of retaining this idea of Israelite greatness.[88] It is, however, interesting to see how scholars have tried to use the age-old technique of reducing the biblical narrative through a paraphrase of its content. Few scholars of the present age seem to be ready to subscribe to the biblical picture of an Israelite empire stretching from the Euphrates to the border of Egypt. As such the biblical picture of the empire is not part of the discussion. The historicity of David is, on the other hand, defended in any possible way. To many scholars it does not matter if David is no longer a great imperial monarch, or a petty chief of a small and insignificant political structure—some would still call it a state[89]—hidden away in the Judean mountains. This was the technique that isolated the Moses group from the multitudes of Israelites who escaped from Egypt, or retained only the framework of the biblical story about the conquest of Canaan. It is also a procedure that without remorse destroyed the narrative as it is written, in order to find and isolate its historical nucleus. It was at the same time forgotten that the ideological framework of the narrative must be destroyed at the same time. The idea of "all Israel," which is governing the mind of the narrators, is at the same time embedded in a narrative, now destroyed. This becomes evident in the case of David and Solomon. If the aim was to protect the idea of a collective Israel consisting of the descendants of the twelve tribes already in force in the days of David and Solomon, it will not be of much help if the David of history was no more than a shadowy figure of Palestine's ancient past. The procedure of the biblical scholars can be compared to the saying "to have your cake and eat it too." Scholars will have to realize that they have a choice to make. They can decide to keep David as a historical figure, however reduced into something quite different from the biblical towering figure of the almighty king. They can also keep the biblical figure that is a literary and not a historical figure. They cannot have it both ways.

CUT AND PASTE

More than a hundred years ago, the French biblical scholar Maurice Vernes published a work that was originally planned to present to a French audience the results of the great German (and Dutch) school of Graff, Kuenen, and Wellhausen. In it Vernes claims that he was originally convinced by the arguments of this school. As he proceeded with his project, he more and more came to believe that its basic assumptions were totally false and misleading, assuming as the point of departure of the study of the biblical text what was in fact intended to be the result of the investigations. Vernes thereafter proceeded to present the following theses concerning the formation of the Old Testament literature:

> 1. The time when the biblical literature was put together will be decided on the basis of the most secure conditions if one starts from a relatively late date, when there can be no doubt about the existence of this literature. If one—using this date as a starting point—works one's way back through the course of the centuries, looking for fitting circumstances which may form the background of the individual books.
>
> 2. We accept as far as the major biblical works of literature are concerned a fundamental unity of composition and time of appearance. At the same time we understand this in the broadest possible sense, and see this literature as the result of a co-operative effort—there can be no doubt that they are the work of the great schools of theology which

flourished in Jerusalem between 400 and 200 B.C. The composition of it lasted about two or three generations.

3. We accept that there exists a uniformity of thought in the biblical literature. Although we may speak of a multitude of forms—the freedom within Judaism of expressing the common dogmatic has always been considerable—the fundamental unity of the main concepts is conspicuous. The individual authors all believe in a monotheism on a high moral and spiritual level, and they confirm that the deity among all the nations of the earth has elected the people of Israel in order to overwhelm it with his gifts if it follows its laws.

4. It is finally possible here and there to trace the remnants of a memory that has changed and has been mixed up. We are confronted with a product of the greatest importance, which has many analogies among ancient and modern literature, but none of them with a similar imaginative force and literary completeness.[90]

Nobody can say that Vernes's ideas took root among the fraternity of biblical scholars. An early verdict was presented by the Danish biblical scholar Frants Buhl, who claimed that according to Vernes the Old Testament came out of the late postexilic period like a shot out of a pistol.[91] Now, Buhl was a respected scholar in his own time, considered in his own milieu to be a radical representative of the German school of Old Testament studies.[92] Therefore few reckoned it worthwhile becoming acquainted with Vernes's work at firsthand, and he soon lapsed into oblivion—in fact, so total an oblivion that he was not accorded even the most minute place in the history of research. Thus no modern summaries of the development of Old Testament study in the nineteenth century include any reference to Vernes. He was already handicapped because he was part of a scholarly tradition that wasn't mainstream either in the Anglo-American or in the German world. He survived only in a note in Robert H. Pfeiffer's erudite and respected introduction to the Old Testament.[93] Otherwise he was totally forgotten, although it is obvious that he is much closer than anybody else from his time—including a respected figure like Julius Wellhausen—to the ideas of the modern school of revisionists, consisting of, among others, Philip R. Davies, Thomas L. Thompson, Keith W. Whitelam, and this author. This circle generally favors a very late date of the composition of the biblical literature. It may originate in the Persian or in the Greco-Roman period.[94] Had Vernes's ideas become accepted, he might have paved the way for a comprehension of the aims and intentions of the biblical literature that took another hundred years to achieve.

As already mentioned, Vernes reacted to the achievement of the Graff-

Kuenen-Wellhausen school of biblical studies, although not so much to the historical investigations of a scholar like Wellhausen. Rather, he objected against what in his eyes was the willful way they pursued their literary studies which centered around the establishment of so-called higher criticism, the acme of which was considered to be the documentary hypothesis. It is not my intention to present anything that even remotely resembles a comprehensive review of the development of this hypothesis. Other scholars like Hans-Joachim Kraus or John Rogerson have contributed with extensive reviews.[95] This author has no intention of multiplying them. The merits of this scholarly trend are conspicuous in liberating the study of the Bible from the dogmatic control of church officials, thereby creating the prerequisites for an independent appraisal of the contents of this literature.

In the end, the higher criticism ended up with an enormously complicated structure, sometimes ridiculed because of its seeming absurdity, nowhere better displayed than in Otto Eissfeldt's synoptic presentation of the various documents, which is generally considered to form the basis of the literary development of the Pentateuchal tradition.[96] In this form, the narratives of the first four books of Moses have been dissolved into a kind of jigsaw puzzle of isolated elements, passages, verses, and half verses. In its mechanical form the documentary hypothesis is monstrous, however necessary in some form or other to understand the compositional character of the historical literature in the Old Testament.

The most popular form of the hypothesis worked with three main documents present in the first four books of Moses, J (the Yahwist [Jahwist]), E (the Elohist), and P (the Priestly document). Of these, the Yahwist was considered to provide the oldest and more original version. The Elohist and especially the Priestly documents were reckoned later and theologically more sophisticated versions of the origin history of Israel.[97] There should, however, be no doubt that the scholars of this period widely preferred the lack of sophistication in J to the detraction of E's and P's elaborate reformulations. The Yahwist was normally placed in the tenth century, the Elohist perhaps a couple of centuries later. The Priestly document belonged to the postexilic period, following Wellhausen's famous assignment of Judaism to two successive stages, the one of the prophetic religion, and the other of the law, the latter one in his eyes being inferior to the first.

The reason why the tenth century was seen as the date of the composition of the oldest part of the Pentateuch—according to some authors with a *Grundlage* in the preceding period of the Judges[98]—has probably never been better explained than in the work of Gerhard von Rad. He considers the time of Solomonic enlightenment to contain all the prerequisites for literary production, including history writing. It was first of all a time of political stability and economic prosperity. On top of this came the need of a new state to provide a history of its past. Finally the creative impetus following in the wake of the establishment of an Israelite state created this new literature.[99]

This date of the oldest strands of history writing in ancient Israel has later been modified. This is not so much because it is historically unlikely. It is, however, founded on the most vicious kind of logical circle—the literature assumed to derive from the Davidic-Solomonic period is the only source of the period from which it is said to come. Nevertheless, the reason for the new date was that scholars persuaded themselves into believing that it was closer to the Babylonian exile, the seventh to sixth century, or to the time of the exile.[100] The reasoning behind the change of date was, as a matter of fact, very much of the same kind as the one behind the Davidic-Solomonic date. External circumstances were thought to provide the most likely background for this kind of literature. It goes without saying that no matter how early or how late such a date is, the logical reasoning is the same. It didn't make a world of difference whether the Yahwist was placed at the court of Solomon or in connection with the reform of Josiah or in Mesopotamia in the sixth century. Whether Davidic or exilic, the date was in itself almost a part of the biblical image of ancient Israel. The Yahwist belonged to the era of Solomon because it provided a picture of the world depicted by the biblical tradition. Conversely, this document was part of the exilic heritage because it looks like something that could be exilic, or Hellenistic because it resembles Greek historical literature, or because . . . The possibilities are certainly legion, although none of them from a methodological angle is very convincing.

The only satisfying procedure, of course, would be to trace the route laid out by Vernes. This says that the starting point for the analysis must be the time where there can be no doubt that this biblical literature existed. When an agreement is reached on this point, we may begin the next step and see whether some part of the tradition has a prehistory. This can sometimes be done on the basis of information given by the literature itself. Regardless, whenever it comes to the fixation of a date, the latest possible one will always be preferable. One example of this is Numbers 22–24. These chapters have sometimes been thought to include some of the most archaic poetic literature in the Old Testament, the poems of the prophet Balaam. This kind of poetry was often seen as premonarchical.[101] Only later was its date lowered to the eighth to seventh century, when Balaam turned up in an Aramaic inscription from this period from Deir 'Alla in Jordan.[102] The poems, however, end with the following passage:

> And ships shall come from the coast of Chittim, and shall afflict Asshur,
> and shall afflict Eber, and he also shall perish forever.
>
> (Num. 24:24)

As Karl David Ilgen said two hundred years ago, this cannot be a reference
to anybody except the Macedonians—something Luther already had made
clear in the notes to his translation of the passage[103]—which would date
these archaic poems to no earlier than the late fourth or third centuries B.C.E.

The problematic—not to say careless—way these literary operations were
executed effectively blocked the way for a correct procedure that would
have enabled the adherents of higher criticism also to *read* their literature
instead of dissecting it. The general idea was to trace the original source in
order to turn it into some kind of historical recollection. In the Pentateuch,
the Yahwist source would in this way probably be reckoned a better source
of historical information than later layers such as the Elohist one, not to
speak of the Priestly document. In this way the "theology" of J would also
be evaluated as more important than the one of the composite work itself,
or put in a different mode. The subject of primary interest would therefore
be the theology of the putative Yahwist, rather than the theology of the Pentateuch taken as a whole. The text would be read and understood in parts,
not as a coherent piece of literature. These critical remarks do not intend to
say that there is no reason at all to do literary-critical studies in some form—
much recent work in this direction is both fruitful and necessary. They
should rather be understood as a warning against removing the literary operations to the historical field under the false presumption that such a study
will provide the investigator the historical source that will provide the modern reader with information about ancient Israel. Also in the case that the
Yahwist writer could indisputably be dated to the tenth century B.C.E., this
strand would not be a primary, that is, contemporary source of events that
were supposed to have happened two or three hundred before. If anything,
the Yahwist source would only be a firsthand witness of the period to which
it belongs, in this case the tenth century. If the date of this piece of literature is postexilic, belonging to, say, the fourth or third century B.C.E., it is of
course not a source about ancient Israel, the Israel before the exile. It is
"only" a source about the concept of ancient Israel nourished by the people
who authored the Yahwist narrative.

There shall be no doubt about the present writer's attitude to the literary
dissection of texts in higher criticism in its traditional form. It has to be admitted, at the same time, that it would be preposterous to say that literary
critics were unable to provide fine exegesis of Old Testament texts. The example of Gerhard von Rad—one of the finest theologians of this century—

militates against such a view. It is also correct that von Rad, like anybody else belonging to his own circle, contributed immensely to the appreciation of the individual literary layers of the Pentateuch, if not of the Old Testament in toto. Thus von Rad subdivided his *Theology of the Old Testament* into a number of subtheologies, one of the Pentateuch, including its different layers, another of the prophets. Von Rad was depending on the traditional position of Wellhausen, that the prophets as seen from an ideological point of view were not of the same age as the Jewish law religion. It must, however, be stressed that the way literary studies were pursued blurred the outlook of the scholars in such a way that they concentrated on the referent of the texts understood to be the period about which the texts talked. They forgot to read the texts as evidence of themselves, of the intentions of their authors. Modern scholars created an image of ancient Israel in this way. It was little more than a repetition of the image of Israel as found in the Old Testament, however, transferred into the historical world of which it had no part, being the creation of the imagination of the biblical authors.

Conclusion

Who invented ancient Israel? According to Keith W. Whitelam, it was the modern scholars. Their "Israel" was a reflection of their own society.[1] According to Philip R. Davies the modern scholars created a curious blend of ancient ideas about Israel as expressed by Old Testament literature—"biblical Israel," historical inscriptions pertinent to Palestine in ancient times, and their own ideas about nationality and ethnicity.[2] In Whitelam's version this invention of an ancient nation seems almost from the beginning a malicious one, which literally took away a history from the people to which it rightfully belonged, the Palestinian people.

Now, this is hardly a fair evaluation, as it is—in Wellhausen's wording—impossible to have a history before we have a people. It still has to be shown that such a societal entity as a Palestinian people ever existed before it was created by the inhabitants of the landscape of Palestine in response to the emergent Jewish community and later state in their midst. Ethnic group identity presupposes that there will be others around who are so different that they can be recognized not to belong, so there must perforce be at least two such units present in an area or nobody would think of ethnic diversity. The famous example of a people living on an isolated island who would never, if not in contact with other similar societies, entertain an idea of ethnicity, is of course true, although constructed. So ethnic identity demands diversity, without which it cannot exist, and if no diversity is present it has to be created if a human group wishes to establish itself as an ethnic unit, whether religious or secular or both.

As far as ancient Israel is concerned, there can be no doubt that it is an artificial creation of the scholarly world of the modern age. It was not, however, created as a contrast to other nations of the ancient Near East, at least not originally intended to be so.[3] It simply developed out of the usual bad habit of paraphrasing the biblical text.

Whenever a modern scholar teaches his students exegesis in the traditional sense of the word, this kind of exegesis presupposes the ability on the part of the student to translate, and then to paraphrase a text. A paraphrase means simply retelling what is the content of the text without analyzing it, in order, for example, to distinguish between early and late layers, or to sort out religious peculiarities or the like embedded in the text under scrutiny. This is an age-old practice reaching back into ancient times, and probably any modern scholar has been brought up within this tradition of paraphrasing the text.

When critical scholarship arose, the scholars participating in this development were still paraphrasing their texts as they had been used to doing since childhood. The only new thing was that they here and there had to revise their opinion about the factual content of the texts themselves. They were told by other authorities—more often than not students of the natural sciences—that some element was, from a scientific point of view, absolutely unlikely, not to say impossible.

The example already referred to a couple of times in the chapters above, the number of Israelites who left Egypt, is illustrative, as the Bible speaks about six hundred thousand Israelites plus their households, easily more than three million persons. Before European explorers started traveling around in the Middle East in numbers, something that did not happen before the seventeenth or eighteenth centuries, very few had any concrete idea about the nature of this landscape, and nobody therefore really questioned the information provided by the biblical writers. Needless to say, any person who has only once visited the Sinai Peninsula will know that this almost moonlike territory could hardly provide food for more than a small number of persons, nothing in the vicinity of the millions presupposed by the biblical authors.

Natural science at the same time taught the scholar that although miracles might have happened (and some scholars as late as the eighteenth century tried to reconcile this new "knowledge" with their biblical studies[4]), these are not easy to handle in a rationalistic study of the Bible. It would certainly be advantageous if the biblical scholar did not in a too obvious fashion have to rest his case on this kind of evidence if he wanted to be au courant with other types of scholarship of his own age. He had to retell the biblical story in such a way that the new knowledge was incorporated while the biblical narrative was at the same time retained as a fact.

It is therefore correct to say that the development of critical biblical scholarship did not lead to a break with earlier tradition of biblical studies. It should rather be seen as a logical continuation of prescientific scholarship that yielded to the impact of the natural sciences only when forced to do so. In principle the biblical scholars continued to paraphrase the biblical text.

They continued to do so although it should have been clear a long time ago to people around that the biblical narrative had vanished in the process. It is evident that the rationale behind the continuous paraphrases had in fact blurred the intentions of the texts themselves, which probably can be best described as bringing information about God's plan for humanity—in the Old Testament the Jewish nation—to human beings.

Parts of this development also included the appearance in humanities of a new worldview connected with the Romantic age and prepared during the century of Enlightenment. This development centered on the concept of a people and a nation, as well as on the newly constructed humanistic science of history. The major political changes in Europe at the end of the eighteenth century and in the first half of the nineteenth century created a new context of humanistic studies. This also became the world of the biblical scholars, who probably without ever realizing the changes—these are never easy to perceive when they happen—simply transferred the changing ideas to their own area of study, the Old Testament.

Modern scholars invented ancient Israel, not because they wanted to invent something new but simply because of a rather naive reading of scripture. It was the Israel of the Old Testament that was carried along by biblical scholars. In the process it was transformed into a nation of modern dimensions (although most of the phraseology connected with this concept was ancient and though at the same time used in a distorted meaning, as with the concept of nation itself).

The decisive part of this invention was probably not the way in which it came into being. It was probably inescapable, as seen in the light of Bible studies through the ages, that the plain biblical paraphrase should in a scholarly context be transformed into a rationalistic paraphrase. It is probably also understandable that this habit of rationalistic paraphrase has proved to be almost impossible to extinguish, even among the most critical scholars of the present day. Not only exegetes, but also archaeologists and sociologists compete in providing their versions of a rationalistic paraphrase of the Bible. The decisive part is rather that the Israel paraphrased by modern scholars in this rationalistic way was already in its original form an invented Israel.

It is one of the theses of this book that the Israel found on the pages of the Old Testament is an artificial creation which has little more than one thing in common with the Israel that existed once upon a time in Palestine, that is, the name. Apart from this not absolutely insignificant element, the Israelite nation as explained by the biblical writers has little in the way of a historical background. It is a highly ideological construct created by ancient scholars of Jewish tradition in order to legitimize their own religious community and its religio-political claims on land and religious exclusivity. This literary society has been built up around a model of the league of twelve tribes of Israel, almost as borrowed from Greek tradition, and has been provided with the necessary features to make it appear to be for a people. It is, however, so far removed from the sociopolitical and religious realities of Palestine in the Iron Age that it can be difficult to find anything of relevance except the name of the god Yahweh. The home of this god may originally have been to the south of Palestine,[5] but he was in the Iron Age clearly a very popular deity in most of Palestine, in contrast to the biblical Yahweh, however, related to the female deity Asherah in some way.[6] When trying to reconstruct this biblical Israel, it can therefore only be done as a reflection of the society and period that created it, not as a reflection of the past.

The Israel of the Iron Age proved to be most elusive, in historical documents as well as in material remains, where hardly anything carries an ethnic tag that helps the modern investigator to decide what is Israelite and what not. Not even the kingdom known in some contexts to have been called Israel seems to have been generally known under this name. Instead of Israel, the dynastic name of the state, "the House of Omri," and the name of the capital Samaria seem to have been more widely used, except of course in the Old Testament imagery of this Palestinian kingdom.

Some may seek help in new definitions of ethnicity and of states and nations that accept, for example, something to be a state that in modern terms had only little to do with it. They may argue in favor of an Israelite ethnicity on the basis of material that does not indicate any such. To identify ethnically Israelite remains demands that it should at the same time be possible to identify remains that are definitely not Israelite. It has to be admitted that archaeology has so far not been able to make such a distinction except in isolated cases.[7] The same applies to sociology, where it is certain that some kind of societal change is happening, for example, in the tenth century B.C.E. in northern and central Palestine. This is a truism. A living society is always, in contrast to the rigid and artificial biblical one, in a state of change from something to something else. The important point is, however, that it is difficult to point to any specifically *Israelite* ethnic identification marks here, peculiar to the historical Israel of the Iron Age and not known in other parts of the southern Levant.

At the end we have a situation where Israel is not Israel, Jerusalem not Jerusalem, and David not David. No matter how we twist the factual remains from ancient Palestine, we cannot have a biblical Israel that is at the same time the Israel of the Iron Age. Here the verdict of Baruch Halpern, that we should talk about two monologues in a dialectical dialogue is very precise, as each of the two monologues has to be listened to and interpreted in isolation, although they are at the same time interrelated.[8] Such a view on the relationship between fact and fiction also provides an answer to the question: How interesting are the Israelites of the Iron Age if they are not to be identified with the biblical Israelites? Are they in any way more interesting than any other group living in this territory at that time?[9] The people who lived in Palestine in ancient times are extremely interesting, probably not in their own right, but because they create a contrasting universe to the Israel of the Old Testament. They at the same time provide the modern reader of this literature with a clue to how to read and understand it.

Abbreviations

ABD	*Anchor Bible Dictionary.* 6 vols. New York: Doubleday, 1992.
ABLAK	Noth, Martin. *Aufsätze zur biblischen Landes- und Altertumskunde.* 2 vols. Edited by Hans Walter Wolff. Neukirchen-Vluyn: Neukirchener Verlag, 1971.
ANEP	Pritchard, James B. *The Ancient Near East in Pictures Relating to the Old Testament.* 2d ed. Princeton, N.J.: Princeton University Press, 1969.
ANET	Pritchard, James B. *Ancient Near Eastern Texts Relating to the Old Testament.* 2d ed. Princeton, N.J.: Princeton University Press, 1969.
AR	Luckenbill, David D. *Ancient Records of Assyria and Babylonia.* 2 vols. Chicago: University of Chicago Press, 1927.
ARE	Breasted, James H. *Ancient Records of Egypt.* 5 vols. Chicago: University of Chicago Press, 1906.
BA	*The Biblical Archaeologist*
BAR	*Biblical Archaeology Review*
BASOR	*The Bulletin of the American Schools of Oriental Research*
BN	*Biblische Notizen*
CAH	Edwards, I.E.S., C. J. Gadd, N.G.L. Hammond, and E. Sollberger, eds. *The Cambridge Ancient History.* 3d ed. Vols. I:1–II:2. Cambridge: Cambridge University Press, 1970–75.
CANE	Jack M. Sasson. *Civilizations of the Ancient Near East,* 4 vols. New York: Charles Scribner's Sons, 1995.
EA	El-Amarna Letter
IEJ	*Israel Exploration Journal*
JARCE	*Journal of the American Research Center in Egypt*
JESHO	*Journal of the Economic and Social History of the Orient*
JBL	*Journal of Biblical Literature*
JNES	*Journal of Near Eastern Studies*
JSOT	*Journal for the Study of the Old Testament*

KAI	Donner, Herbert, and Wolfgang Röllig, *Kanaanäische und aramäische Inschriften.* 3 vols. Wiesbaden: Otto Harrassowitz, 1962–64.
KJV	King James Version
KTU	Dietrich, Manfried, Oswald Loretz, and Joaquín Sanmartín, eds. *The Cuneiform Alphabetic Texts from Ugarit, Ras Ibn Hani and Other Places.* 2d, enlarged ed. Munich: Ugarit-Verlag, 1995.
NAEEHL	Stern, Ephraim. *The New Archeological Encyclopedia of Excavations in the Holy Land.* 4 vols. New York: Simon & Schuster, 1993.
NEB	The New English Bible
PEFQS	*Quarterly Statement,* The Palestine Exploration Fund
RB	*Revue Biblique*
REB	The Revised English Bible
SJOT	*Scandinavian Journal of the Old Testament*
ThLZ	*Theologische Literaturzeitung*
ThZ	*Theologische Zeitschrift*
UF	*Ugarit-Forschungen*
VT	*Vetus Testamentum*
VTSup	*Vetus Testamentum. Supplements*
ZA	*Zeitschrift für Assyriologie*
ZAW	*Zeitschrift für die alttestamentliche Wissenschaft*
ZDPV	*Zeitschrift des Deutschen Palästina-Vereins*

Notes

Prolegomena

1. In recent times the term "the Old Testament" has been questioned, as it is an exclusively Christian term, not paying attention to the fact that it is also the sacred book of Judaism. The term "the Hebrew Bible" has therefore in some quarters become popular. Strictly taken, however, that is a misnomer, as the term the Hebrew Bible is exclusively referring to Hebrew scripture as found in the Tanakh, the traditional Jewish name for the Hebrew Bible. Already the first Christian translations of the books of the Hebrew Bible, in the Latin Vulgate and the Syriac Peshiṭṭa, introduced a number of changes—following the ancient Greek version, the Septuagint—most notably another order of the books of the Old Testament and sometimes including other books as well. As we are here not strictly referring to the study of the Old Testament in its Hebrew form—the King James Version is thus not identical with the Hebrew Bible—the term the Old Testament (sometimes abbreviated OT) will be used hereafter.

2. Matt. 2:15, quoting Hos. 11:1.

3. Matt. 2:16–18.

4. As evidenced, for example, in the catechism of the reformers, with their emphasis on the importance of the Ten Commandments.

5. A short but precise description by R. E. Clements of the development of Pentateuchal research can be found in R. J. Coggins and J. L. Houlden, *A Dictionary of Biblical Interpretation* (London and Philadelphia: SCM Press and Trinity Press, 1990), 527–31.

6. Thus King Christian I of Denmark in 1469 pledged the Orkney Islands to the British Crown as a mortgage for the dowry for his daughter. As a consequence, the islands were in 1590 formally transferred to the British Crown.

7. Except, perhaps, from the Chinese, which were admired for their great age, although hardly for their content.

8. It should be noticed that at the European universities separate chairs in Old and New Testament studies were unusual before the nineteenth century.

9. Some scholars have found it opportune to include the ancient Near East among the forerunners of Greek civilization. An example is C. H. Gordon, *Before the Bible: The Common Background of Greek and Hebrew Civilization* (New York: Harper & Row, 1962). Their perspective is in many ways undoubtedly correct. It is, on the other hand, improper and baseless to argue that the characteristic traits of classical civilization as they developed in Greece in the post-Persian period are mainly (if not

primarily) due to Oriental influence. It is from the Orientalists' vantage point a way to escape the conclusion that Greece through hellenization imposed its culture on the Near East, as happened during the third and second centuries B.C.E. in the wake of Alexander's conquests. Johannes Pedersen's famous *Israel: Its Life and Culture,* Vols. 1–4 (Oxford: Oxford University Press, 1926–47; Danish original, Copenhagen: Branner, 1920–34) may be considered a rather ironic example of this. Most features in Pedersen's *Israel* are also present in his old friend Wilhelm Grønbech's *Hellas,* vols. 1–4 (Copenhagen: Gyldendal, 1942–45), never translated into English; but see also Grønbech's *The Culture of the Teutons* (Copenhagen: Gyldendal, 1931), displaying many of the same characteristics.

10. D. Patte, *Ethics of Biblical Interpretation: A Reevaluation* (Louisville, Ky.: Westminster John Knox Press, 1995).

11. K. W. Whitelam, *The Invention of Ancient Israel: The Silencing of Palestinian History* (London and New York: Routledge, 1996).

12. 1795–1886. Translated into German: *wie es eigentlich gewesen.*

13. A Danish encyclopedia from the beginning of the twentieth century praises von Ranke for "his profound understanding of reality which makes him congenial with the movement that led Prussia to victory." Von Ranke was supposed to be the preferred author of Otto von Bismarck: *Salmonsens Konversationsleksikon* 19 (2d ed., Copenhagen: J. H. Schultz Forlagsboghandel, 1925), 921.

14. Heinrich Ewald 1803–75. The first edition of his *Geschichte des Volkes Israel* in 5 vols., 1843–55. The 3d ed. appeared 1865–68.

15. *Geschichte des israelitisch-jüdischen Volkes,* vols. 1 and 2 (Leipzig: Quelle & Meyer, 1924–32).

16. Julius Wellhausen's book was originally published in German as *Geschichte Israels* vol. 1 (Berlin: G. Reimer, 1878). A second volume was envisaged, but never materialized. English trans. with an introduction by W. Robertson Smith and a preface by Douglas A. Knight, *Prolegomena to the History of Ancient Israel* (Atlanta: Scholars Press, 1994).

17. Julius Wellhausen, *Israelitische und jüdische Geschichte* (1894; 9th ed., Berlin: Walter de Gruyter, 1958).

18. On the "taming" of Wellhausen, see N. P. Lemche, "Rachel and Lea; or, On the Survival of Outdated Paradigms in the Study of the Origin of Israel," pts. 1 and 2, *SJOT* 1:2 (1987): 127–53, and 3:1 (1988): 39–65.

19. Edward Meyer, *Die Israeliten und ihre Nachbarstämme: Alttestamentliche Untersuchungen* (Leipzig: Max Niemeyer, 1906; reprint, Darmstadt: Wissenschaftliche Buchgesellschaft, 1967), 50. Cf. also below, 154.

20. The methodology of *les annales* is best studied in the collection of essays by the best-known representative of the school, Ferdnand Braudel, *On History* (Chicago: University of Chicago Press, 1980).

21. Some of Alt's seminal short studies on the history of Israel have been translated in his *Essays on Old Testament History and Religion* (Oxford: Basil Blackwell, 1966). However, for a full appraisal of his work it is necessary to refer to his much more comprehensive German collection, *Kleine Schriften zur Geschichte Israels,* vols. 1–3 (Munich: Beck, 1953–59), as a number of his most important essays have never been translated.

22. Martin Noth, *Geschichte Israels* (Göttingen: Vandenhoeck & Ruprecht, 1950). English trans.: *The History of Israel* (London: A. & C. Black, 1958).

23. M. Noth, *Das System der zwölf Stämme Israels* (Stuttgart: Kohlhammer, 1930; reprint, Darmstadt: Wissenschaftliche Buchgesellschaft, 1966), which has never been translated. English-speaking readers will have to resort to the description of this tribal league in his *A History of Israel.*

24. It should at the same time not escape the reader's attention that "ethnicity" is a fairly modern convention, the use of which is first recorded in the 1950s. Cf. John Hutchinson and Anthony D. Smith, "Introduction," in J. Hutchinson and A. D. Smith, *Ethnicity* (Oxford and New York: Oxford University Press, 1996), 4. All contemporary anthropologists do not consider it to be of much use. See the very critical appraisal by Marcus Banks, *Ethnicity: Anthropological Constructions* (London: Routledge, 1996).

25. Herodotus VIII:144: αὖτις δὲ τὸ ἑλληνικόν, ἐὸν ὅμαιμόν τε καὶ ὁμόγλωσσον, καὶ θεῶν ἱδρύματά τε κοινὰ καὶ θυσίαι ἤθεά τε ὁμότροπα. The translation is by A. de Sélincourt, *Herodotus: The Histories* (Harmondsworth, Middlesex: Penguin Books, 1954), 550. C.H.J. de Geus has discussed this concept of a nation extensively in connection with the tribal league. Cf. his *The Tribes of Israel: An Investigation into Some of the Presuppositions of Martin Noth's Amphictyony Hypothesis* (Assen and Amsterdam: Van Gorcum, 1976), 156–64. De Geus also demonstrates how German historians in general tended to adopt Herodotus's definition of a nation.

26. Raoul Naroll, "On Ethnic Unit Classification," *Current Anthropology* 5 (1964): 283–312.

27. Pliny, *Naturalis Historiae* V:73 (15:4).

28. H. G. Liddell and R. Scott, *A Greek-English Lexicon: A New Edition Revised and Augmented Throughout by H. S. Jones* (reprint, Oxford: Clarendon Press, 1961), 480.

29. This is not the place to discuss the elusive term of "tribe." On this I can refer to my *Early Israel: Anthropological and Historical Studies on the Israelite Society before the Monarchy* (Leiden: E. J. Brill, 1985), 274–90, and the literature cited there. The Greek understanding of the word—in Greek φυλή or φῦλον—includes also "race." It is mostly used to describe a group of people presumably blood-related but is also used about the repeated but artificial political reorganizations of the populations of the Greek states into such φῦλαι. The word also carries connotations like "kind" or "sex" (male or female).

30. Charlton T. Lewis and Charles Short, *A Latin Dictionary* (1879; Oxford: Clarendon Press, 1962), 1189.

31. On the development of the idea of the nation, see also the convenient review by Uffe Østergård, "What Is National and Ethnic Identity?" in Per Bilde, Troels Engberg-Pedersen, Lise Hannestad, and Jan Zahle, eds., *Ethnicity in Hellenistic Egypt* (Århus: Aarhus University Press, 1992), 16–38. On industrialization and nationalism, Østergård, "What Is National and Ethnic Identity?" 18.

32. On the history of the national Czech movement, J.F.N. Bradley, *Czechoslovakia: A Short History* (Edinburgh: Edinburgh University Press, 1971), 119–39.

33. Anthropologists who participated in this "game" included scholars like Gregory Bateson and Margaret Mead; cf. G. Bateson, "Morale and National Character" (1942), in his *Steps to an Ecology of Mind: Collected Essays in Anthropology, Psychiatry, Evolution, and Epistemology* (San Francisco: Chandler, 1972), and Margaret Mead, *And Keep Your Powder Dry: An Anthropologist Looks at America* (New York: William Morrow & Co., 1942).

34. John Armstrong is emeritus professor of political science at the University of

Wisconsin. Main opus in this genre is *Nations before Nationalism* (Chapel Hill, N.C.: University of North Carolina Press, 1982). Anthony D. Smith is professor of sociology at the London School of Economics; among his works we may mention *Theories of Nationalism* (London: Gerald Duckworth, 1971), and *The Ethnic Origin of Nations* (Oxford: Basil Blackwell, 1986).

35. Cf. Anthony D. Smith, *The Ethnic Origin of Nations,* 11.

36. The legend about Naram-Sin is preserved in, respectively, a series of editions in Akkadian and one in Hittite. The Hittite version has been published by O. R. Gurney, "The Cuthaean Legend of Naram-Sin," *Anatolian Studies* 5 (1955): 93–113, the Akkadian ones by H. G. Güterbock, "Die historische Tradition in ihre literarischen Gestaltung bei Babyloniern und Hethitern bis 1200," *Zeitschrift für Assyriologie* 10 (1938): 49–59. All of them have been translated in B. R. Foster, ed., *Before the Muses: An Anthology of Akkadian Literature,* vols. 1 and 2 (Bethesda, Md.: D. L. Press, 1993), 1:257–69. This passage can be found in its neo-Assyrian version in Foster, *Before the Muses,* 1:265.

37. F. Barth, introduction to F. Barth, ed., *Ethnic Groups and Boundaries* (Oslo: Universitetsforlaget, 1969), 9–37.

38. In order to appreciate the central position of Barth's contribution, it is recommended to consult Hans Vermeulen and Cora Govers, *The Anthropology of Ethnicity: Beyond "Ethnic Groups and Boundaries"* (Amsterdam: Het Spinhuis, 1994), which includes a review of the discussion by Barth himself, "Enduring and Emerging Issues in the Analysis of Ethnicity," pp. 11–32.

39. E. E. Evans-Pritchard, *The Nuer: A Description of the Modes of Livelihood and Political Institutions of a Nilotic People* (Oxford: Clarendon Press, 1940).

40. Cf. A. Southall, "Nuer and Dinka Are People: Ecology, Ethnicity and Logical Possibility," *Man,* n.s., 11 (1976): 463–91.

41. The Baḫtiyari society has been described by Dieter Ehmann, *Baḫtiyāren— Persische bergnomaden im Wandel der Zeit* (Wiesbaden: Ludwig Reichert, 1975), and by Jean-Pierre Digard, *Techniques des nomades Baxtyari d'Iran* (Cambridge: Cambridge University Press, 1981).

42. Cf. Euan Cameron, *The Reformation of the Heretics: The Waldenses of the Alps, 1480–1580* (Oxford: Clarendon Press, 1984). Cf. also Malcolm D. Lambert, *Medieval Heresy: Popular Movements from Bogomil to Hus* (London: Edward Arnold, 1977).

43. An example of such relations between a village and a neighboring major city: the inhabitants of Tell Toqaan and their relationship to rich people from Aleppo; cf. Niels Peter Lemche, *Early Israel,* 172. This example is taken from Louise E. Sweet, *Tell Toqaan: A Syrian Village* (Ann Arbor, Mich.: University of Michigan Press, 1960). Generally on the relations between city and countryside, see Niels Peter Lemche, *Early Israel,* 164–201.

44. On tribal leaders in society, see Michael B. Rowton, "Dimorphic Structure and the Tribal Elite," in *al-bahit = Festschrift J. Henniger zum 70. Geburtstag am 12. Mai 1976* (St. Augustin bei Bonn: Studi Instituti Anthropos 28, 1976), 219–57.

45. Compare the list in Diana Edelman, "Ethnicity and Early Israel," in Mark G. Brett, ed., *Ethnicity and the Bible* (Leiden: E. J. Brill, 1996), 25–55. In her list of "ethnic markers" that relate to early Israel she includes pottery, architecture, site layout, diet, aniconism, social organization, and burial practices.

46. *Early Israel,* 242.

Chapter 1:
Playing the von Ranke Game

1. An inscription found on the Temple of August in Ankara, based on an official document authorized in the last year of August's reign (C.E. 14), partly based, however, on an earlier source, the *Res Gestae,* and edited before it was published. The inscription has been known since 1555.

2. Manetho's history goes back to Ptolemaic times, third century B.C.E. It is, however, only fragmentarily preserved in the works of Josephus (first century C.E.), Africanus (second century C.E.), and Eusebius (third and fourth centuries C.E.). The tale of the Hyksos is found in Josephus's *Contra Apionem* I:14. The fragments have been collected in *Manetho: With an English Translation by W.G. Waddell* (Cambridge, Mass.: Harvard University Press, and London: William Heinemann, 1980).

3. Saxo Grammaticus records the foundation of Copenhagen in his medieval chronicle *Gestae danorum.* Saxo lived to see this "foundation" happen. So far recording of the recent finds have been published only in Danish newspapers.

4. Thus Baruch Halpern is much too optimistic when he talks about Manetho being dependent on the biblical story of the exodus; cf. his "The Exodus from Egypt: Myth or Reality?" in Hershel Shanks, ed., *The Rise of Ancient Israel: Symposium at the Smithsonian Institution October 26, 1991* (Washington, D.C.: Biblical Archaeology Society, 1992), 87–113, esp. 92–93. Manetho's (and Josephus's) version (*Contra Apionem* I:14 §§73–92) is printed as fragment 42 in the edition by Waddell (see above, n. 2).

5. Published in 1650 in his *Annales Veteris Testamenti.*

6. Fragments found in caves 1 and 4. On the most comprehensive of these (4QSam^a), and by Frank Moore Cross once considered probably the oldest manuscript from Qumran ("The Oldest Manuscript from Qumran," *JBL* 74 [1955]: 147–72, see the comprehensive study by Eugene C. Ulrich, *The Qumran Text of Samuel and Josephus* (Chico, Calif.: Scholars Press, 1978).

7. See Chap. 2 below on the so-called "Bet David" inscription from Tel Dan.

8. Josephus, *Jewish History,* 2:10.

9. Cf., however, Moses' Ethiopian wife, Numbers 12:1. The Old Testament never says when and how this marriage happened.

10. The inscription of Idrimi was published by Sydney Smith, *The Statue of Idrimi* (London: British Institute of Archaeology in Ankara, 1949). It is easily available in English translations by A. Leo Oppenheim in *ANET,* 557–58, and by Tremper Longman in William W. Hallo and K. Lawson Younger, eds., *The Context of Scripture,* vol. I., *Canonical Compositions from the Biblical World* (Leiden: E. J. Brill, 1997), 479–80. One author, Jack Sasson, has questioned the date of the inscription and considers it a later commemoration of the founder of the ruling dynasty of Mukish; cf. his "On Idrimi and Šarruwa, the Scribe," in A. M. Morrison and D. I. Owen, eds., *Nuzi and the Hurrians* (Winona Lake, Ind.: Eisenbrauns, 1981), 309–24.

11. Cf. esp. Mario Liverani, "Partire sul carro, per il deserto," *Annali dell'Istituto Universitario Orientale di Napoli,* n.s., 22 (1972): 403–15.

12. Two examples: Livy, in his description of the fighting at Fidenae against the Veientes, mentions some historians who have argued that ships should have participated in the battle. Livy distances himself from this assumption with a reference to the nature of the landscape (*History of Rome* 4.34). Very entertaining is Herodotus's

dismissal of the idea that snow should be found in Ethiopia and melting snow should account for the rise of the Nile (*Histories* II:21).

13. Fundamental to the interpretation of historical documents from ancient times is Mario Liverani, "Memorandum on the Approach to Historiographic Texts," *Orientalia*, n.s., 42 (1973): 178–94. Liverani has published many exquisite examples of literary analysis of such documents. To be especially recommended are his studies in Hittite history writing: "Storiografia politica hittita—I: Shunashshura, ovvero: Della reciprocità," *Oriens Antiquus* 12 (1973): 267–97, and "Storiografia politica hittita—II: Telipinu, ovvero: Della Solidarietà," *Oriens Antiquus* 16 (1977): 105–31.

14. Cf. Elmar Edel, "KBO I 15+19, ein Brief Ramses' II, mit einer Schilderung der Kadeschschlacht," *ZA* 48 (1949): 208–9 (verso. 26). The whole problematic character of the relationship between the two great monarchs of Hatti and Egypt is laid open in Liverani's analysis of the correspondence, in his "Hattushili alle prese con la propaganda ramesside," *Orientalia*, n.s., 59 (1990): 207–17.

15. Another example of historical recollections that are not "historical" in the proper sense of the word because they have no historical context could be the idea of the great kingdom of David and Solomon (a reflection of another period?). It could also be the information that the Israelites worked on Pithom and Rameses (Ex. 1:11), and that the immigration only touched Benjaminite territory. Cf. my "Is It Still Possible to Write a History of Ancient Israel?" *SJOT* 8 (1994): 163–88.

16. Published by D. J. Wiseman, *Chronicles of Chaldean Kings (626–556 B.C.) in the British Museum* (London: The Trustees of the British Museum, 1956). The preserved part of the Chronicle covers the period from 626–594 B.C.E. and 557–556 B.C.E.

17. Cf. F. H. Cryer on Jerusalem in 587 B.C.E., in his "To the One of Fictive Music: OT Chronology and History," *SJOT* 1:2 (1997): 1–27, see esp. 19–25.

18. The "Grundschrift" about this is evidently Eduard Nielsen, *Oral Tradition: A Modern Problem in Old Testament: Introduction* (London: SCM Press, 1954). On this Scandinavian tradition, Douglas A. Knight, *Rediscovering the Tradition of Israel: The Development of the Traditio-Historical Research of the Old Testament, with Special Considerations of the Scandinavian Contribution*, rev. ed. (Missoula, Mont.: Scholars Press, 1975).

19. On oral tradition—apart from Nielsen, already mentioned—cf. now Susan Niditsch, *Oral World and Written Word: Ancient Israelite Literature* (Louisville, Ky.: Westminster John Knox Press, 1996).

20. In order to include three "generations" of scholars related in this view: William F. Albright, *Yahweh and the Gods of Canaan: A Historical Analysis of Two Contrasting Faiths* (London: Athlone Press, 1968), esp. chap. 1, "Verse and Prose in Early Israelite Tradition," 1–46; Frank M. Cross, *Canaanite Myth and Hebrew Epic: Essays in the Religion of Israel* (Cambridge, Mass.: Harvard University Press, 1975); and Ronald S. Hendel, *The Epic of the Patriarch. The Jacob Cycle and the Narrative Traditions of Canaan and Israel* (Atlanta: Scholars Press, 1987).

21. With reference to the last-mentioned event in the Deuteronomistic History, 2 Kings 25:27–30, the release of King Jehoichin from prison after the death of Nebuchadnezzar, an event that happened in 562 B.C.E. Cf. also below on the Babylonian evidence.

22. Very much in the same fashion as in New Testament scholarship the everlasting quest for the ipsissima verba of Christ, supposed to have been preserved in *logia* collections.

23. 2 Kings 16:5.

24. As a general introduction to these developments, see Colin Renfrew with P. Bahn, *Archaeology: Theories, Methods, and Practices,* 2d. ed. (London: Thames & Hudson, 1996). For social archaeology in Palestinian archaeology, cf. Thomas E. Levy, *The Archaeology of Society in the Holy Land* (London: Leicester University Press, 1995).

25. The term "proto-Israelite," which has become common in recent research, may as its forerunner have such ideas as the "protohistory" of Israel. This is probably the best translation of the notion of *"Frühgeschichte,"* applied by Abraham Malamat in his study, "Die Frühgeschichte Israels—eine methodologische Studie," *ThZ* 39 (1983): 1–16, meaning something that is not yet quite history, only a "protohistory." Thus "proto-Israelites" are "Israelites" who did not yet make it as Israelites. According to William G. Dever "proto-Israel is not the same as the 'all Israel' of the later monarchical period [Dever, as a matter of fact, means the "ancient Israelites" of the Old Testament]. . . . These are the progenitors of the later people" (Dever in discussion published in Shanks, ed., *The Rise of Ancient Israel,* 154). We must, however, feel obliged to ask Dever why and how the Israelites in the days of Mernephtah were less Israelite than the later Israelites living in Palestine, say six hundred years later? Is it only that they were less "biblical Israelites"?

26. On this further below. Cf. also my *The Canaanites and Their Land: The Idea of Canaan in the Old Testament* (Sheffield: JSOT Press, 1991).

27. Cf. Yigael Shiloh, "The Four-Room-House—The Israelite Type-House?" *Eretz Israel* 11 (1973): 277–85.

28. Cf. William F. Albright, *The Archaeology of Palestine* (1949; rev. ed., Harmondsworth, Middlesex: Penguin Books, 1960), 118–19. Cf. on the background of Albright's ascription of this ceramic type to the Israelites (something which in the palaver of archaeologists occurred one afternoon in 1929 during a visit to the Danish excavations at Shiloh), Douglas L. Esse, "The Collared Rim Store Jar: Scholarly Ideology and Ceramic Typology," *SJOT* 5:2 (1991): 99–116, esp. 99–103.

29. C. G. Feilberg, *La tente noire: Contribution ethnographique à l'histoire culturelle des nomades* (Copenhagen: Nationalmuseet, 1944).

30. See also the pertinent remarks on this by Kenneth W. Schaar, "The Architectural Traditions of Building 23A/13 at Tell Beit Mirsim," *SJOT* 5:2 (1991): 75–98, who considers the development of this house form in the Early Iron period a kind of compromise between two older house types with a pedigree going back into the Bronze Age.

31. This was already pointed out by Ruth Amiran in her *Ancient Pottery of the Holy Land* (New Brunswick. NJ.: Rutgers University Press, 1970), 232–33. Her discussion of the development of storage jars from the Late Bronze Age to the Early Iron Age, however, seems less than clear.

32. Discussion in, among other places, Israel Finkelstein, *The Archaeology of the Israelite Settlement* (Jerusalem: Israel Exploration Society, 1988), 275–85 (see his recent update in "Pots and Peoples Revisited: Ethnic Boundaries in the Iron Age I," in Neil Asher Silberman and David Small, eds., *The Archaeology of Israel: Constructing the Past, Interpreting the Present* [Sheffield: Sheffield Academic Press, 1997], 216–37, esp. 224–25); Douglas L. Esse, "The Collared Pithos at Megiddo: Ceramic Distribution and Ethnicity," *JNES* 51 (1992): 81–103 (an expanded version of his article in *SJOT* 5:2 [see n. 28 above]); and in a discussion about ethnicity: David B. Small,

"Group Identification and Ethnicity in the Construction of the Early State of Israel: From the Outside Looking In," in Silberman and Small, *The Archaeology of Israel*, 271–88. Recent debate includes the attribution of the type to the introduction of the camel as the carrier animal, cf. Michal Artzy, "Incense, Camels and Collared Rim Jars: Desert Trade Routes and Maritime Outlets in the Second Millennium," *Oxford Journal of Archaeology* 13 (1994): 121–47. It could also be considered as evidence of an Egyptian taxation system; cf. David Wengrow, "Egyptian Taskmasters and Heavy Burdens: Highland Exploitation and the Collared-Rim Pithos of the Bronze-Iron Age Levant," *Oxford Journal of Archaeology* 15 (1996): 307–26.

33. Hazor in upper Galilee is a exception to the general small scale of Palestinian cities. Hazor is the only major tell in Palestine comparable to the tells of Syria. The size of the population may vary according to the method of reckoning, but it will be a safe guess that at the height of its wealth this city counted perhaps no less than 25,000 inhabitants. In many aspects Hazor should probably not be reckoned a Palestinian settlement; it might be closer to the cities of inner Syria. This applies to the situation in the Bronze Age. In the Iron Age, much of this changed, not least the size of the city, which was in the first millennium reduced to only a fraction of its former greatness. Information on Hazor can be obtained from Y. Yadin and Amnon Ben-Tor, "Hazor," in *NAEEHL* (New York: Simon & Schuster, 1993), 2:594–695; and Amnon Ben-Tor, "Hazor," in Eric Meyers, ed., *The Oxford Encyclopedia of Archaeology in the Ancient Near East* (Oxford and New York: Oxford University Press, 1997) 3:1–5.

34. Whether such a pentapolis really existed except as a scholarly theory is unknown. It is supposed to have included the cities of Gath, Ashkelon, Gaza, Ashdod, and Ekron.

35. I owe the information about the Philistine culture to my colleague John Strange. He is about to publish a review in Danish of the material basis for claiming the Philistines to be ethnically diverse from the main stock of the Palestinian population in the transition period between 1250 and 850 B.C.E., "Ethnicitet i Arkæologi: Filisterne som eksempel," in Niels Peter Lemche and Henrik Tronier, eds., *Etnicitet og Bibel* (Copenhagen: Museum Tusculanum, 1998).

Chapter 2: Israel in Contemporary Historical Documents from the Ancient Near East

1. Published by W. Spiegelberg, "Der Siegeshymnus des Merneptah auf der Flinders Petrie-Stele," *Zeitschrift für ägyptischen Sprache und Altertumskunde* 34 (1896): 1–25.

2. *ANET,* 378.

3. The literature on this inscription is extensive. A review of the discussion until the 1970s in Hartmut Engel, "Die Siegesstele des Merenptah," *Biblica* 60 (1979): 373–399. Subsequent contributions include Erik Hornung, "Die Israelstele des Merenptah," in Manfred Görg, ed., *Fontes atque pontes: Eine Festgabe für Hellmut Brunner* (Wiesbaden: Otto Harrassowitz, 1983), 224–33; Gösta W. Ahlström and Diana Edelman, "Merneptah's Israel," *JNES* 44 (1985): 59–61; Lawrence E. Stager, "Merneptah, Israel and Sea Peoples: New Light on an Old Relief," *Eretz Israel* 18 (1985): 56–64; Itamar Singer, "Merneptah's Campaign to Canaan and the Egyptian

Occupation of the Southern Coastal Plain of Palestine in the Ramesside Period," *BASOR* 269 (1988): 1–10; Volkmar Fritz, *Die Entstehung Israels im 12. und 11. Jahrhundert v. Chr.* (Stuttgart: W. Kohlhammer, 1996), 73–75, and Manfred Görg, *Die Bezeihungen zwischen den alten Israel und Ägypten: Von den Anfängen bis zum Exil* (Darmstadt: Wissenschaftliche Buchgesellschaft, 1997), 58–63.

4. Of special interest are the letters concerning Labayu "the major of Shechem" and ÌR-Ḥeba's letters from Jerusalem, EA 237, 244–46, 249–50, 252–53, 155, 263, 280, and EA 285–290, respectively. ÌR-Ḥeba also mentions Labayu, EA 287 and 289.

5. Why pictorial representations should be more trustworthy than textual references goes beyond my comprehension, but the argument of Frank Yurco (see following note) has been accepted by scholars of the caliber of Gösta W. Ahlström; see his *The History of Ancient Palestine from the Palaeolithic Period to Alexander's Conquest: With a Contribution by Gary O. Rollefson,* edited by Diana Edelman (Sheffield: Sheffield Academic Press, 1993), 284.

6. Cf. Frank J. Yurco, "Merenptah's Palestinian Campaign," *The Society for the Study of Egyptian Journal* 8 (1982): 189–215. Cf. also his recent contribution, "Merenptah's Canaanite Campaign and Israel's Origins," in Ernest S. Frerichs and Leonard H. Lesko, eds., *Exodus: The Egyptian Evidence* (Winona Lake, Ind.: Eisenbrauns, 1997), 27–56.

7. The epithet given to Merenptah in an inscription from Amada as the "subduer of Gezer" (Kenneth Kitchen, *Ramesside Inscriptions,* vols. 4, 9 [Oxford: Basil Blackwell, 1982); cf. also Görg, *Die Beziehungen,* 61. The pedigree of the discussion of this inscription among scholars has been confusing, as it is sometimes mixed up with the Amada stele, going back to Amenhotep II. Thus, mistakenly, Gösta W. Ahlström, *Who Were the Israelites?* (Winona Lake, Ind.: Eisenbrauns, 1986), 38. Cf., however, Alan H. Gardiner, *Egypt of the Pharaohs. An Introduction* (Oxford: Clarendon Press, 1961), 273, and R. O. Faulkner, in *CAH* II:2, p.234.

8. In hieroglyphs 〔hieroglyphs〕; transcribed *ja-si₅-'ā-l* (there is no distinction between *-l-* and *-r-* in hieroglyphic writing) by W. Helck, *Die Beziehungen Ägyptens zu Vorderasien im 3. und 2. Jahrtausend v.Chr.* (Wiesbaden: Otto Harrassowitz, 1962), 240. In *Lexikon der Ägyptologie,* vol. 3, ed. Wolfgang Huck and Wolfhart Westendorf (Wiesbaden: Otto Harrassowitz, 1980), 205: *ja-si-r-é-l<a>*).

9. Ahlström, *History,* 285 n. 2.

10. Cf. Ahlström and Edelman in *JNES* 44 (1985): 59–61, and Ahlström in *Who Were the Israelites?* 39, and finally *History,* 284–85.

11. On Gaza as Canaan, Lemche, *The Canaanites and Their Land,* 48–49. Thus also Görg, *Beziehungen,* 60.

12. The Hittite kingdom may have survived the turn of the century 1300 B.C.E. with only a few years; cf. the review of the end of the Hittite kingdom in Oliver R. Gurney, *The Hittites* (reprint with revisions; London; Penguin Books, 1990), 30–32; and in J. G. Macqueen, "The History of Anatolia and of the Hittite Empire: An Overview," in *CANE* 4: 1085–1105, esp. 1097.

13. For example, in his article on Gezer, in *ABD* 2: 1001. He believes stratum XV to have been the victim of Merneptah's aspirations, in contrast to the only vaguely present stratum XIV, whose destruction he reckons to be the handiwork of the Philistines. In his entries on Gezer in *The Oxford Encyclopedia of Archaeology* 2: 396–401, esp. 398, he attributes the end of stratum XIV to Merneptah based on the

evidence of field II. In *NAEEHL* 2: 496–506, esp. 504, he claims that the end of these strata presents a problem; especially the Philistine connection seems doubtful as nothing combines the Philistines with any destruction around 1200 B.C.E.

14. By a Bedouin boy looking for his father's sheep. This tale has been retold again and again and accepted without being questioned. It is, however—despite that it might be true—too close to allow us to be comfortable to tales like the one about King Saul, who as a young boy went out to look for his father's donkeys but found a kingdom.

15. This is not the place to discuss the heated debate that followed the appearance of Michael Baigent and Richard Leigh's, *The Dead Sea Scrolls Deception* (London: Jonathan Cape, 1991), about the Dead Sea Scrolls and the provenience/lack of provenience in early Christianity.

16. The inscriptions were published with a commendable speed: the first one in Avraham Biran and Joseph Naveh, "An Aramaic Stele Fragment from Tel Dan," *IEJ* 43 (1993): 81–98; the two following fragments by the same authors, "The Tel Dan Inscription: A New Fragment," *IEJ* 45 (1995): 1–18.

17. The texts were joined already by Biran and Naveh, *IEJ* 45 (1995): 12–13, without indicating that there should be a safe join. However, other published illustrations of the stone slabs, like the one in *BAR* 23/24 (July/August 1997): 34, clearly present the texts as if the combination of them was already an established fact. In the present exhibition of the inscriptions at the Israel Museum in Jerusalem, the joint is presented as a fact and covered with a "protective" plaster!

18. A close inspection of the fragments shows first the lines of fragment A not to match the lines of fragments B2 and 3. Second, it also tells us that some of letters on fragment A are different in shape from the ones found in fragment B1 and B2—although from a paleographic point of view, all three fragments seem to belong within the same time horizon. The text of fragment A was evidently done by another engraver than the one of fragments B1 and 2. Cf. further on the paleography of the fragments, Frederick H. Cryer, "On the Recently-Discovered 'House of David' Inscription," *SJOT* 8 (1994): 3–19, and "King Hadad," *SJOT* 9 (1995): 223–35.

19. Cf. fragment B2 line 7, in Biran's and Naveh's reconstruction: [*Jeho*]*ram son* [*of Ahab*] and 8: [*Ahaz*]*yahu son*[*of Jehoram*].

20. The major Aramaic inscriptions of this period include the inscriptions of Zakkur of Hamath, from c. 800 B.C.E. (*KAI*, 202), of Panammuwa of Yauda from the middle of the eighth century B.C.E. (*KAI*, 214), of Barrakib from Yauda from the second half of the eighth century (*KAI*, 215–18), and finally, but not least, the treaty of Sfire from shortly after the middle of the eighth century B.C.E.

21. Compare fig. 1 in Joseph Naveh, *The Development of the Aramaic Script* (Jerusalem: The Israel Academy of Sciences and Humanities, 1970), or Ada Yardeni, *The Book of Hebrew Script: History, Palaeography, Script Styles, Caligraphy & Design* (Jerusalem: Carta, 1997), fig. 1 and fig. 14 referring to the Kilamuwa inscription, and p. 17 recording the Mesha style. The Mesha inscription definitely belongs within the Palestinian/Phoenician/Palestine context and not the Aramaic. It suffices to compare the respective form of the *taw* in Mesha and in Aramaic inscriptions.

22. Thus Josef Tropper, "Eine altaramäische Steleninschrift aus Dan," *UF* 25 (1993): 395–406.

23. Thus Cryer, *SJOT* 8:8–9. Cf. also Frederick H. Cryer, "Of Epistemology,

Northwest-Semitic Epigraphy and Irony: The '*BYRDWD*/House of David' Inscription Revisited," *JSOT* 69 (1996): 3–17.

24. Thus Giovanni Garbini, "L'iscrizione aramaica di Tel Dan," *Atti della Accademia Nazionale dei Lincei.* Anno CCCXCI (1994): 461–71.

25. Here we may mention the sad fact that the picture (by Avraham Biran) published by Biran and Naveh in *IEJ 43*, 82, fig. 1, claiming to show the fragment A in situ, was obviously not showing this item to be in situ. However, a photograph by Zev Radovan is said to show the text in its original place (*BAR* 23/24, July/August 1997, p. 35). One of the photos (the one in *BAR* 23/24?) seems, however, to be presented mirror-wise.

26. The Paraiba inscription is a relatively modern example of this. This is sometimes assumed to be a Phoenician inscription that was found in South America. The Paraiba inscription was still as late as the 1960s treated as genuine by a serious scholar, Lienhard Delekat; see his *Phönizier in Amerika: Ein Inschrift des 5. Jh. v. Chr. aus Brasilien in einer unbekannten semitischen Konsekutivtempussprache* (Bonn: Peter Hanstein Verlag, 1969). See also the rejection of this inscription as genuine by Edward Lipiński, "The Phoenicians," *CANE* II, 1321–1333, esp. 1331. Another example would be the so-called "Carian leather inscriptions" announced by William H. Brownlee and George E. Mendenhall, in the *Annual of the Department of Antiquities in Jordan* 15 (1970): 39–40 (pls. 73–75).

27. And should this not be enough, it will always be possible to present an extended reconstruction of the inscription. Compare for example the reconstruction proposed by the well-known French scholar Émile Puech, "La stèle araméenne de Dan: Bar Hadad II et la coalition des omrides et de la maison de David," *RB* 101 (1994): 215–41. Puech reconstructed a text that is at least 200 percent bigger than the original fragment A.

28. The closest parallel being the so-called "Northern Kingdom," Bît Ḥumriya, "the House of Omri" (on this see below). Other names include Bît Adini and Bît Gusi.

29. Cf. Ernst Axel Knauf, "*BaytDawīd* ou *BaytDōd*?" *BN* 72 (1994): 60–69. On the combination of titles and patronymics, *BaytDawīd* ou *BaytDōd*?: 66.

30. On Mesha, see especially the collection of studies published by Andrew Dearman, ed., *Studies in the Mesha Inscription and Moab* (Atlanta: Scholars Press, 1989). Additional literature includes John C. L. Gibson, *Textbook of Syrian Semitic Inscriptions,* vol. 1: *Hebrew and Moabite Inscriptions* (Oxford: Clarendon Press, 1971), 71–83, and Stefan Timm, *Die Dynastie Omri* (Göttingen: Vandenhoeck & Ruprecht, 1982), 158–71.

31. *KAI,* 14. Date shortly around 500 B.C.E. The "discovery" of the Mesha stele and early history of research is covered by M. Patrick Graham, "The Discovery and Reconstruction of the Mesha Inscription," in Dearman (ed.), *Studies in the Mesha Inscription,* 27–92.

32. The genuineness of the Mesha inscription was, furthermore, affirmed beyond any reasonable doubt by the discovery of a fragment of another inscription of this king at Kerak in Jordan. On this, see Gibson, *Textbook,* 1:83–84.

33. Omri reigned for twelve years (1 Kings 16:23), Ahab for twenty-two (1 Kings 16:29).

34. On the length of Omri's and Ahab's reigns and the forty years of Mesha's inscription, cf. Timm, *Die Dynastie Omri,* 162–65; also J. Andrew Dearman, "Historical

Reconstruction and the Mesha Inscription," in Dearman, ed., *Studies in the Mesha Inscription,* 153–210, esp. 164. Dearman accepts the obvious conclusion, that the "forty years" is a round number. So already Martin Noth, *Geschichte Israels* (Göttingen: Vandenhoeck & Ruprecht, 1950), 223.

35. Omri, by the way, was probably an Arab; cf. M. Noth, *Die israelitischen Personennamen in Rahmen der gemeinsemitischen Namengebung* (Stuttgart: W. Kohlhammer, 1928; reprint, Hildesheim: Georg Olms Verlagsbuchhandlung, 1966), 63. Also the name of Ahab is classified by Noth, same place, as probably of Arab origin. Cf. also Noth, *Geschichte,* 210.

36. Cf. on this Thomas L. Thompson, "'House of David': An Eponymic Referent to Yahweh as Godfather," *SJOT* 9 (1995): 59–74, esp. 63–66.

37. Cf. below on the Black Obelisk inscription, 52–53.

38. Which would be something of a catastrophe for the usual way of interpreting the paleographic history of inscriptions from the Levant. Most of the major inscriptions have been found either before scientific archaeology was initiated, or by sheer luck without any precise archaeological context (which is certainly the case of the Mesha inscription). They have often been dated because of imagined references to biblical persons. Very few inscriptions can be dated with absolute certainty. In Palestine the recently found inscription from Ekron (see S. Gitin, T. Dothan, and J. Naveh, "A Royal Dedicatory Inscription from Ekron," *IEJ* 47 [1997]: 1–16), can safely be dated on the basis of references to kings of Ekron also known from Sennacherib's and Asarhaddon's annals to the first part of the 7th century B.C.E.. This inscription may therefore serve as a pivotal point in the study of the paleographic development of Phoenician-paleo-Hebrew writing. This writer has been quoted as maintaining that this inscription could be a fake (See *BAR* 23/24 [July/August 1997]: 37). Its subsequent publication has certainly shown this opinion to be premature.

39. In Moabite ٦ﺍﻭﻪ ﻝﻙ٩ﻙ

40. On *'r'l* see the discussion in K. P. Jackson, "The Language of the Mesha'-inscription," in Dearman, ed., *Studies in the Mesha Inscription,* 96–130, esp. 112–113, and as a supplement to this the entry on אריאל in H. Donner, *Wilhelm Gesenius Hebräisches und Aramäisches Handwörterbuch über das Alte Testament* (18. Aufl.; Berlin, Heidelberg, New York, London, Paris, Tokyo: Springer-Verlag, 1987), 1:98. The interpretation "alter" depends on the expression *'ry'l** in Hezekiah 43:15.

41. The Hebrew root *dwd* has this meaning. Cf. further n. 44 below.

42. On Elhanan and David, L.M. von Pákozdy, "'Elḥånån—der frühe Name Davids?" *ZAW* 68 (1956): 257–59.

43. Cf. Chaim Tadmor, "Historical Implications of the Correct Reading of Akkadian *dâku,*" *JNES* 17 (1958): 129–41. Against Jackson in Dearman, ed., *Studies in the Mesha Inscription,* 113.

44. On the god Dod, Gösta W. Ahlström, *Psalm 89: Eine Liturgie aus dem Ritual des leidenden Königs* (Lund: C.W.K. Gleerups Förlag, 1959), 163–73. On Dod and Mesha, N. Na'aman, "King Mesha and the Foundation of the Moabite Monarchy," *IEJ* 47 (1997): 83–92. Na'aman talks about a god of the name of Daudoh.

45. On Lemaire and the restoration in line 34. A. Lemaire, "La dynastie davidique (Byt Dwd) dans deux inscriptions Ouest-Sémitiques de Iè S. Av. J.-C.," *Studi epigraphici e linguistici* 11 (1994): 17–19, and "'House of David' Restored in Moabite

Inscription," *BAR* 20/23 (1994): 30–37. Absolutely justified criticism of this interpretation can be found in Na'aman, *IEJ* 47: 89.

46. Collections in *KAI*, 183–88, and Gibson, *Textbook* 1:5–13, and complete discussion in Johannes Renz, *Handbuch der althebräischen Epigraphik*, I, II/1, III (Darmstadt: Wissenschaftliche Buchgesellschaft, 1995). André Lemaire accepted these scattered inscriptions to be evidence of an extensive literacy in Palestine in the Iron Age, *Les écoles et la formation de la Bible dans l'ancien Israël* (Fribourg: Éditions universitaires; Göttingen: Vandenhoeck & Ruprecht, 1981).

47. The situation of Tel Jezreel can be considered more typical than the reverse. Here after seven years of excavations only one absolutely insignificant example of a Hebrew text was found, no more than a few incomprehensible signs incised on an ostracon. It had no stratigraphic context, but probably dates from the ninth century. Cf. David Ussishkin and John Woodhead, "Excavations at Tel Jezreel 1994–1996: Third Preliminary Report," *Tel Aviv* 24 (1997): 6–72, esp. 63.

48. Literature on Samaria Ostraca: published by G. Reisner, C. S. Fisher, and D. G. Lyon, *Harvard Excavations at Samaria,* vols. 1 and 2 (Cambridge, Mass.: Harvard University Press, 1908–10), 1:227–46; 2:plate 55. See also the lengthy article by Ivan T. Kaufman, "Samaria (Ostraca)," *ABD* 5:921–26. Indispensable for the study of these texts is Renz, *Handbuch* 1, 79–110.

49. On the *le-melek impressions* and the *rosetta* impressions from the seventh century B.C.E. Peter Welten, *Die Königs-Stempel: Ein Beitrag zur militärpolitik Judas unter Hiskia und Josia* (Wiesbaden: Otto Harrassowitz, 1969). On the Rosette variation, Jane M. Cahill, "Rosette Stamp Seal Impressions from Ancient Judah," *IEJ* 45 (1995): 232–52. Cf. also the discussion in Amihai Mazar, *Archaeology of the Land of the Bible 10,000–586 B.C.E.* (New York: Doubleday, 1990), 455–58.

50. Cf. my "From Patronage Society to Patronage Society," in Volkmar Fritz and Philip R. Davies, eds., *The Origins of the Israelite States* (Sheffield: Sheffield Academic Press, 1996), 106–20. On the system of royal farms in Ugarit, see Mario Liverani, "Economia delle fattorie palatine ugaritiche," *Dialoghi di Archeologia* n.s. 1 (1979): 57–72.

51. *KAI* 189. Cf. now Renz, *Handbuch* 1:178–89.

52. John Rogerson and Philip R. Davies, "Was the Siloam Tunnel Built by Hezekiah?" *BA* 59 (1996): 138–49.

53. Literature on Yavneh Yam (or Meṣad hašavyāhū). The ostracon was published by Joseph Naveh, "A Hebrew Letter from the Seventh Century B.C.," *IEJ* 10 (1960): 129–39. Cf. further *KAI* (no. 200) 2:199–201; Gibson, *Textbook* 1:26–30; and esp. in Renz, *Handbuch* 1:315–29.

54. Literature on the Gezer calendar, Renz, *Handbuch* 1:30–37. Most often this text is dated to the tenth century, without qualifications, although the exact stratigraphy surrounding its discovery may be less than clear (found by Macalister at the beginning of this century, announced in *PEFQS* 1908: 271). The dating to the tenth century was done by Mark Lidzbarski, "An Old Calendar-Inscription from Gezer," *PEFQS* 1909: 26–29, solely on the basis of paleography.

55. The ostraca from Samaria have been collected in Renz, *Handbuch* 1:40–47, 67–74, 111–122, 145–165, 290–306, 347–403. This collection ranges from the late ninth century to the beginning of the sixth century B.C.E., probably with a slip in the first half of the seventh century B.C.E. The *kittim* at Arad: cf. Ostracon 2, 4, 7, 8, 10,

11, 14, and 17. These ostraca mostly deal with delivery of foodstuff to these *kittim*. They belong to the last phase of Iron Age Arad.

56. On the Lachish letters, date, situation, literature, see Renz, *Handbuch* 1:405–27. Although the name of Shallum is well known from the Old Testament—about fourteen different persons including a son of King Josiah who succeeded his father for a few months in 609/608 B.C.E. carry this name—the Shallum of Lachish letter 3, the son of Jaddua, is not among them. The name of the prophet who appears in the same letter and perhaps also in Lachish letter 6 is sometimes believed to be Jeremiah. This is a gratuitous guess, no more than a clear expression of the mania of scholars for finding biblical references among the inscriptions from Palestine and its neighboring countries.

57. J. H. Tigay, *You Shall Have No Other Gods. Israelite Religion in the Light of Hebrew Inscriptions* (Atlanta: Scholars Press, 1986).

58. Cf. the relevant criticism in Tilde Binger, *Asherah: Goddesses in Ugarit, Israel and the Old Testament* (Sheffield: Sheffield Academic Press, 1997), 30–35.

59. In the books of Samuel, Saul's son is called Ishbosheth ("the shameful man") in the KJV, "bosheth" being a pejorative of Ba'al. The correct form is found in 1 Chron. 8:33.

60. The god Shalem is known from the Ugaritic texts. It has been proposed to see the name of this god also as part of the city name of Jerusalem. The Akkadian form of Jerusalem as found in the Amarna letters of ÌR-Ḫeba of Jerusalem, *Urušalim*, might have been understood as "the city of Shalem," the element uru- being otherwise orthographically identical with the ideogram for city, in Akkadian *alu*, the Sumerian URU. In ÌR-Ḫeba's letters the writing of the name is, however, ^{URU}u-ru-$ša_{10}$-lim (EA 287:25; cf. also 287:38, 46, 61, 63; 289:14, 29; 290:15), meaning that the (false) etymology has not been understood or accepted by the scribe who wrote these letters.

61. Cf. Gibson, *Textbook* 1:36–37.

62. In spite of justified criticism (see above), there should be no doubt that the intentions of J. Tigay in his discussion of personal names point in the right direction. Important information can be obtained about the religion of the bearers of theophoric names, provided that the statistics are corrected and adjusted to the material presented by the inscriptions.

63. In general on the Samaria Ostraca, cf. now Renz, *Handbuch* 1:79–109. The name *'glyw* means "The calf of Yahweh" or simply "Yahweh the calf" (Samaria ostracon 41), cf. Gibson, 12. The calf, normally the attribute of the god Ba'al, could here mean either that the divine calf (alias Ba'al) is the son of Yahweh—as Ba'alu in the Ugaritic pantheon is the son of Ilu (El)—or that Yahweh is the calf, i.e., Ba'al.

64. Cf. in the Sfire inscriptions *KAI*, 222, A 11 in a listing of pairs of divinities lined up together with the god El (𐤋𐤏𐤋𐤉𐤍 𐤅𐤒𐤃𐤌 𐤀𐤋 "before El and Elyon"). Also to be included here is the famous passage in Deut. 32:8–9 where in the rendering of the Septuagint the Most High, Greek ὁ ὕψιστος is distributing the nations among the gods, and Yahweh is given Israel as his share.

65. Noth on Gad: "Gilead und Gad," *ZDPV* 75 (1959): 14–73 = *ABLAK* 1:489–543, 533–43. Cf also his *Geschichte,* 63, n. 2.

66. Urs Winter, *Frau und Göttin: Exegetische und ikonographische Studien zum weiblischen Gottesbild im Alten Testament und in dessen Umwelt* (Freiburg, Schweiz:

Universitätsverlag, and Göttingen: Vandenhoeck & Ruprecht, 1983). Cf. also Silvia Schroer, *In Israel Gab es Bilder: Nachrichten von darstellender Kunst in Alten Testament* (Fribourg: Universitätsverlag, and Göttingen: Vandenhoeck & Ruprecht, 1987); Othmar Keel and Christoph Ühlinger, *Göttinnen, Götter und Göttersymbole: Neue Erkenntnisse zur Religionsgeschichte Kanaan und Israel aufgrund bislang unerschlossener ikonographischen Quellen* (Fribourg: Herder, 1992).

67. Kuntillet ʿAjrud: Renz, *Handbuch* 1:59–64.

68. Khirbet el-Qom: Renz, *Handbuch* 1:202–11.

69. Compare Judith M. Hadley, "The Khirbet el-Qom Inscription," *VT* 37 (1987): 50–62, and Judith M. Hadley, "Yahweh and 'His Asherah': Archaeological and Textual Evidence for the Cult of the Goddess," in Walter Dietrich and Martin A. Klopfenstein, eds., *Ein Gott allein? JHWH-Verehrung und biblischer Monotheismus im Kontext der israelitischen und altorientalischen Religionsgeschichte* (Freiburg: Universitätsverlag, 1994), 235–68, 242–45. Now also Renz, *Handbuch* 1:207–10.

70. Zeev Meshel, "Two Aspects in the Excavation of Kuntillet ʿAğrud," in Dietrich and Klopfenstein, eds., *Ein Gott allein?* 99–104, esp. 99.

71. On Asherah in the Bible, cf. Binger, *Asherah,* 110–41.

72. The most "famous" supporter of this goddess may be the notorious Abdi-Ashirta, king of Amurru, and known from the Amarna letters. On his name see Richard S. Hess, *Amarna Personal Names* (Winona Lake, Ind.: Eisenbrauns, 1993), 7–9.

73. The KJV is of no help here: "And he brought out the grove from the house of the LORD." Compare REB, "He took the Ashera from the house of the Lord."

74. Cf. on the development toward a practical monotheism in the ancient Near East, Herbert Niehr, *Der höchste Gott: Alttestamentlicher YHWH-Glaube im Kontext syrisch-kanaanäischer Religion des 1. Jahrtausends v. Chr.* (Berlin: Walter de Gruyter, 1990). Criticism of the way the concept of monotheism is used when applied to the religious situation in the ancient Near East has been delivered by Fritz Stolz, "Der Monotheismus Israels im Kontext der altorientalischen Religionsgeschichte—Tendenzen neuerer Forschung," in Dietrich and Klopfenstein, eds., *Ein Gott allein?* 33–50. Cf. also Fritz Stolz, *Einführung in den biblischen Monotheismus* (Darmstadt: Wissenschaftliche Buchgesellschaft, 1996).

75. Monolith inscription, Luckenbill *AR* 1 § 611; *ANET,* 278–79.

76. A list of the absolute dates and a discussion of their importance for the chronology of the ninth through sixth centuries B.C.E. can be found in the article by Mordechai Cogan, "Chronology," in *ABD* 1:1002–11, esp. 1007.

77. There are two references to Jehu's tribute: Luckenbill, *AR* 1:§ 672; *ANET,* 280 (Shalmaneser III's eighteenth year), and the "Black Obelisk" inscription, Luckenbill, *AR* 1:§ 590; *ANET,* 281.

78. Luckenbill, *AR* §§ 739–40; *ANET,* 281. In this inscription Palestine is written *pa-la-as-tu,* without any indication that it is restricted to the territory of the Philistines. Cf. also his annals from his regnal year 5: Luckenbill *AR* § 734; *ANET,* 82.

79. Cf. his "Rimah-stele," published by S. Page, "A Stela of Adad-Nirari III and Nergal ereš from Tell al Rimah," *Iraq* 30 (1968): 139–63; trans. in J. Maxwell Miller and John H. Hayes, *A History of Ancient Israel and Judah* (Philadelphia: Westminster Press, 1986), 299.

80. *Me-ni-ḫi-im-me* ᵁᴿᵁ*Sa-me-ri-na-a-a* . . . *ANET,* 283 (lines 150–157).

81. Luckenbill, *AR* 1:§§ 815–16; *ANET,* 283–84.

82. Luckenbill, *AR* 1:§§ 815–16; *ANET,* 284. These events of Tiglath-pileser's life are reflected by the Old Testament, 2 Kings 15:27–30; 17:1–2, however, without recognizing that Hoshea was installed by the Assyrian king.

83. Cf. Luckenbill, *AR* 2:§ 99; *ANET,* 284; *AR* 2:§ 5; *ANET,* 285.

84. On the problems concerning the destruction of Samaria: Bob Becking, *The Fall of Samaria: An Historical and Archaeological Study* (Leiden: E. J. Brill, 1992).

85. Sargon on the destruction of Samaria: Luckenbill *AR* 2:§ 5; *ANET,* 284–85.

86. By this I do not say that the Mesha inscription should be dated as late as the end of the eighth century. In this place I shall only indicate that it might, from a methodological point of view, be precarious to use the Mesha inscription to date other inscriptions like the one from Tel Dan.

87. Luckenbill, *AR* 1:§ 801; *ANET,* 282.

88. Luckenbill, *AR* 1:§ 770; *ANET,* 282.

89. Sennacherib *ante portas:* Luckenbill, *AR* 2:§§ 239–40; *ANET,* 287–88. Sennacherib is applying traditional imagery: the bird in the cage is a beloved motif, used, for example, several times in Rib-Adda's correspondence among the Amarna letters, EA 74:45–47; 78:13; 79:35, etc., to describe his situation as "beleaguered" in his own city.

90. Luckenbill, *AR* 2:§ 195.

91. *ANET,* 291.

92. *Luckenbill, AR* 2:§ 876; *ANET,* 294.

93. 10 mina of silver . . . from LÚ.MEŠ ᴷᵁᴿ*Ia-ú-da-a-a, ANET,* 301.

94. Dennis J. Wiseman, *Chronicles of the Chaldaean Kings (626–556 B.C.) in the British Museum:* B.M. 21946 rev. 11–13 (pp. 72–73). Jerusalem is not named but described as ᵁᴿᵁ*ia-a-ḫu-du*. This part is also translated in *ANET,* 564.

95. List over deliveries to Jehoiachin: *ANET,* 308. This document has been compared to the note in 2 Kings 25:27–30, about the release of Jehoiachin from prison after the death of Nebuchadnezzar in 562 B.C.E. and future entertainment at the royal court. This may be correct, but in that case the status of Jehoachin as being kept alive by deliveries from the royal court seems to have predated the death of Nebuchanezzar.

96. The Assyrian use of the term "Palestine" is not always clear. Sometimes it seems to be a general reference to the city-states on the coastal plain, other times a more general one. They never, however, reckon "the House of Omri" as part of this Palestine.

97. On the Greek—written *ia-ma-ni,* "the Ionian"—in Sargon's inscriptions, cf. Luckenbill, *AR* 2:§§ 79–80; *ANET,* 285; Luckenbill, *AR* 2:§ 30; *ANET,* 286, and Luckenbill, *AR* 2:§ 5; *ANET,* 287.

98. According to the estimate followed by W. J. Murnane, "The History of Ancient Egypt: An Overview," in *CANE* 2:691–717, esp. 714, which for this period is identical with the one in A. Gardiner, *Egypt of the Pharaohs,* 448. The chronology is one of the many problems connected with the Twenty-second Dynasty (thus Donald B. Redford gives the date of Shosheng's reign as 931–910, *ABD* 5:1221). See also the reconstruction of the period in Kenneth A. Kitchen, *The Third Intermediary Period in Egypt (1100–650 B.C.)* (Warminster: Aris & Phillips, 1973), 85–122, and 287–361. The various reconstructions of the Egyptian chronology in the tenth century have, however, been criticized by Giovanni Garbini, *History & Ideology in Ancient Israel* (Lon-

don: SCM Press, 1988), 29–30, for being based partly on the problematic biblical chronology of the early period of the monarchy. Cf. also J. Alberto Soggin, *An Introduction to the History of Israel and Judah* (London: SCM Press, 1993), 207–8. Cf. also Kitchen, *Third Intermediary Period,* 72, who opens his discussion of the chronology of this period with the "synchronism" between Shoshenq and Rehoboam, which accepts the biblical evidence at face value.

99. According to the *kětîb* (the consonant text), the name is שׁישׁק; the Egyptian form is *Ššnq.* Manetho has *Sesonkhosis;* see Kitchen, *Third Intermediary Period,* 73 n. 356. There are altogether five pharaohs of this name ranging from the tenth century to the middle of the eighth century.

100. On the list and its itinerary cf., among others, J. Simons, *Handbook for the Study of Egyptian Topographical Lists Relating to Western Asia* (Leiden: E. J. Brill, 1937), 89–101; Martin Noth, "Die Wege der Pharaonenheere in Palästina und Syrien: Untersuchungen zu den hieroglyphischen Listen palästinischer und syrischer Städte," 4: "Die Schoschenkliste," *ZDPV* 61 (1938): 277–304 (= *ABLAK* 2:73–93). See further Siegfried Herrmann, "Operationen Pharao Schoschenks I. Im östlichen Ephraim," *ZDPV* 80 (1964): 55–79. Cf. also the discussion of the list and its implications in Kitchen, *Third Intermediary Period,* 294–300. A fragment of an inscription of Shoshenq from Megiddo (C. S. Fisher, *The Excavations of Armageddon* [Chicago: University of Chicago Press], 1929, 12–4 and figs. 7 and 9) has been taken as a proof that this campaign really happened.

101. On Jeroboam's shift of capital, see for example Noth, *Geschichte,* 211. A more critical position can be found in Herbert Donner, *Geschichte des Volkes Israel und seiner Nachbarn in grundzügen* (Göttingen: Vandenhoeck & Ruprecht, 1986), 2:241, who correctly sees no problem in a king having several residences.

102. Thus if we were to follow the chronology of, e.g., J. H. Hayes and P. K. Hooker, *A New Chronology for the Kings of Israel and Judah* (Atlanta: John Knox, 1988), 16, dating the ascension of Rehoboam to 926 B.C.E. Other systems place this event in 931/930, thus K. T. Andersen, "Noch einmal: Die Chronologie von Israel und Juda," *SJOT* 3:1 (1989): 1–45, esp. 42.

103. Examples of how scholars generally deal with the missing mentioning of Jerusalem: Noth, *Geschichte,* 219; Ahlström, *History of Palestine,* 555; Soggin, *An Introduction to the History,* 208, who is merely paraphrasing the Old Testament. None of these scholars takes into consideration the character of the inscription, including exaggerations, traditional language, boasting. Had Judah been a consolidated state and had it submitted to Shoshenq during his campaign to Palestine, it is safe to assume that Judah and its capital would have been included among the conquered localities mentioned by Shoshenq. The note in 1 Kings 14:25–26 on this campaign and Rehoboam's tribute should rather be attributed to the biblical historian who knew about the tradition of Shoshenq's campaign and had to answer the question: What happened to Judah? It is probably invented history, eventually based on the information about Hezekiah's tribute.

104. On this, Raymond Westbrook, "Biblical and Cuneiform Law Codes," *RB* 92 (1985): 247–64. A detailed comparison between cuneiform and biblical law was published by Shalom M. Paul, *Studies in the Book of the Covenant in the Light of Cuneiform and Biblical Law* (Leiden: E. J. Brill, 1970). On the character of cuneiform written law, see below.

105. The English-speaking public is in possession of several adequate translations

of the Ugaritic epic literature: J.C.L. Gibson, *Canaanite Myths and Legends* (Edinburgh: T. & T. Clark, 1978); Johannes C. de Moor, *An Anthology of Religious Texts from Ugarit* (Leiden: E. J. Brill, 1987); Simon B. Parker, ed., *Ugaritic Narrative Poetry* (Atlanta: Scholars Press, 1997); William W. Hallo with K. Lawson Younger, eds., *The Context of Scripture,* 1:239–83, 333–56.

106. Translations of Gilgamesh can be found in *ANET,* 72–99, and in Stephanie Dalley, *Myths from Mesopotamia: Creation, the Flood, Gilgamesh, and Others* (Oxford: Oxford University Press 1989), 39–153. Atra-ḫasis has been translated in W. G. Lambert and A. R. Millard, *Atra-Ḫasīs: The Babylonian Story of the Flood; With the Sumerian Flood Story by M. Civil* (Oxford: Clarendon Press, 1969); in Dalley, *Myths from Mesopotamia,* 1–38; and in Benjamin R. Foster, *Before the Muses: An Anthology of Akkadian Literature,* vol. 1: *Archaic, Classical, Mature* (Bethesda, Md.: CDL Press, 1993), 158–201.

107. A translation of "The Two Brothers": Hallo and Younger, eds., *Context of Scripture,* 1:85–89.

108. This is, from a theological point of view, a rather unhappy decision. On one side, it removes the Old Testament from its biblical context, leaving a rather amputated New Testament alone. On the other hand, the Christian church is in possession of several different Old Testaments, one in Hebrew, another in Greek or in Latin or in Syriac, Coptic, Ethiopian, Arabic, etc., not to speak of versions of a later date from King James or the Lutherbibel up to modern renditions.

109. The standard edition of the Amarna texts is still J. A. Knudtzon, *Die El-Amarna Tafeln mit Einleitung und Erläuterungen,* vols. 1 and 2 (Leipzig: J. C. Hindrichs, 1915; reprint, Aalen: Otto Zeller Verlagsbuchhandlung, 1964). An appendix has been published by Anson F. Rainey, *El Amarna Tablets 359–379: Supplement to J. A. Knudtzon, Die El-Amarna Tafeln,* 2d ed. (Kevelaer: Verlag Butzon & Bercker; Neukirchen-Vluyn: Neukirchener Verlag, 1978).

110. For historical overviews, see *CANE* 2: Egypt (William J. Murnane), Mesopotamia (Dominique Charpin), Elam (Burchard Brentjes), Asia Minor (J. G. Macqueen), Syria and Palestine (Niels Peter Lemche).

111. ÌR-Ḫeba's letters, EA 286:56; 287:31; 288:38.44; 289:24; 290:13. 24, LÚ.MEŠ *ḫa-bi-ru,* "ḫabiru-people" 288:28, LÚ *ḫa-bi-ru,* "ḫabiru-man.".

112. Egyptian examples are collected in Jean Bottéro, *Le problème des ḫabiru à la 4ᵉ rencontre assyriologique internationale* (Paris: Imprimerie nationale, 1954), 165–75.

113. This had been understood since F. Chabas, "Les Hébreux en Égypte," *Mélanges égyptologique,* 1st ser. (1862), 42–54. Cf. also on the discussion of the Egyptian material Oswald Loretz, *Habiru-Hebraer: Eine sozio-linguistische Studie über die Herkunft des Gentiliziums 'ibrî vom Appellativum ḫabiru* (Berlin: Walter de Gruyter, 1984).

114. A *p* in the transcription of a semitic word instead of a *b* is a common feature. The introductory ' compares to the Hebrew ', the first letter of the word *'ibrî,* "Hebrew." As to *ḫabiru,* the first part of the word, *ḫa,* is a usual rendering in Akkadian of an *'a.* The second syllable, the *bi* could be, in Akkadian, a *pí*—a perfectly sensible rendering. Oswald Loretz, *Habiru-Hebräer,* 43, is, however, evidently correct when he considers the equation LÚ.MEŠ SA.GAZ.ZA *a-bu-ur-ra* in a cuneiform tablet from Kumidi (Kamid el-Loz) to be decisive. The term *aburra* is here used as

a phonetic complement of the Sumeriogram LÚ.MEŠ SA.GAZ.ZA, the normal rendering of *ḫabiru* in Akkadian (see below).

115. Evidence from Hattushash: Bottéro, *Le problème*, 71–84.

116. Basic literature: Apart from Bottéro, *Le problème*, also the less complete collection by Moshe Greenberg, *The Ḫab/piru* (New Haven, Conn.: American Oriental Society, 1955). Most complete discussion: Loretz, *Habiru-Hebräer*.

117. Compare the conclusion in Bottéro, *Le problème*, 187–98.

118. The treaty between the Egyptians and the Hittites: *ANET*, 199–203. Among the most interesting studies of the refugee movement in the Late Bronze Age belongs Mario Liverani, "Il fuoruscitismo in Siria nella Tarda Età del Bronze," *Rivista Storica Italiana* 77 (1965): 315–36.

119. Cf. on this aspect George E. Mendenhall, *The Tenth Generation: The Origin of the Biblical Tradition* (Baltimore and London: The Johns Hopkins University Press, 1973), 65–77; Mario Liverani, "Farsi Habiru," *Vicino Oriente* 2 (1979): 65–77.

120. Thus ÌR-Ḫeba of Jerusalem accuses Labayu of Shechem for having made common cause with the *ḫabiru*, EA 289:21–24; in another letter he accuses the sons of Labayu for having committed the same crime, EA 287:29–31. In EA 280, however, Šuwardata of Qeila accuses ÌR-Ḫeba for being just another Labayu, while Labayu for his part spends his time assuring the pharaoh of his loyalty—perhaps not always very convincing; cf. EA 253–54.

121. Beth Shan stela: *ANET*, 255; Bottéro, *Le problème*, 168.

122. Two otherwise unknown tribal names are included in the Beth Shan stele: the Tayar and the Rahamu.

123. Cf. on this the discussion in Loretz, *Habiru-Hebräer*, 41–44.

124. Cf. on this Niels Peter Lemche, "'Hebrew' as a National Name for Israel," *Studia Theologica* 33 (1979): 1–23. See also Nadav Na'aman, "Khabiru and Hebrews: The Transfer of a Social Term to the Literary Sphere," *JNES* 45 (1986): 271–88.

125. Cf., however, Niels Peter Lemche, "'The Hebrew Slave': Comments on the Slave Law Ex xxi 2–11," *VT* 25 (1975): 129–44, esp. 139–42 on *ḥophšî*. Also Oswald Loretz, "Die hebräischen termini *ḥpšj* 'freigelassen, Freigelassener' und *ḫpšh* 'Freilassung,'" *UF* 9 (1977): 163–67.

126. Niels Peter Lemche, "The Manumission of Slaves—the Fallow Year—the Sabbathical Year—the Jobel Year," *VT* 26 (1976): 38–59.

127. Contra Lemche, "'The Hebrew Slave,'" following Loretz, *Habiru-Hebräer*, 139–41.

128. This literary character of the Babylonian law codes was first established by F. R. Kraus, "Ein zentrales Problem des altmesopotamischen Rechts: Was ist der Codex Hammu-rabi?" *Genava* 8 (1960): 283–96. It is now more or less mainstream among Assyriologists. Cf. Martha T. Roth, *Law Collections from Mesopotamia and Asia Minor,* 2d ed. (Atlanta: Scholars Press, 1997), Introduction, 4–7.

129. On the rules governing the life in court in the Levant, cf. Niels Peter Lemche, "Justice in Western Asia in Antiquity, or: Why No Laws Were Needed!" *The Kent Law Review* 70 (1995): 1695–1716. Cf. also Herbert Niehr, "The Constitutive Principles for Establishing Justice and Order in Northwest Semitic Societies with Special Reference to Ancient Israel and Judah," *Zeitschrift für Altorientalische und Biblische Rechtsgeschichte* 3 (1997): 112–30.

Chapter 3:
Archaeology and Israelite Ethnic Identity

1. Helga Weippert, *Palästina in vorhellenistischer Zeit* (Munich: C. H. Beck'sche Verlagsbuchhandlung, 1988); Amihai Mazar, *Archaeology of the Land of the Bible 10,000–586 B.C.E.* (New York: Doubleday, 1990); Amnon Ben-Tor, ed., *The Archaeology of Ancient Israel* (New Haven, Conn.: Yale University Press, 1992); Thomas E. Levy (ed.), *The Archaeology of Society in the Holy Land* (London: Leicester University Press, 1995).

2. William G. Dever, *Recent Archaeological Discoveries and Biblical Research* (Seattle and London: University of Washington Press, 1990); Israel Finkelstein, *The Archaeology of the Israelite Settlement* (Jerusalem: Israel Exploration Society, 1988); Israel Finkelstein, *Living on the Fringe: The Archaeology and History of the Negev, Sinai and Neighbouring Regions in the Bronze and Iron Ages* (Sheffield Academic Press, 1995); Israel Finkelstein and Nadav Na'aman, eds., *From Nomadism to Monarchy: Archaeological and Historical Aspects of Early Israel* (Jerusalem: Israel Exploration Society, 1994).

3. *La longue durée:* On this concept fundamental to the school of historians called *les annales,* cf. Ferdnand Braudel, *On History* (Chicago: University of Chicago Press, 1980). A discussion concerning its relevance for the study of ancient Israel can be found in the exchange between Niels Peter Lemche and William G. Dever: Niels Peter Lemche, "Early Israel Revisited," *Currents in Research: Biblical Studies* 4 (1996): 9–34, esp. 20–22; William G. Dever, "Revisionist Israel Revisited: A Rejoinder to Niels Peter Lemche," *Currents in Research: Biblical Studies* 4 (1996): 35–50, esp. 38–39. Especially Israel Finkelstein has worked with models of *la longue durée,* e.g., in his "The Emergence of Israel: A Phase in the Cyclic History of Canaan in the Third and Second Millennia B.C.E.," in Finkelstein and Na'aman, eds., *From Nomadism to Monarchy,* 150–78.

4. On this Thomas L. Thompson, *Early History of the Israelite People: From the Written and Archaeological Sources* (Leiden: E. J. Brill, 1992), 215–300: "The Late Bronze–Iron Age Transition." On the continuation of sociopolitical organization, cf. Niels Peter Lemche, "From Patronage Society to Patronage Society," in Volkmar Fritz and Philip R. Davies, eds., *The Origins of the Ancient Israelite States* (Sheffield: Sheffield Academic Press, 1996), 106–20. In this article the argument says that when things got "normal" again after the upheavals at the end of the Late Bronze Age, the cards had been redistributed, but it was still the same cards. Finkelstein and Na'aman, eds., *From Nomadism to Monarchy,* centers on the transition period as its main theme.

5. Christian Jürgensen Thomsen, 1788–1865. His distribution of the past into three successive stages was published in *Ledetraad til nordisk Oldkyndighed* (Copenhagen, 1827), although he had already some years before his publication arranged the collections of the National Museum in Copenhagen according to this technological clue.

6. Updates on the literature of the Sea People: Trude Dothan, "The 'Sea Peoples' and the Philistines of Ancient Palestine," in *CANE* 2:1267–79; furthermore, Ed Noort, *Die Seevölker in Palästina* (Kampen: Kok Pharos Publishing House, 1994).

7. On Aramaeans: Paul E. Dion, "Aramaean Tribes and Nations of First-Millennium Western Asia," in *CANE* 2:1281–94.

8. Cf. on the succession from bronze to iron, Volkmar Fritz, *Die Entstehung Israels im 12. und 11. Jahrhundert v. Chr.* (Stuttgart: W. Kohlhammer, 1996), 101–2. He stresses—following Ora Negbi, "The Continuity of the Canaanite Bronzework of the Late Bronze Age into the Early Iron Age," *Tel Aviv* 1 (1974): 159–72—the continuation of the use of bronze, now procured from a local source. Iron became a viable substitute for bronze only after it became steel, something that happened only in the tenth century B.C.E.; cf. on this Fritz, *Entstehung Israels,* 101, and the literature cited there.

9. For a study in the perspective of *la longue durée* focusing on the negative effects of the disturbance of international trade, cf. Robert B. Coote and Keith W. Whitelam, *The Emergence of Early Israel in Historical Perspective* (Sheffield: Almond Press, 1987).

10. Any person who has been working, e.g., in excavations in Palestine, Jordan, or Syria in summertime will instantly recognize this to be true. To mention the amount of water used by a private soldier participating in the Desert War during the Second World War, it might on hot days run up to, say, twenty-five liters. Although the local population is of course able to do with much less, the amount of water to be reserved for drinking is still considerable. The best (worst) example of what would happen to a large-scale migration is the tragic incidence of the Turkish deportation of the Armenians from Anatolia to Iraq during the First World War. Although the Turks behaved in a highly improper way (which is a friendly way to put it), they did not plan the destruction of 1,500,000 individuals; on the other hand, they had no idea of how to keep the Armenians alive while en route.

11. On drought in the Late Bronze Age, see Thompson, *Early History,* 407.

12. The so-called "spring letter," cf. on this Mario Liverani, "A Seasonal Pattern for the Amarna Letters," in Tzvi Abusch, John Huehnergard, Piotr Steinkeller, eds., *Lingering over Words: Studies in Ancient Near Eastern Literature in Honor of William L. Moran* (Atlanta: Scholars Press, 1990), 337–48.

13. The situation at Sarepta, a settlement that continued to exist right down the Late Bronze–Iron Age transition, may be typical. On Sarepta, cf. Issam Ali Khalifeh, "Sarepta," in *The Oxford Encyclopedia of Archaeology in the Ancient Near East,* 4:488–91. See also James B. Pritchard, *Recovering Sarepta, a Phoenician City* (Princeton, N.J.: Princeton University Press, 1978).

14. One gets a lively literary impression of the situation in Phoenicia around 1100 B.C.E. from the so-called Report of Wenamun (Hallo and Younger, eds., *Context of Scripture,* 1:89–93). This is most likely a fictitious narrative describing the eventful travels of an Egyptian officer in the Eastern Mediterranean, and visiting Byblos in order, in the tradition of the old, to buy wood for construction work. If anything, the Byblian attitude toward the Egyptian envoy is one of contempt, far removed for the doglike servitude of a Rib-Adda of Byblos in the Amarna age. On Tel Achzib, see Moshe W. Prausnitz, *NAEEHL,* 1:32–36.

15. Especially because this area seems at least in places to have been destroyed and then resettled by members of the so-called "Sea People" movement. Cf. concerning the results of the excavations at Tell Keisan and Acco, Rafael Frankel, "Upper Galilee in the Late Bronze–Iron I Transition," in Finkelstein and Na'aman, eds., *From Nomadism to Monarchy,* 18–34, esp. 24.

16. Cf. Papyrus Anastasi VI with the report of the border officer, translated in

ANET, 259, dating from the end of the thirteenth century B.C.E.; and from another time (nineteenth century) the relief showing arriving people from Asia in the grave of Kanhotep at Beni Hasan in *ANEP,* fig. 3, 2–3.

17. An example of such a passport can be found in the EA archive, EA 30.

18. On merchants in the ancient Near East, cf. Horst Klengel, *Handel und Händler im alten Orient* (Vienna: Böhlau, 1979). On the merchant as the king's agent, Mario Liverani, "La dotazione dei mercanti di Ugarit," *Ugarit-Forschungen* 11 (1979): 495–503.

19. On the nomads of Palestine and Syria in the Late Bronze period, Manfred Weippert, "Semitische Nomaden des zweiten Jahrtausends," *Biblica* 55 (1974): 265–80, 427–33. On the Suteans, Michael Heltzer, *The Suteans: With a Contribution by Shoshana Arbeli* (Naples: Istituto Universitario Orientale, 1981). The Egyptian material concerning the Shasu was collected by Raphael Giveon, *Les Bédouins Shosou des documents égyptiens* (Leiden: E. J. Brill, 1971).

20. The literature on nomadism in the Near East is extensive, although—as far as the ancient world goes—not always particularly well informed. In this place I shall refer to the extensive discussion in Niels Peter Lemche, *Early Israel,* 95–163, and to the collection edited by Ofer Bar-Josef and Anatoly Khazanov, *Pastoralism in the Levant: Archaeological Materials in Anthropological Perspectives* (Madison, Wis.: Prehistory Press, 1992).

21. On Hazor in the Late Bronze Age, see Ben-Tor, in *NAEEHL* 2:594–605.

22. On Jerusalem in the Late Bronze Age: Graeme Auld and Margreet Steiner, *Jerusalem I: From the Bronze Age to the Maccabees* (Cambridge: Lutterworth Press; Macon, Ga.: Mercer University Press, 1996), 29. This archaeological situation, of course, makes it hard to use the letters of ÌR-Ḫeba of Jerusalem in the Amarna archive (see above) in a historical analysis concerning literacy and economics in Palestine in the Late Bronze Age, as does Nadav Na'aman, e.g., in his "The Contribution of the Amarna letters to the Debate on Jerusalem's Political Position in the Tenth Century B.C.E.," *BASOR* 304 (1996): 17–27 (cf. already his "Canaanite Jerusalem and its Central Hill Country Neighbours in the Second Millennium B.C.E.," *UF* 24 [1992]: 275–91). It is, however, difficult to see any of this founded in history.

23. The fact that many of the Amarna letters sent from Palestine are of the type: Yes, we obey! (e.g., EA 319–25) has been overshadowed in the scholarly world by the repeated references to letters expressing frustration, complaints, and disconcert. Thus, if we reduce the collection with for example the endless row of complaints from a Rib-Adda (at times driving the Egyptian recipients to despair, see EA 124), it will probably be easier to obtain a more balanced view of the political situation in Palestine in the Amarna age.

24. On this pharaoh and his time see, among others, the studies by Cyril Aldred, *Akhenaten, King of Egypt* (London: Thames & Hudson, 1988) (cf. already Aldred, in *CAH* II:2, chap. 19, 49–63; and Donald B. Redford, *Akhenaten, The Heretic King* (Princeton, N.J.: Princeton University Press, 1984).

25. The traditional view can be found in numerous older studies of the Amarna period. Thus William F. Albright's chapter on the Amarna age in the *CAH* II:2, chap. 20, 98–116, is safely placed within this paradigm, which was probably for the first time seriously questioned by Alan R. Schulman, "Some Observations on the Military Background of the Amarna Period," *JARCE* 3 (1964): 51–69. A scholar like Mario Liv-

erani sees the crisis to be mainly an ideological one, the Amarna letters reflecting a serious lack of mutual understanding between Egyptian overlords and their Palestinian and Syrian subjects: "Contrasti e confluenze di concezioni politiche nell'età di El-Amarna," *Revue Assyriologique* 61 (1967): 1–18. In order to perceive the extension of the Egyptian control, a letter like EA 162 (from pharaoh to Aziru of Amurru) should be scrutinized. It shows beyond doubt the Egyptians in perfect control.

26. This date seems to be generally accepted; cf. J. G. Macqueen in *CANE* 2:1092, and O. R. Gurney, *The Hittites,* 2d ed. (reprint with revisions; London: Penguin Books, 1990), 181.

27. Kenneth A. Kitchen, *Suppiluliuma and the Amarna Pharaohs: A Study in Relative Chronology* (Liverpool: Liverpool University Press, 1962), remains the classic study on the clash between the Egyptians and the Hittites in this period.

28. Cf. Donald B. Redford, *Egypt, Canaan, and Israel in Ancient Times* (Princeton, N.J.: Princeton University Press, 1992), 192–213, on the Egyptian organization of the empire, including the revitalization of their control under the early pharaohs of the Eighteenth Dynasty.

29. Cf. the study by Leon Marfoe, "The Integrative Transformation: Patterns of Sociopolitical Organization in Southern Syria," *BASOR* 234 (1979): 1–42.

30. On this development see especially Israel Finkelstein, *The Archaeology of the Israelite Settlement,* and Finkelstein and Na'aman, eds., *From Nomadism to Monarchy.* And now also the publication of the Samaria survey in Israel Finkelstein and Zvi Lederman, eds., *Highlands of Many Cultures: The Southern Samaria Survey: The Sites,* vols. 1 and 2 (Tel Aviv: Sonia and Marco Nadler Institute of Archaeology, 1997).

31. Albrecht Alt, "Die Landnahme der Israeliten in Palästina" (1925), reprinted in *Kleine Schriften zur Geschichte des Volkes Israel* (Munich: C. H. Beck'sche Verlagsbuchhandlung, 1953), 1:89–125 (also in English trans.: "The Settlement of the Israelites in Palestine," in Albrecht Alt, *Essays on Old Testament History and Religion* [Oxford: Basil Blackwell, 1966], 133–69); and "Erwägungen über die Landnahme der Israeliten in Palästina" (1939), reprinted in *Kleine Schriften zur Geschichte des Volkes Israel,* 1:126–75.

32. Iron Age Agriculture in Palestine: Cf. David C. Hopkins, *The Highlands of Canaan: Agricultural Life in the Early Iron Age* (Sheffield: Almond Press, 1985); Oded Borowski, *Agriculture in Iron Age Israel* (Winona Lake, Ind.: Eisenbrauns, 1987).

33. Cf. Mario Liverani, "Le 'origine' d'Israele progetto irrelizzabile di ricerca etnogenetica," *Rivista Biblica Italiana* 28 (1980): 9–31, 20.

34. Israel Finkelstein has opted for a certain nomadic element in his *Archaeology of the Israelite Settlement,* esp. 345–47 (on the physical layout of early settlements see below). On the development in the Negev, see his *Living on the Fringe.*

35. E.g., Yigael Yadin, *Hazor: The Head of All Those Kingdoms: Joshua 11:10* (London: published for the British Academy by Oxford University Press, 1972), 131–32.

36. Yohanan Aharoni, "Problems of the Israelite Conquest in the Light of Archaeology," *Antiquity and Survival* II, 2/3 (1957): 131–50.

37. Rafael Frankel, "Upper Galilee in the Late Bronze-Iron I Transition," in Finkelstein and Na'aman, eds., *From Nomadism to Monarchy,* 18–34.

38. George E. Mendenhall, "The Hebrew Conquest of Palestine," *BA* 25 (1962):

66–87, reprinted in Edward F. Campbell and David Noel Freedman, eds., *The Biblical Archaeologist Reader* (Garden City, N.Y.: Doubleday & Co., 1970), 3:100–120, and expanded in his *The Tenth Generation: The Origin of the Biblical Tradition* (Baltimore: Johns Hopkins University Press, 1973).

39. Norman K. Gottwald, *The Tribes of Yahweh: A Sociology of the Religion of Liberated Israel 1250–1050 B.C.* (Maryknoll, N.Y.: Orbis Books, 1979). Also to be mentioned in this context: Marvin L. Chaney, "Ancient Palestinian Peasant Movements and the Formation of Premonarchic Israel," in David Noel Freedman and David Frank Graf, eds., *Palestine in Transition: The Emergence of Ancient Israel* (Sheffield: Almond Press, 1983), 39–90.

40. Cf. the settlement with the revolution hypothesis in Niels Peter Lemche, *Early Israel*, 1985. On the problems of sociological methodology, cf. Niels Peter Lemche, "On the Use of 'System Theory,' 'Macro Theories' and Evolutionistic Thinking in Modern OT Research and Biblical Archaeology," *SJOT* 4:2 (1990): 73–88, reprinted in Charles E. Carter and Carol L. Meyers, eds., *Community, Identity, and Ideology: Social Sciences Approaches to the Hebrew Bible* (Winona Lake, Ind.: Eisenbrauns, 1996), 273–86. For an appraisal of the other side of sociology, cf. among other contributions Norman K. Gottwald, "Recent Studies of the Social World of Premonarchic Israel," *Currents in Research: Biblical Studies* 1 (1993): 163–89, and several contributions in his *The Hebrew Bible in Its Social World and in Ours* (Atlanta: Scholars Press, 1993).

41. The French Revolution of 1789 is one example of this, the Gracchi of Rome another. The Arab insurrection against the Turks during the First World War, epitomized in the shape of Lawrence of Arabia, may serve as another example. British intelligence officers in cooperation with the Hashemites of Mecca, an Arab elite family, initiated this "insurrection." As it "rolled onward" the participants shifted. Only the local peasants participated, and when the campaign continued, they returned to their villages in order to be replaced by new peasants. Other examples could be found in ancient as well as modern history. These includes the revolution of Oliver Cromwell in England, of the Kmer Rouge in Cambodia, the Taliban movement in Afghanistan, not forgetting the Russian Revolution of 1917, which had nothing to do with a peasants' revolt. Russian peasant revolts of the nineteenth century were mostly short-lived, local, and disorganized affairs. The Danish peasant was "liberated" in 1787, not by his own initiative but on the initiative of some of the highest-ranking noblemen in the country, by the counts Reventlow and Bernstorff.

42. The question is often put: If there never was a Moses, he would have had to be invented—otherwise it would be impossible to explain the particularities of the Israelite religion! The best answer is probably one once formulated by Mario Liverani: And so they invented him! On the historical position of Moses in the Pentateuchal narratives, cf. Niels Peter Lemche, *Die Vorgeschichte Israels: Von den Anfängen bis zum Ausgang des 13. Jahrhunderts v.Chr.* (Stuttgart: W. Kohlhammer, 1996), 52–68 (English edition in press: *Prelude to Israel's Past: Background and Beginnings of Israelite History and Identity* [Peabody, Mass.: Hendrickson's, 1998]).

43. Niels Peter Lemche, *Early Israel*, 1985, identified by Winfried Thiel, "Vom revolutionären zum evolutionären Israel?" *ThLZ* 113 (1988): 401–10. Israel Finkelstein's ideas of the development in Palestine in the transition period also mostly accord with this idea of an evolution.

44. Cf. above, n. 34.

45. Fredrik Barth's study of the Kurdish nomads of northern Iraq provides ample examples of this. Before the modern state curtailed the influence of the nomads, they were as a matter of fact the scourge of the earth, extracting "protection money" from the other sectors of the society. Cf. Fredrik Barth, *Principles of Social Organization in Southern Kurdistan* (Oslo, 1953; reprinted New York: AMS, 1979). A study of the Luri nomads by Jacob Black-Michaud, *Sheep and Land: The Economics of Power in a Tribal Society,* ed. Jean Pierre Digard (Cambridge: Cambridge University Press, 1986), also helps to break down the romantic stereotype of peaceful nomads living in symbiosis with other parts of the Oriental society.

46. Cf. on this my *Early Israel,* 131–36. Conversely, modern nomadic societies of the Near East are not so much "enclosed" in the greater society (thus, Michael B. Rowton, "Enclosed Nomadism, *JESHO* 17 [1974]: 1–30), as "encapsulated" by it (cf. Fredrik Barth, "A General Perspective on Nomad-Sedentary Relations in the Middle East," in C. Nelson, ed., *The Desert and the Sown: Nomads in the Wider Society* (Berkeley, Calif.: University of California Press, 1973), 11–21.

47. Cf. the circular layouts of several Early Iron I settlements in Palestine, in Finkelstein, *The Archaeology of the Israelite Settlement,* 238–50. Finkelstein compares this layout to the nomadic campsite, and thinks here to find evidence of the presence of people with a nomadic origin: in the courtyard created by the circle of houses the nomads could protect their animals. It is typical of nomadic life, however, that they don't assemble their animals during the night, and that the protection is more often than not placed in the hands of professional herdsmen (members of their families or hired specialists). The layout is, rather, evidence of people with an urban background looking for at least a vestige of protection in a new and insecure environment.

48. Cf. the remarks on this in Niels Peter Lemche, "On Doing Sociology with 'Solomon,'" in Lowell K. Handy, ed., *The Age of Solomon: Scholarship at the Turn of the Millennium* (Leiden: E. J. Brill, 1997), 312–35.

49. *ANET,* 255. Cf. also on this text above, 60.

50. Cf. on the developments in the Negev and especially of the centralized settlement of Tel-Saba (Beer-Sheba), Ze'ev Herzog, "The Beer-Sheba Valley: From Nomadism to Monarchy," in Finkelstein and Na'aman, eds., *From Nomadism to Monarchy,* 122–49; Finkelstein, *Living on the Fringe,* 103–20.

51. Called *Huwa,* i.e. "brotherhood-(money)." On this, my *Early Israel,* 99, 131–32. It is this kind of "activity" that is described in the story in 1 Samuel 25, about David asking for protection money from Nabal.

52. The only source for this empire is the Old Testament, or literature dependent on its narratives. Not a single document from the ancient Near East refers to either of these two kings of Israel. The legendary character of the traditions about this empire is highlighted by the disagreement between the Deuteronomistic version of the founding of the famous Temple in Jerusalem in 2 Samuel and 1 Kings on the one side, and Chronicles on the other. According to 2 Samuel 7, David was not asked to build the Temple. This was an honor reserved for his son. In 1 Chronicles 22, it is David who decides to build a Temple and who prepares everything. The only thing left for Solomon was the accomplishment of the task according to his father's instructions. In the writings of the late Hellenistic historian Dionysius from Halicar-

nassus (late first century B.C.E.), it is Moses who builds the Temple after having led
Israel from Egypt to the Promised Land. This tradition may not be Dionysius's invention in light of the note in 2 Kings 18:4 about Hiskija's destruction of the copper
serpent Nehushtan that Moses had made.

53. Any such estimate is, as far as antiquity is concerned, highly hypothetical.
There is, however, evidence from the Late Bronze Age from Syria that as an average
the nuclear family—by far the most common part of the social structure—counted
little more than five persons. On this, cf. my *Early Israel*, 131–32. The estimate of the
total number of inhabitants is dependent on various methods of calculation based
on experiences from the most crowded and traditional quarters of Middle Eastern
cities of this century, such as the old part of Baghdad. Whereas such estimates are
hypothetical, they at least show the relative size of the population of different settlements, if only the same system of measuring and counting is always used.

54. Israel Finkelstein, "The Archaeology of the United Monarchy: An Alternative
View," *Levant* 28 (1996): 177–87. A response has been published by Amihai Mazar,
"Iron Age Chronology: A Reply to I. Finkelstein," *Levant* 29 (1997): 157–67. Finkelstein's argument includes a general compressing of the ceramic chronology that
leaves the tenth century, the assumed time of David and Solomon, almost without
ceramic attestation. Finkelstein is now supported by David Ussishkin, "Jerusalem in
the Period of David and Solomon: The Archaeological Evidence," so far only in a
preliminary Hebrew version, in Avraham Faust and Eyal Baruch, eds., *New Studies
on Jerusalem: Proceedings of the Third Conference December 11th 1997* (Ramat-Gan:
Bar-Ilan University Faculty of Jewish Studies, 1997), 57–58.

55. Cf., apart from the literature quoted in the preceding note, also Margreet
Steiner, *Jerusalem in the Late Bronze and Early Iron Ages: Archaeological Versus Lit-
erary Sources?* in Avraham Faust, ed., *New Studies on Jerusalem: Proceedings of the
Second Conference November 28th 1996* (Ramat-Gan: Bar-Ilan University Faculty of
Jewish Studies, 1996), 3*–8*.

56. D. Jamieson-Drake, *Scribes and Schools in Monarchic Judah: A Socio-
Archeological Approach* (Sheffield: Almond Press, 1991).

57. It this respect Jamieson-Drake's study must be seen as a rejoinder to A.
Lemaire, *Les écoles et la formation de la Bible dans l'ancien Israel* (Fribourg, Suisse:
Éditions universitaires, Göttingen: Vandenhoeck & Ruprecht, 1981).

58. Jamieson-Drake, *Scribes and Schools*, 48–80.

59. The discussion about these gates and their relation to Solomon or to the early
dynasty of Omri has been long and often intense. It will suffice in this place to mention the general discussion, Weippert, *Palästina in vorhellenistischer Zeit*, 440–41,
and Mazar, *Archaeology*, 384–87, both of whom reckon it to be a tenth century phenomenon. The newly excavated "six-chamber" gate at Jezreel, attached to a "case-
mate wall" (cf. Ussishkin and Woodhead, "Excavations at Tel Jezreel 1994–95,"
13–25, with fig. 5, is definitely ninth and not tenth century B.C.E.

60. An outline of the Ashdod gate in comparison to similar structures at Hazor,
Gezer, Lachish, and Megiddo can be found in Mazar, *Archaeology*, 384.

61. Cf. on "palaces" the comprehensive study by Lorenzo Nigro, *Ricerche sul-
l'architettura palaziale della Palestina nette età del Bronzo e del ferro: Contesto
archeologico e sviluppo storico* (Rome: Università degli Studi di Roma "La sapienza,"
1995). "So-called" because of the tendency among archaeologists to call any build-

ing of importance either a palace or a temple. Very little in the way of the extensive palatial structures of Syria or northern Palestine (Hazor) of the Bronze Age has so far been found dating from the Iron Age in Palestine.

62. On temples (cultic structures), cf. Weippert, *Palästina in vorhellenistischer Zeit,* 447–49 (supposed tenth century B.C.E.). She also includes a longish discussion of the Temple complex of Solomon, *Palästina in vorhellenistischer Zeit,* 461–76, of which hardly a stone "remains" (saying that the Temple was built by Solomon; cf. also above).

63. Cf. Jamieson-Drake, *Scribes and Schools,* 107–35, on luxury items.

64. The socioeconomic structure of Syria and Palestine in the Late Bronze Age has been the subject of many studies. Among the most interesting I would count the essay by Mario Liverani in Paul Garelli, ed., *Le palais et la royauté* (Paris: Geuthner, 1974), 329–56. Cf. also in general terms Mario Liverani, *Antico Oriente. Storia, società, economia* (Bari: Editori Laterza, 1988), 469–80. A case study of one such "palace state" is W. H. van Soldt, "Ugarit: A Second-Millennium Kingdom on the Mediterranean Coast," *CANE* 2:1255–66.

65. Jamieson-Drake, *Scribes and Schools,* 138–45. A similar result was reached on the basis of the study of the biblical evidence by Hermann Michael Niemann, *Herrschaft, Königtum und Staat: Skizzen zur soziokulturellen Entwicklung im monarchischen Israel* (Tübingen: J.C.B. Mohr [Paul Siebeck], 1993). Niemann, as well as Jamieson-Drake, however, does not deny the historicity of David and Solomon (see now also Hermann Michael Niemann, "The Socio-Political Shadow Cast by the Biblical Solomon," in Handy, ed., *The Age of Solomon,* 252–99), although not much is left, except a couple of "robber-barons" on a hilltop hidden away somewhere in the Judean mountains. Also following the results of Jamieson-Drake: Israel Finkelstein, "State Formation in Israel and Judah" (in press).

66. On Arad, cf. Miriam Aharoni, *NAEEHL* 1:75–87.

67. Cf. above on the *le-melek* stamps.

68. Cf. Jane M. Cahill, "Rosette Stamp Seal Impressions from Ancient Judah," *IEJ* 45: 232–52.

69. There is evidence of destruction at the turn of the eighth and seventh centuries in many places. Most famous is at Lachish, a conquest of which Sennacherib was particularly proud of and described in elaborate reliefs in his royal palace. Cf. David Ussishkin, *The Conquest of Lachish by Sennacherib* (Tel Aviv: The Institute of Archaeology, 1982). Other places to be included are Timnah, Ramat Rahel, and Gezer; see Mazar, *Archaeology,* 438.

70. The classic example of this combination of Bible with archaeology is the "conquest model" for the Israelite settlement, in North America personalized by William F. Albright and especially George Ernest Wright, *An Introduction to Biblical Archaeology* (London: Gerald Duckworth, 1957).

71. In his annals, Sennacherib mentions that he, among other things, destroyed forty-six of Hezekiah's cities (Luckenbill, *AR,* vol. II § 240; *ANET,* 288). He may not have exaggerated.

72. In Jamieson-Drake's words: "The end of the Judahite state: a pathology," *Scribes and Schools,* 145. Hans M. Barstad has in a recent study argued for a considerable activity in Judea also in the sixth century, *The Myth of the Empty Land: A Study in the History and Archaeology of Judah During the "Exilic" Period* (Oslo: Scandinavian

University Press, 1996). As a contrast to the claim in 2 Chron. 36:21 that the land was empty during the exile, Barstad is evidently right. However, seen in contrast to the situation in the eighth century, before Sennacherib's destructions, and at the end of Manasseh's long reign in the second half of the seventh century, Judah in the sixth century was hardly a prospering place.

73. This definition, territorial state, versus city-state, goes against the division proposed by Giovanni Buccellati, *Cities and Nations of Ancient Syria. An Essay on Political Institutions with Special Reference to the Israelite Kingdoms* (Rome: Instituto di Studi del Vicino Oriente, 1967). Buccellati characterizes the states of the Late Bronze Age as "territorial," as a contrast to the states in the Iron Age which were in his view "national" states. This distinction is sometimes believed to be true, but is absolutely anachronistic and presupposes that the idea of Israel formulated by the Old Testament writers has anything to do with realities in the ancient world.

74. John Holladay, "The Kingdoms of Israel and Judah: Political and Economic Centralization in the Iron IIA-B (Ca. 1000–750 B.C.E.)," in T. Levy, *The Archaeology of Society in the Holy Land,* 368–98.

75. It is, however, difficult to find a decent review of Jamieson-Drake's study. Sometimes one gets the feeling that it has deliberately been overlooked, probably because its theses are considered "problematic." The criticism leveled here is therefore more or less dependent on discussions with a series of archaeologists who are, on the other hand, in general agreement as to the virtues and deficits of his approach.

76. Israel Finkelstein criticizes him for not paying sufficient attention to the results of the extensive area surveys conducted by, not least, Israeli archaeologists, in his *State Formation in Israel and Judah* (in press).

77. A review of Jericho's archaeological history by Kathleen M. Kenyon can be found in *NAEEHL* 2:674–81. So far little has appeared pertaining to the Italian-Palestinian excavations. I owe my information to a member of the Italian team, Lorenzo Nigro.

78. Finkelstein, *Living on the Fringe,* 1995.

79. On the situation here, cf. above.

80. We already above referred to the discussion about the so-called "Solomonic" building activity at Hazor and other places. Samaria and Jezreel present a different kind of problems, as they *are* supposed to be ninth-century settlements, and are likely to reflect construction work organized by the kings of Bet Omri. There seem to be traces of a pre-Omride settlement on the hilltop of Samaria, cf. *NAEEHL* 4:1303, and the discussion in Ron E. Tappy, *The Archaeology of Israelite Samaria, I: Early Iron Age through the Ninth Century B.C.E.* (Atlanta: Scholars Press, 1992), 15–101.

81. Samaria ivories *NAEEHL* 4:1304–6; Weippert, *Palästina in vorhellenistischer Zeit,* 655–57.

82. For that reason these items belonged among the markers of Jamieson-Drake for a state organization, *Scribes and Schools,* 107–35.

83. On the Samaria ware, its character and provenience, see Weippert, *Palästina in vorhellenistischer Zeit,* 639–41, with fig. 4.69, p. 642; cf. also Mazar, *Archaeology,* 508.

84. Tel Jezreel was excavated 1990–96. Three preliminary reports have been published, by David Ussishkin and John Woodhead, in *Tel Aviv* 19 (1992): 3–56, *Levant*

26 (1994): 1–48, and *Tel Aviv* 24 (1997): 6–72. An updated layout of the huge rectangular structure can be found in *Tel Aviv* 24:11, fig. 4.

85. On the interrelationship between the level of taxation and the amount of royal propaganda, cf. Niels Peter Lemche, "Our Most Gracious Sovereign: On the Relationship between Royal Mythology and Economic Oppression in the Ancient Near East," in Morris Silver, ed., *Ancient Economy in Mythology* (Savage, Md.: Rowman & Littlefield, 1991), 109–34. From this point of view, and in light of the extensive archaeological activity in Palestine over a period of more than a hundred years, it is remarkable that so far not a single monumental inscription of Israelite or Judean provenience has been found. Although this situation may change in the future, it is cause for concern whenever a subject like literacy in the states of Israel and Judah in the Iron Age is discussed.

86. Sargon on deportation: Luckenbill, *AR:* § 55; *ANET,* 285. Sennacherib could do much better than this, or so he claims: His bag of prisoners from 701 B.C.E. counted 200,150 people (Luckenbill *AR* 2:§ 240; *ANET,* 288), something that not only would have left Judah without inhabitants but would probably also have emptied its graveyards.

87. In general on the Assyrian policy of deportations, Bustaney Oded, *Mass Deportation and Deportees in the Neo-Assyrian Empire* (Wiesbaden: Ludwig Reichert, 1979). See also Becking, *The Fall of Samaria,* 61–93.

Chapter 4: The People of God

1. The partition of the book of Isaiah into three books: "Proto-," "Deutero-," and "Trito-Isaiah," a preexilic, exilic, and postexilic part, is a scholarly convention which presupposes that the traditional picture of Israel's history as painted by the biblical authors can be sustained. A study of the redaction of the book without this presupposition may turn out a quite different result. All three parts should not be placed on a vertical time axis; they are more like three different commentaries to the biblical narrative of an Israel doomed to exile, to suffer from the exile, and to be restored again. The book of Isaiah is therefore not a "book" in the usual sense of the word; it is rather a "collage" of scripture. See Knud Jeppesen, *Graeder ikke saa saare: Studier i Mikabogens sigte,* vols. 1 and 2 (Aarhus: Aarhus Universitetsforlag, 1987; English summary, 421–33), according to whom books like Isaiah and Micah are such collages of rags and bits. See also Uwe Becker, *Jesaja: Von der Botschaft zum Buch* (Göttingen: Vandenhoeck & Ruprecht, 1996), who speaks about Isa. 6:1–8* and 8:1–4* as the opening of a tradition that extended like "year-rings" of a tree.

2. The seventy years of Jeremiah is a round number, indicating in itself no more than a very long period, so long that nobody who went into the exile would ever be allowed to return. It has no bearing on the extent of the actual exile, which has traditionally among biblical scholars been said to have lasted from 587 B.C.E. to 538 B.C.E., or about fifty years—making the return almost a Jubilee (cf. Leviticus 25).

3. On the exile and history, see the papers presented at the European Seminar on Methodology in Israel's History, held at the Society of Biblical Literature International Meeting in Lausanne, July 29–30, 1997, to be published by Lester L. Grabbe, *European Seminar in Historical Methodology* 2 (Sheffield: Sheffield Academic Press, 1998).

4. Cf. 2 Chron. 36:21.

5. Livy, *History,* 1.3.

6. A recent translation of the Sargon of Akkad legend in Hallo and Younger, eds., *Context of Scripture,* 461.

7. Exemplified already at the beginning of Abraham's stay in Canaan, when immediately after having arrived there he continues to Egypt because of famine, and almost loses every hope for the future there as his wife becomes part of the Pharaoh's household (Gen. 12:10–20).

8. To which place Abraham's grandson, Jacob, the future Israel, flees to escape the anger of his brother, and to please his mother who is afraid that he will marry a Canaanite woman (Gen. 27:41–45; cf. Gen. 27:46–28:2). The theme that a Jew should not defile himself by marrying a girl of foreign origin is already in evidence in this place.

9. Whether or not any events narrated in connection with this part of Israel's history are historical is immaterial to the argument as presented here, which is a literary one and therefore reflective of the sentiments, ideologies, and interpretations of the narrators and not that of the ancient past.

10. The sermon of the angel is surprising in light of Josh. 24:19–24, according to which the people agreed to remove the foreign gods. Therefore the narrative logic in Judg. 2:1–5 has to do with the future and not the past, although the future is described as something that has already happened. The logic of the narrative in Judges is explained so that anybody should understand it, in Judg. 2:11–23, to be about the behavior of the Israelites following Joshua's death.

11. A study of the peace periods following the "liberation acts" of Yahweh is revealing. Othniel creates a peace that lasts for forty years (Judg. 3:11), Ehud another one for eighty years (Judg. 3:30). Another forty years follows the victory of Deborah and Barak (Judg. 5:31), and also Gideon's victory leads to forty years of rest (Judg. 8:31). After these follows a series of judges ruling for irregular periods, like Tola (23 years, Judg. 10:2), and Jair (22 years, Judg. 10:4). They are followed by Jephta, who, however, rules for only six years (Judg. 12:7), while Ibsan made seven years (Judg. 12:9), Elon ten years (Judg. 12:11), Abdon eight years (Judg. 12:14). Until this moment the periods of peace are always considerably longer than those of oppression: Kushan-Rishataim: eight years (Judg. 3:8), Eglon of Moab: eighteen years (Judg. 3:14), Sisera and the Canaanites: twenty years (Judg. 4:3), the Midianites: seven years (Judg. 6:1), the Philistines and Ammonites: eighteen years (Jud. 10:8). It now changes. After Abdon, the Philistines for forty years oppress Israel (Jud. 13:1), while Samson makes for only twenty years of relative peace (Judg. 17:31). This change could be part of a narrative plot leading first to the final section of Judges, where "in those days there was no king in Israel, but every man did that which was right in his own eyes" (Judg. 17:6; 18:1; 21:25), and second to the introduction of kingship as a substitute for the office of the judge. After all, the two first kings of Israel—disregarding Saul—are both said to have ruled for the vaunted forty years.

12. It has often been maintained by Old Testament theologians that Israel's God is a God who acts in history, i.e. that Yahweh directs history, decides its course. This is the main line, for example, of Gerhard von Rad's idea of the *salvation history,* much simplified in its North American version as "God who acts" (cf. George E. Wright, *God Who Acts: Biblical Theology as Recital* [London: SCM Press, 1952]). From

a theological point of view this is a highly questionable proposition. The Old Testament's image of God and history is rather that God, who created all things as they should be, provided human beings with the option of a blessed future. It is up to humanity itself to decide its future, as happens when it decides for knowledge against eternal life (Genesis 3). Israel is promised a great future, if it follows the way of Yahweh, but when it decides not to follow this course, it is not corrected and put back on the right road. It is punished and thrown out. Yahweh provides the requisites, but history in the Old Testament is the problem of human beings, and they decide the course of history.

13. In Neh. 10:1 the Hebrew phrase is כרתים אמנה, "those who cut an agreement" instead of the usual expression of covenant making כרת ברית "to cut a covenant," אמנה, however, from the root אמן, meaning something that is stable or true being part of the semantics of the covenant.

14. Cf. the repeated references to the burial of "foreign gods," in Gen. 35:2–4 and Josh. 24:23, and the acceptance not so much that Rachel stole her father's house gods as that before Abraham traveled to Canaan the fathers worshiped foreign gods "on the other side of the flood," in Hebrew עבר הנהר, "beyond the River." On this geographical term, see Michael E. Hardwick, "Beyond the River," *ABD* 1:717. He identifies three meanings of this term in the ancient world: (1) the territory east of the Euphrates; (2) from the Persian view the province (satrapy) of Syria, i.e., the territory to the *west* of the Euphrates; and (3) Transjordan. Although Josh. 24:23 is ostensibly a reference to Haran, Haran in the Persian period was part of the satrapy of Ebirnari.

15. Cf. my *The Canaanites and Their Land: The Idea of Canaan in the Old Testament*. Serious criticism has been raised by Nadav Na'aman, "The Canaanites and Their Land: A Rejoinder," *UF* 26 (1994): 397–418 (cf., however, my answer, "Where Should We Look for Canaan? A Reply to Nadav Na'aman," *UF* 28 [1996]: 767–72), and also by Anson F. Rainey, "Who Is a Canaanite? A Review of the Textual Evidence," *BASOR* 304 (1996): 1–15 (cf., however, my rejoinder, "Greater Canaan: The Implications of a Correct Reading of *EA* 151:49–51", *BASOR* 310 [1998]: 19–24).

16. The idea of history as the acts of a god is not peculiar to the Old Testament; rather, it was a common idea in the ancient Near East that the will of some divine being could be seen behind the course of history. The Assyrians conquered the world to please their god, Ashur; the gods fought side by side with kings and heroes, as in the Homeric epic literature. On this, B. Albrektson, *History and the Gods: An Essay on the Idea of Historical Events as Divine Manifestations in the Ancient Near East and in Israel* (Lund: CWK Gleerups, 1967). The difference between the Old Testament and other ancient literature is not so much this idea of the interference of the gods. It is the planning from the side of God, or rather the history seen as one coherent relationship between God and humanity where every single condition has been placed at the beginning, in the constitution (covenant), which hereafter functions like a script for a movie. For that reason, the "gospel" of the biblical theology movement about the "acts of God" (cf. G. E. Wright, *God Who Acts*) is not totally wrong, as long as this has to do with the narrative. It is something else the moment this narrative is translated into real history supposed to have happened—once upon a time.

17. Scholarship on the prophets has continued to be mostly very traditional, considering the prophets to be historical persons with a message of their own, and not literary inventions of a later time. Should it turn out that the imagery of ancient Israel

in the Old Testament is an invention of Judaism, the prophets will have to be clas-
sified in the same category. Preliminary on this is Niels Peter Lemche, "The God of
Hosea," in Eugene Ulrich and John Wright, eds., *Priests, Prophets, and Scribes: Es-
says on the Formation and Heritage of Second Temple Judaism, in Honor of Joseph
Blenkinsopp* (Sheffield: Sheffield Academic Press, 1992), 241–57. An example of how
a prophetic book might have been constructed on the basis not least of
Mesopotamian tradition of oracle sayings is published by Martti Nissinen, *Prophetie,
Redaktion und Fortschreibung im Hoseabuch: Studien zur Werdegang eines
Prophetenbuches im Lichte von Hos 4 und 11* (Neukirchen-Vluyn: Neukirchener Verlag, 1991). A recent contribution in the same direction is Uwe Becker, *Jesaja: Von
der Botschaft zum Buch.*

18. Shiloh was excavated by Hans Kjær and Aage Schmidt between 1926 and
1929, with a final season in 1932; by Marie-Louise Buhl and Svend Holm-Nielsen in
1963; and finally by Israel Finkelstein between 1981 and 1984. Cf. *NAEEHL* 4:1364–70
(by Aron Kempinski and Israel Finkelstein), and Israel Finkelstein, Zvi Lederman,
and Shlomo Bunimowitz, *Shiloh: The Archaeology of a Biblical Site* (Tel Aviv: Tel Aviv
University, 1993).

19. Cf. Niels Peter Lemche, "Mysteriet om det forsvundne tempel: Overleveringen om Silos ødelæggelse i Jer 7,12.14," *Svensk Eksegetisk Årsbok* 54 (1989): 118–26.

20. Apart from the monographs by Jeppesen and Nissinen already mentioned, a
revision of the biblical prophetism has also been prepared by scholars such as Otto
Kaiser (see his *Isaiah 1–12;* 2d ed., completely rewritten; Old Testament Library
[London: SCM Press, 1983]), and Robert Carroll (*From Chaos to Covenant: Uses of
Prophecy in the Book of Jeremiah*) [London: SCM Press, 1981]). See also Carroll's com-
mentary, *Jeremiah: A Commentary* (London: SCM Press, 1986).

21. Denmark is mentioned not only because it is the homeland of this author but
also because it is, if not the oldest state in the Western world, one with more than a
thousand years of uninterrupted history. It arose as a unified state around 900 C.E.,
and is still ruled by the same royal dynasty (although it is now by a side-side-side-
line).

22. Just a couple of examples: In the annals of Shalmaneser III, he fights a coalition assembled by Hadadezer of Damascus, consisting of twelve princes (Luckenbill,
AR 1:§ 681; *ANET,* 280). In another text he describes this coalition as Hadadezer together with twelve kings of Hatti (i.e., Syria) (Luckenbill, *AR* 1:§ 691; *ANET,* 281).His
famous mentioning of Ahab of Sirla'a places Ahab among twelve named members
of the Levantine–North Arabian coalition against the Assyrians, including both
Hadadezer and Irḫuleni among the twelve members (Luckenbill, *AR* 1:§ 611; *ANET,*
278–79).

23. The same Shalmaneser III mentions in another sequence in his annals a coalition of Hadadezer and Irḫuleni together with fifteen kings from the towns of the region along the sea (Luckenbill, *AR* 1:§ 691; *ANET,* 280).

24. Cf. on the Greek amphictyony Niels Peter Lemche, "The Greek 'Amphictyony': Could It Be a Prototype for the Israelite Society in the Period of the Judges?"
JSOT 4 (1977): 48–59, and the literature cited there.

25. Martin Noth, *Das System der zwölf Stämme Israels.*

26. On Noth's refusal to see the stories about the patriarchs as anything except
traditions of the amphictyony, *Geschichte Israels,* 114–20.

27. Cf. Noth, *Geschichte Israels,* 120–30. Cf., however, also the problems created by Gerhard von Rad, when he separated the Sinai tradition from the exodus tradition, in his *Das formgeschichtliche Problem des Hexateuch* (Stuttgart: W. Kohlhammer, 1938; reprinted in his *Gesammelte Studien zum Alten Testament* [Munich: Christian Kaiser, 1958], 9–86).

28. One such element that was attached to the early Israelite concept of Yahweh was the expression *El Qana,* "the jealous God," which appears in Yahweh's self-representation in Ex. 20:4, in connection with the Second Commandment. See further on this below.

29. The classic work on this is Kurt Galling, *Die Erwählungstraditionen Israels* (Giessen: Alfred Töpelmann, 1928). Also this idea is now placed within a Deuteronomistic theological framework; cf. Albertz, *A History of Israelite Religion* 1:228–29, following Rolf Rendtorff, "Die Erwählung Israels als Thema der deuteronomischen Theologie," in Jörg Jeremias and Lothar Perlitt, eds., *Die Botschaft und die Boten: Festschrift Hans Walter Wolff* (Neukirchen-Vluyn: Neukirchener Verlag, 1981), 75–86.

30. See, in spite of their harsh criticism of Noth and Alt, the complete acceptance of this part of Noth's reconstruction of early Israel by the circle of William F. Albright, in John Bright, *A History of Israel* (London: SCM Press, 1960), 142–60.

31. On holy war, cf. Gerhard von Rad, *Der Heilige Krieg im alten Israel* (Zurich: Zwingli-Verlag, 1951); Rudolf Smend, *Jahwekrieg und Stämmebund: Erwägungen zur ältesten Geschichte Israels,* 2d rev. ed. (Göttingen: Vandenhoeck & Ruprecht, 1966).

32. A.D.H. Mayes, *Israel in the Period of the Judges* (London: SCM Press, 1974).

33. C.H.J. de Geus, *The Tribes of Israel. An Investigation into Some of the Presuppositions of Martin Noth's Amphictyony Hypothesis* (Assen and Amsterdam: Van Gorcum, 1978), 69–119, on the twelve-tribe system.

34. *The Tribes of Israel,* 120–64. His discussion of social matters can, seen from a twenty-years-later vantage point, only be reckoned as preliminary in light of such studies as Norman K. Gottwald, *The Tribes of Yahweh,* and Niels Peter Lemche, *Early Israel.*

35. *The Tribes of Israel,* 193–207.

36. Niels Peter Lemche, *Israel i Dommertiden: En oversigt over diskussionen om Martin Noths "Das System der zwölf Stämme Israel"* (Copenhagen: G.E.C. Gads Forlag, 1972).

37. *Israel i Dommertiden,* 39–44. Cf. also the revised English version, "The Greek 'Amphictyony,'" *JSOT* 4:48–59.

38. Otto Bächli, *Amphiktyonie im Alten Testament. Forschungsgeschichtliche Studie zur Hypothese von Martin Noth* (Basel: Friedrich Reinhardt, 1977).

39. As a matter of fact, many scholars still entertain this idea—some like Volkmar Fritz, *Die Entstehung Israels,* 180–83, however, only after having removed so-called "late" additions.

40. Machir being artificially reckoned a half-tribe, the son of Joseph's son Manasseh; see Gen. 50:23. Machir in Judg. 5:14, however, is not thought of as different from the other tribes mentioned here.

41. Fritz Stolz, *Jahwes und Israels Kriege: Kriegstheorien und Kriegserfahrungen im Glauben des alten Israels* (Zurich: TVZ, 1972).

42. Cf. George E. Mendenhall, "Covenant Forms in Israelite Tradition," *BA* 17

(1954): 25–53 (reprinted in Campbell and Freedman, *The Biblical Archaeologist Reader,* 3:25–53). Mendenhall was in the following decade to win a widespread support, not only in North America, but also in Germany; cf. among others, Walter Beyerlin, *Herkunft und Geschichte der ältesten Sinaitraditionen* (Tübingen: J.C.B. Mohr [Paul Siebeck], 1961).

43. The hypothesis never overcame the difficulties raised against it by von Rad, seeing the Sinai tradition as an integral tradition belonging in the framework of the "original" Pentateuch, in his *Das formgeschichtliche Problem des Hexateuch.*

44. Lothar Perlitt, *Bundestheologie im Alten Testament* (Neukirchen-Vluyn: Neukirchener Verlag, 1969).

45. Cf. Perlitt's well-formulated and reasonable defense of Wellhausen against the accusations by, among others, William F. Albright, *From the Stone Age to Christianity: Monotheism and the Historical Process* (1940; 2d ed., Garden City, N.Y.: Doubleday, 1957), 88, for being influenced by Hegel's philosophy of history, in Lothar Perlitt, *Vatke und Wellhausen: Geschichtsphilosophische Voraussetzungen und historiographische Motive für die Darstellung der Religion und Geschichte Israels durch Wilhelm Vatke und Julius Wellhausen* (Berlin: de Gruyter, 1965). Perlitt beyond doubt showed Wellhausen to be a romantic, having as his spiritual forefather the great German "Sturm und Drang prophet," Johann Gottfried Herder, one of the spiritual forefathers of the Romantic period.

46. Wellhausen's *Prolegomena,* (1878), 1, opens programmatically with the following statement: "In the following pages it is proposed to discuss the place in history of the 'law of Moses;' more precisely, the question to be considered is whether that law is the starting-point for the history of ancient Israel, or not rather for that of Judaism, *i.e.,* of the religious communion which survived the destruction of the nation by the Assyrians and Chaldæans."

47. Cf. my *Israel i Dommertiden,* (1972), 87.

48. Noth mentions the possibility of a six-tribe amphictyony consisting of the tribes of Lea, *Das System,* 91–93. For an original ten-tribe amphictyony, cf. Sigmund Mowinckel, *Israels opphav og eldste historie* (Oslo: Universitetsforlaget, 1967), 171–75. Mowinckel believes that the number twelve is the result of learned speculation at the court of David.

49. The first list can be found in Gen. 39:31–30:24 (& 35:22–26); 46:8–25; 49:2–27; Ex. 1:2–4; the second in Ex. 1:5–15, 20–43; 2:3–31; 7:12–83; 10:14–28; 13:4–15; 26:5–51; 34:16–29; Deut. 27:12–13; 33:6–25.

50. Cf. Lemche, *Israel i Dommertiden,* 106–13.

51. This excursus builds on and improves a never-published part of my early study on the amphictyony in my student thesis from 1968, "Forudsætningerne for Davids Imperium i og uden for Israel: Studier i trehundrede års nærorientalsk historie" (Copenhagen, 1968), 41–49, and subsequently excluded from the almost strictly historical discourse in my *Israel i Dommertiden.*

52. The story of the loss of the ark, 1 Samuel 4–6, and its recovery, 2 Samuel 6, should from a narrative point of view be seen as brackets around a parentheses in Israel's history, to which the stories of Samuel and Saul belong. Although Samuel worked hard in the service of the Lord, his duty—to find a new savior for an Israel in distress—was only accomplished when he anointed the youngest son of Jesse (1 Sam. 16:1–13).

53. The parallel in Ezra 2:1, which seems to be the more corrupted version, contains only eleven names.

54. Cf. his Martin Noth, *Überlieferungsgeschichte des Pentateuch* (Stuttgart: W. Kohlhammer, 1948. Reprint, Darmstadt: Wissenschaftliche Buchgesellschaft, 1966). Included in this original tradition was a series of themes: exodus, immigration, promise to the patriarchs, the Israelite sojourn in the desert, and Sinai. Other themes belonged to the supplementary layers, such as the story of the plagues, Jacob in Sechem, Caleb in Hebron, and so on.

55. All too few scholars have admitted this, continuing in the ways of their fathers and assuming an original tradition about the nation of Israel to have existed without a home. They generally tended to down-date the traditions of the past, by Noth thought to be amphictyonic traditions, to the time of the United Monarchy. Thus see recently J. Alberto Soggin, *An Introduction to the History of Israel and Judah* (London: SCM Press, 1993), 87–193, in a way that strictly resembles the way Noth introduced the discussion of these parts of the biblical tradition in *Geschichte Israels,* 105–39. A few saw the problem raised by the deconstruction of the amphictyony and tried to retain the basic ideas of a historic tribal league, e.g., N. K. Gottwald, *The Tribes of Yahweh,* passim. Gottwald's evaluation of the biblical tradition closely follows Noth's, but he did not succeed in creating a new life for the league, which had already effectively vanished into Israel's literary past.

56. On the classic definition, cf. above 8–9.

57. On this type of marriage, cf. my *Early Israel,* 224–28.

58. The foreign woman is a mixed blessing to the writers of the Old Testament. Zipporah is accepted without blemishes, whereas the Midianite woman in Numbers 25 is killed. Jael, the Kenite woman, is praised for killing Sisera the enemy of Israel (Judg. 5:24–27), as Ruth is in her own book for her acts as a trickster becoming the maternal ancestor of King David.

59. Cf. Herodotus' merry story about how the Egyptians found out which was the original language in *Histories* II.2.

60. Deut. 32:8–9, "Hebrew-wise," the Greek version having the famous variant that Yahweh was given his people by the highest God, El Elyon.

61. On this world especially, John Van Seters, *Abraham in History and Tradition* (New Haven and London: Yale University Press, 1975), part 2, 123–312. Van Seters's argument is that the Abraham tradition is a literary invention from the time of the exile. Cf. also Niels Peter Lemche, *Die Vorgeschichte Israels,* 34–47.

62. In Hebrew יהודית. Hebrew is in fact never used to describe the language of the Israelites in the Old Testament.

63. In Hebrew אשדודית.

64. The curse is repeated in Jer. 5:15.

65. Hebrew לשון אחרת.

66. In Hebrew מכל לשנות הגוים, "from all the tongues of the foreign people;" KJV's "nations" is reflecting a preromantic European understanding of the term "nation" as meaning just "foreign people," rather than nation in the sense of the inhabitants of a national state (cf. above, 11). The NEB's and REB's "ten men [people] from nations of every language" is thoughtlessly repeating this usage, a clear example of how the terminology of the premodern world continued and was inherited without reflection also in the modern world, when a quite different idea of nationality had developed.

67. Nation here being used in the usual English translations in the same sense as in Zech. 8:23.

68. Cf., however, also the discussion in Lemche, *Canaanites,* 123–25.

69. Remembering the incident in Judg. 12:6 when Ephraimite refugees trying to cross the Jordan in disguise were unmasked because they were unable to pronounce the *shin* in *shibbolet.*

70. Ekron inscription, cf. 182 no. 38 above.

71. Cf. above 8–9.

72. The classical language did not, in fact, contain a word that covers the modern concept of religion. Closest to this meaning are terms like the Greek εὐσέβεια, meaning such things as piousness. The Latin *religio* was not confined to religious matters, but developed into a concept that had to do with religion. Cf. *Oxford Classical Dictionary* (Oxford: Clarendon Press, 1949), article "Religion, Terms Relating to," 758.

73. Ex. 20:5; 34:14; Deut. 4:24; 5:9; 6:15. Ex. 34:14 also has קנא יהוה, "Yahweh is jealous." Cf. on this expression above, n. 28.

74. On this expression, Eduard Nielsen, *The Ten Commandments* (London: SCM Press, 1968), Johann Jacob Stamm and Maurice Edward Andrew, *The Ten Commandments in Recent Research* (London: SCM Press, 1967), 86. More recent scholarship reckons this to be a term of God that originated in connection with Deuteronomistic theological thinking. Cf. Rainer Albertz, *A History of Israelite Religion in the Old Testament Period,* 1:215 with n. 134 (p. 357).

75. Ex. 34:11–26; cf. on this as an ancient text the comprehensive study by Jürgen Halbe, *Das Privilegrecht Jahwes: Ex 34,10–26: Gestalt und Wesen, Herkunft und Wirken in vordeuteronomistischer Zeit* (Göttingen: Vandenhoeck & Ruprecht, 1975). I feel no difficulty in subscribing to the verdict of Rainer Albertz, that it is a late composition: *History,* 1:61.

76. As correctly pointed out by Norman K. Gottwald, "Domain Assumptions and Societal Models in the Study of Pre-Monarchic Israel," *VTS* 28 (1975): 89–100.

77. On modern examples of this, including an evaluation of Rainer Albertz, *A History of Israelite Religion in the Old Testament World,* vol. 1, see the following chapter.

78. On this above, 98 with no. 29.

79. F. A. J. Nielsen, *The Tragedy in History: Herodotus and the Deuteronomistic History* (Sheffield: Sheffield Academic Press, 1997).

80. See below on the *nostoi* tradition. Among such belong the traditions about the ill-fated Ajax, Agamemnon's return to Mycenae, and Idomeneus's return to Crete, some of which formed the themes of beloved plays by the Greek tragedians. It should not be forgotten that the theme of the return fills half of the *Odyssey,* Odysseus arriving at Ithaca already in the XIIIth song.

81. *Odyssey* XVII, 290–327.

82. Apollonius of Rhodes, *Argonautica* (third century B.C.E.).

83. From the second half of the first century B.C.E., never finished.

84. It is a peculiar fact that scholars have not used this information to date this narrative, as Babylon was never deserted before Hellenistic times. Once it was raided and destroyed by Sennacherib in 689 B.C.E., a feat from which he earned little praise, not even accepted by his successor Asarhaddon, who rebuilt Babylon (Luckenbill,

AR 2:§ 507). It continued to exist down to the time of Alexander, who had his base here for his campaign to Afghanistan and India, and who returned here to die (323 B.C.E.). However, his successor, Seleuchos I (321–280 B.C.E.) founded his own capital, Seleucia, in 312 B.C.E. (modern Baghdad) close to Babylon. Over the next hundred years Babylon was slowly deserted by its inhabitants. By c. 200 B.C.E., the formerly flowering city did not exist anymore. Is the biblical story a reflection of the fate of one of the marvels of the world?

85. In my *Die Vorgeschichte Israels,* 29, I compared this "geography" to the one we find in a theater, a stage that can revolve: Abraham leaves the scene called "Haran," and immediately after that enters the scene called "Canaan," from where he continues to the scene called "Egypt." The narrative revolves around these three scenes. It is not a geography of the living world; it is the highly stylized geography of a playwright.

86. Compare the *Odyssey.* Odysseus is prevented from reaching his home because of a deadly sin committed by his men, the abduction of the oxen of the Helios (*Odyssey,* XII:260–450), whereupon his seven-year-long sojourn with Calypso can begin.

87. Examples of this from the ancient Near East are Idrimi of Alalakh and David. Cf. above 24–25 on Idrimi.

88. One example is Sinuhe in the Middle Kingdom tale of this Egyptian's exile in Retenu and subsequent return (Hallo and Younger, eds., *Context of Scripture,* 1:77–82). Another is the Idrimi story, although the motif of return will here cover up for the fact that the hero did not return to the place of birth, but rather usurped the throne of a neighboring kingdom.

89. The name derives from Greek νόστος, "return home." *Nostoi* was the name of one of the Cylic epics, which dealt with the fate of the Greek heroes after the fall of Troy.

90. Livy on the early history of Rome, *History,* vol. 1, which opens with a short résumé of Aeneas's travel from Troy to Italy.

91. Showing, however, an awareness of the dilemma: what to do with a righteous enemy? never so poignantly exposed as in H. von Kleist's play the "Hermannschlacht," when the first Roman soldier to die in the Teutoburger Forest is the one who saved a German child from a burning house: A just enemy is opposing the order of nature and creates confusion, so a radical decision is called for, one that the Israelites were never able to make.

92. It is one of the "hidden" codes of the Bible, as it is in classical literature, that a transgression is a transgression, which although temporarily corrected must at the end lead to some kind of punishment. Modern scholars have not always been good at discovering such codes, living in a world with different norms and rules. Another example of such a hidden code becoming operative is the fate of Lot, who decides as the first where to live, invited to this by his uncle Abraham, who should of course have decided as the elder and more important person (Gen. 13:5–13). Abraham's invitation is no excuse for Lot's behavior that he assumed for himself the right of the elder uncle. His fate was in fact doomed because of this transgression.

93. Probably best expressed by Judges 1, with an emphasis on a listing of territories not conquered by the Israelites. This should be seen in light of admonitions like Ex. 23:20–33; 34:10–16.

94. Herodotus on circumcision, 2.104.

95. The Egyptians usually cut off the foreskins of enemies killed in battle in order to count their number. However, in the cases where the enemies were circumcised, they cut off hands instead of foreskins. In an account of the battle against the Sea-people, the Egyptians counted hands! Cf. Breasted, *ARE,* 3:§ 588. Although this text (from the time of Merneptah) does not mention the Philistines (Peleset), it makes clear that the Egyptians distinguished between *uncircumcised* Libyans and Sea-people.

96. In Hebrew אשר לא מזרעד.

97. On genealogies, see Lemche, *Die Vorgeschichte Israels,* 31.

98. On this discussion, cf. the studies by Antonius H. J. Gunneweg, *Leviten und Priester* (Göttingen: Vandenhoeck & Ruprecht 1965), and Aelred Cody, *A History of Old Testament Priesthood* (Rome: Pontifical Biblical Institute, 1969); also Eduard Nielsen, "The Levites in Ancient Israel," in his *Law, History and Tradition: Selected Essays by Eduard Nielsen* (Copenhagen: G.E.C. Gads Forlag, 1983), 71–81, and the comprehensive but very traditional article "Levites and Priests," by Merlin D. Rehm, in *ABD* 4:297–310.

99. The Hebrew of Gen. 15:18 is often corrected from נהר מצרים to נחל מצרים as proposed by the text-critical apparatus in *Biblia hebraica stuttgartensia* (cf. the description of the southern border of Judah in Josh. 15:4, 47; cf. also Solomon's kingdom in 1 Kings 8:65), meaning the Brook of Egypt (i.e., Wadi el-Arish in the northern part of Sinai) instead of the River of Egypt. That the other tradition was known (if it is not a testimony to the antiquity of the Masoretic text) can be seen from the passage in the Genesis Apocryphon, where Abraham from Ramat Hazor can see his country stretching from the River of Egypt to the Euphrates (GenAp XXI:8–13).

100. The passage in 1 Kings 5:1 is difficult and the text probably not in order. The KJV represents no more than the most common restoration of it.

101. Lebo-hamath, or "the entrance of Hamath" (thus KJV) is sometimes in the Old Testament maintained to be Israel's northern border (Num. 34:7–9; Josh. 13:5; Ezek. 47:16). It is often associated with the modern place-name in Syria, Lebweh, c. twenty miles south of modern Hamath, most likely also mentioned in Egyptian and Assyrian sources (Laba'um), where in early antiquity a famous wood was situated. Cf. on this Martin Noth, "Studien zu den historisch-geographischen Dokumenten des Josuabuches" (1935), *ABLAK,* 1:229–54, 271–75, and esp. "Das Reich von Hamath als Grenznachbar des Reiches Israel" (1937), *ABLAK* 2:148–60.

102. Cf., among others, Noth (see preceding note). Cf. also Yohanan Aharoni, *The Land of the Bible: A Historical Geography* (London: Burns & Oates, 1967), 65–67, and Nadav Na'aman, "The Canaanites and Their Land: A Rejoinder," *UF* 26 (1994): 397–418.

103. Cf. above 77–80.

104. Palestine was in Herodotus's opinion a part of Syria. Cf. the evidence collected in Niels Peter Lemche, "Clio Is Also among the Muses! Keith W. Whitelam and the History of Palestine: A Review and a Commentary," in Lester L. Grabbe, *Can a "History of Israel" Be Written* (Sheffield: Sheffield Academic Press, 1997), 123–155, 131–2.

105. David W. Baker, "Girgashite," in *ABD* 2:1028, refers to Ugaritic *grgš/bn grgš,* as people coming from a place of this name. However, according to Frauke Grön-

dahl, *Die Personennamen der Texte aus Ugarit* (Rome: Pontifical Biblical Institute, 1967), 129, partly followed by G. del Olmo Lete and J. Sanmartín, *Diccionario de la lengua ugaritica* (Barcelona: Editorial Ausa, 1996), 1:151, the Ugaritic parallel is a compound of *gr* (= Hebrew גר "foreign resident") and a word of unknown origin, *gš*.

106. Cf. on the Kenites the well-informed article "Kenites," by Baruch Halpern, in *ABD* 4:17–22.

107. The "identity" of the Rephaim as "ghosts" has been confirmed by their appearance in Ugaritic texts, including *KTU* 1.161, an incantation of the spirits of deceased kings of Ugarit. Cf. on this (with an outlook to similar phenomena in the Old Testament) Oswald Loretz, *Ugarit und die Bibel. Kanaanäische Götter und Religion im Alten Testament* (Darmstadt: Wissenschaftliche Buchgesellschaft, 1990), 128–39.

108. Hebrew קדם, carrying both spatial and chronological connotations. A study of the double meaning of, among other Hebrew words, קדם is being prepared by Tilde Binger of Copenhagen.

109. The first Amorite example being the two "confederates" of Abraham, Mamre and Eshcol (Gen. 14:13). Other examples include the Amorite king of Transjordan, Sihon (Num. 21:21–31), also mentioned in combination with the Rephaim King Og of Bashan (Num. 21:33–35; cf. Josh. 12:1–6).

110. Cf. on the term Amorite in late Mesopotamian sources, John Van Seters, "The Terms 'Amorite' and 'Hittite' in the Old Testament," *VT* 22 (1972): 64–81, and Van Seters, *Abraham in History and Tradition,* 20–26. On the Amorites in general, cf. Mario Liverani, "The Amorites," in Dennis J. Wiseman, ed., *Peoples of Old Testament Times* (Oxford: Oxford University Press, 1973), 100–33.

111. On Amurru, cf. Horst Klengel, *Geschichte Syriens im 2. Jahrtausend v.u.Z. Teil 2: Mittel- und Südsyrien* (Berlin: Akademie-Verlag, 1969), 245–99; and Itamar Singer, "A Concise History of Amurru," in Shlomo Izre'el, *Amurru Akkadian: A Linguistic Study,* vols. 1 and 2 (Atlanta: Scholars Press, 1991), 135–95.

112. Thus already in the Execration Texts from Egypt nineteenth and eighteenth centuries B.C.E. (cf. *ANET,* 329). On Jerusalem in the Amarna letters and the problems caused by these, cf. above 192 no. 22.

113. Cf. above 30–31 and 201 no. 15 and n. 15 on the Canaanites and the discussion between this author and Nadav Na'aman and Anson F. Rainey.

114. Cf. above on the ethnic situation in the Late Bronze Age and Early Iron Age in places like Achzib and Tell Keisan, 68 with no. 15.

115. Cf. Niels Peter Lemche, *The Canaanites,* 56–57, with a reference to Augustine, *E ad Romanos inchoata expositio* 13 (Migne, *Patrologia Latina* XXXV, 2096).

116. Lemche, "Is It Still Possible to Write a History of Ancient Israel?" *SJOT* 8 (1994): 163–88.

117. It is hardly fortuitous, but in accordance with the logic of the narrative, that this priest settles in Bethel, the center of the apostasy from Yahweh (2 Kings 17:28; cf. 1 Kings 12:26–33; and the rejection of Bethel in 1 Kings 13, with the appendix in 2 Kings 23:15–18).

118. Cf. above 81 on the socioeconomic situation in Judea in the sixth century B.C.E., and the literature cited there.

119. Cf. above 85 on deportations.

120. Such cities included probably Sepphoris, Straton's Tower (the place of the later Caesarea), Joppa, and Aszotus, to mention only a selection of these.

121. Cf. John Strange, "The Book of Joshua: A Hasmonaean Manifesto?" in André Lemaire and Bendedikt Otzen, eds., *History and Traditions of Early Israel: Studies Presented to Eduard Nielsen May 8th 1993* (Leiden: E. J. Brill, 1993), 136–41.

Chapter 5: The Scholar's Israel

1. A challenging perspective on the school of Albright and its influence in North American biblical studies has recently been published by Burke O. Long, *Planting and Reaping Albright: Politics, Ideology, and Interpreting the Bible* (University Park, Pa.: Pennsylvania State University Press, 1997). On Albright and his relationship to Alt and Noth, *Planting and Reaping Albright,* 53–59.

2. This seems the case with: Siegfried Herrmann, *Israels Aufenhalt in Ägypten* (Stuttgart: Verlag Katholisches Bibelwerk, 1970), and his *Geschichte Israels in alttestamentlicher Zeit* (Munich: Christian Kaiser, 1973; English trans.: *A History of Israel in Old Testament Times,* 2d ed. [London and Philadelphia: Fortress Press, 1981]).

3. "The history of a nation cannot be traced beyond the people itself, back to a period when this nation did not exist at all" in J. Wellhausen, *Israelitische und jüdische Geschichte,* 10.

4. I have chosen to use his *Israelitische und jüdische Geschichte,* and especially the paragraph herein, "Die Anfänge des Volkes," 10–33, instead of his *Prolegomena to the History of Ancient Israel.* This is not because this history is a superior work, which it is certainly not, but because it is much easier to use in order to get an impression of Wellhausen's ideas about Israelite ethnicity. The *Encyclopaedia Britannica* from the end of the nineteenth century should also include an article by Wellhausen on Israelite history (according to Rudolf Smend, in Julius Wellhausen, *Grundrisse zum Alten Testament,* ed. R. Smend [Munich, Christian Kaiser, 1965], 6). A German version of this article was published for the first time in the same volume, as "Geschichte Israels" 1880, 13–64.

5. "Quite malicious Alexandrine legends," *Israelitische und jüdische Geschichte,* 11.

6. *Israelitische und jüdische Geschichte,* 14. This was going to be a continuous theme in Old Testament historical studies over the next many generations, the last serious contributers to this discussion being probably O. Eissfeldt and S. Mowinckel. As a paradigm for historical-critical investigations into the early history of ancient Israel, from Wellhausen to Albrecht Alt, cf. my articles "Rachel and Lea," I. *SJOT* 1:2 (1987): 127–53, and "Rachel and Lea," II. *SJOT* 2:1 (1988): 39–65.

7. *Israelitische und jüdische Geschichte,* 16, 122–32.

8. *Israelitische und jüdische Geschichte,* 15.

9. *Israelitische und jüdische Geschichte,* 19.

10. *Ibid.* Cf. Judg, 17:6; 18:1; 19:1; 21:25.

11. *Israelitische und jüdische Geschichte,* 20.

12. *Israelitische und jüdische Geschichte,* 22.

13. "Das ist der Anfang und das bleibende Prinzip der folgenden politisch-religiösen Geschichte," *Israelitische und jüdische Geschichte,* 23.

14. *Israelitische und jüdische Geschichte,* 28: "Zu einer politischen Einheit wurde Israel erst allmählich, durch die Vorarbeit der Religion, als Volk Jahves."

15. In less than a generation this was mainstream OT scholarship and dominates

the histories of Israelite religion, such as the one by the Scandinavian scholar Helmer Ringgren, *Israelite Religion* (Philadelphia: Fortress Press, 1975), and the German Werner H. Schmidt, *Alttestamentlicher Glaube und seine Umwelt: Zur Geschichte des alttestamentlichen Gottesverständnisses* (Neukirchen-Vlyun: Neukirchener Verlag, 1968). Cf. also emphatically, Gösta W. Ahlström, *Aspects of Syncretism in Israelite Religion* (Lund: C.W.K. Gleerups, 1963). A very elegant study of this alleged syncretism was published by Walter Dietrich, *Israel und Kanaan: Vom Ringen zweier Gesellschaftssysteme* (Stuttgart: Verlag Katholisches Bibelwerk, 1979).

16. This is sometimes—mostly in oral communications (cf., however, Friedemann W. Golka, "German Old Testament Scholarship," in R. G. Coggins and J. L. Houlden, *A Dictionary of Biblical Interpretation,* 258–66, esp. 259)—among scholars taken as proof of Wellhausen's alleged anti-Semitism. This view of Wellhausen sometimes, surfaces, however, as in William B. Dever's accusations of this writer's entertaining "antipathy to Judaism (akin to Wellhausen's jaundiced view)," "Revisionist Israel Revisited," *Currents in Research: Biblical Studies* 4: 35–50.

17. See my articles on "Rachel and Lea" (note 6 above), where one of the themes concerns the way Wellhausen was "tamed" by subsequent scholarship, including that of his own students.

18. Martin Noth, *Geschichte Israels,* 8–15.

19. Noth, *Geschichte Israels,* 12.

20. Cf. the Prolegomena to this book on the development of Czech nationalism.

21. Cf. on the grave of Moses, Noth, *Geschichte,* 128 n. 2. Cf. also, *Überlieferungsgeschichte des Pentateuchs,* 186–87. Herbert Donner, writing a history in the tradition of Noth (delayed, however, by one generation) goes further into the traditional roles of Moses, thereby isolating twelve different functions of Moses in the biblical literature; *Geschichte* 1:110–12.

22. Thus already Leonhard Rost (who "invented" this story: cf. his *Die Überlieferung von der Thronnachfolge Davids* [Stuttgart: W. Kohlhammer, 1926]; reprinted in Leonhard Rost, *Das kleine Credo und andere Studien zum Alten Testament* [Heidelberg: Quelle & Meyer, 1965], 119–244) reckoned the so-called "succession narrative" (2 Sam.7–2 Kings 2) to be at least in parts based on an "Ebiathar-source," i.e., on a source composed by one of David's officers.

23. Rudolf Kittel (1853–1929) was for many years professor in Leipzig and the teacher of Albrecht Alt and at the end of his career also Martin Noth. Alt studied in Erlangen and Leipzig from 1902 to 1906, Noth became a member of Kittel's seminar in the 1920s. Cf. Rudolf Smend, *Deutsche Alttestamentler in drei Jahrhunderten* (Göttingen: Vandenhoeck & Ruprecht, 1989), 182–207, 188 (Alt), and 255–75, 255 (Noth). His main work was *Geschichte des Volkes Israel* (2d. ed., Gotha: Friedrich Andreas Perthes A.-G., 1909–12). It appeared originally as *Geschichte der Hebräer,* vols. 1 and 2 (Gotha: Friedrich Andreas Perthes, 1888–98).

24. Martin Metzger, *Grundriß der Geschichte Israels,* (Neukirchen-Vluyn: Neukirchener Verlag, 1983); Siegfried Herrmann, *Geschichte Israels in alttestamentlicher Zeit,* 1973; Antonius J. H. Gunneweg, *Geschichte Israels bis Bar Kochba* (Stuttgart: W. Kohlhammer, 1972); Georg Fohrer, *Geschichte Israels von den Anfängen bis zur Gegenwart* (Heidelberg: Quelle & Meyer, 1977); Herbert Donner, *Geschichte des Volkes Israel,* vols. 1 and 2 (Göttingen: Vandenhoeck & Ruprecht, 1984–86).

25. Aage Bentzen, *Israels Historie* (Copenhagen: Haase & Søns Forlag, 1930);

Eduard Nielsen, *Grundrids af Israels Historie,* 2d. ed. (Copenhagen: G.E.C. Gads Forlag, 1960); Benedikt Otzen, *Israeliterne i Palæstina: Det gamle Israels historie, religion og litteratur* (Copenhagen: G.E.C. Gads Forlag, 1977). This also includes the
otherwise idiosyncratic history by Sigmund Mowinckel, *Israels opphav og eldste historie,* 1967, and can still be traced in Gösta W. Ahlström, *The History of Ancient Palestine from the Palaeolithic Period to Alexander's Conquest,* ed. Diana Edelman, 1993,
at least from the time of the monarchy and onward (sections that he did not man-
age to revise before his death in January 1992). The major English work from this
period is W.O.E. Oesterley and Theodore H. Robinson, *A History of Israel,* vols. 1
and 2 (Oxford: Clarendon Press, 1932).

26. J. Alberto Soggin, *A History of Israel: From the Beginnings to the Bar Kochba
Revolt, AD 135* (London: SCM Press, 1984; Italian edition, Brescia: Casa Editrice
Paideia, 1985). The speed with which this view on ancient Israel was changing is re-
flected by the second edition of this work, now published as *An Introduction to the
History of Israel and Judah* (1993) (an intermediary stage is represented by the Ger-
man edition *Einführung in die Geschichte Israels und Judas: Von den Ursprüngen bis
zum Aufstand Bar Kochbas* [Darmstadt: Wissenschaftliche Buchgesellschaft, 1991]).
Soggin is a student of Noth.

27. Cf. not least Siegfried Herrmann, *Israels Aufenhalt in Ägypten,* 1970.

28. Roland de Vaux, *Histoire ancienne d'Israël,* vol. 1: *Des origines à l'installation en Canaan* (Paris: Librairie Lecoffre, J. Gabalda et Cie, Éditeurs, 1971). The second volume was published as a fragment: *Histoire ancienne d'Israël,* vol. 2: *La
période des juges* (Paris: Librairie Lecoffre, J. Gabalda et Cie, Éditeurs, 1973). (English trans.: *The Early History of Israel* [London: Darton, Longman & Todd, 1978]).

29. Cf. already de Vaux's "Les Patriarches hébreux et les découvertes récentes,"
Revue Biblique 53 (1946): 321–48; 55 (1948): 321–47; 56 (1949): 5–36. Repeated in
Histoire ancienne, 1:150–273. A very comprehensive, harsh, however precise, review
of de Vaux's *Histoire ancienne* was published by Mario Liverani in *Oriens Antiquus*
15 (1976): 145–59. Liverani stresses the arbitrariness of de Vaux's position, standing
"in the middle" between on one side the school of Albright, and on the other that of
Alt and Noth. De Vaux forgot at the same time that another direction (represented
by George E. Mendenhall) was to the left of the positions of Alt and Noth. The result is a history of Israel with a definite conservative bent.

30. John Bright's *A History of Israel,* which appeared in its first edition in 1959,
underwent two major revisions, the last one in 1981 (Philadelphia: Westminster,
1981), when Mendenhall's model for the origin of Israel greatly influenced Bright.

31. The closest Albright ever came to publishing a history of Israel was his *The
Biblical Period from Abraham to Ezra* (New York: Harper & Row, 1963), based on
an essay in Louis Finkelstein, ed., *The Jews: Their History, Culture, and Religion* (New
York: Harper & Row, 1949).

32. The attitude and tactics of the Albright circle toward Alt and Noth is reviewed
in Long, *Planting and Reaping Albright,* 53–59. It is an ironic fact that the third generation of this circle—exemplified by William G. Dever—is carrying on the same tactics, although it has a long time ago accepted most of Alt's and Noth's ideas about
early Israel and given up many fundamental parts of Albright's position. Cf. for example William G. Dever, *Recent Archaeological Discoveries and Biblical Research,*
and his well-aimed crusade against the concept of "biblical archaeology," a major
point in the Albright armory.

33. Cf. Yehezkel Kaufmann, *The Biblical Account of the Conquest of Palestine* (Jerusalem: Magnes Press, 1953).

34. Cf. Niels Peter Lemche, "Rachel and Lea," 2:45–48, on Kittel.

35. Bright, *History of Israel,* 128–60. If possible, Bright rather increased the importance of the amphictyony in early Israel.

36. Ibid., 120–27.

37. Ibid., 120. "The Bible also offers evidence that the people of Israel was formed by a complex process and included components of exceedingly diverse origin." In the following Bright refers to Ex. 12:38 and Num. 11:4, to the expression "a mixed multitude" meaning a "rabble." This "multitude" is, however, not reckoned a part of the 600,000 Israelites either in Exodus 12 or Numbers 11; in Num. 11:4 they are, as a matter of fact, seen as a problem to the Israelites because of their greediness.

38. Ibid., 121. He refers to a study of A. Lucas, according to which the column of Israelites walking in rows of four would extend for 350 miles, (*History of Israel,* 121 n. 56). The controversy about the size of the Israelite exodus from Egypt goes back at least two centuries, to Gottholdt Ephraim Lessing (based on notes from Hermann Samuel Reimarus); cf. John Rogerson, *Old Testament Criticism in the Nineteenth Century: England and Germany* (London: SPCK, 1984), 24–25.

39. This motif, which opens in Ex. 16:2, was isolated as part of the secondary motives by Noth, in his *Überlieferungsgeschichte des Pentateuchs,* 134–43. For a more recent discussion, cf. esp. John Van Seters, *The Life of Moses: The Yahwist as Historian in Exodus-Numbers* (Kampen: Kok Pharos Publishing House, 1994), 220–44.

40. On this narrative technique, cf. Niels Peter Lemche, *Die Vorgeschichte Israels,* 61. 65.

41. Bright, *History of Israel,* 121.

42. It is of no importance to the argument here that Gibeon was hardly founded when Joshua is supposed to have conquered the land. It is just an obstacle to accepting the biblical version of the Israelite conquest at face value. Cf. on Gibeon, James B. Pritchard, *NAEEHL* 1:511–14, esp. 513. In his popular book *Gibeon, Where the Sun Stood Still: The Discovery of a Biblical City* (Princeton, N.J.: Princeton University Press, 1962), 157–58, Pritchard tried to cover up for the fact that there is little that speaks in favor of a Late Bronze settlement. In his article "Arkeologiens plats i studiet av Gamla Testamentet," *Svensk Exegetisk Årsbok* 30 (1965): 5–20, esp. 15, Pritchard emphatically stresses the lack of remains of a city from this time.

43. Cf. above (57–62) on the *ḫabiru.*

44. Bright, *History of Israel,* 125–26.

45. A not very adept means to bypass what in Bright's days was a heatedly discussed problem, the relation between the Sinai traditions and the Kadesh traditions, the Sinai complex probably being secondary to the Kadesh one. Cf. on this above (100 with no. 43) with reference to the distinction made between the Sinai and the exodus traditions by Gerhard von Rad.

46. Bright, *History of Israel,* 125.

47. Mendenhall, "The Hebrew Conquest" (1962).

48. English translation, Louisville, Ky.: Westminster John Knox Press, 1994.

49. On this hypothesis, cf. above (65–77).

50. Cf. Rainer Albertz, "Religionsgeschichte Israels statt Theologie des Alten Testaments! Plädoyer für eine Forschungsgeschichtliche Umorientierung," *Jahrbuch für Biblische Theologie* 10 (1995): 3–24.

51. Rainer Albertz, *A History of Israelite Religion*, 1:23–103.

52. Ibid., 60, accepting at the same time that Yahweh was not originally the God of Israel, but rather had an independent "life" in the regions to the south of Palestine.

53. Ibid.

54. Ibid., 49.

55. Ibid., 71f., 77.

56. Ibid., 76–77.

57. Ibid., 91.

58. Niels Peter Lemche, *Early Israel*, as against Norman K. Gottwald, *The Tribes of Yahweh*.

59. Niels Peter Lemche, "On the Problem of Studying Israelite History: Apropos Abraham Malamat's View of Historical Research," *BN* 24 (1984): 94–124, cf. esp. 111–14.

60. Niels Peter Lemche, "On the Problem," 111. The quotation is my translation of a passage taken from M. Liverani, "Storiografia politica hittita II: Telipino, ovvero: Della Solidarietà," *Oriens Antiquus* 16 (1977): 105–31, esp. 105.

61. English translation in Hallo and Younger, eds., *Context of Scripture*, 1:194–98.

62. In order to understand the nature of historical literature in the ancient Near East it is recommended that the reader should consult Mario Liverani, "Memorandum on the Approach to Historiographic Texts," *Orientalia*, n.s., 42 (1973): 178–94.

63. The primeval history, Genesis 1–11 was reluctantly reduced to myth and literature during the eighteenth and nineteenth centuries, although W.M.L. de Wette already in 1807 confidently could write "Die Schöpfungsgeschichte 1 Mose 1. wird ausser Hrn. Henschler heut zu Tage niemand mehr für Geschichte nehmen . . . ," ["Except for Mr. Henschler nobody will take the Creation story in Genesis 1 to be history."] in *Beiträge zur Einleitung in das Alte Testament, Zweiter Band: Kritik der israelitischen Geschichte. Erster Theil. Kritik der mosaischen Geschichte* (Halle: Schimmelpfennig & Compagnie), 27–28. When stating this, he was probably somewhat premature.

64. John H. Hayes and J. Maxwell Miller, eds., *Israelite and Judaean History* (London: SCM Press, 1977); on the patriarchal period, pp. 70–148 (this chapter written by W. G. Dever and W. M. Clark).

65. De Wette's critique of the patriarchal narratives as historical sources was published in *Beiträge zur Einleitung in das Alte Testament. Zweiter Band*, 48–168.

66. Wellhausen's *Israelitische und jüdische Geschichte* does not include a session on the patriarchs, neither does his *Prolegomena*, as far as history is concerned. For Wellhausen, the history of Israel began in the desert at Kadesh before the immigration.

67. Noth, *Geschichte*, 114–20.

68. Rudolf Kittel, *Geschichte des Volkes Israel*, 1:408–80; Ernst Sellin, *Geschichte des Israelitisch-jüdischen Volkes*, 1:29–40, although Sellin admits that we have only a little historical information about the three patriarchs.

69. Cf. William F. Albright, *From the Stone Age to Christianity*, 236–49, "The Biblical Period," 1–9; John Bright, *History of Israel*, 60–93.

70. Thomas L. Thompson, *The Historicity of the Patriarchal Narratives: The Quest for the Historical Abraham* (Berlin: Walter de Gruyter, 1974); John Van Seters, *Abra-*

ham in History and Tradition (New Haven, Conn., and London: Yale University Press, 1975).

71. Albright's circle never gave up fighting for the historicity of these events, in some form or other. See, best of all, Albright's emphatic defense of the Mosaic tradition in his *From the Stone Age to Christianity,* 249–72.

72. Noth, *Geschichte,* 105–14, 120–30.

73. Cf. Alt, "Die Landnahme der Israeliten in Palästina," and "Erwägungen über die Landnahme der Israeliten in Palästina."

74. George E. Mendenhall, "The Hebrew Conquest"; Norman K. Gottwald, *The Tribes of Yahweh.*

75. The Old Testament is very particular here; cf. the number given in Num. 1:46: 603,550, and the result of the census in Numbers 26: 601,730 (Num. 26:51; some 24,000 had died as a consequence of the sin at Baal-peor (Num. 25:9).

76. Alt, "Erwägungen über die Landnahme der Israeliten in Palästina." Alt was here partly preceded by Bernhard Stade, *Geschichte des Volkes Israel,* (Zweite Auflage. Berlin: G. Grote'sche Verlagsbuchhandlung, 1887), 1:134–35, who talks about an Israelite prolonged sojourn in Transjordan, and a move toward the west as a consequence of a growing population.

77. I have reviewed this discussion twice, in *Early Israel,* 35–65, and "Early Israel Revisited," *Currents in Research: Biblical Studies* 4 (1996): 9–34.

78. According to Judges 1, the Israelites were not able from the beginning to conquer all of Palestine. Parts of the country remained Canaanite. As a matter of fact, according to the Old Testament, the conquest is only at an end when David conquers Jerusalem (2 Samuel 5).

79. There is no reason to dwell on this theme, although Baruch Halpern's defense of the historicity of the Ehud episode in Judg. 3:12–30 is from more than one point of view "amusing." Cf. Baruch Halpern, *The First Historians: The Hebrew Bible and History* (San Francisco: Harper & Row, 1988), 39–75.

80. Cf. the famous study on this phenomenon by Henry M. Chadwick, *The Heroic Age* (Cambridge: Cambridge University Press, 1912).

81. Although to be fair to the biblical scholars, colleagues in other fields might entertain similar ideas about historicity of ancient legend, most notably the Homeric epic literature, which formed the background of Heinrich Schliemann's activities in Turkey and Greece. Even in the middle of the twentieth century we find scholars close to the Albright circle believing in the basic historicity of the Trojan War, such as T.B.L. Webster, *From Homer to Mycenae* (London: Methuen, 1958); D. L. Page, *History and the Homeric Iliad* (Berkeley and Los Angeles: University of California Press, 1959).

82. Niels Peter Lemche, *Ancient Israel: A New History of Israelite Society* (Sheffield: JSOT Press, 1988. Reprint, Sheffield: Sheffield Academic Press, 1995). This work reflects—as does also the one by J. Maxwell Miller and John H. Hayes, *A History of Ancient Israel and Judah*—the dichotomy in Old Testament historical research in the 1980s. This scholarship was split between on one hand advanced methodological ideas and on the other, the inability to carry the critical program out in praxis. In his usual pointed way, Bernd Jörg Diebner noted this in his review of this writer's *Ancient Israel,* "Traditionen über Israels Vorzeit, die keine Geschichtsquelle sind," *Dielheimer Blätter zum Alten Testament* 21 (1985): 246–51.

83. Donner, *Geschichte des Volkes Israel,* 1:117–67.

84. Nobody reading Ahlström's textbook, *The History of Ancient Palestine from the Palaeolithic Period to Alexander's Conquest,* can escape being surprised by the difference between the first sections of this book and a chapter like the one on Judges, pp. 371–90.

85. Quotation from E. Meyer, *Die Israeliten und ihre Nachbarstämme: Alttestamentliche Untersuchungen,* 50 (author's translation).

86. Cf. the description of the tribal society in Niels Peter Lemche, *Ancient Israel,* 88–104, following chap. 2: "Text and History," *Ancient Israel,* 29–73; and in Miller and Hayes, *A History of Ancient Israel and Judah,* 91–107, following a very critical assessment of the book of Judges as a historical source, on pp. 85–90.

87. J. Alberto Soggin, *An Introduction to the History of Israel and Judah,* 44–86. Cf. also Lemche, *Ancient Israel,* 119–28, and Miller and Hayes, *A History of Ancient Israel and Judah,* 120–217.

88. The debate concerning the historicity of David opened for serious with the chapter "David's Empire" in Giovanni Garbini, *History and Ideology in Ancient Israel,* 21–32. Among Garbini's supporters we should count—aside from the present writer–Thomas L. Thompson, *Early History of the Israelite People,* 108–12. The following discussion of the transition period in Thompson, *Early History,* 215–300, has no room to spare for this part of Israel's past. Status of the debate can be glimpsed from the works published by Volkmar Fritz and Philip R. Davies, eds., *The Origins of the Ancient Israelite States,* 1996, and Lowell K. Handy, ed., *The Age of Solomon,* 1997. Cf. also the perhaps too optimistic review in Walter Dietrich, *Die frühe Königszeit in Israel: 10. Jahrhundert v. Chr* (Stuttgart: W. Kohlhammer, 1997), 94–201.

89. It is sometimes maintained, against scholars who will not leave room for an early Israelite kingdom already in the tenth century, that an ancient state is not the same as a modern one. No informed person would ever maintain anything like that. However, the argument is nonsense. Speaking about a definition of state, this will involve certain structures and functions believed to belong to this stage of sociopolitical organization. If none of the political functions or structures relevant to such a definition is present, then it is meaningless to speak about a state, whether modern or ancient.

90. M. Vernes, *Précis d'histoire juive depuis les origines jusqu'à l'époque persane (Vᵉ siècle avant J.-C.)* (Paris: Librairie hachette et Cⁱᵉ, 1889), 7–9 (author's translation).

91. F. Buhl, *Det israelitiske Folks Historie* (1st ed., 1892, here quoted according to the 6th printing; Copenhagen, Kristiania, London, Berlin: Gyldendalske Boghandel Nordisk Forlag, 1922), 12.

92. Frants Buhl (1850–1932), best known as the editor of the seventeenth edition of Wilhelm Gesenius, *Hebräisches und Aramäisches Handwörterbuch über das Alte Testament bearbeitet von Dr. Frants Buhl* (Unveränderte Neudrück der 1915 erschienenen 17. Auflage. Berlin, Göttingen, Heidelberg: Springer Verlag, 1959), was denied the professorship in Old Testament studies in Copenhagen and had to turn to Germany (Leipzig) to obtain a position. He later returned to Copenhagen as professor of the Semitic languages and became the teacher of Johannes Pedersen.

93. R. H. Pfeiffer, *Introduction to the Old Testament* (rev. ed., New York: Harper

& Brothers Publishers, 1941), 528. I owe these references to my teacher, Eduard Nielsen, who made use of the example of Vernes to warn me against a fate like his: E. Nielsen, "En hellenistisk bog?" *Dansk Teologisk Tidsskrift* 55 (1992): 161–74; see 169–73.

94. P. R. Davies, *In Search of "Ancient Israel"* (Sheffield: JSOT Press, 1992), could easily be considered a modern version of a work like the one by Vernes, although Davies himself has obviously never read Vernes.

95. John Rogerson, *Old Testament Criticism in the Nineteenth Century.* Cf. also Hans-Joachim Kraus, *Geschichte der historsch-kritischen Erforschung des Alten Testaments,* 3d ed. (Neukirchen-Vluyn: Neukirchener Verlag, 1982).

96. Otto Eissfeldt, *Hexateuch-Synopse: Die Erzählung der fünf Bücher Mose und des Buches Joshua mit den Anfange des Richterbuches in ihre vier Quellen zerlegt und in deutscher Übersetzung dargeboten samt einer in Einleitung und Anmerkungen gegebenen Begründung* (Leipzig: J. C. Hindrichs, 1922. Reprint, Darmstadt: Wissenschaftliche Buchgesellschaft, 1962). Apart from the usual three sources, the Jahwist, the Elohist, and the Priestly sources, Eissfeldt also operated with a fourth, the "Laienquelle," best translated as the "secular source," older than the Jahwist.

97. Cf. the early criticism of this by Johannes Pedersen, "Die Aufassung vom Alten Testament," *ZAW* 49 (1931): 161–81.

98. Thus Noth, *Überlieferungsgeschichte des Pentateuchs.*

99. Cf. Gerhard von Rad, "Der Anfang der Geschichtsschreibung im Alten Israel" (1944), in his *Gesammelte Studien zum Alten Testament,* 148–88.

100. The list of recent contributions to the vexed problem of the literary composition of the Pentateuch is too long to be quoted here. Among the more valuable studies are the ones by Hans Heinrich Schmid, *Der sogenannte Jahwist* (Zurich: TVZ, 1976), who opted for a late preexilic date; by Rolf Rendtorff, *The Problem of the Process of Transmission in the Pentateuch* (Sheffield: JSOT Press, 1990), who asks for a revision of the documentary hypothesis at large; by John Van Seters, *Abraham in History and Tradition,* his *Prologue to History: The Yahwist as Historian in Genesis* (Louisville, Ky.: Westminster/John Knox Press, 1992) and his *The Life of Moses: The Yahwist as Historian in Exodus-Numbers.* Like Erhard Blum, *Studien zur Komposition des Pentateuch* (Berlin and New York: Walter de Gruyter, 1990), Van Seters favors an exilic date.

101. Reckoned to belong to the so-called archaic poetry in the Old Testament, including such texts as the victory hymn, Exodus 15; the Song of Deborah, Judges 5; a few psalms (including 68 and the hymn in Habakkuk 3); and several other short poetic passages scattered around in the prose narrative. Cf., for example, William F. Albright, *Yahweh and the Gods of Canaan: A Historical Analysis of Two Contrasting Faiths* (London: The Athlone Press, 1968), chap. 1, "Verse and Prose in Early Israelite Tradition," 1–46; on the Balaam songs, 29. For an excellent review of the discussion, cf. Jo Ann Hacket, "Balaam," *ABD* 1:569–72, who still favors a rather early date, sometime during the Hebrew monarchy.

102. Cf. Jean Hoftijzer and G. van der Kooij, *Aramaic Texts from Deir 'Alla* (Leiden: E. J. Brill, 1976).

103. Cf. concerning Ilgen's opinion on Num. 24:24, Bodo Seidel, *Karl David Ilgen und die Pentateuchforschung im Umkreis der sogenannten älteren Urkundenhypothese: Studien zur Geschichte der exegetischen Hermeneutik in der späten*

Aufklärung (Berlin and New York: Walter de Gruyter, 1993), 173. Cf. also Martin Luther: *Die gantze Heilige Schrifft deudsch,* Wittenberg, 1545 (reprint, Darmstadt: Wissenschaftliche Buchgesellschaft, 1972), 310: Randnotiz to Num. 24:24: "(Chittim) Sind die aus Europa / Als der grosse Alexander /und Römer / welche auch zu letzt untergehen." Luther of course (and maybe also Ilgen) takes it to be prophecy. Here Luther follows the Vulgate: "Venient in trieribus de Italia."

Conclusion

1. Cf. above, the Prolegomena, 5.

2. Philip R. Davies, *In Search of "Ancient Israel,"* 16–8. Davies distinguishes between three "Israels": ancient Israel, the scholars' Israel; biblical Israel, the Israel of the Old Testament; and historical Israel, the Palestinian state of this name in the Iron Age.

3. Whitelam's discussion, not least of the attitude of the members of the Albright circle—*The Invention of Ancient Israel,* 79–101—is revealing, showing a definite bias and inability—or better, unwillingness—to understand and accept ancient cultures for what they were. Instead of a proper appraisal of these civilizations, Albright, Wright, and Bright in several places expressed opinions that can only be characterized as Eurocentric, if not openly racist.

4. The so-called "Neologists." Cf. on these John Rogerson, *Old Testament Criticism in the Nineteenth Century,* 16–18; Kraus, *Geschichte der historisch-kritischen Erforschung des Alten Testaments,* 104–13.

5. Although other occurrences of the name are known, from Lebanon where a deity according to Philo of Byblus is called Ἰευώ, cf. Harold W. Attridge and Robert A. Oden, *Philo of Byblos: The Phoenician History: Introduction, Critical Text, Translation, Notes* (Washington, D.C.: The Catholic Biblical Association of America, 1981), 20. Maybe also the Ugaritic passage *KTU* 1.1:IV:14–15 should be included in the discussion: *šm . bny . yw . ilt,* translated by Mark S. Smith in Simon B. Parker, ed., *Ugaritic Narrative Poetry* (Atlanta: Scholars Press, 1997), 89, as "The name of my son (is?) Yw, O Elat." This occurrence may, however, be no more than the consequence of a scribal error, *yw* instead of *ym* (the sea god Yammu), cf. *KTU,* 4, note. Interesting in light of West Semitic name giving are the "Yahwistic" names from Hama. Cf. on these Stephanie Dalley, "Yahweh in Hamath in the 8th Century BC: Cuneiform Material and Historical Deductions," *VT* 40 (1990): 21–32.

6. Cf. above 50–51 on Asherah and Yahweh.

7. A new development in this discussion about ethnic identification in archaeology concerns the diet. In this case, archaeologists have been concentrating on pig consumption. Cf. on this Brian Hesse and Paula Wapnish, "Can Pig Remains Be Used for Ethnic Diagnosis in the Ancient Near East?" in Silberman and Small, eds., *The Archaeology of Israel,* 238–70; also Israel Finkelstein, "Pots and People Revisited: Ethnic Boundaries in the Iron Age I," in Silberman and Small, eds., *The Archaeology of Israel,* 216–37, esp. 227–30.

8. Cf. Baruch Halpern, "Text and Artifact: Two Monologues?" in Silberman and Small, eds., *The Archaeology of Israel,* 311–40, esp. 340.

9. Cf. Hershel Shanks, "When 5613 Scholars Get Together in One Place: The Annual Meeting, 1990," *BAR* 17:2 (1991): 62–68.

Bibliography

Aharoni, Miriam. "Arad," *NAEEHL* 1:75–87.

Aharoni, Yohanan. "Problems of the Israelite Conquest in the Light of Archaeology." *Antiquity and Survival* 2, 2/3 (1957): 131–50.

———. *The Land of the Bible: A Historical Geography*. London: Burns & Oates, 1967.

Ahlström, Gösta W. *Psalm 89: Eine Liturgie aus dem Ritual des leidenden Königs*. Lund: C.W.K. Gleerups, 1959.

———. *Aspects of Syncretism in Israelite Religion*. Lund: C.W.K. Gleerups, 1963.

———. *Who Were the Israelites?* Winona Lake, Ind.: Eisenbrauns, 1986.

———. *The History of Ancient Palestine from the Palaeolithic Period to Alexander's Conquest: With a Contribution by Gary O. Rollefson*. Edited by Diana Edelman. Sheffield: Sheffield Academic Press, 1993.

Ahlström, Gösta W., and Diana Edelman. "Merneptah's Israel." *JNES* 44 (1985): 59–61.

Albertz, Rainer. *A History of Israelite Religion in the Old Testament Period*. Vols. 1 and 2. London: SCM Press, 1994.

———. "Religionsgeschichte Israels statt Theologie des Alten Testaments! Plädoyer für eine Forschungsgeschichtliche Umorientierung." *Jahrbuch für biblische Theologie* 10 (1995): 3–24.

Albrektson, Bertil. *History and the Gods: An Essay on the Idea of Historical Events as Divine Manifestations in the Ancient Near East and in Israel*. Lund: C.W.K. Gleerups, 1967.

Albright, William F. *The Archaeology of Palestine*. (1949). Rev. ed. Harmondsworth, Middlesex: Penguin Books, 1960.

———. *From the Stone Age to Christianity: Monotheism and the Historical Process* (1940) 2d ed. Garden City, N.Y.: Doubleday, 1957.

———. *The Biblical Period from Abraham to Ezra*. New York: Harper & Row, 1963.

———. *Yahweh and the Gods of Canaan: A Historical Analysis of Two Contrasting Faiths*. London: Athlone Press, 1968.

———. "The Amarna Letters from Palestine." In *CAH* 2:2, chap. 20, 98–116.

Aldred, Cyril. "Egypt: The Amarna Period and the End of the Eighteenth Dynasty." In *CAH,* 2:2, chap. 19, 49–63.

———. *Akhenaten, King of Egypt*. London: Thames & Hudson, 1988.

Alt, Albrecht. "Die Landnahme der Israeliten in Palästina" (1925). Reprinted in *Kleine Schriften zur Geschichte des Volkes Israel*, 1:89–125. Munich: C. H. Beck'sche Verlagsbuchhandlung, 1953. Also English trans., "The Settlement of the Israelites in Palestine," in Alt, *Essays on Old Testament History and Religion,* 133–69 Oxford: Blackwell, 1966.

219

————. "Erwägungen über die Landnahme der Israeliten in Palästina" (1939). Reprinted in *Kleine Schriften zur Geschichte des Volkes Israel,* 1:126–75.

Amiran, Ruth. *Ancient Pottery of the Holy Land.* New Brunswick, N.J.: Rutgers University Press, 1970.

Andersen, Knud T. "Noch einmal: Die Chronologie von Israel und Juda," *SJOT* 3:1 (1989): 1–45.

Armstrong, John. *Nations before Nationalism.* Chapel Hill, N.C.: University of North Carolina Press, 1982.

Artzy, Michal. "Incense, Camels and Collared Rim Jars: Desert Trade Routes and Maritime Outlets in the Second Millennium." *Oxford Journal of Archaeology* 13 (1994): 121–47.

Attridge, Harold W., and Robert A. Oden. *Philo of Byblos: The Phoenician History: Introduction, Critical Text, Translation, Notes.* Washington, D.C.: Catholic Biblical Association of America, 1981.

Auld, Graeme, and Margreet Steiner. *Jerusalem I: From the Bronze Age to the Maccabees.* Cambridge: Lutterworth Press; Macon, Ga.: Mercer University Press, 1996.

Bächli, Otto. *Amphiktyonie im Alten Testament: Forschungsgeschichtliche Studie zur Hypothese von Martin Noth.* Basel: Friedrich Reinhardt, 1977.

Baigent, Michael, and Richard Leigh. *The Dead Sea Scrolls Deception.* London: Jonathan Cape, 1991.

Baker, David W. "Girgashite." In *ABD* 2:1028.

Banks, Marcus. *Ethnicity: Anthropological Constructions.* London: Routledge, 1996.

Bar-Josef, Ofer, and Anatoly Khazanov. *Pastoralism in the Levant: Archaeological Materials in Anthropological Perspectives.* Madison, Wis.: Prehistory Press, 1992.

Barstad, Hans M. *The Myth of the Empty Land: A Study in the History and Archaeology of Judah During the "Exilic" Period.* Oslo: Scandinavian University Press, 1996.

Barth, Fredrik. *Principles of Social Organization in Southern Kurdistan.* Oslo, 1953. Reprint, New York: AMS, 1979.

————. "Introduction." In *Ethnic Groups and Boundaries,* edited by F. Barth, 9–37. Oslo: Universitetsforlaget, 1969.

————. "A General Perspective on Nomad-Sedentary Relations in the Middle East." In *The Desert and the Sown: Nomads in the Wider Society,* edited by Cynthia Nelson, 11–21. Berkeley, Calif.: University of California Press, 1973.

————. "Enduring and Emerging Issues in the Analysis of Ethnicity." In *The Anthropology of Ethnicity: Beyond "Ethnic Groups and Boundaries,"* edited by Hans Vermeulen and Cora Govers, 11–32. Amsterdam: Het Spinhuis, 1994.

Bateson, Gregory. "Morale and National Character" (1942). In *Steps to an Ecology of Mind: Collected Essays in Anthropology, Psychiatry, Evolution, and Epistemology.* San Francisco: Chandler, 1972.

Becker, Uwe. *Jesaja: Von der Botschaft zum Buch.* Göttingen: Vandenhoeck & Ruprecht, 1996.

Becking, Bob. *The Fall of Samaria: An Historical and Archaeological Study.* Leiden: E. J. Brill, 1992.

Ben-Tor, Amnon, ed. *The Archaeology of Ancient Israel.* New Haven, Conn.: Yale University Press, 1992.

————. "Hazor," in *NAEEHL* 2:594–605.

————. "Hazor." *The Oxford Encyclopedia of Archaeology in the Ancient Near East*, 3:1–5. Oxford and New York: Oxford University Press, 1997.

Bentzen, Aage. *Israels Historie*. Copenhagen: Haase & Søns Forlag, 1930.

Beyerlin, Walter. *Herkunft und Geschichte der ältesten Sinaitraditionen*. Tübingen: J.C.B. Mohr (Paul Siebeck), 1961.

Binger, Tilde. *Asherah: Goddesses in Ugarit, Israel and the Old Testament*. Sheffield: Sheffield Academic Press, 1997.

Biran, Avraham, and Joseph Naveh. "An Aramaic Stele Fragment from Tel Dan." *IEJ* 43 (1993): 81–98.

————. "The Tel Dan Inscription: A New Fragment." *IEJ* 45 (1995): 1–18.

Black-Michaud, Jacob. *Sheep and Land: The Economics of Power in a Tribal Society*. Edited by Jean Pierre Digard. Cambridge: Cambridge University Press, 1986.

Blum, Erhard. *Studien zur Komposition des Pentateuch*. Berlin and New York: Walter de Gruyter, 1990.

Borowski, Oded. *Agriculture in Iron Age Israel*. Winona Lake, Ind.: Eisenbrauns, 1987.

Bottéro, Jean. *Le problème des habiru à la 4e rencontre assyriologique internationale*. Paris: Imprimerie nationale, 1954.

Bradley, J.F.N. *Czechoslovakia: A Short History*. Edinburgh: Edinburgh University Press, 1971.

Braudel, Ferdnand. *On History*. Chicago: University of Chicago Press, 1980.

Bright, John. *A History of Israel*. London: SCM Press, 1960.

Brownlee, William H., and George E. Mendenhall. Announcement in the *Annual of the Department of Antiquities in Jordan* 15 (1970): 39–40 (pl. 73–75).

Buccellati, Giovanni. *Cities and Nations of Ancient Syria: An Essay on Political Institutions with Special Reference to the Israelite Kingdoms*. Rome: Instituto di Studi del Vicino Oriente, 1967.

Buhl, Frants. *Det israelitiske Folks Historie* (1892). Copenhagen, Kristiania, London, Berlin: Gyldendalske Boghandel Nordisk Forlag, 1922.

Cahill, Jane M. "Rosette Stamp Seal Impressions from Ancient Judah," *IEJ* 45 (1995): 232–52.

Cameron, Euan. *The Reformation of the Heretics: The Waldenses of the Alps, 1480–1580*. Oxford: Clarendon Press, 1984.

Carroll, Robert. *From Chaos to Covenant: Uses of Prophecy in the Book of Jeremiah*. London: SCM Press, 1981.

————. *Jeremiah: A Commentary*. London: SCM Press, 1986.

Chabas, F. "Les Hébreux en Égypte." In *Mélanges égyptologique*. Ière série (1862), 42–54.

Chadwick, Henry M. *The Heroic Age*. Cambridge: Cambridge University Press, 1912.

Chaney, Marvin L. "Ancient Palestinian Peasant Movements and the Formation of Premonarchic Israel." In *Palestine in Transition: The Emergence of Ancient Israel*, edited by David Noel Freedman and David Frank Graf, 39–90. Sheffield: Almond Press, 1983.

Cody, Aelred. *A History of Old Testament Priesthood*. Rome: Pontifical Biblical Institute, 1969.

Cogan, Mordechai. "Chronology." In *ABD* 1:1002–11.

Coote, Robert B., and Keith W. Whitelam. *The Emergence of Early Israel in Historical Perspective*. Sheffield: Almond Press, 1987.

Cross, Frank M. "The Oldest Manuscript from Qumran." *JBL* 74 (1955): 147–72.

————. *Canaanite Myth and Hebrew Epic: Essays in the Religion of Israel.* Cambridge, Mass.: Harvard University Press, 1975.

Cryer, Frederick H. "On the Recently-Discovered 'House of David' Inscription." *SJOT* 8 (1994): 3–19.

————. "King Hadad," *SJOT* 9 (1995): 222–35.

————. "Of Epistemology, Northwest-Semitic Epigraphy and Irony: The '*BYRDWD*/ House of David' Inscription Revisited," *JSOT* 69 (1996): 3–17.

————. "To the One of Fictive Music: OT Chronology and History." *SJOT* 1:2 (1997): 1–27.

Dalley, Stephanie. *Myths from Mesopotamia: Creation, the Flood, Gilgamesh, and Others.* Oxford: Oxford University Press, 1989.

————. "Yahweh in Hamath in the 8th Century BC: Cuneiform Material and Historical Deductions." *VT* 40 (1990): 21–32.

Davies, Philip R. *In Search of "Ancient Israel."* Sheffield: JSOT Press, 1992.

Dearman, J. Andrew, ed. *Studies in the Mesha Inscription and Moab.* Atlanta: Scholars Press, 1989.

————. "Historical Reconstruction and the Mesha Inscription." In *Studies in the Mesha Inscription and Moab,* edited by J. Andrew Dearman, 153–210. Atlanta: Scholars Press, 1989.

Delekat, Lienhard. *Phönizier in Amerika: Ein Inschrift des 5. Jh. v. Chr. aus Brasilien in einer unbekannten semitischen Konsekutivtempussprache.* Bonn: Peter Hanstein Verlag, 1969.

Dever, William G. *Recent Archaeological Discoveries and Biblical Research.* Seattle and London: University of Washington Press, 1990.

————. "Gezer." In *ABD* 2:998–1003.

————. "Gezer." In *NAEEHL* 2:496–506.

————. "Revisionist Israel Revisited: A Rejoinder to Niels Peter Lemche." *Currents in Research: Biblical Studies* 4 (1996): 35–50.

————. "Gezer." In *The Oxford Encyclopedia of Archaeology in the Ancient Near East,* 2:396–401.

Diebner, Bernd Jörg. "Traditionen über Israels Vorzeit, die keine Geschichtsquelle sind." *Dielheimer Blätter zum Alten Testament* 21 (1985): 246–51.

Dietrich, Walter. *Israel und Kanaan: Vom Ringen zweier Gesellschaftssysteme.* Stuttgart: Verlag Katholisches Bibelwerk, 1979.

————. *Die frühe Königszeit in Israel. 10. Jahrhundert v. Chr.* Stuttgart: W. Kohlhammer, 1997.

Digard, Jean-Pierre. *Techniques des nomades Baxtyari d'Iran.* Cambridge: Cambridge University Press, 1981.

Dion, Paul E. "Aramaean Tribes and Nations of First-Millennium Western Asia." In *CANE* 2:1281–94.

Donner, Herbert. *Geschichte des Volkes Israel und seiner Nachbarn in grundzügen.* Vols. 1 and 2. Göttingen: Vandenhoeck & Ruprecht, 1984–86.

————. *Wilhelm Gesenius Hebräisches und Aramäisches Handwörterbuch über das Alte Testament.* Vol. 1. 18. Aufl.; Berlin, Heidelberg, New York, London, Paris, Tokyo: Springer-Verlag, 1987.

Dothan, Trude. "The 'Sea Peoples' and the Philistines of Ancient Palestine." In *CANE* 2:1267–79.

Edel, Elmar. "KBO I 15+19, ein Brief Ramses' II. mit einer Schilderung der Kadeschschlacht." *ZA* 48 (1949): 208–9.

Edelman, Diana. "Ethnicity and Early Israel." In *Ethnicity and the Bible,* edited by Mark G. Brett, 25–55. Leiden: E. J. Brill, 1996.

Ehmann, Dieter. *Baḫtiyāren—Persische bergnomaden im Wandel der Zeit.* Wiesbaden: Ludwig Reichert, 1975.

Eissfeldt, Otto. *Hexateuch-Synopse: Die Erzählung der fünf Bücher Mose und des Buches Joshua mit den Anfange des Richterbuches in ihre vier Quellen zerlegt und in deutscher Übersetzung dargeboten samt einer in Einleitung und Anmerkungen gegebenen Begründung.* Leipzig: J. C. Hinrichs, 1922. Reprint, Darmstadt: Wissenschaftliche Buchgesellschaft, 1962.

Engel, Hartmut. "Die Siegesstele des Merenptah." *Biblica* 60 (1979): 373–99.

Esse, Douglas L. "The Collared Rim Store Jar: Scholarly Ideology and Ceramic Typology." *SJOT* 5:2 (1991): 99–116.

———. "The Collared Pithos at Megiddo: Ceramic Distribution and Ethnicity." *JNES* 51 (1992): 81–103.

Evans-Pritchard, E. E. *The Nuer: A Description of the Modes of Livelihood and Political Institutions of a Nilotic People.* Oxford: Clarendon Press, 1940.

Faulkner, R. O. "Egypt from the Inception of the Nineteenth Dynasty to the Death of Ramesses III." In *CAH* 2:2, chap. 23, 217–51

Feilberg, C. G. *La tente noire: Contribution ethnographique à l'histoire culturelle des nomades.* Copenhagen: Nationalmuseet, 1944.

Finkelstein, Israel. *The Archaeology of the Israelite Settlement.* Jerusalem: Israel Exploration Society, 1988.

———. *Living on the Fringe: The Archaeology and History of the Negev, Sinai and Neighbouring Regions in the Bronze and Iron Ages.* Sheffield: Sheffield Academic Press, 1995.

———. "Pots and People Revisited: Ethnic Boundaries in the Iron Age I." In *The Archaeology of Israel: Constructing the Past, Interpreting the Present,* edited by Neil Asher Silberman and David Small, 216–37. Sheffield: Sheffield Academic Press, 1997.

———. "The Emergence of Israel: A Phase in the Cyclic History of Canaan in the Third and Second Millennia B.C.E." In *From Nomadism to Monarchy: Archaeological and Historical Aspects of Early Israel,* edited by Israel Finkelstein and Nadav Na'aman, 150–78. Jerusalem: Israel Exploration Society, 1994.

———. "The Archaeology of the United Monarchy: An Alternative View." *Levant* 28 (1996): 177–87.

———. "State Formation in Israel and Judah." In press.

Finkelstein, Israel, and Zvi Lederman, eds. *Highlands of Many Cultures: The Southern Samaria Survey: The Sites.* Vols. 1 and 2. Tel Aviv: Sonia and Marco Nadler Institute of Archaeology, 1997.

Finkelstein, Israel, Zvi Lederman, and Shlomo Bunimowitz. *Shiloh: The Archaeology of a Biblical Site.* Tel Aviv: Tel Aviv University, 1993.

Fisher, C. S. *The Excavations of Armageddon.* Chicago: University of Chicago Press, 1929.

Fohrer, Georg. *Geschichte Israels von den Anfängen bis zur Gegenwart.* Heidelberg: Quelle & Meyer, 1977.

Foster, Benjamin R. *Before the Muses: An Anthology of Akkadian Literature.* Vols. 1 and 2. Bethesda, Md.: CDL Press, 1993.

Frankel, Rafael. "Upper Galilee in the Late Bronze-Iron I Transition." In *From Nomadism to Monarchy: Archaeological and Historical Aspects of Early Israel,* edited by Israel Finkelstein and Nadav Na'aman, 18–34. Jerusalem: Israel Exploration Society, 1994.

Fritz, Volkmar. *Die Entstehung Israels im 12. und 11. Jahrhundert v. Chr.* Stuttgart: W. Kohlhammer, 1996.

Fritz, Volkmar, and Philip R. Davies, eds. *The Origins of the Ancient Israelite States.* Sheffield: Sheffield Academic Press, 1996.

Galling, Kurt. *Die Erwählungstraditionen Israels.* Giessen: Alfred Töpelmann, 1928.

Garbini, Giovanni. *History and Ideology in Ancient Israel.* London: SCM Press, 1988.

———. "L'iscrizione aramaica di Tel Dan." *Atti della Accademia Nazionale dei Lincei.* Anno CCCXCI (1994): 461–71.

Gardiner, Alan H. *Egypt of the Pharaohs: An Introduction.* Oxford: Clarendon Press, 1961.

Geus, Cornelius H. J. de. *The Tribes of Israel. An Investigation into Some of the Presuppositions of Martin Noth's Amphictyony Hypothesis.* Assen and Amsterdam: Van Gorcum, 1976.

Gibson, John C. L. *Textbook of Syrian Semitic Inscriptions.* Vol. 1: *Hebrew and Moabite Inscriptions.* Oxford: Clarendon Press, 1971.

———. *Canaanite Myths and Legends.* Edinburgh: T. & T. Clark, 1978.

Gitin, Seymour, Trude Dothan, and Joseph Naveh. "A Royal Dedicatory Inscription from Ekron." *IEJ* 47 (1997): 1–16.

Giveon, Raphael. *Les Bédouins Shosou des documents égyptiens.* Leiden: E. J. Brill, 1971.

Golka, Friedemann W. "German Old Testament Scholarship." In *A Dictionary of Biblical Interpretation,* edited by Richard J. Coggins and J. L. Houlden, 258–66. London and Philadelphia: SCM Press and Trinity Press International, 1990.

Gordon, Cyrus H. *Before the Bible: The Common Background of Greek and Hebrew Civilization.* New York: Harper & Row, 1962.

Görg, Manfred. *Die Beziehungen zwischen dem alten Israel und Ägypten: Von den Anfängen bis zum Exil.* Darmstadt: Wissenschaftliche Buchgesellschaft, 1997.

Gottwald, Norman K. "Domain Assumptions and Societal Models in the Study of Pre-Monarchic Israel." *VTSUP* 28 (1975): 89–100.

———. *The Tribes of Yahweh: A Sociology of the Religion of Liberated Israel 1250–1050 B.C.* Maryknoll, N.Y.: Orbis Books, 1979.

———. "Recent Studies of the Social World of Premonarchic Israel." *Currents in Research: Biblical Studies* 1 (1993): 163–89.

———. *The Hebrew Bible in Its Social World and in Ours.* Atlanta: Scholars Press, 1993.

Grabbe, Lester L. *European Seminar in Historical Methodology.* Vol. 2: *Leading Captivity Captive: "The Exile" as History and Ideology.* Sheffield: Sheffield Academic Press, 1998.

Graham, M. Patrick. "The Discovery and Reconstruction of the Mesha Inscription." In *Studies in the Mesha Inscription and Moab,* edited by J. Andrew Dearman, 27–92. Atlanta: Scholars Press, 1989.

Greenberg, Moshe. *The Hab/piru*. New Haven, Conn.: American Oriental Society, 1955.

Grønbech, Wilhelm. *Hellas*. vols. 1–4. Copenhagen: Gyldendal, 1942–45.

———. *The Culture of the Teutons*. Copenhagen: Gyldendal, 1931.

Gröndahl, Frauke. *Die Personennamen der Texte aus Ugarit*. Rome: Pontifical Biblical Institute, 1967.

Gunneweg, Antonius H. J. *Leviten und Priester*. Göttingen: Vandenhoeck & Ruprecht, 1965.

———. *Geschichte Israels bis Bar Kochba*. Stuttgart: W. Kohlhammer, 1972.

Gurney, Oliver R. "The Cuthaean Legend of Naram-Sin." *Anatolian Studies* 5 (1955): 93–113.

———. *The Hittites*. Reprinted, with revisions, London: Penguin Books, 1990.

Güterbock, Hans G. "Die historische Tradition in ihre literarischen Gestaltung bei Babyloniern und Hethitern bis 1200." *Zeitschrift für Assyriologie* 10 (1938): 49–59.

Hacket, Jo Ann. "Balaam," In *ABD* 1:569–72.

Hadley, Judith M. "The Khirbet el-Qom Inscription." *VT* 37 (1987): 50–62.

———. "Yahweh and "His Asherah": Archaeological and Textual Evidence for the Cult of the Goddess." In *Ein Gott Allein? JHWH-Verehrung und biblischer Monotheismus im Kontext der israelitischen und altorientalischen Religionsgeschichte,* edited by Walter Dietrich and Martin A. Klopfenstein, 235–68. Freiburg: Universitätsverlag, 1994.

Halbe, Jürgen. *Das Privilegrecht Jahwes: Ex 34,10–26: Gestalt und Wesen, Herkunft und Wirken in vordeuteronomistischer Zeit*. Göttingen: Vandenhoeck & Ruprecht, 1975.

Hallo, William W., and K. Lawson Younger, eds., *The Context of Scripture*. Vol. 1: *Canonical Compositions from the Biblical World*. Leiden: E. J. Brill, 1997.

Halpern, Baruch. *The First Historians: The Hebrew Bible and History*. San Francisco: Harper & Row, 1988.

———. "The Exodus from Egypt: Myth or Reality?" In *The Rise of Ancient Israel: Symposium at the Smithsonian Institution October 26, 1991,* edited by Hershel Shanks, 87–113. Washington, D.C.: Biblical Archaeology Society, 1992.

———. "Kenites." *ABD* 4:17–22.

———. "Text and Artifact: Two Monologues?" In *The Archaeology of Israel: Constructing the Past, Interpreting the Present,* edited by Neil Asher Silberman and David Small, 311–40. Sheffield: Sheffield Academic Press, 1997.

Hardwick, Michael E. "Beyond the River." In *ABD* 1:717.

Hayes, John H., and Paul K. Hooker. *A New Chronology for the Kings of Israel and Judah*. Atlanta: John Knox, 1988.

Hayes, John H., and J. Maxwell Miller, eds. *Israelite and Judaean History*. London: SCM Press, 1977.

Helck, Wolfgang. *Die Beziehungen Ägyptens zu Vorderasien im 3. und 2. Jahrtausend v.Chr.* Wiesbaden: Otto Harrassowitz, 1962.

Heltzer, Michael. *The Suteans: With a Contribution by Shoshana Arbeli*. Naples: Istituto Universitario Orientale, 1981.

Hendel, Ronald S. *The Epic of the Patriarch: The Jacob Cycle and the Narrative Traditions of Canaan and Israel*. Atlanta: Scholars Press, 1987.

Herrmann, Siegfried. "Operationen Pharao Schoschenks I. Im östlichen Ephraim." *ZDPV* 80 (1964): 55–79.

————. *Israels Aufenhalt in Ägypten.* Stuttgart: Verlag Katholisches Bibelwerk, 1970.

————. *Geschichte Israels in alttestamentlicher Zeit.* Munich: Christian Kaiser, 1973. English translation: *A History of Israel in Old Testament Times.* 2d ed. Philadelphia: Fortress Press, 1981.

Herzog, Ze'ev. "The Beer-Sheba Valley: From Nomadism to Monarchy." In *From Nomadism to Monarchy: Archaeological and Historical Aspects of Early Israel,* edited by Israel Finkelstein and Nadav Na'aman, 122–49. Jerusalem: Israel Exploration Society, 1994.

Hess, Richard S. *Amarna Personal Names.* Winona Lake, Ind.: Eisenbrauns, 1993.

Hesse, Brian, and Paula Wapnish. "Can Pig Remains Be Used for Ethnic Diagnosis in the Ancient Near East?" In *The Archaeology of Israel: Constructing the Past, Interpreting the Present,* edited by Neil Asher Silberman and David Small, 238–70. Sheffield: Sheffield Academic Press, 1997.

Hoftijzer, Jean, and G. van der Kooij. *Aramaic Texts from Deir 'Alla.* Leiden: E. J. Brill, 1976.

Holladay, John S. "The Kingdoms of Israel and Judah: Political and Economic Centralization in the Iron IIA-B (Ca. 1000–750 B.C.E.)." In *The Archaeology of Society in the Holy Land,* edited by T. Levy, 368–98. London: Leicester University Press.

Hopkins, David C. *The Highlands of Canaan: Agricultural Life in the Early Iron Age.* Sheffield: Almond Press, 1985.

Hornung, Erik. "Die Israelstele des Merneptah." In *Fontes atque pontes: Eine Festgabe für Hellmut Brunner,* edited by Manfred Görg, 224–33. Wiesbaden: Otto Harrassowitz, 1983.

Hutchinson, John, and Anthony D. Smith. *Ethnicity.* Oxford and New York: Oxford University Press, 1996.

Jackson, K. P. "The Language of the Mesha'-inscription." In *Studies in the Mesha Inscription and Moab,* edited by J. Andrew Dearman, 96–130. Atlanta: Scholars Press, 1989.

Jamieson-Drake, D. *Scribes and Schools in Monarchic Judah: A Socio-Archeological Approach.* Sheffield: Almond Press, 1991.

Jeppesen, Knud. *Graeder ikke saa saare: Studier i Mikabogens sigte.* Vols. 1 and 2. Aarhus: Aarhus Universitetsforlag, 1987.

Kaiser, Otto. *Isaiah 1–12.* 2d ed., completely rewritten. London: SCM Press, 1983.

Kaufman, Ivan T. "Samaria (Ostraca)." In *ABD* 5:921–26.

Kaufmann, Yehezkel. *The Biblical Account of the Conquest of Palestine.* Jerusalem: Magnes Press, 1953.

Keel, Othmar, and Christoph Ühlinger. *Göttinnen, Götter und Göttersymbole: Neue Erkenntnisse zur Religionsgeschichte Kanaans und Israels aufgrund bislang unerschlossener ikonographischen Quellen.* Freiburg: Herder, 1992.

Kempinski, Aron, and Israel Finkelstein. "Shiloh." In *NAEEHL* 4:1364–70.

Kenyon, Kathleen M. "Jericho." *NAEEHL* 2:674–81.

Khalifeh, Issam Ali. "Sarepta." In *The Oxford Encyclopedia of Archaeology in the Ancient Near East,* 4:488–91.

Kitchen, Kenneth A. *Suppiluliuma and the Amarna Pharaohs: A Study in Relative Chronology.* Liverpool: Liverpool University Press, 1962.

————. *The Third Intermediary Period in Egypt (1100–650 B.C.).* Warminster: Aris & Phillips, 1973.

————. *Ramesside Inscriptions,* 4:9. Oxford: Basil Blackwell, 1982).

Kittel, Rudolf. *Geschichte des Volkes Israel.* 2d ed. Gotha: Friedrich Andreas Perthes, 1909–12.

Klengel, Horst. *Geschichte Syriens im 2. Jahrtausend v.u.Z,* Teil 2: *Mittel- und Südsyrien.* Berlin: Akademie-Verlag, 1969.

————. *Handel und Händler im alten Orient.* Vienna: Böhlau, 1979.

Knauf, Ernst Axel. "**BaytDawīd ou *BaytDōd?*" *BN* 72 (1994): 60–69.

Knight, Douglas A. *Rediscovering the Tradition of Israel: The Development of the Traditio-Historical Research of the Old Testament, with Special Consideration of Scandinavian Contributions.* Rev. ed. Missoula, Mont.: Scholars Press, 1975.

Knudtzon, J. A. *Die El-Amarna Tafeln mit Einleitung und Erläuterungen.* Vols. 1 and 2. Leipzig: J. C. Hinrichs, 1915. Reprint, Aalen: Otto Zeller Verlagsbuchhandlung, 1964.

Kraus, F. R. "Ein zentrales Problem des altmesopotamischen Rechts: Was ist der Codex Hammu-rabi?" *Genava* 8 (1960): 283–96.

Kraus, Hans-Joachim. *Geschichte der historisch-kritischen Erforschung des Alten Testaments.* 3d ed. Neukirchen-Vluyn: Neukirchener Verlag, 1982.

Lambert, Malcolm D. *Medieval Heresy: Popular Movements from Bogomil to Hus.* London: Edward Arnold, 1977.

Lambert, W. G., and A. R. Millard. *Atra-Ḫasīs: The Babylonian Story of the Flood; With the Sumerian Flood Story by M. Civil.* Oxford: Clarendon Press, 1969.

Lemaire, André. *Les écoles et la formation de la Bible dans l'ancien Israël.* Fribourg: Éditions Universitaires; Göttingen: Vandenhoeck & Ruprecht, 1981.

————. "La dynastie davidique (Byt Dwd) dans deux inscriptions Ouest-Sémitiques de Iè S. Av. J.-C." *Studi epigraphici e linguistici* 11 (1994): 17–19.

————. "'House of David' Restored in Moabite Inscription." *BAR* 20/3 (1994): 30–37.

Lemche, Niels Peter. *Israel i Dommertiden: En oversigt over diskussionen om Martin Noths "Das System der zwölf Stämme Israel."* Copenhagen: G.E.C. Gads Forlag, 1972.

————. "'The Hebrew Slave': Comments on the Slave Law Ex xxi 2–11." *VT* 25 (1975): 129–44.

————. "The Manumission of Slaves—the Fallow Year—the Sabbathical Year the Jobel Year." *VT* 26 (1976): 38–59.

————. "The Greek 'Amphictyony': Could It Be a Prototype for the Israelite Society in the Period of the Judges?" *JSOT* 4 (1977): 48–59.

————. "'Hebrew' as a National Name for Israel." *Studia Theologica* 33 (1979): 1–23.

————. "On the Problem of Studying Israelite History: Apropos Abraham Malamat's View of Historical Research." *BN* 24 (1984): 94–124.

————. *Early Israel: Anthropological and Historical Studies on the Israelite Society Before the Monarchy.* Leiden: E. J. Brill, 1985.

————. "Rachel and Leah, or: On the Survival of Outdated Paradigms in the Study of the Origin of Israel." Pts. 1 and 2. *SJOT* 1:2 (1987): 127–53, and 3:1 (1988): 39–65.

————. *Ancient Israel: A New History of Israelite Society.* Sheffield: JSOT Press, 1988. Reprint, Sheffield: Sheffield Academic Press, 1995.

————. "Mysteriet om det forsvundne tempel: Overleveringen om Silos ødelæggelse i Jer 7,12.14." *Svensk Eksegetisk Årsbok* 54 (1989): 118–126.

————. "On the Use of 'System Theory,' 'Macro Theories' and Evolutionistic Thinking in Modern OT Research and Biblical Archaeology." *SJOT* 4:2 (1990): 73–88. Reprinted in *Community, Identity, and Ideology: Social Sciences Approaches to the Hebrew Bible,* edited by Charles E. Carter and Carol L. Meyers, 273–86. Winona Lake, Ind.: Eisenbrauns, 1996.

———. *The Canaanites and Their Land: The Idea of Canaan in the Old Testament.* Sheffield: JSOT Press, 1991.

———. "Our Most Gracious Sovereign: On the Relationship between Royal Mythology and Economic Oppression in the Ancient Near East." In *Ancient Economy in Mythology,* edited by Morris Silver, 109–34. Savage, Md.: Rowman & Littlefield, 1991.

———. "The God of Hosea." In *Priests, Prophets, and Scribes: Essays on the Formation and Heritage of Second Temple Judaism in Honor of Joseph Blenkinsopp,* edited by Eugen Ulrich and John Wright, 241–57. Sheffield: Sheffield Academic Press, 1992.

———. "Is It Still Possible to Write a History of Ancient Israel?" *SJOT* 8 (1994): 163–88.

———. "Justice in Western Asia in Antiquity; Or: Why No Laws Were Needed!" *Kent Law Review* 70 (1995): 1695–1716.

———. "From Patronage Society to Patronage Society." In *The Origins of the Israelite States,* edited by Volkmar Fritz and Philip R. Davies, 106–20. Sheffield: Sheffield Academic Press, 1996.

———. "Early Israel Revisited." *Currents in Research: Biblical Studies* 4 (1996): 9–34.

———. *Die Vorgeschichte Israels. Von den Anfängen bis zum Ausgang des 13. Jahrhunderts v.Chr.* Stuttgart: W. Kohlhammer, 1996. English edition: *Prelude to Israel's Past: Background and Beginnings of Israelite History and Identity* (Peabody, Mass.: Hendrickson's, 1998), in press.

———. "Where Should We Look for Canaan? A Reply to Nadav Na'aman." *UF* 28 (1996): 767–72

———. "Clio Is Also among the Muses! Keith W. Whitelam and the History of Palestine: A Review and a Commentary." In *Can a "History of Israel" Be Written?* edited by Lester L. Grabbe, 123–55. Sheffield: Sheffield Academic Press, 1997.

———. "On Doing Sociology with 'Solomon'." In *The Age of Solomon: Scholarship at the Turn of the Millennium,* edited by Lowell K. Handy, 312–35. Leiden: E. J. Brill, 1997.

———. "Greater Canaan: The Implications of a Correct Reading of EA 151:49–51." *BASOR* 310 (1998):19–24.

Levy, Thomas E., ed. *The Archaeology of Society in the Holy Land.* London: Leicester University Press, 1995.

Lewis, Charlton T., and Charles Short. *A Latin Dictionary* (1879). Oxford: Clarendon Press, 1962.

Liddell, Henry G., and Robert Scott. *A Greek-English Lexicon: A New Edition Revised and Augmented Throughout by H. S. Jones.* 1940. Reprint, Oxford: Clarendon Press, 1961.

Lidzbarski, Mark. "An Old Calendar-Inscription from Gezer." *PEFQS* 1909: 26–29.

Liverani, Mario. "Il fuoruscitismo in Siria nella Tarda Età del Bronze." *Rivista Storica Italiana* 77 (1965): 315–36.

———. "Contrasti e confluenze di concezioni politiche nell'età di El-Amarna." *Revue Assyriologique* 61 (1967): 1–18.

———. "Partire sul carro, per il deserto." *Annali dell'Istituto Universitario Orientale di Napoli,* n.s., 22 (1972): 403–15.

———. "Memorandum on the Approach to Historiographic Texts." *Orientalia* n.s., 42 (1973); 178–94.

———. "Storiografia politica hittita–I: Shunashshura, ovvero: Della reciprocità." *Oriens Antiquus* 12 (1973): 267–97.

———. "The Amorites." In *Peoples of Old Testament Times,* edited by Dennis J. Wiseman, 100–33. Oxford: Oxford University Press, 1973.

———. "La royauté syrienne de l'age du Bronze Récent." In *Le palais et la royauté,* edited by Paul Garelli, 329–56. Paris: Geuthner, 1974.

———. "Review of Roland de Vaux: Histoire ancienne d'Israël. I-II." *Oriens Antiquus* 15 (1976): 145–59.

———. "Storiografia politica hittita—II: Telipinu, ovvero: Della Solidarietà." *Oriens Antiquus* 16 (1977): 105–31.

———. "Farsi Habiru." *Vicino Oriente* 2 (1979): 65–77.

———. "Economia delle fattorie palatine ugaritiche." *Dialoghi di Archeologia,* n.s., 1 (1979): 57–72.

———. "La dotazione dei mercanti di Ugarit." *Ugarit-Forschungen* 11 (1979): 495–503.

———. "Le "origine" d'Israele progetto irrelizzabile di ricerca etnogenetica." *Rivista Biblica Italiana* 28 (1980): 9–31.

———. *Antico Oriente. Storia, società, economia.* Bari: Editori Laterza, 1988.

———. "Hattushili alle prese con la propaganda ramesside." *Orientalia,* n.s., 59 (1990): 207–17.

———. "A Seasonal Pattern for the Amarna Letters." In *Lingering over Words: Studies in Ancient Near Eastern Literature in Honor of William L. Moran,* edited by Tzvi Abusch, John Huehnergard, and Piotr Steinkeller, 337–48. Atlanta: Scholars Press, 1990.

Long, Burke O. *Planting and Reaping Albright: Politics, Ideology, and Interpreting the Bible.* University Park, Pa.: Pennsylvania State University Press, 1997.

Loretz, Oswald. "Die hebräischen termini *ḥpšj* 'freigelassen, Freigelassener' und *ḥpšh* 'Freilassung.'" *UF* 9 (1977): 163–67.

———. *Habiru-Hebräer. Eine sozio-linguistische Studie über die Herkunft des Gentiliziums ʿibrî vom Appellativum ḫabiru.* Berlin: Walter de Gruyter, 1984.

———. *Ugarit und die Bibel: Kanaanäische Götter und Religion im Alten Testament,* 128–39. Darmstadt: Wissenschaftliche Buchgesellschaft, 1990.

Luckenbill, Daniel D. *Ancient Records of Assyria and Babylonia.* Vols. 1 and 2. Chicago: University of Chicago Press, 1926–27.

Macqueen, J. G. "The History of Anatolia and of the Hittite Empire: An Overview." In *CANE* 2:1085–1105.

Malamat, Abraham. "Die Frühgeschichte Israels—eine methodologische Studie." *ThZ* 39 (1983): 1–16.

Manetho. With an English translation by W. G. Waddell. Cambridge, Mass.: Harvard University Press, London: William Heinemann, 1980.

Marfoe, Leon. "The Integrative Transformation. Patterns of Sociopolitical Organization in Southern Syria." *BASOR* 234 (1979): 1–42.

Mayes, A.D.H. *Israel in the Period of the Judges.* London: SCM Press, 1974.

Mazar, Amihai. *Archaeology of the Land of the Bible 10,000–586 B.C.E.* New York: Doubleday, 1990.

———. "Iron Age Chronology: A Reply to I. Finkelstein." *Levant* 29 (1997): 157–67.

Mead, Margaret. *And Keep Your Powder Dry: An Anthropologist Looks at America.* 1942. Reprint, Salem, N.H.: Ayer Co., Pubs., 1977.

Mendenhall, George E. "Covenant Forms in Israelite Tradition." *BA* 17 (1954): 25–53. Reprinted in *The Biblical Archaeologist Reader,* edited by Edward F. Campbell and David N. Freedman, 3:25–53. Garden City, N.Y.: Doubleday, 1970.

———. "The Hebrew Conquest of Palestine." *BA* 25 (1962): 66–87. Reprinted in *The Biblical Archaeologist Reader,* edited by Edward F. Campbell and David Noel Freedman, 3:100–120. Garden City, NY: Doubleday, 1970.

———. *The Tenth Generation: The Origin of the Biblical Tradition.* Baltimore: John Hopkins University Press, 1973.

Meshel, Zeev. "Two Aspects in the Excavation of Kuntillet ʿAğrud." In *Ein Gott Allein? JHWH-Verehrung und biblischer Monotheismus im Kontext der israelitischen und altorientalischen Religions-geschichte,* edited by Walter Dietrich and Martin A. Klopfenstein, 99–104. Freiburg: Universitätsverlag, 1994.

Metzger, Martin. *Grundriß der Geschichte Israels.* 6. Aufl. Neukirchen-Vluyn: Neukirchener verlag, 1983

Meyer, Eduard. *Die Israeliten und ihre Nachbarstämme: Alttestamentliche Untersuchungen.* Leipzig: Max Niemeyer, 1906; reprint, Darmstad: Wissenschaftliche Buchgesellschaft, 1967.

Miller, J. Maxwell, and John H. Hayes. *A History of Ancient Israel and Judah.* Philadelphia: Westminster Press, 1986.

Moor, Johannes C. de. *An Anthology of Religious Texts from Ugarit.* Leiden: E. J. Brill, 1987.

Mowinckel, Sigmund. *Israels opphav og eldste historie.* Oslo: Universitetsforlaget, 1967.

Murnane, William J. "The History of Ancient Egypt: An Overview." In *CANE,* 2:691–717.

Na'aman, Nadav. "Khabiru and Hebrews: The Transfer of a Social Term to the Literary Sphere." *JNES* 45 (1986): 271–88.

———. "Canaanite Jerusalem and Its Central Hill Country Neighbours in the Second Millennium B.C.E.." *UF* 24 [1992]: 275–91.

———. "The Canaanites and their Land: A Rejoinder." *UF* 26 (1994): 397–418.

———. "The Contribution of the Amarna Letters to the Debate on Jerusalem's Political Position in the Tenth Century B.C.E." *BASOR* 304 (1996): 17–27.

———. "King Mesha and the Foundation of the Moabite Monarchy." *IEJ* 47 (1997): 83–92.

Naroll, Raoul. "On Ethnic Unit Classification." *Current Anthropology* 5 (1964): 283–312.

Naveh, Joseph. "A Hebrew Letter from the Seventh Century B.C." *IEJ* 10 (1960): 129–39.

———. *The Development of the Aramaic Script.* Jerusalem: The Israel Academy of Sciences and Humanities, 1970.

Negbi, Ora. "The Continuity of the Canaanite Bronzework of the Late Bronze Age into the Early Iron Age." *Tel Aviv* 1 (1974): 159–72.

Niditsch, Susan. *Oral World and Written Word: Ancient Israelite Literature.* Louisville, Ky.: Westminster John Knox Press, 1996.

Niehr, Herbert. *Der höchste Gott: Alttestamentlicher YHWH-Glaube im Kontext syrisch-kanaanäischer Religion des 1. Jahrtausends v. Chr.* Berlin: Walter De Gruyter, 1990.

———. "The Constitutive Principles for Establishing Justice and Order in Northwest Semitic Societies with Special Reference to Ancient Israel and Judah." *Zeitschrift für Altorientalische und Biblische Rechtsgeschichte* 3 (1997): 112–30.

Nielsen, Eduard. *Oral Tradition: A Modern Problem in Old Testament. Introduction.* London: SCM Press, 1954.

———. *Grundrids af Israels Historie.* 2d ed. Copenhagen: G.E.C. Gads Forlag, 1960.

———. *The Ten Commandments.* London: SCM Press, 1968.

———. "The Levites in Ancient Israel." In *Law, History and Tradition: Selected Essays by Eduard Nielsen,* 71–81. Copenhagen: G.E.C. Gads Forlag, 1983.

———. "En hellenistisk bog?" *Dansk Teologisk Tidsskrift* 55 (1992): 161–74.

Nielsen, Flemming A.J. *The Tragedy in History: Herodotus and the Deuteronomistic History.* Sheffield: Sheffield Academic Press, 1997.

Niemann, Hermann Michael. *Herrschaft, Königtum und Staat: Skizzen zur soziokulturellen Entwicklung im monarchischen Israel.* Tübingen: J.C.B. Mohr (Paul Siebeck), 1993.

———. "The Socio-Political Shadow Cast by the Biblical Solomon." In *The Age of Solomon: Scholarship at the Turn of the Millennium,* edited by Lowell K. Handy, 252–99. Leiden: E. J. Brill, 1997.

Nigro, Lorenzo. *Ricerche sull'architettura palaziale della Palestina nette età del Bronzo e del ferro: Contesto archeologico e sviluppo storico.* Roma: Università degli Studi di Roma "La Sapienza," 1995.

Nissinen, Martti. *Prophetie, Redaktion und Fortschreibung im Hoseabuch: Studien zur Werdegang eines Prophetenbuches im Lichte von Hos 4 und 11.* Neukirchen-Vluyn: Neukirchener Verlag, 1991.

Noort, Ed. *Die Seevölker in Palästina.* Kampen: Kok Pharos Publishing House, 1994.

———. *Die israelitischen Personennamen in Rahmen der gemeinsemitischen Namengebung.* Stuttgart: W. Kohlhammer, 1928. Reprint, Hildesheim: Georg Olms Verlagsbuchhandlung, 1966.

———. *Das System der zwölf Stämme Israels.* Stuttgart: W. Kohlhammer, 1930. Reprint, Darmstadt: Wissenschaftliche Buchgesellschaft, 1966.

———. "Studien zu den historisch-geographischen Dokumenten des Josuabuches." 1935. *ABLAK* 1:229–54, 271–75.

———. "Das Reich von Hamath als Grenznachbar des Reiches Israel." 1937. *ABLAK* 2:148–60.

———. "Die Wege der Pharaonenheere in Palästina und Syrien: Untersuchungen zu den hieroglyphischen Listen palästinischer und syrischer Städte," 4: "Die Schoschenkliste," *ZDPV* 61 (1938): 277–304 = *ABLAK* 2:73–93.

———. *Überlieferungsgeschichte des Pentateuch.* Stuttgart: W. Kohlhammer, 1948. Reprint, Darmstadt: Wissenschaftliche Buchgesellschaft, 1966.

Noth, Martin. *Geschichte Israels.* Göttingen: Vandenhoeck & Ruprecht, 1950.

———. "Gilead und Gad," *ZDPV* 75 (1959): 14–73 = *ABLAK* 1:489–543.

Oded, Bustaney. *Mass Deportation and Deportees in the Neo-Assyrian Empire.* Wiesbaden: Ludwig Reichert, 1979.

Østergård, Uffe. "What Is National and Ethnic Identity?" In *Ethnicity in Hellenistic*

Egypt, edited by Per Bilde, Troels Engberg-Pedersen, Lise Hannestad, and Jan Zahle, 16–38. Århus: Aarhus University Press, 1992.

Oesterley, W.O.E., and Theodore H. Robinson. *A History of Israel.* Vols. 1 and 2. Oxford: Clarendon Press, 1932.

Olmo Lete, G. del, and J. Sanmartín. *Diccionario de la lengua ugaritica.* Vol. 1. Barcelona: Editorial Ausa, 1996.

Otzen, Benedikt. *Israeliterne i Palëstina: Det gamle Israels historie, religion og litteratur.* Copenhagen: G.E.C. Gads Forlag, 1977.

Page, D. L. *History and the Homeric Iliad.* Berkeley and Los Angeles: University of California Press, 1959.

Page, S. "A Stela of Adad-Nirari III and Nergal ereš from Tell al Rimah." *Iraq* 30 (1968): 139–63.

Pákozdy, L.M. von. "'Elḥânân—der frühe Name Davids?" *ZAW* 68 (1956): 257–59.

Parker, Simon B. *Ugaritic Narrative Poetry.* Atlanta: Scholars Press, 1997.

Patte, Daniel. *Ethics of Biblical Interpretation: A Reevaluation.* Louisville, Ky.: Westminster John Knox Press, 1995.

Paul, Shalom M. *Studies in the Book of the Covenant in the Light of Cuneiform and Biblical Law.* Leiden: E. J. Brill, 1970.

Pedersen, Johannes. *Israel: Its Life and Culture.* Vols. 1 and 4. Oxford: Oxford University Press, 1926–47.

———. "Die Aufassung vom Alten Testament." *ZAW* 49 (1931): 161–81.

Perlitt, Lothar. *Vatke und Wellhausen: Geschichtsphilosophische Voraussetzungen und historiographische Motive für die Darstellung der religion und Geschichte Israels durch Wilhelm Vatke und Julius Wellhausen.* Berlin: Walter de Gruyter, 1965.

———. *Bundestheologie im Alten Testament.* Neukirchen-Vluyn: Neukirchener Verlag, 1969.

Pfeiffer, R. H. *Introduction to the Old Testament.* Rev. ed. 1948.

Prausnitz, Moshe W. "Tel Achzib." In *NAEEHL* (1993), 1:32–36.

Pritchard, James B. *Gibeon, Where the Sun Stood Still: The Discovery of a Biblical City.* Princeton, N.J.: Princeton University Press, 1962.

———. "Arkeologiens plats i studiet av Gamla Testamentet." *Svensk Exegetisk Årsbok* 30 (1965): 5–20.

———. *Recovering Sarepta, a Phoenician City.* Princeton, N.J.: Princeton University Press, 1978.

———. "Gibeon." In *NAEEHL,* 1 (1993): 511–14.

Puech, Émile. "La stèle araméenne de Dan: Bar Hadad II et la coalition des omrides et de la maison de David." *RB* 101 (1994): 215–41.

Rad, Gerhard von. *Das formgeschichtliche Problem des Hexateuch.* 1938. Reprinted in his *Gesammelte Studien zum Alten Testament,* 9–86. Munich: Christian Kaiser, 1958.

———. "Der Anfang der Geschichtsschreibung im Alten Israel." 1944. Reprinted in his *Gesammelte Studien zum Alten Testament,* 148–88. Munich: Christian Kaiser, 1958.

———. *Der Heilige Krieg im alten Israel.* Zurich: Zwingli-Verlag, 1951.

Rainey, Anson F. *El Amarna Tablets 359–379. Supplement to J. A. Knudtzon, Die El-Amarna Tafeln.* 2d ed. Kevelaer: Verlag Butzon & Bercker; Neukirchen-Vluyn: Neukirchener Verlag, 1978.

————. "Who Is a Canaanite? A Review of the Textual Evidence." *BASOR* 304 (1996): 1–15.

Redford, Donald B. *Akhenaten: The Heretic King.* Princeton, N.J.: Princeton University Press, 1984.

————. *Egypt, Canaan, and Israel in Ancient Times.* Princeton, N.J.: Princeton University Press, 1992.

Rehm, Merlin D. "Levites and priests." In *ABD* 4 (1992): 297–310.

Reisner, G., C. S. Fisher, and D. G. Lyon. *Harvard Excavations at Samaria.* Vols. 1 and 2. Cambridge, Mass.: Harvard University Press, 1908–10.

Rendtorff, Rolf. "Die Erwählung Israels als Thema der deuteronomischen Theologie." In *Die Botschaft und die Boten. Festschrift Hans Walter Wolff,* edited by Jörg Jeremias and Lothar Perlitt, 75–86. Neukirchen-Vluyn: Neukirchener Verlag, 1981.

————. *The Problem of the Process of Transmission in the Pentateuch.* Sheffield: JSOT Press, 1990.

Renfrew, Colin, with Peter Bahn. *Archaeology: Theories, Methods, and Practices.* 2d ed. London: Thames & Hudson, 1996.

Renz, Johannes. *Handbuch der althebräischen Epigraphik.* Vols. 1, 2/1, and 3. Darmstadt: Wissenschaftliche Buchgesellschaft, 1995.

Ringgren, Helmer. *Israelite Religion.* Philadelphia: Fortress Press, 1975.

Rogerson, John. *Old Testament Criticism in the Nineteenth Century: England and Germany.* London: SPCK, 1984.

Rogerson, John, and Philip R. Davies. "Was the Siloam Tunnel Built by Hezekiah?" *BA* 59 (1996): 138–49.

Rost, Leonhard. *Die Überlieferung von der Thronnachfolge Davids.* 1926. Reprinted in his *Das kleine Credo und andere Studien zum Alten Testament,* 119–244. Heidelberg: Quelle & Meyer, 1965.

Roth, Martha T. *Law Collections from Mesopotamia and Asia Minor.* 2d ed. Atlanta: Scholars Press, 1997.

Rowton, Michael B. "Enclosed Nomadism. *JESHO* 17 (1974): 1–30.

————. "Dimorphic Structure and the Tribal Elite." In *al-bahit = Festschrift J. Henniger zum 70: Geburtstag am 12. Mai 1976,* 219–57. St. Augustin bei Bonn: Studi Instituti Anthropos 28, 1976.

Sasson, Jack. "On Idrimi and Šarruwa, the Scribe." In *Nuzi and the Hurrians,* edited by A. M. Morrison and D. I. Owen, 309–24. Winona Lake, Ind.: Eisenbrauns, 1981.

Schaar, Kenneth W. "The Architectural Traditions of Building 23A/13 at Tell Beit Mirsim." *SJOT* 5:2 (1991): 75–98.

Schmid, Hans Heinrich. *Der sogenannte Jahwist.* Zurich: TVZ, 1976.

Schmidt, Werner H. *Alttestamentlicher Glaube und seine Umwelt: Geschichte des alttestamentlichen Gottesverständnisses.* Neukirchen-Vluyn: Neukirchener Verlag, 1968.

Schroer, Silvia. *In Israel Gab es Bilder: Nachrichten von darstellender Kunst in Alten Testament.* Fribourg: Universitätsverlag; Göttingen: Vandenhoeck & Ruprecht, 1987.

Schulman, Alan R. "Some Observations on the Military Background of the Amarna Period." *JARCE* 3 (1964): 51–69.

Seidel, Bodo. *Karl David Ilgen und die Pentateuchforschung im Umkreis der sogenannten älteren Urkundenhypothese: Studien zur Geschichte der exegetischen Hermeneutik in der späten Aufklärung.* Berlin and New York: Walter de Gruyter, 1993.

Sélincourt, Aubrey de. *Herodotus: The Histories.* Harmondsworth, Middlesex: Penguin Books, 1954.

Sellin, Ernst. *Geschichte des israelitisch-jüdischen Volkes.* Vols. 1 and 2. Leipzig: Quelle & Meyer, 1924–32.

Shanks, Hershel. "When 5613 Scholars Get Together in One Place: The Annual Meeting, 1990." *BAR* 17:2 (1991): 62–68.

Shiloh, Yigael. "The Four-Room-House—The Israelite Type–House?" *Eretz Israel* 11 (1973): 277–85.

Simons, J. *Handbook for the Study of Egyptian Topographical Lists Relating to Western Asia.* Leiden: E. J. Brill, 1937.

Singer, Itamar. "Merneptah's Campaign to Canaan and the Egyptian Occupation of the Southern Coastal Plain of Palestine in the Ramesside Period." *BASOR* 269 (1988): 1–10.

———. "A Concise History of Amurru." In Shlomo Izre'el, *Amurru Akkadian: A Linguistic Study,* vols. 1 and 2, Atlanta: Scholars Press, 1991, 135–95.

Small, David B. "Group Identification and Ethnicity in the Construction of the Early State of Israel: From the Outside Looking In." In *The Archaeology of Israel: Constructing the Past, Interpreting the Present,* edited by Neil Asher Silberman and David Small, 271–88. Sheffield: Sheffield Academic Press, 1997.

Smend, Rudolf. *Jahwekrieg und Stämmebund: Erwägungen zur ältesten Geschichte Israels.* 2d rev. ed. Göttingen: Vandenhoeck & Ruprecht, 1966.

———. *Deutsche Alttestamentler in drei Jahrhunderten.* Göttingen: Vandenhoeck & Ruprecht, 1989.

Smith, Anthony D. *Theories of Nationalism.* London: Gerald Duckworth, 1971.

———. *The Ethnic Origin of Nations.* Oxford: Basil Blackwell, 1986.

Smith, Sydney. *The Statue of Idri-mi.* London: The British Institute of Archaeology in Ankara, 1949.

Soggin, J. Alberto. *A History of Israel: From the Beginnings to the Bar Kochba Revolt, AD 135.* London: SCM Press, 1984.

———. *Einführung in die Geschichte Israels und Judas: Von den Ursprüngen bis zum Aufstand Bar Kochbas.* Darmstadt: Wissenschaftliche Buchgesellschaft, 1991.

———. *An Introduction to the History of Israel and Judah.* London: SCM Press, 1993.

Soldt, Wilfred H. van. "Ugarit: A Second-Millennium Kingdom on the Mediterranean Coast." In *CANE* 2:1255–66.

Southall, A. "Nuer and Dinka Are People: Ecology, Ethnicity and Logical Possibility." *Man,* n.s., 11 (1976): 463–91.

Spiegelberg, Wilhelm. "Der Siegeshymnus des Merneptah auf der Flinders Petrie-Stele," *Zeitschrift für ägyptischen Sprache und Altertumskunde* 34 (1896): 1–25.

Stade, Berhard. *Geschichte des Volkes Israel.* Vol. 1, 2d ed. Berlin: G. Grote'sche Verlagsbuchhandlung, 1887.

Stager, Lawrence E. "Merneptah, Israel and Sea Peoples: New Light on an Old Relief." *Eretz Israel* 18 (1985): 56–64.

Stamm, Johann Jacob, and Maurice Edward Andrew. *The Ten Commandments in Recent Research.* London: SCM Press, 1967.

Steiner, Margreet. "Jerusalem in the Late Bronze and Early Iron Ages: Archaeological Versus Literary Sources?" In *New Studies on Jerusalem. Proceedings of the Second*

Conference November 28th 1996, edited by Avraham Faust. Ramat-Gan: Bar-Ilan University Faculty of Jewish Studies, 1996, 3*–8*.

Stolz, Fritz. *Jahwes und Israels Kriege: Kriegstheorien und Kriegserfahrungen im Glauben des alten Israels.* Zurich: TVZ, 1972.

————. "Der Monotheismus Israels im Kontext der altorientalischen Religionsgeschichte—Tendenzen neuerer Forschung." In *Ein Gott Allein? JHWH-Verehrung und biblischer Monotheismus im Kontext der israelitischen und altorientalischen Religionsgeschichte,* edited by Walter Dietrich and Martin A. Klopfenstein, 33–50. Freiburg: Universitätsverlag, 1994.

————. *Einführung in den biblischen Monotheismus.* Darmstadt: Wissenschaftlichen Buchgesellschaft, 1996.

Strange, John. "The Book of Joshua: A Hasmonaean Manifesto?" In *History and Traditions of Early Israel: Studies Presented to Eduard Nielsen May 8th 1993,* edited by André Lemaire and Bendedikt Otzen, 136–41. Leiden: E. J. Brill, 1993.

————. "Ethnicitet i Arkëologi. Filisterne som eksempel." In *Etnicitet og Bibel,* edited by Niels Peter Lemche and Henrik Tronier. Copenhagen: Museum Tusculanum, 1998. In press.

Sweet, Louise E. *Tell Toqaan: A Syrian Village.* Ann Arbor, Mich.: University of Michigan Press, 1960.

Tadmor, Chaim. "Historical Implications of the Correct Reading of Akkadian *dâku.*" *JNES* 17 (1958): 129–41.

Tappy, Ron E. *The Archaeology of Israelite Samaria,* I: Early Iron Age Through the Ninth Century B.C.E. (Atlanta: Scholars Press, 1992).

Thiel, Winfried. "Vom revolutionären zum evolutionären Israel?" *ThLZ* 113 (1988): 401–10.

Thompson, Thomas L. *The Historicity of the Patriarchal Narratives: The Quest for the Historical Abraham.* Berlin: Walter de Gruyter, 1974.

————. *Early History of the Israelite People: From the Written and Archaeological Sources.* Leiden: E. J. Brill, 1992.

————. "'House of David': An Eponymic Referent to Yahweh as Godfather." *SJOT* 9 (1995): 59–74.

Tigay, Jeffrey H. *You Shall Have No Other Gods: Israelite Religion in the Light of Hebrew Inscriptions.* Atlanta: Scholars Press, 1986.

Timm, Stefan. *Die Dynastie Omri.* Göttingen: Vandenhoeck & Ruprecht, 1982.

Tropper, Josef. "Eine altaramäische Steleninschrift aus Dan." *UF* 25 (1993): 395–406.

Ulrich, Eugene C. *The Qumran Text of Samuel and Josephus.* Chico, Calif.: Scholars Press, 1978.

Ussishkin, David. *The Conquest of Lachish by Sennacherib.* Tel Aviv: The Institute of Archaeology, 1982.

————. "Jerusalem in the Period of David and Solomon: The Archaeological Evidence." In *New Studies on Jerusalem: Proceedings of the Third Conference December 11th 1997,* edited by Avraham Faust and Eyal Baruch, 57–58 (Hebr.). Ramat-Gan: Bar-Ilan University Faculty of Jewish Studies, 1997.

Ussishkin, David, and John Woodhead. "Excavations at Tel Jezreel 1990–1991: First Preliminary Report." *Tel Aviv* 19 (1992): 3–56.

————. "Excavations at Tel Jezreel 1992–1993: Second Preliminary Report." *Levant* 26 (1994): 1–48.

————. "Excavations at Tel Jezreel 1994–1996: Third Preliminary Report." *Tel Aviv* 24 (1997): 6–72.

Van Seters, John. "The Terms 'Amorite' and 'Hittite' in the Old Testament." *VT* 22 (1972): 64–81.

————. *Abraham in History and Tradition.* New Haven and London: Yale University Press, 1975.

————. *Prologue to History: The Yahwist as Historian in Genesis.* Louisville, Ky.: Westminster/John Knox Press, 1992.

————. *The Life of Moses: The Yahwist as Historian in Exodus-Numbers.* Kampen: Kok Pharos Publishing House, 1994.

Vaux, Roland de. "Les Patriarches hébreux et les découvertes récentes." *Revue Biblique* 53 (1946): 321–48; 55 (1948): 321–47; 56 (1949): 5–36.

————. *Histoire ancienne d'Israël.* Vol. 1: *Des origines à l'installation en Canaan.* Paris: Librairie Lecoffre, J. Gabalda et Cie, Éditeurs, 1971.

————. *Histoire ancienne d'Israël.* Vol. 2: *La période des juges.* Paris: Librairie Lecoffre, J. Gabalda et Cie, Éditeurs, 1973.

————. *The Early History of Israel.* London: Darton, Longman & Todd, 1978.

Vernes, M. *Précis d'histoire juive depuis les origines jusqu'à l'époque persane (Ve siècle avant J.-C.).* Paris: Librairie hachette et Cie, 1889.

Webster, T.B.L. *From Homer to Mycenae.* London: Methuen, 1958.

Weippert, Helga. *Palästina in vorhellenistischer Zeit.* Munich: C.H. Beck'sche Verlagsbuchhandlung, 1988.

Weippert, Manfred. "Semitische Nomaden des zweiten Jahrtausends." *Biblica* 55 (1974): 265–80, 427–33.

Wellhausen, Julius. *Geschichte Israels.* Vol. 1. Berlin: G. Reimer, 1878.

————. "Geschichte Israels," 1880. In *Grundrisse zum Alten Testament,* edited by R. Smend, 13–64. Munich: Christian Kaiser, 1965.

————. *Israelitische und jüdische Geschichte.* 1894. 9th ed. Berlin: Walter de Gruyter, 1958.

————. *Grundrisse zum Alten Testament,* edited by R. Smend. Munich: Christian Kaiser, 1965.

————. *Prolegomena to the History of Ancient Israel,* with an introduction by W. Robertson Smith and a preface by Douglas A. Knight. Atlanta: Scholars Press, 1994.

Welten, Peter. *Die Königs-Stempel: Ein Beitrag zur militärpolitik Judas unter Hiskia und Josia.* Wiesbaden: Otto Harrassowitz, 1969.

Wengrow, David. "Egyptian Taskmasters and Heavy Burdens: Highland Exploitation and the Collared-Rim Pithos of the Bronze-Iron Age Levant." *Oxford Journal of Archaeology* 15 (1996): 307–26.

Westbrook, Raymond. "Biblical and Cuneiform Law Codes." *RB* 92 (1985): 247–64.

Wette, Wilhelm Martin Leberecht de. *Beiträge zur Einleitung in das Alte Testament: Zweiter Band. Kritik der israelitischen Geschichte. Erster Theil. Kritik der mosaischen Geschichte.* Halle: Bei Schimmelpfennig und Compagnie, 1806–7.

Whitelam, Keith W. *The Invention of Ancient Israel: The Silencing of Palestinian History.* London and New York: Routledge, 1996.

Winter, Urs. *Frau und Göttin: Exegetische und ikonographische Studien zum weiblischen Gottesbild im Alten Testament und in dessen Umwelt.* Freiburg, Schweiz: Universitätsverlag; Göttingen: Vandenhoeck & Ruprecht, 1983.

Wiseman, Dennis J. *Chronicles of Chaldean Kings (626–556 B.C.) in the British Museum.* London: The Trustees of the British Museum, 1956.

Wright, George Ernest. *God Who Acts: Biblical Theology as Recital.* London: SCM Press, 1952.

———. *An Introduction to Biblical Archaeology.* London: Gerald Duckworth, 1957.

Yadin, Yigael. *Hazor: The Head of All Those Kingdoms. Joshua 11:10.* London: Published for the British Academy by Oxford University Press, 1972.

Yadin, Yigael, and Amnon Ben-Tor. "Hazor." In *NAEEHL,* 2:594–695 New York: Simon & Schuster, 1993.

Yardeni, Ada. *The Book of Hebrew Script: History, Palaeography, Script Styles, Caligraphy & Design.* Jerusalem: Carta, 1997.

Yurco, Frank J. "Merenptah's Palestinian Campaign." *The Society for the Study of Egyptian Journal* 8 (1982): 189–215.

———. "Merenptah's Canaanite Campaign and Israel's Origins." In *Exodus: The Egyptian Evidence,* edited by Ernest S. Frerichs and Leonard H. Lesko, 27–56. Winona Lake, Ind.: Eisenbrauns, 1997.

Index of Biblical Passages and Ancient Sources

ANCIENT NEAR EASTERN SOURCES

CLASSICAL SOURCES

Index of Names and Subjects

la longue durée, 65
Lachish ostraca, 48, 49
Land of Israel, 125–26
Landsberger, Benno, 59
Language, 9, 17, 18, 33, 111–13
le-melek stamps, 46, 81
Levy, Thomas, 65
literacy, 46
Liverani, Mario, 72, 148–49
Livy, 22, 89
Loretz, Oswald, 61, 62
Lot, 108, 118
Luther, Martin, 160

Manetho, 22, 23
marriage, 108–10
Matthew, 2
Mayes, Andrew, 99
Mazar, Amihai, 65
Megiddo, 79, 84
Mendenhall, George E., 73–74, 134, 145, 146, 148
Merneptah, 35–38, 42, 57
Mesha, 41, 44–46, 63
Metzger, Martin, 141
Meyer, Eduard, 7, 154
Miller, J. Maxwell, 150, 153, 154
Moab, 44–46
Monumentum Ancyranum, 22
Mormons, 96
Moses, 3, 6, 23, 24, 73, 89, 90, 92, 109, 111, 125, 136, 140, 143

Naram-Sin, 16
Naroll, Raoul, 9–10
nation, 3, 8–20
nationalism, 11, 12, 15
nationality, 4
Naveh, Joseph, 40, 41, 43
Nebuchadnezzar, 54, 121
Nehemiah, 6, 29
Nielsen, Flemming A., 116
nomadism, nomads, 18, 68–69, 75
nostoi traditions, 119
Noth, Martin, 7, 8, 97–98, 101, 105, 107, 130, 133, 138–41, 142, 145, 147, 150, 153, 155

Nuer, 17

Odyssey, 118
Omri, 44, 45, 52
oral tradition, 27

patronage, 19
Paraiba inscription, 44
Patte, Daniel, 5
peasants' revolt, 73
Pentateuch, 27, 158, 160
Perlitt, Lothar, 100
Pfeiffer, Robert H., 157
Philistines, 33, 83
Philo from Alexandria, 2
Pliny, 10
Priestly writer, 26, 158
prophets, 27–28, 94–95
Proto-Israelites, 31

Rab-shakeh, 112
Rad, Gerhard von, 27, 158, 160–61
Ramses II, 25, 60, 76
Ranke, Leopold von, 5, 6, 7, 12, 22
rationalistic paraphrase, 148–56
Rehoboam, 56
religion, 113–17
Rephaim, 127
Rogerson, John, 158
Romulus, 89

Samaria, Samerina, 31, 51, 53, 55, 62, 63, 83, 84, 166
Samaria ostraca, 46, 49–50
Sargon of Akkad, 89
Sargon II, 53
Sellin, Ernst, 6, 82
Sennacherib, 26, 47, 54, 56–57, 81
Shalmaneser III, 52
Shasu, 69
Shiloh, 95
Shoshenq, 56, 64
Shishak. See Shoshenq
Shuppiluliumash I, 70
Siloam inscription, 47
Smith, Anthony, 16
Soggin, J. Alberto, 141, 153, 155